Introduction
to
Aviation Insurance

by
Alexander T. Wells, Ed.D.
Broward Community College

ROBERT E. KRIEGER PUBLISHING COMPANY
MALABAR, FLORIDA
1986

Original Edition 1986

Printed and Published by
ROBERT E. KRIEGER PUBLISHING COMPANY, INC.
KRIEGER DRIVE
MALABAR, FL 32950

Library of Congress Cataloging in Publication Data

Wells, Alexander T.
    Introduction to aviation insurance.

    Includes index.
    1. Insurance, Aviation—United States.   I. Title.
HG9972.3.W44   368.5′76′00973   85-7589
ISBN 0-89874-862-3
10 9 8 7 6 5 4 3 2

Dedication

To my friend Bruce D. Chadbourne, a highly respected professor of aviation management who has taught a course in aviation insurance at Embry-Riddle Aeronautical University for over ten years and has truly been an inspiration to many students who have entered all segments of the aviation industry.

Contents

Preface

Preface

INTRODUCTION TO AVIATION INSURANCE

Introduction to Aviation Insurance was designed to serve a threefold purpose: (1) it underscores the great economic and social importance of an understanding of risk and the means of dealing with risk, including insurance; (2) it should provide a foundation of general knowledge in a subject area which plays a significant role in any aviation related business; and (3) it initiates specialized education for someone beginning a career in insurance or aviation.

Other than marketing information prepared by the aviation insurers for their agents and the general public as well as several books designed for the private pilot, there are no text books on the subject of aviation insurance. It was my intention from the outset of this undertaking to write a book which included the typical textbook pedagogical features. It was designed to enable a student with little or no background in insurance to proceed through the material in a step-by-step approach beginning with general principles and following through with the more specialized aviation lines. Students should find the book easily readable and understandable. The approach taken is introductory, not exhaustive. The book is not a treatise on aviation insurance; it does not pretend to offer the last word on the subject for that would take a working knowledge of underwriting. It should offer a logical approach to building a foundation for future study in this important area for any aviation enterprise.

CHARACTERISTICS OF THIS BOOK

This book employs a number of features that are designed to facilitate student learning. The main ones are:

1. *Chapter outlines.* Each chapter opens with an outline of the major topics to be covered.
2. *Chapter objectives.* After the outline, each chapter includes a list of objectives that the student should be able to accomplish upon completing the chapter.
3. *Logical organization and frequent headings.* Insurance can easily become overwhelming in its multitude of topics, concepts, practices, and examples. The material covered has been put in a systematic framework so that students know where they have been, where they are, and where they are going in the text. Frequent headings and subheadings aid organization and readability.
4. *Key Terms.* Each chapter concludes with a list of key terms used in the text.
5. *Review Questions.* Review questions at the end of each chapter cover all of the important points.
6. *Appendixes.* Each separate appendixes are included at the end of the text. They include Appendixes A, B, and C, applications, policies, and endorsements used by aviation underwriters. Appendix D includes objective self-tests.
7. *Complete Index.* The book includes a complete index to help the student find needed information.

ORGANIZATION OF THE TEXT

INTRODUCTION TO AVIATION INSURANCE is designed to acquaint the student with the basic principles of insurance and risk with its special application to the aviation industry. The book should provide a foundation of general insurance principles and practices and an introduction to the specialized field of aviation insurance.

The following is an outline of INTRODUCTION TO AVIATION INSURANCE:

THE AVIATION INSURANCE INDUSTRY

Aviation Insurance in the United States: A Historical Perspective. Chapter 1 provides a historical sketch of the aviation insurance industry in the United States from its beginning at the end of World War I through the emergence of underwriting in the space age.

Types of Insureds. This relatively short chapter introduces the student to the market for aviation insurance including aerospace manufacturers, the air carriers, the various segments of the general aviation industry, airports, and individual pilots.

Types of Insurers. Chapter 3 concludes the first part of the book with a review of major domestic aviation underwriters and Lloyd's of London. Other topics include selecting an insurer and selecting an agent or broker.

PRINCIPLES OF INSURANCE

Risk and Insurance. The opening chapter of Part Two introduces the student to the concept of risk including its classifications, factors affecting it, and methods of dealing with risks including insurance. Insurance is clearly defined including its purpose and the requirements for an insurable risk. The process of risk management is thoroughly explored in this chapter.

The Legal Foundation for Insurance. Chapter 5 introduces the student to the nature and types of law including the principle of indemnity on which insurance is founded. This is followed by a comprehensive review of legal liability including the principle of negligence and liability under contracts.

Insurance Contracts. This is one of the most important chapters because it sets the stage for delving into the various aviation contracts which follow the next part of the text. Chapter 6 begins with a discussion of the characteristics of the insurance contract in general. This is followed by a review of the powers of agents and brokers in forming the contract and the prerequisites to an enforceable contract. The chapter concludes with a discussion of the standard layout of an insurance contract including its parts.

INSURANCE FOR THE AVIATION INDUSTRY

Aircraft Hull Insurance. The opening chapter of Part Three introduces the student to the hull portion of the combined aircraft hull and liability contract. Coverage, exclusions, limit of liability, and conditions applicable to the hull coverage are thoroughly explored.

Aircraft Liability Insurance. Chapter 8 covers the liability portion of the combined aircraft hull and liability contract including the coverages, exclusions, limits of liability, and conditions. Medical payments and guest voluntary settlement (admitted liability) are reviewed as well as other conditions applicable to the hull and liability portion of the contract.

Airport Premises, Products, Hangarkeepers, and Other Aviation Liability Coverages. This chapter rounds out our discussion of the principal lines of aviation insurance by covering airport premises, products, and hangarkeepers liability plus several additional liability coverages written in conjunction with premises liability.

Other Lines of Insurance. Aviation insurance is just one aspect of an aviation firm's overall insurance needs. Chapter 10 completes the insurance package by reviewing fire and allied lines; business automobile insurance; workers' compensation; crime, fidelity, and surety coverages as well as life and health insurance. This is followed by a discussion of the principles of insurance buying and determining essential, desirable, and available coverages. The closing portion of this chapter deals with the important subject of loss prevention and safety.

Chapter 11

Underwriting and Pricing Aviation Risks. Chapter 11 completes Part Three by analyzing the process of underwriting and pricing aviation risks. The need for underwriting is reviewed followed by an indepth discussion of the nature of aviation exposures. The major factors in underwriting aircraft and airport risks is then explored. This chapter concludes with a discussion on pricing and reinsuring aviation risks.

ACKNOWLEDGMENTS

Although this textbook has been written by a single author, it owes its existence to many people with whom I have had the pleasure of working over the years. It is difficult to single out the many people working for insurance agencies, brokers, and companies who, at least indirectly, have had an effect on this undertaking, but several come to mind.

Larry Robinson, who hired me as an aviation underwriter trainee with the Royal-Globe Insurance Companies in April 1960. Dave Cassell, now vice president of the aviation department at Johnson and Higgins in Atlanta, whose patience and understanding as senior underwriter at Royal assisted me greatly during the first several years. Jack Bowater, now a vice president with Richard J. Berlow & Company in New Jersey, who was my supervisor in the Chicago office of Royal during the mid 1960s and was a great motivating factor by his leadership example. Two other individuals who played a significant part later in my career were Don Wilson, senior vice president with Rollins Burdick Hunter Company and Waller Smith, formerly director of insurance for United Airlines—unquestionably two of the most knowledgeable aviation insurance individuals in the country.

Thanks are also due to the industry sources who provided material that was extremely helpful in putting together this textbook. In this regard, I am indebted to personnel of the Associated Aviation Underwriters, Avemco Insurance Company, Aviation Office of America, Insurance Company of North America, National Aviation Underwriters, and United States Aviation Underwriters.

I am grateful to Professor Jack Hinman, head of the aviation management program at Florida Institute of Technology, for his content review of the manuscript.

I would like to give special thanks to Robert Krieger for his foresight in agreeing to publish the first textbook in this growing field of insurance. Thanks are also due the other members of the Krieger Publishing team. This text has benefited greatly from the comprehensive review of the manuscript by Mary Roberts, whose copy editing expertise smoothed out many rough edges.

Finally, thanks to my wife Mary, my daughter Jeannie, and my son John for their continuous support and encouragement.

Chapter 1

Aviation Insurance in the United States: A Historical Perspective

OUTLINE

Introduction
The Formative Period
Establishment of the United States Aviation Insurance Market
Aviation Insurance Reaches Maturity
Conclusion

OBJECTIVES

At the end of this chapter you should be able to:
Describe some of the early attempts in underwriting aviation risks in the immediate post–World War I period.
Identify several of the early aviation underwriters and discuss their contribution to the field of aviation insurance.
Explain the factors which caused the establishment of the aviation insurance market during the mid-to-late 1920s.
Identify the three leading aviation insurance groups up to World War II.
Recognize several of the independent insurers who entered the market in the post–World War II period.
Describe the challenge faced by the aviation insurance market with the introduction of jet aircraft in the late 1950s.
Summarize the reasons for and the findings of the Senate investigation into aviation insurance during August 1958.

INTRODUCTION

In 80 years aviation has changed from a few test flights to orbiting celestial bodies, from sliding along sand dunes to spanning oceans, from feats of isolated daring to casual acceptance. Speeds have increased a thousandfold, as have altitude and range capabilities. No longer is the sky the limit. Ahead lie risks and rewards as vast as space itself. We have new airplanes that fly with greater fuel efficiency, huge air freighters that move the nation's goods, an expanding general aviation fleet, and the vehicles for space exploration and research.

A little over 70 years ago, aviation insurance was barely recognized. Today it is part of the space age. Aviation insurance began in 1911 when the first policy was developed by Lloyd's of London. In July 1912 Lloyd's agreed to cover legal liability only on some aircraft participating in an air meet. Unfortunately, the weather was bad, the crashes were numerous, and the losses on the policies were so bad that the underwriters gave up completely the insurance of airplanes.

Few policies were issued before World War I, and those few were more or less confined to legal liability or personal accident coverages. The risk of insuring against loss from physical damage to the unstable and frail aircraft of those days was more than even the most courageous underwriter would undertake. World War I ended civilian aviation and until 1919 the demand for insurance coverage lapsed. The return of peace set underwriters to thinking again about the possibilities of this form of travel. There was comparatively little flying at the time however, and what flying existed did not produce enough business to feed a competitive market with an adequate premium income.

THE FORMATIVE PERIOD

After World War I civilian air transportation and the aviation insurance market began in the United States. Many returning pilots bought surplus war aircraft—Curtis Jennies, de Havilland DH-4's, and S.E. 5's—and went into business. A Curtis Jenny which had cost the government close to $17,000 sold for as high as $750 including a new OX-5 engine and as low as $50. These happy-go-lucky barnstormers toured the country putting on shows and giving rides to the local townsfolk. Some insurance companies experimented with the risk of insuring them, but the loss experience was poor and withdrawals from the market were frequent.

Nevertheless, in meeting the needs, the Travelers Insurance Company announced on May 1, 1919, a comprehensive insurance program for air risks. Aviation insurance became a reality.

The lines of insurance written by the Travelers applied to the maintenance, operation, and use of aircraft for private and commercial purposes, including the transportation of passengers. The program assumed that airplanes use for business as well as pleasure purposes would increase vastly in the next few years.

According to the announcement the lines of aviation business to be written included:

1. **Life Insurance.** The company was prepared to issue aviation risk life insurance upon the one year nonrenewable term plan, with a $5,000 limit.

2. **Accident insurance for owners and pilots.** The policy provided death, dismemberment, and loss of sight benefits, also indemnity for total and partial disability.

3. **Trip accident ticket insurance.** The company prepared to furnish transportation-by-air companies with an accident ticket to be sold to passengers. These tickets were issued to take effect as of date and hour of issue and to end at 4 A.M. the following day. The ticket provided $5,000 for accidental death benefit and disability benefits.

4. **Workers' Compensation insurance.**

5. **Public liability and property damage insurance.**[1]

The stated purpose was "offering insurance to encourage the manufacture, improvement and use of aircraft."

Public liability policies were designed for injuries occasioned by collision in the air resulting in injuries to occupants of other aircraft. They did not include the passenger hazard of the insured's aircraft. Public liability policies also included injuries caused to others on the ground while landing or taking off or because of articles accidently dropped from the aircraft while in flight. Property damage coverage provided for the liability of the insured for damage to the property of others not carried on the aircraft. This early Travelers' program did not include coverage against damage to the aircraft itself (the aircraft hull insurance).

A few days after the travelers' announcement, on May 6th, at a convention of the Aero Club of America in Atlantic City, New Jersey, the agency of Payne and Richardson issued Aero Tickets to an illustrious group of Americans, including President Woodrow Wilson and the Wright brothers. Aero Ticket Number One was sold to President Wilson at a premium of $5.00 for $5,000 accidental death benefits. "In issuing aircraft trip tickets,' commented the *Weekly Underwriter* that week, "the Travelers increase the reputation of that company for initiative in the insurance business."[2]

Unfortunately, the early development of air transportation did not measure up to the Travelers' expectations. After struggling to write aviation insurance business independently for 12 years, the Travelers was finally forced to cease in 1931, after several tragic air disasters that year wiped out the company's reserves for aviation business. The Travelers did not reenter the aviation insurance market until 1939, when the company joined the United States Aircraft Insurance Group (USAIG).

In the next three years after 1919 there were, besides the Travelers, five other companies active in aviation insurance:

1. The Home Insurance Company

2. Queen Insurance Company of America

3. Globe and Rutgers Insurance Company

4. National Liberty Insurance Company

5. Fireman's Fund Insurance Company

Early Aviation Underwriters

In May 1920 Horatio Barber, an underwriter at Lloyd's, came to the United States and became aviation underwriter for the Hartford Accident and Indemnity Company. In 1924 the Hartford dropped out of all aviation coverages except public liability and property damage liability and in 1925 they and the Travelers were the only American companies writing any aviation insurance. Finally the Hartford group dropped out entirely in 1926.[3] Hartford joined the USAIG on September 1, 1929.

Following the termination of his contract with the Hartford, Barber and his partner, Baldwin, in 1926 became the aviation underwriting managers for the Independent Fire Insurance Company and its casualty affiliate, the Independent Indemnity Company of Philadelphia. This initial entry of Barber and Baldwin, as an organization, into the field of aviation insurance in America lasted three years. In September 1929 the Independent withdrew from the office of Barber and Baldwin and entered the field as a competitor. Finally in October 1930 the Independent retired from the aviation insurance field. The Barber and Baldwin Agency remained in business until 1948, writing business through Lloyd's and other British companies. Their success was largely attributable to underwriting hull coverages with very high deductibles, using very difficult and complicated policy conditions and charging very high rates.

Since the very early days another individual, and the company he organized, has continuously played an important role in the development of the aviation insurance market in the United States. This man was the late J. Brooks B. Parker. The firm he organized, Parker & Co., International, Inc. (now the Parker Aviation Division of Frank B. Hall and Company) has been recognized as the world's first brokerage house specializing in aviation insurance and a pioneer in aviation since its founding in 1919.

One of the original founders of the Aero Club of the University of Pennsylvania in 1908, Mr. Parker joined Chubb & Son as a marine underwriter upon graduation in 1911. He entered the first class of Army flying schools in May 1917, graduated as a pilot, and because of his marine insurance training, he established his own brokerage firm.

In exploring ever-broadening coverages to meet the insuring needs of clients, Parker & Co. originated many of the forms and methods of writing this type of coverage. In addition to his insurance qualifications, Mr. Parker knew aircraft manufacturing and airlines from having assisted in the formation of several carriers. For example, Parker & Co. has placed insurance coverages for Pan American World Airways since its formative days to the present time. Parker & Co. induced the Continental Casualty Company to enter the aviation insurance field so that flight insurance for international air passengers could be sold by Pan American ticket agents.

Parker & Co. modernized the merchandising method of air travel insurance by selling the policy over the counter in airports. Later, Parker & Co. expanded its operation in the international market, particularly in Latin American countries, and became a significant reinsurance broker.

ESTABLISHMENT OF THE UNITED STATES AVIATION INSURANCE MARKET

Gradually, commercial aviation became stabilized. Several factors were responsible. The Air Mail Act of 1925 provided for the carriage of mail by private carriers. The Air Commerce Act of 1926 established the first airway rules and regulations as well as the licensing of aircraft and airmen. In 1927 the successful transatlantic flight of Charles Lindbergh brought about the release of large amounts of capital for the building up of the aviation industry. Public attention focused on the almost forgotten possibilities of flying as a means fo transportation. Between 1926 and 1928 17 domestic airlines commenced air mail services. At the same time, two American airlines started foreign operations. Altogether in 1928 there were 294 airplanes in service, having flown 10,472,024 miles and carried 52,934 passengers.[4] In addition, there were also airplanes conducting aerial service operations (which means all acitivtes that may not be properly classified as scheduled transport or private flying). In 1929 the aviation industry included 6,684 licensed aircraft in the United States, 10,215 licensed pilots, and 948 established airports. During the first six months of 1929, 153 manufacturers produced some 970 commercial aircraft and 22 manufacturers each produced more than 10 aircraft. The average value of the aircraft, including engines, constructed during 1929 was $9,519.[5]

Lindbergh's historical flight had also stimulated popular interest in the aviation insurance business in the Western Hemisphere. Consequently, the competition for this business really began in the period 1927–1929, when three major groups of aviation underwriters established themselves in the market.

USAIG

On July 1, 1928, the first entry, the United States Aircraft Insurance Group with the United States Aviation Underwriters, Inc., serving as managers, commenced the acceptance of aviation risks in New York City. The group had as a nucleus eight members in all, four fire insurance companies and four casualty companies. The original four fire members were National Union Fire Insurance Company, United States Fire Insurance Company, North River Insurance Company, and Pacific Insurance Company. The first four casualty members were Maryland Casualty Company, New Amsterdam Casualty Company, New York Indemnity Company, and United Fidelity and Guarantee Company.

The necessity for including within the same management-organization both fire and casualty companies arose because in many states legislation permitted an insurance company to write only one of the three major lines of business, i.e., fire (and marine), casualty, or life. By joining together a number of companies, the underwriting manager could meet all the insurance needs of various aviation interests.

On August 24, 1928, the first policy, No. AF251, was issued to Canadian Colonial Airways, Inc. During the year, the USAIG suffered its first catastrophic loss. A Colonial & Western Airway's Ford Tri-Motor crashed on the edge of the Newark, New Jersey airport, killing all 14 passengers, the pilot being the sole survivor. The group paid $29,680 on account of the total destruction of the aircraft and ultimately paid a liability loss amounting to $193,000, which included $189,119 for passenger liability, and the balance for workers' compensation and for the liability for property damage to others.[6]

AAU

The catastrophe occurred on March 17, 1929. On the very next day, the Associated Aviation Underwriters (AAU) entered the aviation insurance field. The idea was hatched when Owen C. Torrey (then vice president of the Marine Office of America) and J. Russell Parsons (a partner of Chubb & Son) met and decided that insurance for airplanes would be required. A partnership was established that continues to this day.

Initially AAU included 17 companies in its group. Later that year it reinsured the outstanding liability of the Transportation Companies when these companies retired from the aviation field. Again in 1930 when the Independent Companies retired from the aviation insurance field, the AAU reinsured their outstanding liabilities.

Later, when the Aero Insurance Underwriters retired from the writing of scheduled airlines, the burden of providing insurance for the airlines fell on the Associated Aviation Underwriters and the USAIG.

Aero Insurance Underwriters

The Aero Insurance Underwriters came into the aviation business as successors to the original firm of Barber & Baldwin, Inc. After the Independent Companies withdrew from the office of Barber and Baldwin, the Aero Underwriters Corporation was organized as a holding company for the newly created Aero Insurance Company, Aero Indemnity Company, Aero Engineering and Advisory Company, and the old firm of Barber and Baldwin, Inc. In 1932 the Aero Underwriters Corporation and its subsidiaries were placed in liquidation. Barber retired and returned to Europe and in November of that year the Aero Insurance Underwriters came into being under the management of George L. Lloyd. The major companies in the Aero Insurance Underwriters group were the Royal-Globe Insurance Companies and the Great American Insurance Companies. Later when the Aero dissolved in 1948, the Royal-Globe Group entered the aviation market independently and the Great American Companies joined the USAIG.

Many of the companies previously associated with the Barber and Baldwin office joined Aero Insurance Underwriters which then became a group that followed a pattern initially established by the USAIG.

The National Continental Aviation Insurance group was formed in Chicago in the summer of 1929, but it did not make adequate progress and later retired from the business in April 1933. Thereafter until the end of the Second World War, AAU and the USAIG, representing over one hundred insurance companies, handled practically all the insurance transactions in the aviation market.

The Group Approach to Underwriting

The group, as an approach to underwriting aviation risks, has spanned the period between the day when the financial speculator first saw an opportunity in civil aviation for those who were willing to take a risk and the present time when airlines and the aerospace industry have become an accepted part of our complex economic structure. The success of the group approach represents the finest example in American insurance of the pooling of faith, knowledge, and facilities in a common undertaking involving the fortunes of both fire and casualty companies, which have been inseparably intertwined in providing the insurance protection for the American aerospace industry.

It all started from the idea of two comparatively young men who foresaw the need for better insurance facilities for the aviation industry. One was David C. Beebe, who had a background of flying experience and insurance experience in the marine field. In 1927 Beebe resigned from Marsh & McLennan and traveled to England, Germany, and other European countries on his own to study problems of aviation insurance and to learn, if possible, how it could be underwritten successfully in America. At that time aviation insurance, though still experimental, was developed more thoroughly in Europe. His research convinced him that this form of indemnity could be handled safely only by insurance pools or groups of companies.

Upon his return Beebe approached Major Reed M. Chambers and convinced him to enter the insurance field. Together they hoped to build up aviation insurance where it could be of real service to American aviation. Major Chambers was a leading figure in American aviation. Following a brilliant flying career in the Army in France during World War I, he remained in aviation and in 1926, along with Eddie Rickenbacker, organized Florida Airways, the forerunner of Pan American World Airways. Major Chambers knew the technical end of aviation and the industry had complete confidence in his judgment. He gave the new insurance organization immediate prestige among possible buyers of coverage.

In the formation of their group, Beebe and Chambers approached the initial insurance companies on three grounds:

1. To promote American patriotism. American aviation was deserving of support to bring it up to the standard of other countries.

2. The most economical way to write aviation insurance was to pool the facilities that might be of service to each member company.

3. The proposed new group would be composed of specialists in aviation.

With Beebe as president and Chambers as vice president, the United States Aviation Underwriters, Inc., (USAU) began operation to serve as underwriting managers for the United States Aircraft Insurance Group. The group approach initially selected by the USAU for the handling of aviation risks has been followed ever since.

Shortly after the formation of USAIG, AAU, and Aero Insurance Underwriters the country experienced its great depression. Commencing in 1930, there was a serious decline in the volume of aviation insurance business. This trend continued for three or four years, but in the middle of the decade the business began to come back. In 1935 and 1936, aviation insurance business took a distinctly upward trend and in the late 1930s prior to World War II, it started to climb at a rapid pace. During the war years premium volume receded for a while but then increased slightly. United States entry into World War II cast an ever-increasing influence over American aviation and American aviation insurance.

The war changed the business of aviation insurance underwriting considerably. In the prewar days aviation insurance was written principally for:

1. Scheduled airlines
2. Manufacture of civil aircraft
3. Fixed base operators and flying schools
4. Private owners
5. Aircraft sales distributors
6. A small amount of military manufacturers

During the war, the available business for the aviation underwriting market changed to:

1. Scheduled airlines
2. Manufacturers of military aircraft
3. Civilian pilot training program
4. Civil Air Patrol
5. Army training schools

All these businesses were directly or indirectly under government control or influence. Consequently, the three groups pooled resources and placed their full facilities at the service of the government—a valuable contribution to the war effort. Still they continued to dominate the American aviation insurance market. In 1942 over 96 percent of the aviation insurance business reported to the New York State Insurance Department was written by the three underwriting groups.

On June 10, 1932, the Superintendent of Insurance of New York State called a meeting of all insurance companies engaged in transacting aviation insurance. The purpose was to establish some coordination and uniformity in rates and rules so that the required regulation could be properly administered. An industry committee was appointed to accomplish this purpose. On September 27, 1932, a plan subscribed to by all existing elements of the aviation insurance market was presented to the department and was accepted on September 30, 1932. The original subscribers to this plan were: Associated Aviation Underwriters, Aero Insurance Underwriters (successors to Barber and Baldwin, Inc.), National Continental Aviation Insurance Association, United States Aircraft Insurance Group, and The Travelers Insurance Companies.

On October 7, 1932, these groups and the companies they represented organized a rather loose advisory rating and statistical organization and adopted articles of association containing rules and regulations. The name agreed upon for this organization was the Board of Aviation Underwriters and it assumed countrywide jurisdiction. Over the years its importance diminished and finally in 1945 the Board of Aviation Underwriters ceased functioning. Thereafter the various companies and groups writing aviation insurance filed their rates directly with the New York State Insurance Department.

AVIATION INSURANCE REACHES MATURITY

The growth of aviation insurance has paralleled the growth of the aviation industry itself. As American aviation achieved world supremacy during and after World War II, American aviation insurance business established a strong position in the world aviation insurance market. As was true of the post–World War I years, the postwar years of 1946 and 1947 brought increased aviation activities and the further expansion of aviation insurance business. A great number of returning pilots and new air carriers expanded the aviation industry. At the same time a considerable number of new underwriting organizations staffed with inexperienced underwriters entered the aviation insurance field.

The overexpansion of the aviation insurance business resulted in poor loss ratios for all underwriters and a reduction of rate levels below those necessary to write the business successfully. As a result, many withdrew from the market in 1947, including one of the major groups, the Aero Insurance Underwriters. During 1947 the remaining underwriting groups increased rates significantly for all types of coverage and cancelled or refused to renew a large number of accounts which had shown poor loss experience. After these years of painful adjustment, the aviation insurance market gradually stabilized by 1948.

Entry of Independent Underwriters

The vast expansion of general aviation in the postwar years prompted several insurance companies to write the aviation business independently. Numerous companies tried but soon withdrew. Among the survivors were the Royal-Globe Insurance Companies, the Insurance Company of North America, the American Mercury Insurance Company, and several mutual insurance companies associated in the Mutual Aviation Casualty Underwriters group.

Following its withdrawal from the Aero Insurance Underwriters at the end of 1947, the Royal-Globe Insurance Companies entered the aviation insurance field on January 1, 1948, by establishing its own aviation department. Specializing in the business and pleasure risks including corporate aircraft operators, this market continued to underwrite aviation business until the early 1970s when the combination of recession in the general aviation industry and severe competition in the aviation insurance field forced them to withdraw as an independent and subsequently join the USAIG.

As early as 1927 the Insurance Company of North America (INA) expressed its interest in aviation insurance and conducted an investigation to determine whether it would be advisable to write the various forms of aviation insurance. Seven years later, in 1934, the Insurance Company of North America and affiliated fire companies joined the Hull section of the USAIG. The Indemnity Company of North America, however, stayed outside the group and commenced writing aviation liability business on its own during World War II as an accommodation to its agents.

Immediately after the war, the North American Companies decided that they could best serve the industry and their agents by divorcing themselves from any underwriting syndicate and by writing this form of insurance directly through their agents. On January 1, 1946, INA announced its entry into the aviation field, and established a new aviation department.

INA started with those lines of aviation insurance which were most valuable to the local agency system and endeavored to confine writings largely to owners of private airplanes, including corporate operators, aircraft dealers, and fixed base operators. At present INA continues to write these classes of business as well as several air carriers and aircraft manufacturers. It has also widened its interest by participating in the excess insurance on a number of major carriers.

An entirely new firm, the American Mercury Insurance Company, with its headquarters in Washington, D.C., entered the aviation insurance market in 1949. Unlike North America and the Royal-Globe Companies, the American Mercury was organized to write aviation business exclusively, although its charter powers authorized it to write all lines of business except surety, life, and annuity. The company obtained its business, to a considerable extent, from members of the Aircraft Owners and Pilots Association and the National Aviation Trades Association. The company terminated its agreement with the Aircraft Owners and Pilots Association on January 1, 1963. On the same date, the Aircraft Owners and Pilots Association entered a new agreement with the newly organized Aviation Employees Insurance Company (AVEMCO) to solicit members' business through direct mail.

At the close of World War II, several mutual insurance companies also saw the prospect of the expansion of general aviation activities and thus began the growth of the general aviation insurance market. In order to strengthen their entry into the field and to obtain a meaningful share of the business, these mutual companies decided, in 1945, after a careful study, to associate themselves together in a new group called Mutual Aviation Casualty Underwriters. With the group facilities available, the agency-writing companies among the group were also enabled to accommodate their agents in writing aviation risks. Only two of the original nine members of this group are still active in the aviation insurance business. They are Liberty Mutual and Employers Mutual of Wausau.

Challenge of the Jet Era

The real test of strength of the American aviation insurance market came in 1954 when the industry entered the jet age. In July 1954 a Boeing 707 took off from Renton, Washington, to Baltimore, Maryland, on a test flight. This prototype was the first of a long line of jet aircraft to follow in the next three decades.

This development presented an unprecedented challenge to the USAIG when the group was called upon to provide insurance coverage of over $5 million on a single plane in test flight. To meet the huge requirements, the USAIG not only utilized the full capacities of its member companies but mobilized the world insurance market through Lloyd's. The test flight was successful, and the American aviation insurance market has since built up a substantially large capacity to meet the ever-increasing needs for far larger amounts.

The enlarged underwriting capacities of the two groups did not meet the entire insurance requirements of the aviation industry, particularly in the area of products liability for aircraft manufacturers. Since the early 1950s, the liability of an aircraft manufacturer to a third party for alleged defective products has become a serious problem. An aircraft crashing into a heavily populated area with resulting fire and explosion could prove to be disastrous to the manufacturer of the aircraft or of the component part which may have caused the accident. Furthermore, grounding liability coverages were not available on the market then.

Consequently, in 1952 certain members of the Aerospace Industries Association became concerned and initiated a study of the aviation insurance market. To explore the possibilities of providing adequate insurance protection against products liability, the Aircraft Builders Counsel, Inc., was organized. The counsel developed a plan of aircraft products liability insurance and the so-called ABC Plan became operative in 1955.

The Plan provided manufacturers with the third party liability insurance for damages arising out of the products hazard, with a limitation of $5,000,000 for personal injury or property damage for any one occurrence and, in addition, third party liability insurance for damages arising out of the products hazard for loss of use of completed aircraft, caused by grounding, up to a limit of $5,000,000. The insurance was available for a qualified manufacturer of aircraft, aircraft engines, propellers, missiles, and component parts thereof. Coverage applied to both the sales of military and commercial aircraft, aircraft parts, and missiles. Military and commercial coverages could not be purchased separately. The Plan was underwritten by two domestic mutual companies and Lloyd's of London and British companies. The two domestic companies are Liberty Mutual Insurance Company and Employers Mutual of Wausau.

Senate Investigation of the Industry

Aero Insurance Underwriters, as previously mentioned, went out of existence on January 1, 1948. Subsequently another group called Aero Associates was formed in 1949 by an insurance broker, George Stewart, president of Stewart, Smith & Co. The group originally consisted of the American Fidelity and Casualty Company and the American Fidelity Fire Insurance Company. In 1950 the Eagle Star Insurance Company joined the group, and in 1954 Zurich Insurance Company was substituted for American Fidelity and Casualty Company. As originally formed, 50 percent of Aero was owned by Stewart, Smith & Co. and the other 50 percent by the American Fidelity Companies. When Stewart entered the market in 1949 through the formation of Aero Associates, he conducted a market survey which indicated there was room for another group to provide more capacity.

In the early days Aero Associates was quoting prices approximately 20 percent less than the other two groups. Stewart was satisfied that additional business could be obtained at rates lower than those charged by the two existing groups. From 1954 to 1958 Aero Associates showed underwriting losses for each year. Zurich offered to buy out Stewart, Smith's 50 percent ownership in Aero Associates, but was not able to interest any other underwriters in entering the group after it took control of Aero Associates. As a result, Aero Associates ceased operations and Zurich joined the USAIG on January 1, 1958.

Despite the enormous growth of the aviation industry and the vast increase in insurance that such growth entails, where formerly there were three available American groups, now there were only two. It was against this background that the Subcommittee on Antitrust and Monopoly of the Committee of the Judiciary of the United States Senate, headed by the late Senator O'Mahoney, started its investigation of the situation and commenced public hearings which lasted from August 6, 1958, through August 15, 1958. Throughout the hearings, the Subcommittee indicated that its overriding concern was with the extent and effectiveness of competition.

In summarizing its findings, the Subcommittee made its conclusions and recommendations in a report published in August 1960. The major items among its conclusions were:

1. In 1943, a report of the Civil Aeronautics Board criticized the concentration of the aviation insurance business in the hands of three competing groups or markets. Despite the phenomenal growth of the commercial aircraft industry in the intervening years, only two groups or syndicates were available to furnish the insurance for the operation and continued growth of the industry.

2. Adequate reinsurance facilities had not developed in the United States.

3. Reverse competition had occurred in the air trip insurance business where the three insurers were engaged in a struggle for market position, not through lower rates or wider coverages to buyers, but through the payment of enormous rentals to airports.

4. State regulation of aviation insurance was not completely effective in eliminating the restrictive market practices discovered by the Subcommittee.

No specific actions aimed at correcting the above situations were undertaken by the federal government or by the New York State Insurance Department. The Justice Department, however, and a Federal Grand Jury later conducted lengthy investigations and hearings on the allegations of the Subcommittee. The conclusion of both was that no action was warranted.

The Emergence of Competition in the Sixties and Seventies

The tremendous growth in all segments of the aviation/aerospace industry during the 1960s and 1970s brought a host of new aviation insurance markets onto the scene, particularly in the general aviation field. This factor has fostered a comparatively higher degree of competition for business over the years and has been one of the reasons for the reduction in the level of premium rates.

Some of the more prominent markets which started writing aviation risks during the 1960s and are still in business today include Aviation Insurance Managers, American Aviation Underwriters, and Aviation Office of America. Aviation Insurance Managers was organized in 1962 by Southern Marine and Aviation Underwriters, international surplus lines brokers, and serves as aviation insurance managers for eight companies. American Aviation Underwriters, managed by Cravens, Dargen & Co. for two companies, is based in Houston, Texas. Aviation Office of America, based in Dallas, Texas, has become a significant market, participating in all lines of aviation insurance.

A number of other companies, primarily writing general aviation risks, have withdrawn from the market. Included are Airway Underwriters out of Ann Arbor, Michigan; General Aviation Insurance Group and International Aviation Underwriters, both formerly based in Dallas, Texas; and Ohio Casualty Company.

Another company who attained prominence during the 1960s and is still an active insurer today is National Aviation Underwriters based in St. Louis, Missouri. Formed in 1945 as a reciprocal exchange whose members predominantly included a number of midwestern fixed base operators, this company now underwrites a broad range of general aviation aircraft.

Underwriting in the Space Age

Insurers have been covering space payloads, mostly satellites for over 20 years. The business has been maturing in recent years because of the Shuttle program and the growing rush of communication satellites. Space insurance policies are custom-tailored for each launch. Pioneering insurance brokers in this field are Caroon & Black Inspace, Inc., Johnson & Higgins, and Marsh & McLennan. More recently, Washington-based International Technology Underwriters has become a leading source in assembling insurers of space policies.

About 60 percent of the coverage is typically provided by Lloyd's of London, with the rest coming from U.S. companies. By some estimates, there are 300 to 400 insurance companies world-wide that can join to offer space coverage.

CONCLUSION

In conclusion, it is worth repeating that few chapters in the annals of human history have been as romantic as man's conquest of the sky. The fact that the air age began only 80 years ago at Kitty Hawk and has now soared into outer space is evidence of the tremendous resourcefulness of imagination, skill, fortitude, and capital that have been dedicated to the accelerated expansion of the aviation industry. Many factors have contributed to this expansion of the industry. Of no less significance is the strong backing it has received from the American insurance industry. Willingness to underwrite and accept the risks of flight, particularly in the formative and uncertain years of aviation, has been a mighty factor in getting people to invest their money in aircraft manufacturing and air transportation and in fostering the confidence of the air travelers. The recognition of aviation's needs did not come easily to the insurance underwriters and they should be highly complimented for their pioneering study of the industry and for their coverage in venturing into an extremely hazardous new field without the stabilizing protection of past experience. It is this coverage that has made the aviation insurance business what it is today, and as Lloyd's of London aided in awarding in England "supremacy of the seas," so does our aviation insurance business give to America supremacy of the air. Today the American aviation underwriters prepare to meet the gigantic challenge of the space era.

REVIEW QUESTIONS

1. Who was the first company to write aviation insurance in the post–World War I period? What lines did they underwrite? Why did they withdraw from the market?

2. Describe the contributions to the field of aviation insurance made by the following pioneer underwriters: Horatio Barber, J. Brooks, B. Parker, and David C. Beebe

3. What factors caused the aviation industry to become stabilized during the mid-to-late 1920s and thus permitted the growth of aviation insurance? Who were the three major aviation insurance groups to become established in the late 1920s?

4. Why has the group approach to underwriting aviation insurance been so successful over the years? How did the nature of insuring aviation risks change during the war years? Why do you think that the Board of Aviation Underwriters was not successful?

5. Who were the leading independent aviation insurers during the fifties and sixties? Which one is the only survivor today?

6. Why did the introduction of the jet equipment into the airline fleets during the late 1950s present such a problem to the underwriters? Why was the Aircraft Builders Counsel formed? Why did the select Senate committee investigate the aviation insurance industry in August 1958? What were its findings?

7. What was the reason for the growth in the number of aviation insurers during the sixties and seventies?

REFERENCES

1. The Travelers Insurance Companies, *The Travelers 100 years,* published by the Travelers in commemorating the Companies' 100th anniversary on April 1, 1964, pp. 90–93.
2. The Travelers Insurance Companies, ibid.
3. Beebe, David C., Comments of the United States Aviation Underwriters, Inc., on *A Study of Aviation Insurance by the Civil Aeronautics Board.* New York, May 8, 1944.
4. Aeronautical Chamber of Commerce, *Aircraft Year Book,* 1929.
5. Beebe, ibid., p. 98
6. Beebe, ibid., p. 93

Axe, J. H., *Aviation Insurance.* Insurance Institute of America, New York, 1931.

Civil Aeronautics Board, *A Study of Aviation Insurance.*

Rhyne, Charles S., *Aviation Accident Law.* Columbia Law Book Company, Washington, D.C., 1947.

Sweeney, S. B., *Nature and Development of Aviation Insurance.* University of Pennsylvania Press, Philadelphia, 1927.

Chapter 2

Types Of Insureds

OUTLINE

The Challenges of Space
The Aerospace Manufacturers
Aircraft Owners and Operators
Airport Owners and Operators
Individual Pilots

OBJECTIVES

At the end of this chapter you should be able to:
Recognize the potential for aviation insurance with the growth of space exploration.
Identify some of the members of the AIA and GAMA and describe the primary aviation insurance coverage purchased by them.
Distinguish between the following air carriers: major, national, and regional.
Describe the primary aviation insurance coverages purchased by the air carriers.
Distinguish between the following classes of general aviation aircraft business: industrial aid, business and pleasure, commercial operators, and special use.
Describe the airport and individual pilot as a market for aviation insurance.

THE CHALLENGES OF SPACE

Forty years ago, science fiction writer Ray Bradbury wrote about a spacecraft capable of transporting hundreds of Earthlings and diverse agricultural and scientific equipment to the developing Martian colonies, and then shuttling back to Earth for another load.

Considering the success and routine nature of the recent Space Shuttle flights, the fictional writings of Mr. Bradbury and his *Martian Chronicles* have turned into real possibilities. During the next decade, the insurance industry will come face to face with these possibilities. From an insurance standpoint, the space industry is emerging from the formative stages of the 1960s and 70s and insurance will become an important instrument of finance in future space ventures.

Most space insurers anticipate their industry ultimately will be asked to insure such property risks as outer space manufacturing facilities, earth observation satellites, liability and bodily injury exposures, workers' compensation exposures, and much more.

Since the beginning of the satellite programs, all communications satellites have required some form of insurance, including property and liability coverage. The suitability of insurance to outer space ventures is a foregone conclusion. Many insurance analysts predict that by the year 2000 leisure space travel will be an opportunity for many. By the year 2025 space travel may be an everyday occurrence, and extraterrestrial communities populated by as many as 10,000 people may be commonplace.

To the insurance industry these developments all pose unique risk challenges. A demand for sophisticated insurance coverages is expected within a few years. Major corporations such as IBM, General Electric, Ford, and RCA already have made firm commitments to the industrialization of outer space.

THE AEROSPACE MANUFACTURERS

The *aerospace manufacturers* include those companies engaged in research, development, and manufacture of aerospace systems, including manned and unmanned aircraft; space-launch vehicles and spacecraft; propulsion, guidance, and control units for all of the foregoing; and a variety of airborne and ground-based equipment essential to the testing, operation, and maintenance of flight vehicles. Virtually all of the major aerospace manufacturers are members of the *Aerospace Industries Association* (AIA) or the *General Aviation Manufacturers Association* (GAMA).

The aerospace manufacturers include about 80 major firms operating over 1,200 facilities, backed by thousands of subcontractors, vendors, and suppliers. The principal product line—aircraft, missles, space systems, and related engines, parts, and equipment—is characterized by high performance and high reliability, hence high technology and high unit value.

Members of the AIA include such firms as:

Aerojet-General Corporation	Martin Marietta Corporation
The Bendix Corporation	McDonnell Douglas Corporation
The Boeing Company	Northrop Corporation
Gates Learjet Corporation	Ratheon Company
General Dynamics Corporation	RCA Corporation
General Electric Company	Rockwell International Corporation
The BF Goodrich Company	The Singer Company
Goodyear Aerospace Corporation	Sperry Corporation
Grumman Corporation	Teledyne CAE
Honeywell, Inc.	Textron, Inc.
Hughes Aircraft Company	TRW, Inc.
IBM Corporation	United Technologies Corporation
Lockheed Corporation	Westinghouse Electric Corporation

Members of the GAMA include such firms as:

AVCO Corporation	The Garrett Corporation
Beech Aircraft Corporation	Gulfstream American Corporation
Cessna Aircraft Company	King Radio Corporation
Champion Spark Plug Company	McCreary Tire and Rubber Company
Collins Avionics	Mooney Aircraft Corporation
EDO Corporation	Parker Hannifin Corporation
Fairchild Swearingen Aviation Corporation	Piper Aircraft Corporation

While these manufacturers and subcontractors require all forms of insurance coverage, the principal aviation industry insurance coverage is products liability. The products liability policy provides a coverage for damage arising out of the use of goods or products manufactured, sold, handled, or distributed by the company. Grounding coverage is also provided which protects the company if the aircraft is withdrawn from service because of the existence or alleged or suspected existence of a like fault, defect, or condition in two of more such aircraft.

Beyond the more obvious aerospace manufacturers whose prime product is destined to be part of an aircraft, a great deal of the aviation product business is generated by manufacturers of small parts, off-the-shelf items, and raw materials which may find their way into aircraft production without the knowledge of the company. Most general liability policies exclude aviation liability and consequently many of these subcontractors and suppliers must purchase aviation products liability to obtain protection in the event that their products become part of an aircraft.

AIRCRAFT OWNERS AND OPERATORS

The Airline Industry

The airline industry consists of a vast network of routes connecting cities throughout the country, and indeed the world. Over this network, a large number of airlines carry passsengers and cargo on scheduled service. The largest of these, United Airlines, earns revenues in excess of $4 billion a year, while the smallest may operate a single plane only several months a year.

Certificated carriers linking the high density cities and earning annual gross revenues in excess of $1 billion are classified as *major air carriers*. Included in this group are some of the most familiar names in the airline industry such as United, American, Delta, Eastern, Pan American, and Trans World Airlines. In 1985 there were 12 major air carriers.

Next in line, generally serving lower density cities, are the *national air carriers* whose annual revenues fall between $75 million and $1 billion and include such airlines as Alaska, Frontier, Ozark, Hawaiian, Southwest, and World. In 1985 there were 15 national air carriers.

The *regional air carriers* fall into three groups: large, medium, and small. A large regional is one whose annual gross revenue falls between $10 million and $75 million. A medium regional carrier is one with annual gross revenue of less than $10 million. In 1985 there were 18 large regionals and 46 medium regionals. These scheduled air carriers operate over 2,500 aircraft of all sizes and are required to hold a Certificate of Public Convenience and Necessity issued by the Department of Transportation.

The small regional air carriers, which are non-certificated and commonly referred to as *commuters*, operate smaller aircraft such as Beechcraft 99's and de Havilland Twin Otters. In 1985 these approximately 250 air carriers provided regular scheduled airline service with over 1,200 aircraft between smaller cities and major hub airports.

The principal lines of aviation insurance carried by the airlines include the following:

Aircraft Hull—Loss of or damage to the insured's aircraft including disappearance.

Aircraft Liability—Covers liability arising out of the ownership or operation of aircraft.

Workers' Compensation—Protects employees for job related injuries in accordance with state compensation laws.

Airport Liability—Covers the liability arising out of the existence or operation of the insured airport premises.

Products Liability—Covers the liability of the air carrier arising out of the sale or servicing of aircraft or other products.

Hangarkeepers Liability—Covers liability for aircraft of others in the air carrier's care, custody, or control for storage, repair, servicing, or safekeeping.

Contractual Liability—Covers the carriers for liability assumed under provisions of a lease or contract agreement with others such as the airport operator, the gasoline or oil supplier, and fuel equipment supplier.

Construction and Alterations—Covers the carrier's liability arising out of renovations and new construction.

The airlines as a class of business represent a tremendous volume of premium for a relatively few insurance markets which can provide the substantial limits of liability required. This class has also enjoyed a favorable loss experience over the years resulting in extremely competitive rates.

The General Aviation Industry

Corporate operated aircraft flown by professional pilots are referred to as the *industrial aid* class of business. Industrial aid is considered the preferred type of business in aviation insurance. A unique branch of aviation, it embraces a select group of highly skilled, professional pilots flying on behalf of corporations. Over 16,000 aircraft fall into this class and their loss experience compares very favorably with that of the scheduled air carriers.

Aircraft, which range from large jets to single-engine and twin-engine piston aircraft, may be owned or leased by corporations for the purpose of transporting guests and employees primarily for business purposes. Many corporations operating aircraft have their own flight department with an operations manual detailing such procedures as pilot training, maintenance, and flight procedures. Others contract with a flying service to schedule, maintain, and pilot the aircraft. The use of corporate aircraft complements and supplements the corporate utilization of regularly scheduled airlines.

Aircraft hull and liability coverage is a prime consideration of corporate aircraft operators. Other major aviation insurance coverages carried by corporate operators include:

Medical Payments—Covers the insured for injuries sustained by passengers regardless of liability.

Guest Voluntary Settlement (Admitted Liability)—A form of liability protection under which voluntary settlement can be made, whether or not the aircraft owner is liable, with respect to the death or dismemberment of a passenger.

Non-Ownership Liability—Covers the insured's liability arising out of the use of non-owned aircraft.

Single-engine or multiengine aircraft owned by an individual, corporation, or less than three individuals, and operated by the owner for personal recreational or for business use, is considered as a *business and pleasure* class. If owned by three or more individuals it is termed a *flying club*. Flying clubs refer to nonprofit organizations formed for the purpose of owning and operating aircraft at a reasonable per capita cost.

The majority of aircraft fall into the business and pleasure or flying club class. An estimated 145,000 active general aviation aircraft fall under this category. As with the industrial aid class, usage does not contemplate operating the aircraft for a charge in excess of reimbursement at no profit. Business and pleasure is generally considered to be a desirable class of business. Underwriting and rating in this category can vary considerably, however, depending upon the capability and ability of pilots to operate the aircraft to be insured. Factors that are considered include the pilot's total time as well as the time in the particular make and model aircraft, and the year of manufacture of the aircraft. Owners of aircraft used for business and pleasure purposes normally carry hull and liability coverage as well as medical payments coverage.

The *fixed base operators* (FBO's) class refers to the airport-based, commercial operations which provide some or all of the following activities: aircraft charter, rental, instruction, and cargo carrying, as well as ground operations consisting of providing tie-down and/or hangar space, new and used aircraft sales, repairs and service, and parts and fuel sales.

The best educated guess is that there are 3,500 fixed base operations of different sizes at public-use airports in the United States. These FBO's operate about 33,000 aircraft for air taxi, instructional and rental purposes. Some extremely specialized aviation operations found on public airports do not qualify as true fixed base operations but are nevertheless necessary to aviation. These include engine manufacturers and remanufacturers, avionics specialists, propeller specialists, and certain flight training specialists who do nothing but recurrent flight training for professional and semi-professional pilots of high-performance aircraft.

Fixed base operators vary widely in size, scope of services offered, type of facility, size of investment, and management expertise. Consequently, as a class, underwriting and rating individual risks can vary considerably.

The primary coverages considered by commercial operators include aircraft hull and liability, airport liability, hangarkeepers liability, and products liability. Two additional coverages are quite frequently purchased by FBO's. They are in-flight hangarkeepers and non-ownership physical damage liability. In-flight hangarkeepers extends the basic hangarkeepers coverage to include in-flight uses in connection with storage, repair, service, or safekeeping of aircraft. Non-ownership physical damage liability insures the operator's liability when, in the course of his own business, he uses aircraft owned by others.

It is estimated that an additional 13,000 aircraft are used for *special use*. These include aircraft used for aerial applications, aerial advertising, aerial photography, fire fighting, fish spotting, mosquito control, police traffic control, pipeline/powerline surveillance, weather modifications, and wildlife conservation.

While the risks presented by special use aircraft represent some of the most perilous activities in aviation, the class as a whole is generally considered to be a favorable one by underwriters. Insurance coverages include the basic aircraft hull and liability and airport premises liability protection.

Other owners and operators of aircraft used exclusively for pleasure purposes include gliders, ultralights, and experimental aircraft. Special aircraft hull and liability contracts have been designed to meet the needs of these individuals.

AIRPORT OWNERS AND OPERATORS

There are over 16,000 airports in the United States ranging in size from Chicago O'Hare and Atlanta Hartsfield to private grass strips. Included in this number are heliports, stolports, and seaplane bases. Airports generally fall into one of the following three categories: private-use, public-use publicly owned, and public-use privately owned.

Private-use airports are those that are not open to the general public, but are restricted to the use of their owners and invited guests of the owners on an exclusive basis. *Public-use Publicly owned airports* range in size from the major airports serving a metropolitan area to a small single grass strip owned by a local community. *Public-use privately owned airports* generally are located on the outskirts of a metropolitan area and serve as the general aviation airport for the community.

From an insurance standpoint, the primary coverage is airport premises liability. Other coverages frequently purchased are contractual liability and alterations and repairs. Another coverage unique to airports is air meet liability. Air meet liability covers the insured's liability arising out of the sponsorship of an air meet or air show.

INDIVIDUAL PILOTS

There are close to 720,000 active pilots in the United States, including approximately 320,000 private pilots, many of whom do not own, but instead rent, borrow, or lease small aircraft for business and pleasure purposes. The personal non-owned aircraft policy is designed for such individuals. It provides liability and medical payments coverage. Optional non-owned aircraft physical damage liability coverage may be purchased. This coverage provides protection for damage to a rented or borrowed aircraft if the insured is held legally liable.

KEY TERMS

Aerospace manufacturers
Aerospace Industries Association
General Aviation Manufacturers
  Association
Major air carriers
National air carriers
Regional air carriers
Commuters

Industrial aid
Business and pleasure
Commercial operations
Fixed base operators
Flying club
Special use
Private-use airports
Public-use publicly owned airports
Public-use privately owned airports

REVIEW QUESTIONS

1. Discuss some of the challenges of space exploration that will face aviation underwriters into the twenty-first century.
2. Name some of the leading aerospace manufacturers who are members of AIA and GAMA. What is the purpose of products liability? Why do subcontractors and suppliers need this form of coverage?
3. Name several of the major and national air carriers. Who are the commuters? What are the principal lines of aviation insurance carried by the air carriers?
4. Why is the industrial aid class of business considered one of the best by aviation underwriters? Describe one unique coverage provided industrial aid accounts.
5. Most aircraft risks fall into which class of business? What are some of the commercial uses of aircraft? List the principal aviation insurance coverages purchased by FBO's. What are special use aircraft?
6. Discuss the variety of airport risks. What type of aviation insurance is sold to active pilots who do not own an aircraft?

Chapter 3

Types Of Insurers

OUTLINE

Overview of the Industry
Major Aviation Insurers
Lloyd's of London
Selecting an Insurer
Insurance Agents and Brokers

OBJECTIVES

At the end of this chapter you should be able to:
Identify the two major direct-writing aviation insurance companies and the classes of aviation business written by them.
Recognize the four major aviation insurers who sell their security and services through the agency system.
Describe how aviation insurance is placed through Lloyd's of London.
Summarize the important considerations an insured must make in selecting an insurer.
Distinguish between an agent and broker.
Identify several of the largest aviation insurance brokerage firms in the United States.
Discuss some of the factors an insured must consider in selecting an agent or broker.

OVERVIEW OF THE INDUSTRY

Today there are over 5,000 insurers in the United States organized under a variety of ownership forms and writing a variety of coverages. It is estimated that probably no more than 300 of these write aviation insurance and the majority are a member of some pool or association.

The divisions of the insurance business according to underwriting lines are somewhat arbitrary, as a result of the gradual development of different branches of insurance and of the laws which controlled them. The original charters were so broad that the early U.S. insurance companies wrote all lines of insurance. Over the years state insurance laws were tightened restricting companies to one or another of the following lines:

1. Life and health coverages
2. Fire, marine, and allied forms of property insurance
3. Casualty and surety business

Companies were prohibited from engaging in more than one of the three categories. Up until the late 1940s it was quite common for an insurer to write separate hull (physical damage to the aircraft) and liability (protection against the insured's negligent acts) policies. The method of evading the restrictions imposed by state laws was to organize subsidiary companies, owned in part or wholly by the parent company.

During the 1940s there was great pressure to abandon the strict categories and gradually the state laws were amended. One state after another passed multiple-line laws. At present, such laws exist in all states. This makes it possible for any company except a life insurance company to engage in all forms of property and liability insurance.

The first combined aircraft hull and liability policies appeared during the 1950s and soon became a significant marketing factor. This multiple-line underwriting approach continues today with the result that many life insurance companies are buying property and liability insurance companies, and the latter are buying life insurance companies. Although combinations of life and property companies have existed for years, recently the tempo of acquisition has been speeded up. Some industry analysts foresee only two policies in the future, one covering life and health insurance and the other covering all property and liability losses.

Aviation insurance has remained as one of the few specialty lines of insurance and although there has been a trend to combine policies within the aviation insurance field, it has not been caught up with the tide of combining the major property and casualty lines of insurance. The reason for this relates to the basic nature of the aviation risk. Aircraft and the perils of flight present many unique problems for the aviation insurer. One factor is the constant exposure to a catastrophy loss. Another is the wide diversity of risks resulting in a relatively limited number of insureds (spread of risk) in any one category. Finally, the rapidity of change in aircraft and aviation risks compared to other lines of insurance has required the need for a specialist to underwrite such risks.

MAJOR AVIATION INSURERS

Direct-Writing Companies

Aviation insurance in the United States is written by two types of insurers: direct-writing companies and underwriters who deal exclusively through brokers and agents.

Direct-writing companies sell their policies directly to the public either through the home office or through company representatives located throughout the country. The two major direct-writing companies are Avemco Insurance Company and National Aviation Underwriters.

Avemco Insurance Company
Frederick Municipal Airport
411 Aviation Way
Frederick, Maryland 21701

Avemco Insurance Company, the Aircraft Owners and Pilots Association (AOPA) designated insurer, is part of the Avemco Group which was organized in 1950 as the parent company to supervise and coordinate the activities of all its subsidiaries. Regional offices are located in Maryland, Georgia, Florida, Tennessee, Ohio, Illinois, Texas, California, and Washington State.

Avemco Insurance Company sells all types of aviation insurance on a direct basis primarily to aircraft owners and pilots of general aviation aircraft, including commercial coverages to fixed base operators. Other aviation-related insurance coverages are sold to lending institutions and to manufacturers of component parts used in aircraft. Avemco has become a leading carrier in insuring ultralight aircraft. The company does not underwrite air carrier risks.

Other companies in the Avemco Group include Eastern Aviation and Marine Underwriters, a managing general agency, selling aviation and marine insurance through agents and brokers; Avemco Insurance Brokerage, an all-lines general insurance agency; Brooks Shettle Company, a general insurance brokerage and reinsurance facility; Avemco Sales Corporation, a direct marketer for products and services to individuals, groups, and associations; Linden Corporation, which handles Avemco's real estate activities and owns commercial and residential properties; Avemco Aircraft Investment Corporation, which finances and leases general aviation aircraft; and Loss Management Services, which provides claims and non-claims services for insurance companies with particular regard to aviation and marine insurance.

National Aviation Underwriters
Lambert St. Louis International
Airport
P.O. Box 10155
St. Louis, Missouri 63145

Formed in 1945, *National Aviation Underwriters (NAU)* is part of NAVCO Corporation which in 1984 became part of the Crum and Foster insurance organization, a subsidiary of Xerox Corporation. In addition to the home office in St. Louis, there are division offices in California, Minnesota, Missouri, and New Jersey.

National Aviation Underwriters started out as a specialty market primarily insuring FBO's but quickly expanded their writings to all types of general aviation risks. Today NAU writes all classes of general aviation business and has become a major market in writing FBO's, helicopters, and agricultural operators.

American Aviation Services Corporation (AASC). Formed in 1978, AASC provides professional safety engineering services for aviation, surface, and marine transportation industries. As a member company, they are the prime reason for the excellent claims service which NAU has traditionally provided policyholders. In addition, they provide a full range of aviation safety engineering programs to the general aviation industry—helicopter and fixed wing safety evaluations, heliport and fixed base operators analysis, landing site studies, and aviation cost analysis and aircraft feasibility studies.

National General Insurance Company. National General is the personal lines carrier under NAVCO, offering homeowners and automobile insurance directly to members of sponsoring organizations.

Companies Dealing Exclusively Through Agents and Brokers

The following companies sell their policies through agents and brokers (independent businesses) who have a contract with the company. The four major carriers are Associated Aviation Underwriters, United States Aircraft Insurance Group, Aviation Office of America, and Insurance Company of North America.

Associated Aviation Underwriters
90 John Street
New York, New York 10038

One of the two largest multicompany aviation insurance pools, *Associated Aviation Underwriters (AAU)* is owned by Chubb & Son, Inc., and The Continental Company. It was formed in 1929 to insure the risks of ownership, operating, and maintenance of aircraft, airlines, aircraft and parts manufacturers, and related exposures. Today, as the aviation department for 30 participating and affiliated companies, AAU underwrites all classes of aviation business including the major air carriers, airports, and manufacturers.

Staffed with aviation insurance specialists in underwriting and claims, AAU maintains branch offices in Atlanta, Chicago, Dallas, Detroit, New York, Kansas City, Los Angeles, San Francisco, and Seattle. All of AAU's representatives are licensed pilots and have at their access a fleet of company aircraft to service the agents and brokers in their territory. In addition to insuring risks, trained personnel in each office inspect aircraft premises, manufacturing plants, individual aircraft, and other prospective risks with special conditions.

Because AAU operates as the aviation department for its member companies, the licensing or appointing of agents is handled exclusively by the member companies. Business is written only through qualified agents of member companies and licensed insurance brokers. However, all aviation insurance business is transacted directly with AAU offices rather than the member company.

United States Aircraft Insurance
Group
110 William Street
New York, New York 10038

Largest of the domestic aviation underwriters, USAIG was formed in 1928 and today includes over 70 of the world's major insurance companies. *United States Aviation Underwriters (USAU)* functions as manager of the group and has worldwide authority to accept or reject proposals, specify rates, bind risks, settle claims, and issue aviation insurance policies on behalf of the USAIG. Like AAU, USAU underwrites all classes of aviation insurance and has aviation insurance underwriting and claims specialists located in branch offices throughout the country.

Branch offices are located in Atlanta, Anchorage, Boston, Chicago, Dallas, Denver, Houston, Los Angeles, Memphis, Minneapolis, New York, Orlando, Phoenix, Pittsburgh, Richmond, San Francisco, Seattle, St. Louis, Toledo, and Wichita. Agents and brokers representing the member and associate member companies of the USAIG pool are entitled to full use of its facilities and services.

Aviation Office of America
Love Field Terminal Building
Dallas, Texas 75235

The *Aviation Office of America (AOA)* is a relatively new aviation insurance market, formed in 1962. In 1977 it became a unit of Crum and Forster, a New York based insurance holding company. AOA now represents 35 insurance companies and handles their business much in the same manner as AAU and USAU. Regional offices are located in Atlanta, Chicago, Kansas City, Los Angeles, San Francisco, and Morris Plains, New Jersey.

The group underwrites all classes of aviation insurance and has become a leading underwriter in the commuter/regional airline market.

Insurance Company of North America
1600 Arch Street
Philadelphia, Pennsylvania 19101

One of the oldest insurance markets in the United States, *Insurance Company of North America (INA)* started doing business in 1792. In 1982, INA Corporation merged with Connecticut General Corporation, the parent of Aetna Insurance Company, to form CIGNA, one of the nation's largest insurance and financial organizations. Today, CIGNA's affiliated companies operate around the world, offering insurance products and services through selected independent agents and brokers. INA/Aetna is CIGNA's property/casualty insurance division.

INA started writing aviation liability business during World War II as an accommodation to its agents. Aircraft hull coverage was written through the USAIG. In 1945, INA decided that it could best serve the industry and their agents by divorcing themselves from the USAIG pool and writing aircraft hull and liability directly through their agents. Management ultimately decided this could best be accomplished by establishing an aviation department. In entering the business, INA started with those lines of aviation insurance which were most valuable to the local agency system by writing private aircraft operators, aircraft dealers and other fixed base operators, and corporate operators using aircraft in furtherance of their business. Today INA continues to write these same classes of business as well as major airports and regional/commuter airlines.

Other Aviation Insurance Markets

There are a number of smaller aviation insurance markets which tend either to specialize in a particular class of business such as agricultural aircraft, helicopters, or antique and experimental aircraft or to restrict their writings to single-engine and light-twin business and pleasure risks. These markets include:

American Aviation Underwriters P.O. Box 1660 Houston, Texas 77251	Pacific Aviation Managers 3600 Wilshire Boulevard Los Angeles, California 90010
Crump Aviation Underwriters 5350 Popular Avenue Memphis, Tennessee 38117	Southeastern Aviation Underwriters Inc. 1373 Broad Street Clifton, New Jersey 07013
Liberty Mutual Insurance Co. 175 Berkeley Street Boston, Massachusetts 02117	Southern Marine & Aviation Underwriters Inc. 610 Poydras Street New Orleans, Louisiana 70130

In addition to these 12 aviation insurance markets, there are at least 6 or 7 additional markets, several of which specialize in such lines as loss-of-license insurance. During the 1960s and 1970s, about 30 or 40 markets were in business. Many of them dropped out, victims of increased competition and a leveling off of the number of active general aviation aircraft. There were simply too many companies for the amount of premium available. Until the aircraft market expands to the level experienced during the late 1970s, the available aviation insurance market should remain fairly stable.

LLOYD'S OF LONDON

In a colorful history spanning three centuries, *Lloyd's of London* has created a tremendous impact on the world's insurance business. Lloyd's was originally a market exclusively for marine insurance, writing the first policies in the 1680s. Today, however, nearly two-thirds of its annual premium writings come from non-marine sources. Risks of every conceivable description are accepted by Lloyd's underwriters from all continents and most countries either directly or by means of reinsurance.

The first standard aviation insurance ever written was accepted at Lloyd's in 1911, and Lloyd's aviation syndicates today represent a substantial part of the London aviation market as a whole. It is estimated that Lloyd's underwriters write about 20 percent of the world's aviation premiums.

Lloyd's is not a company as such but an association of individuals formed into syndicates whose underwriters actually accept the risks. Underwriting members, of whom there are over 23,000 known as *Names*, are the people who provide the capital to finance the insurance accepted on their behalf. By tradition they leave the choice of risks entirely to the active underwriter as they themselves do not necessarily know anything about the insurance business. Underwriting members, although primarily British, include men and women of all nationalities who must satisfy stringent conditions in order to qualify. To be a Lloyd's underwriting member, individuals must be recommended by other members, transact business with unlimited personal liability, satisfy the Council of Lloyd's of his or her financial integrity, and furnish security in an approved form to be held in trust by the corporation of Lloyd's. The amount of security varies according to the wealth of the member and the volume of business to be transacted. The amount of premiums that can be underwritten on the member's behalf is governed by the size of the deposit and the extent of the member's wealth.

In practice new underwriting members are introduced by firms of underwriting agents who see to most of the formalities connected with joining, advise the new members as to which *syndicate* they should join, and deal with their accounts. There are some 400 syndicates. Each specializes in some class of insurance—marine, non-marine, or aviation. They vary in size from a few members to a thousand or more. In a syndicate each member who joins participates to an extent governed by the amount of premium that the proportion of his deposit applicable to that syndicate entitles him to write. For example, suppose an air carrier needs hull coverage with an insured value of $5,000,000 at a premium of 1 percent, that is $50,000, and an underwriting member has a 1 percent share in a syndicate which includes 125 Names with varying shares. If the lead underwriter accepts a 10 percent line on the insurance on behalf of the syndicate, it will receive a premium of $5,000 of which the underwriting member will be entitled to $50. Should the aircraft suffer a total loss the underwriting member will be liable for 1 percent of 10 percent of $5,000,000 or $5,000. He is not liable for the sums due from any other member of his syndicate.

Lloyd's Brokers

The only persons who may present business to underwriters at Lloyd's are the approximate 270 insurance brokers who are approved by the Committee of Lloyd's and are known as *Lloyd's brokers*. A few are very large, with thousands of employees, but many are quite small. American agents and brokers doing business with Lloyd's must work through an approved Lloyd's broker.

The Lloyd's broker's primary duty is to negotiate the best available terms for his clients. To this end he is free to place risks wherever he thinks fit whether at Lloyd's, with other British companies, or both. On receiving a request for insurance coverage, a Lloyd's broker first makes out the "slip"—a sheet of folded paper with details of the risk. The next step is to negotiate a rate of premium with underwriters expert in that particular type of business. Lloyd's thrives on competition and the broker may obtain several quotes before deciding on the best one—bearing in mind what his client will be prepared to pay and what level of premium is required to get the risk adequately covered in the market. The lead underwriter, having set the rate, takes a proportion of the risk on behalf of his syndicate.

Armed with this lead the broker approaches as many other syndicates as are needed to get the slip fully subscribed. Large aircraft liability risks are usually spread over the whole London market, coverage being shared by Lloyd's underwriters and the insurance companies. Spreading a risk as widely as possible is one of the principles of insurance which enables Lloyd's and the London market to withstand the pressure of heavy claims which might otherwise be ruinous.

In addition to the underwriters at Lloyd's, there are over 2,000 other staff members employed as lawyers, claims adjusters, actuaries, data processing personnel, and clerical staff. Lloyd's maintains a policy signing office through which all policies issued as Lloyd's pass, and a central accounting system for Lloyd's transactions, thus relieving underwriters of all this detailed work.

SELECTING AN INSURER

In many respects the most important consideration an insured faces in selecting insurance is the integrity of the insurer. The company's financial condition, underwriting philosophy, claims policy, service, and price are more important in selecting an insurer than whether it is a direct writer or sells its policies through agents and brokers. Alfred M. Best, Inc., publishes an annual book entitled *Best's Insurance Reports* which covers all property and casualty companies including their history, personnel, investments, operating results, underwriting results, and other financial data.

Theoretically, direct-writing companies, employing their own *captive agents*, should offer lower prices because of the absence of the agent's or broker's commission (generally 15 percent of the gross premium); however, this is not necessarily true. It pays the insured to shop around and get various quotations before selecting an insurer. Another complicating factor is that aviation insurance policies vary tremendously, particularly in rates and policy wording, neither of which is established by state insurance departments or rating bureaus. Each policy differs in some aspect—even policies from the same company. The same company which is very competitive in writing corporate aircraft flown by professional pilots may be very uncompetitive in both policy wording and rating when it comes to low time pilots in high performance single-engine aircraft.

Aviation insurance companies can range from a small department in a large general insurer to a company which only writes aviation business. While most companies accept some of the risk before reinsuring the balance, some organizations accept none of the risk but pass it all off through various reinsurance treaties to other insurers. These so-called *front companies* generally last as long as they protect their reinsurance companies. Once underwriting results deteriorate, the reinsurers pull out and the front companies are forced out of business.

Most aviation insurers are good. Unfortunately, as in any industry marginal firms appear during growth periods in the aviation industry and then retire during recessionary periods. As noted, there are fewer markets now than during the 1960s and 1970s. It behooves an insured to find out how long the insurer has been in business. What is its reputation for paying claims? Does it have experienced claims personnel? Having an experienced agent or broker review a specimen policy from the company is also a wise procedure before selecting an insurer.

INSURANCE AGENTS AND BROKERS

An insurance *agent* is an independent business person who is authorized (under a contract with an insurer) to solicit, modify, or terminate contracts of insurance between the insurer and the insuring public. A typical agency will normally represent 10 to 20 different companies. The problem with representing too many is the difficulty in generating enough premium volume for each insurer which significantly reduces the agent's leverage with the company should loss experience deteriorate. Also involved in the marketing process are insurance brokers. An insurance *broker* is a person who, for a consideration, solicits and negotiates contracts of insurance for an insured and is looked upon as the agent of the insured and not of the insurer. In practice, the distinction between agents and brokers in placing aviation risks is of minor importance.

While there are relatively few aviation insurance companies, there are many agents and brokers who place aviation insurance. The insurance section of the *World Aviation Directory* lists the major agents and brokers in the United States. The following names include some of the largest brokers who place a major percent of the airline and corporate fleets. These companies have an aviation department staffed with experienced personnel, many of whom were former underwriters with the major aviation insurers.

Alexander & Alexander, Inc.
1185 Avenue of the Americas
New York, New York 10036

Johnson & Higgins
95 Wall Street
New York, New York 10005

Bayly, Martin & Fay International, Inc.
660 Newport Center Drive
Newport Beach, California 92660

Marsh & McLennon, Inc.
1221 Avenue of the Americas
New York, New York, 10020

Caroon & Black of Pennsylvania, Inc.
1530 Chestnut Street
Philadelphia, Pennsylvania 19102

Reed Stenhouse, Inc.
88 Pine Street
New York, New York 10005

Frank B. Hall & Co., Inc.
International Aviation Division
261 Madison Avenue
New York, New York 10016

Rollins Burdick Hunter Company
10 S. Riverside Plaza
Chicago, Illinois 60606

Insurance agencies and brokerage firms come in all sizes from one or two person operations specializing in aviation to a large corporation placing all classes of business with separate departments staffed with specialists. Some of the large brokerage firms with offices throughout the country place millions of premium dollars and are as large as some insurance companies.

Selecting an Agent or Broker

Agents and brokers representing various companies can get quotations from the non-direct-writing underwriters but not the direct-writing companies. While it may be faster and more convenient to deal with the direct-writing companies, an independent agent or broker enables the insured to have a local contact who will shop around among the underwriters for the best policy and coverages for the insured's operation. Perhaps the most important factor is that in the event of a claim the local agent or broker as the middle man will represent the insured in his dealings with the company. This is not to say that the direct-writing companies are incompetent. They are very competent, and in many cases they are less expensive. National Aviation Underwriters, a direct-writer has an exceptionally fine reputation in the industry in handling fixed base operator accounts including fair claim treatment and loss prevention and engineering services.

An insured must select an agent or broker carefully. The agent or broker must have an in depth knowledge of the insurance business; time and facilities for providing necessary services; good contacts with the insurance market so that prompt and favorable action for clients can be obtained; knowledge of insurers to use for special situations; an effective claim follow-up service; and finally, the respect and cooperation of the clients, competitors, insurers, and claims adjusters. An agent's competitors are a valuable source of information.

It has been said that "if you have the right agent or broker, the price is right. If you have the wrong agent or broker, no price is right." Many agents and brokers have a considerable amount of experience in placing the more familiar lines of property and casualty insurance. Most of the risks the general agent or broker handles are far more standardized than aviation lines. For example, the average FBO presents a number of risks which the average agent or broker, being unaware of how an FBO operates, would have no idea how to handle. How can an agent recognize loss exposures if unable to recognize the differences in methods of operation.

We might use a general practitioner for our more common medical ailments, but not for open heart surgery. The analogy holds for the insurance industry. While an agent may be extremely competent in the general areas of property and casualty insurance, the individual may have very little aviation insurance experience or it might be limited to a few business and pleasure risks.

An insured must consider an agent or broker years of experience in the insurance business and the breadth of exposure to the various lines. Does the agent primarily handle personal lines, small or large accounts, or across-the-board business? Does the agent specialize in aviation insurance? What type of risks are handled? Which markets are represented? Is there any experience in dealing with aviation claims? How long has the agent been placing aviation risks? Has the agent attended seminars, courses, or received other specific instructions on aviation insurance such as a company correspondence course? Is anyone in the office an active pilot? Answers to these questions help the insured make an informed decision.

Independent Adjusting Services

Normally an insured will notify the agent or broker first in the event of a loss. While all of the aviation insurers have claims personnel, the company will generally assign the loss to one of a number of independent adjusters located throughout the country. Agents and brokers work very closely with these adjusters as well as company claims personnel in handling the claim. An organization which represents many of these independent adjusters is called the *Organized Flying Adjusters*. The following listing includes several of the largest aviation adjusting firms.

Airclaims, Inc.
7315 Wisconsin Avenue
Bethesda, Maryland 20814

Golding and Desveaux
3325 Wilshire Boulevard
Los Angeles, California 90010

Aircraft Investigation & Research Co.
11771 Natural Bridge
Bridgeton, Missouri 63044

Peter J. McBreen & Associates, Inc.
20 North Wacker Drive
Chicago, Illinois 60606

KEY TERMS

Direct-writing companies
Avemco Insurance Company
National Aviation Underwriters (NAU)
Associated Aviation Underwriters (AAU)
United States Aviation Underwriters (USAU)
Aviation Office of America (AOA)
Insurance Company of North America (INA)
Lloyd's of London
Names

Syndicate
Lloyd's brokers
Best's Insurance Reports
Captive agents
Front companies
Agent
Broker
World Aviation Directory
Organized Flying Adjusters

REVIEW QUESTIONS

1. When did the first combined aircraft hull and liability policies appear in the market? Why did it take until this time?
2. Who are the two major direct-writing aviation insurance companies? What are the primary classes of business they underwrite?
3. Who are the two major domestic aviation insurance groups? Describe the classes of business they write. Which major insurance company underwrites aviation risks for its own account and is not a member of a group? Name four other aviation insurance markets.
4. What is a Lloyd's syndicate? Can any agent or broker place business directly with Lloyd's of London? What is the role of the lead underwriter?
5. What is *Best's Insurance Reports*? What are the advantages and disadvantages of selecting a direct-writing company?
6. Discuss some of the things which an insured must consider in selecting an insurer. Why might it not be a good practice to buy aviation insurance on price alone?
7. What is the difference between agents and brokers? Name several of the largest brokerage firms in the United States. Why do you think they place the bulk of the air carrier business?
8. Why is it important for an agent or broker placing aviation business to have an understanding of aviation industry. What characteristics should an insured consider in selecting an agent or broker?

Chapter 4

Risk And Insurance

OUTLINE

The Concept of Risk
Methods of Dealing With Risks
Insurance as a Method for Handling Risk
Uses of Insurance
Risk Management

OBJECTIVES

At the end of this chapter your should be able to:
Describe the fundamental concept of risk and how it relates to insurance.
Define loss and chance of loss.
Recognize the difference between speculative risks and pure risks.
Identify the three types of loss exposures to which an individual or organization is exposed.
Distinguish between perils and hazards.
List six methods of dealing with risks.
Define insurance from a legal, social, and accounting standpoint.
Discuss the requirements for an insurable risk and relate how some of these present a problem for aviation underwriters.
Understand the significant role of insurance in our economy.
Explain what is meant by risk management and highlight the steps in the risk management process.

THE CONCEPT OF RISK

Risk is the basis of insurance. Although every person, business, or organization faces risk every day, a sound understanding of the concept of risk is the foundation for any type of insurance. *Risk* is uncertainty. Risk involves the possibility of loss and therefore makes for insecurity. The *major function of insurance is to substitute certainty for uncertainty* in one's personal and business activities. We cannot say that insurance removes the risk of misfortune, since the mere fact that an article is insured is no guarantee that it will not be lost or damaged. What insurance does accomplish is to provide for full or partial compensation in the event an insured article is damaged or destroyed.

Uncertainty, or risk, represents insecurity and individuals and businesses have a natural desire for a reasonable amount of security in their personal and business lives. Examples of risk are everywhere, ranging from the unavoidable to those assumed by choice, i.e., the risk of losing one's pilot license because of poor health or the risk of starting a new commuter airline. Indeed, anyone who owns property automatically assumes the risk of such perils as fire, windstorm, theft, or liability lawsuits. The inability to predict when or if these perils may cause losses is a risk that property owners acquire with their ownership.

Underwriters often use the word risk in a different manner to describe the object of potential loss, or the object insured. Thus, an aircraft may be referred to as "the risk" in a hull and liability policy. Underwriters will also refer to the different uses of aircraft such as business and pleasure, industrial aid, airline, flight instruction, and so forth as different "classes of risk."

Loss

It was mentioned earlier that risk involves the possibility of loss. Insurance is widely sold because people are anxious to avoid loss. *Loss* may be defined as unintentionally parting with something of value. The theft of a radio is an obvious loss, since the owner has unintentionally parted with the value of the property. There are other types of losses besides physical ones. For example, a person who insures another while flying an airplane and becomes liable for damages has lost property as surely as a person who loses possession of a physical object.

Chance of loss is the relative probability of a loss occurring. The greater the chance of loss, the more likely a person will be to seek insurance. If the property is certain to be destroyed, the chance of loss is 100 percent; if the property cannot be destroyed, the chance of loss is zero. In both of these cases, there is no risk, because there is no uncertainty. The chance of loss may conveniently be expressed as a fraction, the numerator representing the number of times that event can be expected to occur and the denominator representing the number of times that the event could possibly occur. For example, if 100 aircraft are exposed to the risk of theft and 3 of them can be expected to be stolen each year, we may say that the chance of loss is 3 percent.

Insurance companies generally find it impossible to insure events which are likely to occur in a large percentage of cases, say 25 percent or 50 percent of the total number of risks outstanding. Chance of loss, including frequency and severity, is important in insurance because it is the basis on which risks are established. A reasonable degree of accuracy in measuring loss probabilities is necessary if adequate and equitable insurance rates are to be developed. In addition, the chance of loss affects the decision concerning how risk should be handled. If the chance of loss is high, risk avoidance or risk assumption coupled with a major loss-prevention effort might be the best method of dealing with risk. If the chance of loss is very small, the best approach may be to simply ignore the risk.

Classifications of Risk

A risk may be classified as either speculative or pure. A *speculative risk* is one which involves the possibilities of profit or loss. Gambling, for example, is a speculative risk. Similarly, when an airline embarks on a new route it assumes a speculative risk. They are exposing themselves to the possibility of profits, losses, or breaking even. It is the possibility of gain that motivates individuals and companies to incur speculative risks. A *pure risk*, on the other hand, involves only the possibilities of loss or no loss. An aircraft owner is exposed to the risk of loss as a result of an engine fire in flight. Understandably, insurance deals with pure risks. Insurance is not designed to enable the insured to realize a profit, but to protect assets which he already has. The insurance contract, therefore, does not bring into existence any new risk but offers protection against a risk which is already present. By taking out insurance, the insured is not seeking to enrich himself at the expense of anyone else, but merely to protect what he already has.

Types of Loss Exposures

The pure risks that confront individuals and businesses may cause personal, property, or liability exposures. The term *exposure* is used in insurance to describe the property or person facing a condition in which loss or losses are possible.

Personal Loss Exposures

The exposures to accidental death or dismemberment, sickness, disability, and even unemployment are *personal loss exposures* which can result in loss of income or assets, or mental or physical suffering. Life and accident coverage and loss of license coverage would be examples of insurance designed to protect against personal loss exposures.

Property Loss Exposures

Aircraft owners and operators face the possibility of both direct and indirect losses. If your aircraft is damaged in a crash, the *direct loss* is the cost of repairs. The *indirect losses* are the time and effort required to arrange for repairs, the loss of use of your aircraft while repairs are being made, and the additional cost of renting another plane while repairs are being made. Aircraft hull coverage or fire coverage on a hangar would be examples of coverages designed to protect against direct (so sometimes referred to as first party) *property loss exposures.*

Liability Loss Exposures

Under our system of law, a person can be held responsible for causing injury or damage to the person or property of others. Thus a person is exposed to the possibility of *liability loss exposures* (referred to as third party claims) by having to defend himself against a lawsuit. In addition, a person may become legally obligated to pay for the injury or damage to the person or property of others.

Factors Affecting Risk

There are two factors which work together in causing losses. They are perils and hazards.

Perils

The *peril* is the actual cause of a given loss (the loss producing agent) which may be fire, theft, windstorm, explosion, riot, or any number of possible causes. Whether or not a peril is covered by the policy can be determined only by examining the wording of the policy itself.

In the early days of aviation insurance, most hull (physical damage to the aircraft itself) coverage was written on a specified perils basis. Today, virtually all policies are written on an all risks basis.

Hazards

Hazards are the various factors which contribute to uncertainty in any given situation. It is common to speak of a hazard as anything which may conceivably bring about a loss, whereas a peril is used to denote the factor which actually causes the loss. Another way of looking at hazards is to consider them as factors which contribute to the possibility of loss.

There are physical, moral, and morale hazards. Location, construction (in the case of a building), and use can represent *physical hazards* that affect risk. An aircraft tied down at an airport located near a high crime area would certainly be susceptible to loss by theft.

Construction affects the probability and severity of loss. While no building is fireproof, some types of construction are less susceptible to loss from fires than others. Use may also create a physical hazard. A light single-engine aircraft used exclusively for student instruction by a fixed base operator will have a greater probability of loss or damage than the same aircraft operated by an individual private pilot owner with a total of 500 hours in the aircraft.

Moral hazard is an individual characteristic of the insured that increases the probability of loss. Dishonesty or lack of integrity in an individual can increase the chance of loss to 100 percent. For example, dishonest insureds increase arson losses. Insureds have been known to try to overinsure or inflate the value of an aircraft and then destroy it by some means to collect the insurance. The moral hazard is generally determined by an inspection report. Insurance companies make every effort to avoid the moral hazard since in theory it is uninsurable. Underwriters attempt to determine if there is a moral hazard from such things as credit reports and character references.

Morale hazards, unlike moral hazards, do not involve dishonesty. Instead, morale hazards represent an attitude of carelessness and lack of concern that increases the chance a loss will occur. Poor housekeeping on the part of an FBO by allowing spare parts, oily rags, and trash to accumulate in a hangar would be an example.

Because some hazards exist in all lines of insurance, companies are interested in the individuals and companies they insure. *Adverse selection* may be defined as the insuring of a group of risks which represents an above-average expectation of loss. Adverse selection may also be defined as the tendency of poor risks to seek insurance.

It is not the purpose of the insurance company in making physical examinations and inspections to insure only the very best risks. Rather, its purpose is to make sure that it obtains an average spread or risks. It is a motto in insurance circles that companies must select or they will be selected against.

METHODS OF DEALING WITH RISKS

The concept of risk is universal. All individuals and businesses face risks. The methods of dealing with economic risks faced by individuals and businesses can be categorized under the following headings.

1. *The risk may be avoided or ignored.* A company may decide not to use private aircraft or allow any employee to fly aircraft for business purposes and as such avoid the risk. An insured may decide not to purchase hull coverage on his low valued aircraft because of the high premium and as such, ignore the risk.

2. *Loss prevention may be practiced (reducing the hazard).* Individuals or companies may attempt to prevent losses or reduce the chance of loss rather than obtain adequate insurance. Of course, they may wish both to purchase insurance and to practice loss prevention methods. If they do not procure insurance, there will be a greater incentive to survey all the exisiting hazards to the property and prevent these by every reasonable method. An FBO may establish certain procedures in parking aircraft and bringing them in and out of the hangar to avoid "hangar rash" type claims. Establishing certain visitor areas, posting no smoking signs in the hangar, improving housekeeping procedures, and giving proficiency check rides to all renter pilots are all loss prevention techniques which can be initiated at a moderate cost but significantly improve a risk.

3. *Losses may be reduced, once they occur.* Here the individual or company does not purchase insurance, but wisely makes provision to minimize any losses which do occur. The maintenance of firefighting equipment such as fire extinguishers in the hangar is a method, not of actually preventing losses, but of minimizing such losses should they occur. Posting signs which indicate "In case of fire call _____" or giving adequate evacuation procedures from buildings are examples.

4. *The risk may be shifted to another party.* Instead of assuming the risk, the individual may decide to shift the risk of loss to some third party. Fixed base operators quite commonly request that transient aircraft operators sign an agreement holding the the FBO harmless in the event of loss while the aircraft is temporarily parked on their ramp. The U.S. government requires that all civilian aircraft operators using military bases assume all liability for any loss or damage to property arising out of the aircraft use at the base.

5. *Self-insurance may be practiced.* Self-insurance is often confused with noninsurance. Noninsurance simply means not taking out insurance, whereas self-insurance actually involves the insurance mechanism. It should be emphasized that self-insurance is practical only for large organizations. An example might be a large corporate fleet operator which has 20 aircraft and wishes to self-insure against physical damage to the aircraft up to a limit of $500 thousand. A reserve would be created and funds would be paid into it each year on a systematic basis. The reserve should be sufficient to meet the losses which the organization expects in the future. Understandably, self-insurance involves someone performing all of the functions of an insurance company.

6. *Risk may be reduced through combination (purchasing insurance).* Being a group operation, insurance involves the combining of risks in sufficient numbers so that the losses will be predictable, and so that each insured may pay a small premium in exchange for a desired protection.

INSURANCE AS A METHOD FOR HANDLING RISK

The major purpose of insurance is to provide security for individuals and companies by means of a group operation of combining risks. Insurance enables the individual or company to obtain greater protection by combining with others who are also exposed to this risk than he could obtain by meeting it himself. The major social advantage of insurance is that it permits a spreading of risks so that a loss which would be unbearable for one person or company may be borne with relative ease by a large number of insureds.

Insurance is sold primarily by corporations which are licensed to sell policies in one or more states. In order to meet losses and to pay for their operating expenses, insurance companies establish rates, which are the prices for a given amount of insurance. The insurance contract is often referred to as a *policy* to distinguish it from other legal documents.

Insurance is often referred to as an "intangible" since the policyholder receives in essence a piece of paper rather than a physical product. In exchange for a premium, the company promises to pay in the event of loss. Because the benefits of insurance often lie in the future and individuals and companies are not aware of all the risk which they are exposed, insurance companies have generally found it necessary to employ agents to sell their products to the public. The purpose of the agent is to explain policies to the public and to convince potential clients of the benefits of insurance.

Definition of Insurance

Insurance may be defined in many ways, depending upon the standpoint from which it is viewed.

1. From a legal standpoint, insurance is a contract whereby the insurance company agrees to make payments to a party, generally called the *insured*, should the event insured against in the contract occur. Thus, we may look upon all insurance as a series of contracts whereby the insurance company agrees to indemnify the insured against certain losses. The principle of indemnity applies to all lines of insurance except life, accident, and sickness. *Indemnify* simply means to make the insured whole, to return his property to the state that it was in prior to the loss—no better and no worse.

2. From a social standpoint, we may look upon insurance as a method of combining a large enough group of units to make the loss predictable. This method enables individuals or companies to obtain insurance at a reasonable rate and thus to protect themselves against the possibilitiy of unforseen losses.

3. From an accounting standpoint, insurance may be defined as a method of substituting a small certain loss for a large uncertain loss. In other words, in purchasing insurance the insured suffers a monetary loss by paying a small premium which he would otherwise not have to pay; in return, however, he obtains protection against the possibility of a large loss which may or may not occur.

Requirements for an Insurable Risk

It is not possible to insure every personal and business risk. Certain criteria or requirements must be met.

1. *A large number of homogeneous risks must be present.* Since insurance depends upon the law of large numbers, it is essential that the insurance company be able to insure a large number of homogeneous risks so that losses will be predictable and an adequate premium may be determined before policies are sold. Where the insurance is of such a type that few persons would be interested in its purchase, its issuance is usually not practical. Insurance in such cases is not impossible, however, and policies to cover unusual hazards are written by a few markets.

Unlike automobile insurance, aircraft risks represent a considerably smaller number of exposure units. In addition, aircraft risks can vary a great deal depending upon the use and the qualifications of the pilot. Aircraft types and values include a wide range, from low valued older single-engine aircraft to multimillion dollar jets. All these factors compound the underwriter's problem of developing a homogeneous grouping of risks for rating purposes and still having a large enough number to obtain credibility in the rating structure.

2. *The number of losses must be predictable to a reasonable degree.* The price which an insurance company charges is directly related to the number and extent of the losses which they expect. In order to set a rate, the underwriter must have some basis upon which to determine the probable losses. Because of the catastrophic nature of aviation risks, this also is a difficult factor. A company may enjoy reasonably good experience for a period of years and then several catastrophes could wipe out all accumulated reserves. The ultimate nightmare of any aviation underwriter is to have two jumbo jets colliding over New York City at rush hour.

In the case of new risks, such as the insurance on the first jets or a new satellite, there is no adequate basis for determining the rate; the insurance must either be refused or else must be written at a premium which is only a guess.

3. *The object to be insured must be of sufficient value to warrant the purchase of insurance.* Insurance is only practical when the loss of the insured article will cause some hardship to the individual. People generally do not insure objects of very small value such as fountain pens and pencils. Insurance is not practical since the cost of insuring such articles would be disproportionate to their value. Where the article may easily be replaced from current income, insurance is seldom feasible. In this connection it should also be noted that insurance is not designed to cover ordinary repair and maintenance costs. When the article is of such a nature that it will gradually wear out, insurance cannot be written to cover the "wear and tear hazard."

4. *The loss must be accidental.* Insurance is not designed to cover losses which are certain to occur. Preferably the loss should be both accidental and outside the control of the insured. An *accident* normally means an event which is unexpected, unforeseen, and outside the control of the insured.

Underwriters exclude damage, under the physical damage portion of an aircraft hull and liability policy, which is *"due and confined to the wear and tear deterioration"* and so forth. Consequently, an engine that breaks down because it is improperly maintained would not be covered. However, if the engine stopped while in flight, causing a crash with resulting damage, the aircraft would be covered including the engine.

5. *The event insured against must be unlikely to occur to all insured risks simultaneously.* Insurance companies are interested primarily in situations where the loss may be expected to occur to only a very small percentage of the exposed units at any given time.

Underwriters normally exclude losses arising out of war, rebellion, insurrection, and so forth because any of these events could affect all insureds at the same time.

In addition, it is quite common for underwriters to maintain mapping books in which they keep track of all aircraft risks at a particular airport. Too many risks at one location could result in a catastrophic loss, for instance, if a tornado hit that particular airport.

6. *The loss must be definite.* It must be difficult or impossible for the insured to pretend that he has suffered a loss when he has not done so. Life insurance is ideal from this standpoint, since it is rather difficult to feign death.

USES OF INSURANCE

Insurance plays an important role in our economy in a number of ways.

1. *Insurance introduces security into personal and business situations.* The purpose of all forms of insurance is to provide payment in the event of unexpected losses. Insurance acts as a stabilizing factor in protecting both businesses and individuals against unexpected losses. The unique value of insurance lies in its

ability to grant a large amount of protection in return for a small premium. It is only by the insurance method that many of the personal and business risks which confront every individual can be successfully met.

2. *Insurance serves as a basis of credit, especially in business situations.* Without adequate insurance protection no financial institution would lend money for the purchase of capital goods.

3. *Insurance provides a means of capitalizing earning power.* Every person, in a materialistic sense, possesses a monetary value based upon his future earnings. The greater the future earnings, the greater is the present "life value" of the person. The death of a working individual is no less disastrous from a monetary standpoint than is the destruction of an income producing machine.

Payments in the event of death or disability injuries are largely based upon an estimate of the deceased individual's future earnings. Future earnings will depend upon such factors as the individual's annual income, present age, and state of health.

4. *Insurance aids in the development of the economy.* Large reserves are set up to meet future policy obligations, and these reserves are invested throughout the economy. Life insurance companies, such as Metropolitan and Prudential, were a major source of funding the major air carriers when they accepted their first jumbo jets in the early 1970s.

5. *Insurance performs a social function by analyzing risks and making protection available at a reasonable cost.* Since risk is their business, insurance companies have become experts at analyzing the risks to which businesses and individuals are all exposed. Insurance companies maintain large loss prevention and engineering staffs which assist companies in reducing hazards. Safety inspectors from the insurance company are often located at a major insured's facility and work closely with company personnel in developing and managing safety programs.

6. *Insurance distributes the cost of accidents among a large group of persons.* We have seen that insurance may be defined as a method of substituting a small certain loss for a large uncertain loss. By distributing the cost of accidents among a very large group of persons, the cost of such misfortunes can be easily borne.

7. *Loss-prevention methods are encouraged.* By allowing discounts for certain types of loss-prevention methods, insurance companies provide a financial incentive for business firms to improve their safety measures. For example, the introduction of sprinkler systems is often financially advantageous to an insured because of the consequent reduction in fire insurance rates. Companies will offer the most attractive rates to corporate fleet operators who have provided for recurrent flight training for their crews.

8. *Insurance agents provide a professional service.* The tendency today is not to sell policies on a hit-or-miss basis; rather the goal of the better agencies and brokers is to develop a clientele of satisfied policyholders who will look to them for their insurance needs and who will recommend their services to others. Agents survey the needs of their clients in a systematic manner and tailor coverages to fit these needs.

9. *Insurance reduces cost.* Insurance may actually enable a company to sell its products or services at a lower cost, because through insurance the insured is able to cover many business risks for a small premium. If the company were unable to do so, it would be necessary to charge a higher price for products or services to compensate for these risks.

RISK MANAGEMENT

Risk management deals with the systematic identification of a company's exposures to the risk of loss, and with decisions on the best methods for handling these exposures in relation to corporate profitability. Risk managers are responsible for identifying all exposures that create pure risks and for creating programs to handle them. They are expected to protect the organization's income and assets from pure-risk losses as much as is possible at minimum cost.

A company faces the challenge to assess an almost unlimited number of possible events which have financial consequences. Risk management calls for close familiarity with all facets of the business as well as a seasoned, balanced judgment. In larger corporations, such as the major air carriers, aircraft manufacturers or large corporate fleet operators, risk management is directed by a professional insurance staff. In smaller firms, such as a fixed base operator, it may be a part-time responsibility of the treasurer or controller, or even of the president. In any event it is essential to fix responsibility for this vital activity so that it receives the attention it warrants, and is not perceived as simply the purchasing of insurance. Whether the function is performed by a professional risk manager or by another top officer, it is that person's responsibility to assure the financial solvency of the firm against the consequences of loss, at the lowest possible cost.

The history of modern risk management traces its origin to 1931 when the insurance section of the American Management Association was formed. In 1932 the Insurance Buyers of New York was organized by representatives of several large New York firms concerned with problems involving insurance buying for their business. They met regularly to exchange information and ideas in risk management. This organization was succeeded by the American Society of Insurance Management which changed its name in 1975 to the Risk and Insurance Management Society (RIMS). RIMS has local chapters throughout the country.

The Process of Risk Management

The risk management process involves the following steps.

Identifying Risks

Within a company, risk management starts with a comprehensive review of the possibilities of loss to which the firm is exposed. An extensive physical inspection of company facilities and operations is often the first move. Such a survey may be reinforced by the use of risk analysis questionnaires intended to uncover hidden exposures common to many firms. Flow charts, detailing the firm's entire operating processes, may suggest further hazards. Reports on past losses experienced can be invaluable, as can analysis of financial statements and future plans.

The risk manager, often working closely with an agent or broker, looks for five major kinds of risk. They are: (1) physical damage to property; (2) loss of income due to property damage; (3) liability-loss of the firm's assets due to its responsibility for damage or injury to other's property or person; (4) losses through fraud or criminal acts; and (5) loss to the business resulting from the death or disability of employees.

For example, an FBO might identify the following risks:
- Loss or damage to personally owned aircraft
- Liability incurred as a result of operating owned and non-owned aircraft
- Aircraft of others left in the FBO's care and custody for storage, maintenance, or repair
- Loss or damage to buildings
- Injury to employees and customers or visitors while on the premises
- Liability incurred as a result of negligence on the part of employees while working on aircraft of others
- Loss or damage to shop equipment including theft
- Life insurance on the FBO and key employees

This list is by no means all inclusive but merely shows the types of risk which must be identified.

Risk Measurement

Once the risks of loss have been identified, the next step is to measure both the greatest possible loss and the greatest probable loss that can occur. This will determine the relative importance of potential losses and serve as a guide to the best techniques for risk handling and limits of coverage to be carried.

There are four dimensions to be measured. *Frequency* involves the number of losses that may occur and their probabilities. *Severity* has to do with the size of losses that may occur and their probabilities. *Predictability* refers to the credibility of frequency and severity predictions, based on the nature of the risk. *Probability* is the relative frequency with which an event can be expected to occur in the long run.

Of these factors, severity is the most important, since a single catasrophe could wipe out the firm. Therefore all losses from a single event must be considered, as must the ultimate financial impact and the potential adverse impact on financial planning. For example, on an average day an FBO may have anywhere from three to five single-engine transient aircraft stored in the tie-down area. On the weekend this number may double including several multiengine aircraft. Several times during the year around holidays or special events this number may quadruple. What limit of liability should be carried under the hangarkeepers coverage while these aircraft are there? This is just one of a number of questions which must be answered in the risk measurement process.

On the other hand, losses that occur with frequency, such as minor injuries to employees and "hangar rash" type losses are relatively small and more predictable.

Risk Handling Techniques

Risk management-techniques were discussed earlier in this chapter under methods of dealing with risks so it is only necessary to review. Basically, we can place the methods previously discussed under two headings.

One is risk control—minimizing at the least possible cost the risk of losses to which the firm is exposed. The other is risk finance, accomplished either through company funds, such as self-insurance, or through transfer to others, principally insurers.

Risk control can be achieved by simply avoiding the risk in the first place. For example, our FBO might require that all transient multiengine aircraft be hangared and not tied down over night. It can involve reduction of hazards such as better housekeeping or requiring wing walkers when moving aircraft. It can aim at loss reduction—reducing the severity of loss by fire, for example, by installing a sprinkler system or having an adequate number of workable fire extinguishers installed in the hangar.

Risk finance, the second broad option, can be divided between risk retention and risk transfer. *Risk retention* means that the risk has been identified and measured and a decision made to pay any losses out of company resources. For example, our FBO may decide not to insure against theft of shop tools. *Risk transfer,* as opposed to retention, usually means insuring the risk through an insurer, although it also includes transfer to other parties through "hold harmless" clauses in contracts. For example, an FBO may require that all transient aircraft owners sign a hold harmless agreement in an attempt to relieve himself of liability for overnight parking.

Selection of Specific Techniques

After reviewing the techniques available for treating identified and measured risks, the risk manager must determine the best technique for handling each specific risk. Basic to most risk handling decisions is the formulation of alternative strategies for a given situation. Such strategies can then be compared in terms of the possible amount of losses involved as well as their net benefit to the company. For example, an airline risk manager, after deciding to cover the company's aircraft against physical damage, might consider the following alternatives:

• Full coverage with a limit of up to $10 million for each aircraft and no deductibles

- Full coverage with a limit of up to $10 million for each aircraft and $20 million deductible for the year
- Full coverage with a limit of up to $10 million for each aircraft and a disappearing deductible depending upon loss experience

Periodic Evaluation

To be effective, any risk management program must be regularly reviewed. Among the results which should be monitored are those relating to costs, safety activities carried out, and loss prevention efforts effected. Loss records should be examined to determine changes in frequency and severity. Developments that affect original risk handling decisions should be considered. Premiums should reflect any credits due for loss control activities.

Finally the risk manager will want to be assured that the company's overall risk management policy is being carried out and that the company as a whole is cooperating in this vitally important area.

KEY TERMS

Risk	Morale hazards
Loss	Adverse selection
Chance of loss	Policy
Speculative risk	Insurance
Pure risk	Insured
Exposure	Indemnify
Personal loss exposures	Accident
Property loss exposures	Risk management
Direct loss	Frequency
Indirect loss	Severity
Liability loss exposures	Predictability
Peril	Probability
Hazards	Risk retention
Physical hazards	Risk transfer
Moral hazard	

REVIEW QUESTIONS

1. How does the concept of risk relate to insurance? Define loss. What is meant by chance of loss?
2. Give several examples of speculative and pure risks. What is meant by direct and indirect property loss exposures?
3. What is a peril? Distinguish between physical, moral, and morale hazards.
4. List six methods of dealing with risks. How can risks be shifted to another party? Is self-insurance the same as no insurance? Explain. What is the purpose of insurance? How would you define it from a legal, social, and accounting standpoint?
5. One of the requirements for an insurable risk is a large number of homogeneous exposure units subject to the same degree of loss. Why does this requirement present a problem for aviation underwriters? Why does insurance require that the loss must be accidental?
6. Explain the multifaced role that insurance plays in our economy.
7. Describe what is meant by the risk management process. Who is responsible for carrying it out? Define risk management?

REFERENCES

Athern, James L., and S. Travis Pritchett. *Risk and Insurance* (5th ed.). West Publishing Company, St. Paul, Minnesota, 1984.

Bickelhaupt, David L. *General Insurance* (11th ed.). Richard D. Irwin, Inc., Homewood, Illinois, 1983.

Mehr, Robert I., and Emerson Cammack. *Principles of Insurance* (7th ed.). Richard D. Irwin, Inc., Homewood, Illinois, 1980.

Reigel, Robert, Jerome S. Miller, and C. Arthur Williams Jr. *Insurance Principles and Practices: Property and Liability* (6th ed.).Prentice-Hall, Inc., Englewood Cliffs, New Jersey, 1976.

Chapter 5

THE LEGAL FOUNDATION FOR INSURANCE

OUTLINE

Nature and Types of Law
Indemnity
Legal Liability
Summary

OBJECTIVES

At the end of this chapter you should be able to:
Distinguish between the traditional division of law.
Discuss the legal principles of indemnity, insurable interest, and subrogation as they pertain to insurance contracts.
Describe the legal basis for liability and explain why this is important to insurance consumers.
Define torts and explain how they arise.
Describe the four requirements which must be met before a person can be held legally responsible for a negligent act.
Explain what is meant by "degree of care required."
Define guest laws and discuss their purpose.
Summarize three common defenses for a negligent act.
Identify and define five intentional torts.
Describe how liability may be incurred under contract.

NATURE AND TYPES OF LAW

Since the insurance policy is a legal contract, a knowledge of certain fundamental legal principles is useful for understanding its nature and the manner in which it is interpreted. The general purposes of our legal system are to keep order, to settle disputes, and to prescribe a code of conduct for its members.

Law is traditionally divided into two general types—statutory and common. The *statutory law* consists of laws which have been passed by duly authorized bodies, such as the federal and state governments. The *common law* is often referred to as "unwritten law" and as "judge-made law," since it consists of the great body of past court decisions. Under our English system of common law, courts are bound by the traditions of the legal profession to follow precedents which have been well established by prior decisions. It is somewhat misleading to speak of the common law as "unwritten," since past court decisions are published and available to all members of the legal profession and to the public.

A third type of law—*administrative law*—has become of increasing importance. Administrative bodies, such as the Federal Aviation Administration, are often given power to "interpret" legislation which they enforce, and thus have in effect limited legislative powers. Thus, rulings of the state insurance commissioner are theoretically only interpretations of the state insurance law but often have the practical effect of new legislation.

Statutory law on insurance consists of applicable legislation passed by the federal and various state governments. Since 1944, insurance has been held to be subject to regulation by the federal government. *Public Law 15*, however, provided that it was the intention of Congress that states should continue to regulate insurance to the extent that they did so effectively and for the most part, statutory regulation of insurance remains on the state level.

INDEMNITY

The basic legal principle which affects the operation of insurance is the concept of indemnity. Webster defines *indemnity* as "compensation or remuneration for loss or injury sustained." Simply stated, it means that the insurer agrees to pay for no more than the actual loss suffered by the insured (to make him whole: no better, no worse off). Obviously, if insureds could gain by having an insured loss, some would deliberately cause losses.

Insurance is not designed to enable the insureds to realize a profit (such as gambling), but to protect assets which they already have. The insurance contract, therefore, does not bring into existence any new risk but offers protection against a risk which is already present. By taking out insurance, the insureds are not seeking to enrich themselves at the expense of anyone else, but merely to protect what they already have. Therefore, gambling and insurance are opposites: one creates risk, the other reduces it.

The concept of indemnity is supported by several legal principles. They are insurable interest and subrogation.

Insurable Interest

An *insurable interest* is a prerequisite to any valid contract. It is defined as an interest such that its possessor would be financially injured by the occurrence of the event insured against. From a legal standpoint, the absence of an insurable interest at the required time means that the contract is a wagering contract and therefore is unenforceable. If, for example, a life insurance company discovers that the applicant on a policy has no insurable interest in the person whom they insured, the company could refuse to make payment.

The amount of the insurable interest in most lines of property and liability insurance is determined by the value of the property involved or the value of the legal obligation in question. In life insurance the amount of the insurable interest is immaterial. If an insurable interest exists in life insurance, it is legally sufficient to support any amount of life insurance which the person is able to secure.

An insurable interest in property contracts is normally based upon the ownership of the property. This is not essential, however, as a person who has an equitable title in the property or who has a relationship such that he is financially dependent upon the existence of the property may also have an insurable interest. A mortgagee has an insurable interest in the property pledged as security for a debt. For example, a bank holding a loan on an aircraft certainly has an insurable interest in the aircraft. Leasors and leasees of aircraft also have an insurable interest.

Possession may give the holder of property an insurable interest. Thus a bailee (one holding property of another) has an insurable interest in property left in his care and custody. A fixed base operator who provides hangarage, maintenance, repair, or even tie-down space is a bailee.

Generally speaking, an insurable interest in the property or liability field must exist only at the time of loss, and need not necessarily exist when the policy was originally taken out. The amount of the insurable interest is determined by the interest of the policyholder in the property which is insured.

In the case of life insurance, every person has an insurable interest in his own life. He also has an insurable interest in those persons to whom he is related by blood, marriage, or business in such a way that he may reasonably expect to benefit financially by the continuation of their lives. In the case of life insurance, an insurable interest need exist only at the time the policy was originally issued.

Subrogation

The principle of indemnity is also supported by the right of subrogation. *Subrogation* is the right of the insurance company, after paying the insured's loss in full, to take over all the insured's legal rights against negligent third parties. It is not the purpose of insurance to enable policyholders to realize a profit. If it were not for the right of subrogation, the policyholder might recover twice, once from the insurance company and once from the third party who caused the accident or the negligent party (tort-feasor) could escape liability although responsible for the loss. The right of subrogation exists in most lines of property and liability insurance and is applicable independently of any policy provision. To bring it to the attention of the policyholder, most property and liability contracts contain a specific provision that the insurance company will take over all legal rights against third parties upon payment of a loss. A subrogation clause is also included in many proof-of-loss forms.

Subrogation is of great importance in the case of aircraft hull coverage. Because pilot negligence is a leading factor in aircraft accidents, an individual who rents an aircraft from an FBO may be subrogated against in the event of loss or damage to the FBO's aircraft caused by his negligence.

The right of subrogation does not accrue to the insurance company until the insured has been fully indemnified for his loss. This is to prevent any third party who may have caused the loss from being subjected to two lawsuits—one from the policyholder and one from the insurance company. The policyholder must be careful not to take any actions which would defeat the company's right of subrogation, such as signing statements admitting his liability for an accident.

LEGAL LIABILITY

Aviation liability exposures often result in large losses. On June 30, 1984, a jury awarded $10.1 million to a couple whose 11-year-old daughter was killed in the second–worst air disaster in U.S. history. The young girl was among eight people on the ground when a Pan Am Boeing 727 plunged into her home on July 9, 1982. All 146 people aboard were killed.

On June 8, 1984, a jury in Camden, New Jersey, ordered Cessna Aircraft Company to pay $30 million in damages to the estates of three men killed in a Cessna 172 crash and to the lone survivor because it did not warn pilots of a defective seat latch.

The jury found the company negligent for failing to notify the 55,000 owners of the Cessna 172 planes of a faulty seat latching mechanism. A defective seat latch in that type of plane caused the 1980 crash at Cape May Airport. The jury's award included $25 million in punitive damages and $5 million in compensatory damages.

Punitive damages are awards to plaintiffs in excess of *compensatory damages* (full compensation for injuries sustained) and are made to punish the defendent and discourage others from engaging in conduct causing injuries. Defective products have produced large liability settlements.

Nature of Legal Liability

In order to understand the nature of the liability risk, it is helpful to make a division of the various types of legal wrongs. Any action which results in harm to another person may be either a criminal act or a civil act. A *criminal act,* such as arson or theft, is a crime against society and is punished by the state. A *civil wrong* is a wrong against a specific person and constitutes an invasion of the rights of this third party. Civil wrongs are divided into two types: torts and breaches of contracts.

A *tort* is defined as a wrongful act committed by one person against another (other than a breach of contract) for which the law provides a civil remedy in the form of damages. Contracts may involve legal wrong when implied warranties are violated, bailee responsibilities are not fulfilled, or contract obligations are breached.

Torts

1. Negligence

Torts arise out of (1) negligence, (2) liability without fault, and (3) intentional interference. Most tort claims are based on negligence.

Negligence may be defined as "a failure to exercise due care" or "failure to do what a reasonable person would have done under the circumstances, or doing something which a reasonable man would not have done under the circumstances." No one is expected to be perfect, and the law does not require perfection. There are numerous unavoidable accidents for which it would be unfair to hold anyone legally responsible.

The right of recovery for damages due to negligence arises because society expects every person to conduct himself in such a way as not to injure other members of society. As a matter of self-protection, society requires that every person take into account the result of his actions on other persons. If a person fails to exercise such due care and bodily injury or property damage results, the injured party may have a right to reimbursement.

Before a person can be held legally responsible for bodily injury or property damage, four requirements must be met: (1) a legal duty, (2) a wrong, (3) a proximate relationship between the wrong and an injury or damage, and (4) an injury or damage.

A *legal duty* to act, or not to act, depends on the circumstances and persons involved. A bystander has no legal duty to try to prevent a robbery, but a security officer does. Whether or not a legal duty is owed to someone else is decided by the courts, and many factors may determine the degree of care required (to be discussed shortly). The judge decides questions of law and the jury, questions of fact.

A *wrong* is a breach of legal duty, based upon a standard of conduct that is determined by what a prudent person would have done or not done in similar circumstances. Criminal wrongs and other kinds of civil wrongs (breach of contract or warranty) are not so pertinent as negligence is in this description of liability. To do a wrong, the act or omission must be voluntary. Thus, if a person in the course of avoiding great danger injures another person without intent, there is held to be no voluntary act and hence no liability. Negligence usually involves injury that is unintentional. On the other hand, it is no defense if the act which injures a party was done without intent to do an injury or if the motive behind the act was good and praiseworthy.

A third requisite for the fixing of liability is found in the rule that the voluntary act of the wrongdoer must have been the proximate cause of the injury. A person is responsible only for damages which are the direct result of negligence on his part. *Proximate cause* is a legal term which refers to the major cause of injury or damage. The test of proximate cause which is generally applied is whether or not the injury or damage would have occurred in the absence of negligence on the part of the defendant. This means that a person cannot be held responsible for injuries or damages which are an unexpected, or unnatural, result of negligence on his part. For example, suppose a pilot crashed on takeoff when his engine malfunctions, and a spectator became so excited watching the accident that he had a heart attack. By no stretch of the imagination could the pilot be held responsible for the spectator's heart attack.

The fourth requirement for negligence liability is that there be *injury or damage*. The guilty person must pay an amount that reasonably compensates the injured party for: (1) bodily and other personal injuries, (2) loss of income due to disability, (3) pain and suffering, (4) disfigurement, and (5) any other losses for which the negligence is the proximate cause.

Loss of income due to inability to work often comprises a large proportion of *bodily injury* liability cases. As an example of other losses, a husband or wife may collect for the value of the mate's services as well as for *consortium*, the term which the law applies to the companionship of the mate.

Two South Florida couples recently filed suit against Eastern Airlines, claiming the near ditching of Flight 855M between Miami and Nassau on May 5, 1984, caused them permanent mental anguish. The couples contended that Eastern's negligence in failing to install O-rings on the engines, resulting in engine oil losses and near ditching, caused the losses of the "society, services, and consortium" of their spouses.

A parent may also collect for the loss of the services of an injured child and for the expenses associated with the injury. In the case of death, the heirs or next of kin may collect damages for the loss of the life. Some states fix a statutory limit for an instantaneous "wrongful" death; but if the party retains or regains consciousness after the injury and ultimately dies, the damage for conscious suffering is added to the damage for the death. Sometimes bodily injury is extended to include cases where no actual physical injury is suffered, but mental anxiety results from near accidents.

Compensation for *property damage* is measured by the difference in the value of the property before and after injury. Although the cost of repair and replacement may serve as a measure of damage, this does not always reflect the actual amount of the damage. If the cost to repair the damaged property is in excess of its value, then the measure of damage would be the value of the property immediately before the accident, less its salvage value immediately following the accident. Indirect losses resulting from the loss of use of the property may also be a part of property damage liability.

a. Degree of care required. The owner of real estate owes a duty to the public in connection with its care and upkeep, and may be held responsible to persons injured on his property if he allows a nuisance to be present. The word *nuisance* is a legal term meaning a dangerous or defective condition. Thus, an FBO may be held responsible for accidents on the apron area in front his hangar if he fails to keep it free of oil spills or harmful objects. Persons who own or lease property are responsible to members of the public who are injured on it under certain circumstances. The degree of care owed to the public depends upon whether such third parties are legally trespassers, licensees, or invitees.

A *trespasser* is one who ventures upon the property of others without the latter's knowledge or consent. The property owner owes no duty to a trespasser except not to willfully set traps for him. It would not be legal for an airport owner to set up an electric fence around his property without proper warning, even though those who are injured are trespassers. By the same token, a person may not set a trained attack dog upon trespassers without warning.

A *licensee* is one who enters upon the premises of another, with the owner's express or implied consent, principally for his own benefit. An example of a licensee is a salesman. It is often said that a licensee "takes the premises as he finds them." The duty of care owed to a licensee is only slightly greater than that owed to a trespasser. The owner, of course, cannot willfully harm a licensee.

An *invitee* is a person who is invited, either expressly or by implication, to enter a premises. Examples of invitees are customers entering an FBO's office. The fact that an FBO is open for business is an implied invitation for the public to come in. The duty owed to an invitee is a positive one, namely, to keep the premises in a reasonably safe condition. An FBO, for example, is expected to maintain his hangar area in such a manner that members of the public are not injured. His failure to do so constitutes negligence, and members of the public who are injured as a direct result may sue and recover.

A person owes a greater degree of care to someone whom he has invited on his premises (an invitee or guest) than he does to a licensee or trespasser. Some states distinguish between the degree of care owed to business guests or invitees and that owed to social guests to whom a lesser degree is required. If his premises are accessible to children, he may be required to exercise greater care than otherwise.

The degree of care required will also depend on the nature of the activities conducted by the individual or firm and on the type of product being handled. A company who manufactures or sells an inherently dangerous item is expected to take more precautions to prevent it causing injury than a firm which handles less dangerous items. The degree of care expected in each instance is commensurate with the risk involved.

An individual pilot operating his own aircraft for business and pleasure purposes owes invited guests (no charge is made) ordinary or reasonable care in the operation of his aircraft. An injured guest may have a cause of action if he can prove that the pilot did not exercise ordinary or reasonable care in the operation of the aircraft.

An FBO renting (short-term) or leasing (long-term) aircraft to the public must exercise a higher degree of care than the business and pleasure risk. Similarly, air taxi operators and airlines who charge for their services must exercise the highest degree of care to passengers.

b. Guest laws. Originally a great many states enacted laws which severely restricted persons who ride as guests in automobiles or other conveyances like boats and airplanes in their right to sue for injuries sustained by them. By the early 1980s this number had been reduced to 13. The exact terminology of the *guest laws* differs considerably from state to state, but the impact is similar. In general, the guest passenger is not allowed to recover for damage incurred while riding as a passenger, unless the host operator is found to have been guilty of "gross' or "willful and wanton" negligence.

A *guest* is usually defined as one who has not paid for his transportation, although the courts have on occasion interpreted the word more literally in favor of the injured person. Thus, in specific cases, some court decisions have held that where the pilot or owner of an aircraft stood to benefit from the presence of his passenger, the passenger was not a guest, and therefore could recover for damages if ordinary negligence was the proximate cause of the accident. Generally, however, guest laws operate to restrict the right of suit of most ordinary passengers in privately owned conveyances.

c. Res ipsa loquitor. Although the general rule is that the plaintiff (claimant) must prove the negligence of the defendant, the occurrence of an accident under certain conditions is deemed to be prima facie evidence of negligence. This is known as the doctrine of *res ipsa loquitor*—the thing speaks for itself. Generally, this rule will apply when the thing that caused the accident clearly of a kind that does not occur when proper care is exercised.

The doctrine of res ipsa loquitor is not invoked except when necessary evidence is absent or not readily available. Thus, after a plane crash, it may not be possible to determine the cause of the accident. The injured parties are not burdened with proving the negligence of the airline. The doctrine has the effect of justifying an inference of negligence or in some jurisdictions, of establishing a presumption of this nature.

d. Vicarious liability. *Vicarious liability*, sometimes referred to as imputed negligence, makes one person responsible for negligent acts of others. All employers are obligated to protect the public from the wrongful acts of their employees. The courts hold an employer liable for the torts committed by his employees in the course of their employment. When an employee in the course of his employment commits a tort, both the employee and his employer may be sued. The plaintiff may satisfy his judgement against one or both.

In addition to the liability of employers for the torts of their employees, most states provide by statute that a person may be liable for damages caused by another's negligence in operating a motor vehicle. In some states, the rules have been extended to cover aircraft and boats as well as automobiles.

e. Defenses against negligence suits. An important defense against a suit based upon negligence is that no negligence was actually present. This involves proving that the actions of the defendant were those of a reasonable prudent man.

An *assumption of risk* on the part of the injured party is sometimes used as a defense. Assumption of risk argues that the plaintiff by consenting either expressly or by implication to relieve the defendant of the duty to protect had accepted the risk of injury. The risk may be assumed by written agreement (such as a lease for hangar space) or implied (by taking a ride in an open cockpit stunt plane).

Another possible defense is that the injured party was also negligent and was therefore not entitled to collect. Contributory negligence on the part of the injured party is an important reason for many negligence suits being decided in favor of the defendant. *Contributory negligence* is any degree of negligence on the part of the injured party in connection with an accident. In many states, a person who is claiming damages due to another's acts must himself be free of contributory negligence.

The *last-clear-chance* doctrine is an exception to the doctrine of contributory negligence. It states that even though the injured party was negligent, the defendant may be held responsible if he did not take any last clear chance he had of avoiding an accident. A transient pilot who parked his aircraft on an active taxiway is clearly negligent but another pilot using the same taxiway must take a reasonable amount of care to avoid the other aircraft.

In its strict application, the old common law doctrine of contributory negligence does not always produce equitable results. A very slight degree of negligence on the part of an injured person would prohibit recovery. Some 36 states have enacted statutes which provide that contributory negligence shall not prohibit recovery for damages. Such statutes apply the concept of *comparative negligence* and provide that damages shall be diminished in proportion to the amount of negligence attributable to the person injured or to the owner or person in control of the property damaged. As an example, in the case of a midair collision, we might find negligence apportioned among the two aircraft owners and even the Federal Aviation Administration and the manufacturers.

2. Liability Without Fault

The magnitude of liability exposures is seen in a trend in which courts have held firms in particular situations responsible for injuries or damages no matter how careful they may have been in trying to avoid losses to others. Under what is called *strict or absolute liability* certain firms are held liable for damages, regardless of whether or not fault or negligence can be proved against them. Although this doctrine is applied only in particular circumstances, the courts and statutes have been applying it with increasing frequency to the scheduled airlines. The broadest application of the liability regardless of fault idea is demonstrated by workers' compensation laws which hold the employer liable for most employee work injuries and diseases.

3. Intentional Interference

Lawsuits sometimes arise out of injuries or damage caused by intentional torts. Examples include battery, assault, defamation, trespass, and false arrest or detention.

Battery is the offensive or harmful contact of another without his or her express or implied consent. *Assault* is a second example, and this involves threatened battery. Other examples include *defamation,* such as *libel* (written) and *slander* (oral), involving false statements made about someone else, which cause damage to character or invasion of privacy.

Trespass to real property is the wrongful entry on the land of another without permission. *False arrest* or *detention* involves the unprivileged restriction of another's freedom of movement.

Liability Under Contracts

Liability under contract law is based on the invasion of another's right under contract. It occurs only as a result of a contract between one party and another. Liability under tort law is based on the breach of one's duty to respect the rights of the general public. It may result from either common law or statute law.

A *breach of contract* arises when one party to a contract refuses to fulfill his part of the bargain. Liability for breach of contract primarily arises out of the sale of products or services. Under certain circumstances a manufacturer, distributor, or dealer may be held liable for breach of an implied or express contract.

Warranties may be either expressed or implied in connection with the sale of products. An *express warranty* is one which is definitely spelled out, while an *implied warranty* is one which is implied in the sales process. The Consumer Products Safety Act of 1972 has the effect of imposing certain implied warranties on the seller. It is generally the rule that when a buyer makes known to a seller the purpose for which the products are to be used, and the buyer relies on the skill and judgement of the seller, there is an implied warranty that the products will be reasonably fit for the purpose specified. If they are not, the buyer may recover on the basis of breach of an implied contract. Where an express warranty has been made, the purchaser has an obvious right of recovery if the goods do not measure up to the warranty.

Bailee liability

When property is given over to the care of another party, a legal relation of *bailment* arises. Although the ownership of the property is unchanged, it enters the control of the party to whom it is entrusted, known as the *bailee*. This can be in the form of a contract such as a maintenance agreement between two air carriers or simply a handshake as in the case of a private pilot leaving his aircraft with an FBO to be overhauled.

Usually, the bailee is charged with ordinary and reasonable care of the property entrusted to him, and his liability for the safety of the aircraft does not go beyond such degree of care. Negligence on the part of the bailee would establish his liability in case the property were damaged, lost, or destroyed.

SUMMARY

Figure 5.1 includes a summary and synthesis of the legal foundation for insurance discussed in this chapter. This figure should provide a good review of the material covered.

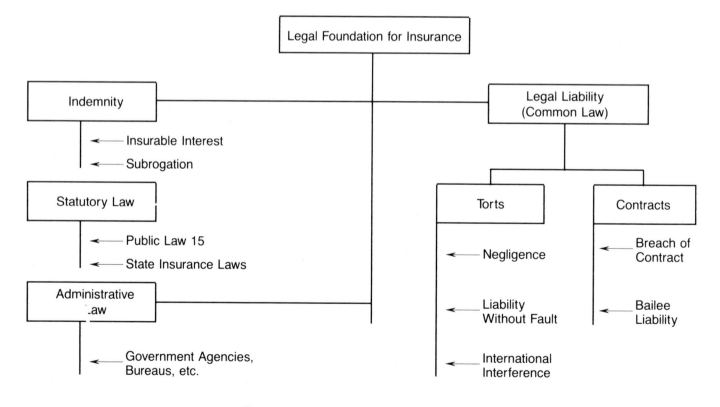

Figure 5.1 Legal Foundation for Insurance.

KEY TERMS

Statutory law	Trespasser
Common law	Licensee
Administrative law	Invitee
Public Law 15	Guest laws
Indemnity	Guest
Insurable interest	Res ipsa loquitor
Subrogation	Vicarious liability
Punitive damages	Assumption of risk
Compensatory damages	Contributory negligence
Criminal act	Last-clear-chance
Civil wrong	Comparative negligence
Tort	Strict or absolute liability
Negligence	Battery
Legal duty	Assault
Wrong	Defamation (libel and slander)
Proximate cause	Trespass
Injury or damage	False arrest (detention)
Bodily injury	Breach of contract
Consortium	Warranties (express and implied)
Property damage	Bailment
Nuisance	Bailee

REVIEW QUESTIONS

1. Distinguish between statutory law, common law, and administrative law.
2. Why is insurance based on the concept of indemnity? Insurance is a form of gambling. Do you agree? How does an insurable interest in life insurance differ from property insurance? What are some relationships other than ownership that can create an insurable interest? How does subrogation relate to indemnity?
3. What is the distinction between punitive damages and compensatory damages? What is the relationship among civil wrongs, torts, negligence, and liability insurance? What is the difference between liability under contracts and under torts?
4. Describe the requirements for negligence. Distinguish between the degree of care owed trespassers, licensees, and invitees. What is the justification for different degrees of care? Explain the types of liability hazards to which an FBO is exposed?
5. What are guest laws? Explain the logic behind their enactments.
6. Discuss assumption of risk and contributory negligence as defenses against negligence suits. What is the purpose of comparative negligence?
7. What are intentional torts? Why might an airline risk manager be concerned with them?
8. Give some examples of liability arising out of contracts. What is a bailment?

REFERENCES

Athern, James L., and S. Travis Pritchett. *Risk and Insurance* (5th ed.). West Publishing Company, St. Paul, Minnesota, 1984.

Mehr, Robert I., and Emerson Commack. *Principles of Insurance* (7th ed.). Richard D. Irwin, Inc., Homewood, Illinois, 1980.

Riegel, Robert, Jerome S. Miller, and C. Arthur Williams Jr. *Insurance Principles and Practices: Property and Liability* (6th ed.). Prentice-Hall, Inc., Englewood Cliffs, New Jersey, 1976.

Chapter 6

Insurance Contracts

OUTLINE

Introduction
Characteristics of the Insurance Contract
Powers of Agents and Brokers
Prerequisites to an Enforceable Contract
Formation of the Contract
The Policy Layout

OBJECTIVES

At the end of this chapter you should be able to:
Define the following characteristics of the insurance contract:
Aleatory, conditional, unilateral, personal, contract of adhesion,
and utmost good faith.
Explain the differences between representations and warranties.
Understand how the parol (oral) evidence rule works.
Distinguish between the terms "concealment" and "fraud".
Discuss the three types of authority possessed by an agent or broker.
Recognize the difference between agents and brokers.
Describe how the doctrines of waiver and estoppel affect the powers of
agents and brokers.
Identify the prerequisites to an enforceable contract.
Discuss the importance of applications and binders in connection with
insurance contracts.
Describe the major components of an insurance contract.

INTRODUCTION

The insurance contract is usually called a policy. It is generally governed by the rules of contract law and will be interpreted in the same manner as all other contracts. Policyholders sometimes forget that the insurance contract is a legal obligation both on the part of the company and also on their part. Policyholders will frequently request the company to waive minimum pilot requirements or extend territorial limits under the policy. It would be unfair to other policyholders not to enforce the insurance contract fairly and impartially.

Those aspects of law which have the greatest importance in insurance are contract law and agency law, because the insurance policy is a legal contract and insurance companies must carry on most of their relations with the public through their agents. A fundamental rule of contract law is that any contract will be interpreted more strongly in favor of the party that did not draw it up. Since the insurance company invariably prepares the insurance contract without consultation or assistance from the insured, any ambiguities in the contract will be interpreted in favor of the policyholder. It is also noteworthy that juries have a natural tendency to favor the injured party. This prejudice exists to some extent against all large corporations, but seems to be particularly potent in the case of insurance companies.

CHARACTERISTICS OF THE INSURANCE CONTRACT

The insurance policy is a legal contract and as such is governed by the general rules of contract law. There are, however, several features of the insurance policy which distinguish it from most other contracts. The following are among the more important.

Aleatory Contract

Both insurance and gambling are *aleatory contracts* in that the person may receive back a greater amount of money than he has put into the transaction. The ordinary commercial contract is known legally as a commutative contract, and each party expects to receive approximately the same value as he is giving. The person who pays $20,000 for an aircraft expects that the aircraft is worth $20,000, and the FBO selling the aircraft is also satisfied with the sale. In both insurance and gambling the party involved may recover far more than his premium or his wager. The individual who pays $1,000 for hull coverage may recover $20,000 if his aircraft is damaged.

Conditional Contract

Insurance is a *conditional contract* since the promises of the insurance company are conditioned upon the insured paying the initial and subsequent premiums and also fulfilling any requirements of the contract. The insured does not promise to continue paying premiums on the policy, but the promises of the insurance company are conditional upon his doing so and upon his fulfilling any policy requirements, such as giving notice of an accident, protecting the aircraft from further damage, filing a proof of loss, and so forth. See the conditions section under the sample hull and liability policy in Appendix B.

Unilateral Contract

From the legal standpoint, insurance is a *unilateral contract*. There is an act in exchange for a promise. The ordinary commercial contract is a *bilateral contract*, which means that the promise of one party is given in return for the promise of another. For example, the purchaser of a radio promises to pay $750 in return for the promise of the dealer to deliver the radio to him. In insurance, the act is on the part of the insured, namely, paying the premium on the policy. The essential duty of the insurance company is to furnish a guarantee (promise) of payment in the event a loss occurs.

Personal Contract

The insurance contract is a *personal* one, which means that its issuance depends upon such things as the personal characteristics of the applicant, his pilot qualifications, and use of the aircraft. For this reason, the insured cannot transfer the protection of his policy to another without the consent of the company. See "assignment" under the conditions section of the sample hull and liability policy in Appendix B.

Contract of Adhesion

The insurance contract is prepared entirely by the insurance company; there is no element of bargaining over the terms of the contract. With few exceptions, the insured must either accept or reject the contract as a whole. In other words, the insured either adheres to the contract as it has been prepared by the insurance company or else he does not accept it. It is a *contract of adhesion*. The legal importance of this is that, since the buyer has no part in preparing the contract, any ambiguities in the contract will be resolved more strongly against the insurance company. The insured will therefore receive the benefit of any doubt in the legal interpretation of the contract.

Utmost Good Faith

In ordinary commercial contracts the rule of "let the buyer beware" prevails because in most businesses the buyer can inspect the product and obtain a reasonable idea as to its quality. In insurance, the buyer is not in a good position to inspect the product; even if the insurance company furnishes specimen policies for his examination, the interpretation of these is often beyond his ability. However, the company may also be at a disadvantage because it is unable to determine all the facts concerning the risk. The phrase *utmost good faith* means that the insurance contract must contain a greater degree of good faith, both on the part of the insured and of the company, than is true of ordinary commercial contracts.

Representations and Warranties

In applying for insurance, the person seeking coverage makes certain statements to the insurance company or to its agent or broker. The company must rely to a greater or lesser extent upon the truth of these statements in deciding whether to issue the policy. In some cases, it is possible to verify these statements from other sources, such as credit reports, but in many cases it is not. The insurance company, therefore, is at the mercy of the applicant to the extent that it must rely upon these statements being true. Although most statements made to insurance companies are true, it is important to determine the result when false statements are made, either intentionally or unintentionally. This is determined in large part by the application of the law regarding representations and warranties.

A *representation* is a statement by the applicant made prior to, or at the time of, making the contract. Its purpose is to give the insurance company information upon which to base its decision as to whether or not to underwrite the risk and to establish the proper premium for the policy. A representation is a statement of knowledge or opinion by the applicant, generally made in the application but also done orally. The answers to questions such as the following are representations: Is your aircraft normally hangared or tied down? Where? Have you had any aircraft accidents during the past five years? Do you hold a valid and current pilots license and medical certificate? How many pilot-in-command hours do you have in the model aircraft to be insured? How many hours have you flown during the past 90 days? When and where did you first learn to fly? From a technical standpoint a representation does not form part of the contract, but rather is an inducement to enter into the contract.

A representation which is untrue is called a *misrepresentation;* it may be used by the company to void the contract only if the misrepresentation is material. A misrepresentation is material if the insurance company, had it known the facts, would have refused to issue the policy or would have issued it only on a different basis. Representations concerning the insured's piloting experience are generally material since they have an important bearing upon whether the company will entertain the risk and for what premium. Statements about the insured's place of birth, where and when he learned to fly, and how many driving tickets he received during the past year are generally immaterial. Where the representation is merely a statement of opinion or belief on the part of the applicant, it is obvious that if the representation is false he cannot be held to be at fault. Some courts have held that there must be bad faith on the part of the applicant before the insurance company is able to cancel the contract or deny coverage on this basis. For example, a company might have a difficult time defending their denial of coverage in the event of an accident because an insured inadvertently let his medical certificate lapse for two months. Not having a valid medical certificate for two years might be another story. The best legal authority is that where the insurance company is relying upon representations of fact in underwriting the contract, it is immaterial whether a misrepresentation is made purposely or in innocence. If a misrepresentation is material, the insurance company generally has the right to refuse payment under the contract.

A warranty is a statement or promise set forth in the policy, the untruth or nonfulfillment of which in any respect renders the policy voidable by the insurer, wholly irrespective of the materiality of such statement or promise.

Warranties are of two types, promissory and affirmative. A *promissory warranty* is an absolute guarantee on the part of the insured that he will perform some duty in the future. For example, stating that a burglar alarm will be installed on the aircraft while it is hangared or tied down at All American Airport would be a promissory warranty included in the contract. Another example might be a clause to the effect that a co-pilot will be utilized at all times when the aircraft is operated under instrument flight rules (IFR) or flown into high density traffic areas.

An *affirmative warranty* is the more common type and is a guarantee as to the absolute accuracy of some statement or condition. This type of warranty may be defined as a statement included in the policy which must be literally true. If an affirmative warranty is untrue to the slightest extent, the insurance company may void the contract. For example, a pilot warranty requiring a valid private pilots license and current medical certificate with a minimum of 200 pilot-in-command hours would be an affirmative warranty.

The question of materiality does not enter into a consideration of warranties since by their very definition the question of materiality is not an issue. A warranty forms an essential part of a contract and must be included in it. It will be readily seen that a warranty may sometimes work an undue hardship on the insured because a slight misstatement may allow the insurance company to refuse payment.

Warranties may be distinguished from representations in the following ways:

1. Warranties form a part of the contract and are agreed to be essential to it; representations are collateral inducements to a contract being formed.
2. Warranties are written into the policy; representations may be contained in other documents such as lease agreements or applications or may even be oral statements given to an agent.
3. Warranties are conclusively presumed to be material; representations must be proved to be material by the insurance company.
4. Warranties must be strictly complied with; only substantial truth is required in the case of representations.

Thus the most important difference between a warranty and a representation is the question of materiality. If a warranty is breached, it does not matter whether the breach is small or large; but a misrepresentation must be material before it will affect the enforceability of the contract.

Some courts have held that a misrepresentation must actually contribute to the loss before the insurance company will be able to refuse payment.

Parol (Oral) Evidence Rule

An imporant rule in interpreting insurance contracts is what is known as the *parol (oral) evidence rule*, or the entire contract rule. This rule states that in the absence of mistake or fraud, the document that is prepared is presumed to represent the intent of the parties, and no oral evidence will be admissible to contradict its written terms. The parol evidence rule generally prohibits the incorporation of any warranty into the policy by reference. Incorporation by reference is a legal method whereby the policy makes reference to a separate document and states that it is incorporated in the policy. Generally speaking, it is impossible to incorporate either a warranty or representation into the policy by this method. If the application is not physically attached to the policy, it is not part of the policy and warranties or statements made in the application cannot be used against the insured.

Concealment

Concealment may be defined as remaining silent when there is a duty to speak. Thus it involves the deliberate withholding of information which the insured is under a legal obligation to furnish to the insurance company. The question naturally arises as to what information the insured is obligated to give. Over the years, the doctrine of concealment has gradually been liberalized, so that at the present time the insured is generally required to answer only those questions which appear in the printed application form. He is not, in most lines of insurance, obligated to volunteer any additional information. It is assumed that the insurance company, in drawing up a detailed survey questionnaire or application, has asked for all the information needed to make a fair evaluation of the risk.

The concealment of a fact which is material to the risk need not be intentional or fraudulent in order to allow the insurance company to void the policy. In a strict sense, the applicant is required to answer all of the questions in the application with complete truth. It is not necessary that there be a fraudulent intent to deceive on the part of the applicant for the policy to be voidable. As a practical measure, the more liberal insurance companies tend to interpret concealment to mean that the insured has wilfully concealed facts which were known to him.

The difference between misrepresentation and concealment should be noted. A misrepresentation is a positive misstatement of fact, whereas concealment is the failure to speak when there is a legal duty to do so. Assume that an applicant is asked to provide a statement concerning his health. He mentions a number of trivial matters but neglects to mention that he is suffering from heart trouble and is flying subject to a waiver from the FAA. In this case, his silence cannot be defended, since he is under a legal duty to answer the questions fully and completely. The failure to answer the question fully is the legal equivalent of a fraudulent misrepresentation that he does not have heart trouble.

Fraud

Fraud is the deliberate attempt to mislead or cheat a third party. An innocent misstatement of fact, no matter how important, does not constitute fraud. Fraud on the part of the insured may occur either before the contract is written, while it is in force, or after a loss has occurred. Where there is fraud before the completion of a contract, it may be said that no legal contract ever came into existence, because the two parties did not contemplate the same thing when the contract was drawn up.

It is a general rule of contract law that fraud at any stage makes a contract voidable by the injured party. This is equitable since each party is entitled to rely upon a minimum degree of honesty and fair-dealing from the other party.

POWERS OF AGENTS AND BROKERS

Because most insurance is placed in force through the efforts of agents and brokers, the relationships between insurance companies and their agents and between insurance agents and the general public are of considerable importance. Agents may possess three different types of authority: contractual, implied, and apparent authority.

The *contractual authority* of the agent is that granted to him by his contract with the insurance company. *Implied authority* is that which is necessarily granted in order for the agent to carry out his contractual duties and obligations. *Apparent authority* is that which the public believes the agent to possess, and which he may or may not actually possess.

The insurer is liable for any fraud or other wrong perpetrated by its agent in the course of his employment. Consequently, insurance companies are very careful in the selection of their representatives. The *agent* is deemed to be acting for the principal, and public policy demands that acts done in the performance of regular duties should be imputed to the principal.

Any important information which is known to the agent, either at the time of the formation of the contract or acquired by him prior to its completion, is deemed to be known by the insurer. This rule applies even if the information was not communicated to the insurance company.

The powers of insurance agents differ considerably in the various lines of insurance. Because of the specialized nature of aviation insurance and the catastrophe exposure, most insurers restrict binding authority or changes in coverage to authorized company underwriters. All binders, policies, and endorsements are prepared and issued by the aviation insurers. To avoid misunderstanding, insurance companies make every attempt to notify the public of any limitations upon their agents' authority. This is best accomplished by statements in the application which specifically limit the authority of the agent.

The question of whether any given act of an agent is binding upon the insurer depends upon whether the third party had reasonable grounds for believing, in the light of all surrounding circumstances, that the insurance company had authorized the act in question. If such reasonable grounds did exist, the insurer will be bound regardless of what authority the agent possesses.

Brokers

An insurance *broker* is one who is engaged in obtaining insurance for those persons who apply to him for this service. The broker normally represents a number of insurance companies. Insurance brokers are particularly important in major metropolitan areas; in rural areas and small cities, the broker is likely to be unimportant or nonexistent. The primary function of the broker is to obtain the best coverage for the client. Therefore the broker normally deals with a number of companies in all lines of insurance.

The legal distinction between a broker and agent is that the broker is the agent of the insured, rather than of the insurance company. In actual practice, the distinction between the broker and agent is often slight. The broker in major metropolitan areas solicits insurance in the same manner as the full line agent. The major advantage of brokers is that they may place the coverage with various companies. The larger brokers who place insurance for the air carriers and corporate accounts generally have a staff of aviation insurance specialists.

Waiver and Estoppel

The doctrines of waiver and estoppel affect the powers of agents and brokers as well as an insurer's position regarding the contract of insurance. An estimated one-third to one-half of the lawsuits between insured and insurer involving the validity or enforceability of the contract, involve a claim by the insured and denied by the insurer that the latter has waived a defense that he is now asserting.

Waiver

A *waiver* may be defined as the voluntary relinquishment of a known right or privilege. In most cases involving an alleged waiver, it is claimed that the insurance company has waived, or relinquished, one of its rights (provisions in the policy) and therefore must make a loss payment which it would not otherwise have had to make. Underwriters are quite often asked to waive such provisions in the policy as the territorial limits, the minimum pilot requirements, or the assumed liability exclusion.

The definition of waiver as a "voluntary" relinquishment often does not describe the situation accurately, since the insurance company may insist that it has not waived a provision of the contract, whereas the insured will insist that the provision has been waived. In many cases it is claimed that the insurance company's agent has waived a provision of the policy. Consequently, where the company has agreed to waive a policy provision, agents generally require that evidence in writing be sent to them as soon as possible. A telegram or letter will suffice until the endorsement to the policy arrives.

Estoppel

Estoppel may be defined as the prohibition against asserting a right because of inconsistent action or conduct. The insurance company is estopped - that is, prohibited - from asserting one of its rights because it has acted inconsistently. The doctrine of estoppel is applied in order to allow the insured to recover in those cases where the insurance company has acted inconsistently and has led the insured to assume that things were true which were untrue. It is often applied to situations involving the investigation and settlement of claims. For example, suppose the agent informed an insured that it was all right to rent his aircraft on occasion despite the fact that the policy use provided for business and pleasure purposes only. Following an accident and investigation in which it was determined that the aircraft was rented, the company may be estopped from denying liability (asserting a right) because of the inconsistant action of the agent which led the insured to believe it was all right to rent his aircraft.

PREREQUISITES TO AN ENFORCEABLE CONTRACT

As in all contracts, there are certain prerequisites before an insurance policy will be legally valid. These general characteristics are as follows.

1. *The purpose of the insurance must be legal.* An insurable interest must be present; otherwise the contract is a gambling contract and unenforceable. However, insurance can be written to cover property used in an illegal enterprise and still be valid. For example, insurance which has been procured on

an aircraft designed to carry cargo which is used to haul contraband would still be valid, despite the fact that the purpose of the aircraft was illegal when carrying contraband.

2. *There must be a definite offer and an unconditional acceptance.* An insurance offer is made by the buyer when submitting an application. The insurance company accepts the offer by agreeing to insure the risk. This is sometimes done orally followed by a completed application.

3. *There must be a valid consideration.* All contracts must be supported by a legal consideration, which means that there must be an exchange of values. Gratuitous promises are generally unenforceable because of a lack of consideration. The insurance company promises to pay for losses as provided by the terms of the policy. The consideration on the part of the policyholder usually consists of the premium.

4. *The parties to the contract must be legally competent.* The insurance company is legally competent to contract if it is licensed to do business in the state in which the contract is written and if it is authorized to write the line of insurance in question. The applicant is legally competent to contract if he is of legal age and of sound mind.

A contract entered into by a minor is not void or illegal; however, the contract, while binding on the insurance company, may be disaffirmed by the minor if he so desires.

FORMATION OF THE CONTRACT

Two basic instruments used in connection with insurance contracts are the application and the binder.

The Application

The *application* is generally required as a basis for the contract, and the insurer relies upon its statements for much of the underwriting information. The application can be looked upon as the inducement for the applicant to make an offer. There is no standard form of application and there are different applications for various lines of insurance. However, all applications follow a general pattern. For example, the hull and liability application includes information that will: (1) identify the applicant; (2) give all the particulars concerning the aircraft to be insured; (3) give detailed pilot information; (4) identify previous accidents; and (5) indicate the coverages and limits desired.

In addition underwriters will generally require a completed pilot qualification report to accompany the application. See Appendix A for examples of aviation insurance applications.

The Binder

In some cases insurance coverage may be provided while the application is being processed. This is done through the use of a *binder*, which is a temporary contract, pending the issuance of the policy. Binders may be written or oral. Many times an insured will contact his agent to advise him of a change such as the acquisition of a new aircraft in which case the agent, after advising the company, will contact the insured and confirm "you are bound." Written binders are preferred since they clearly evidence the understanding between the insured and insurer.

Major items included under a hull and liability binder are: (1) the name and address of the insured; (2) a description of the aircraft; (3) loss payee in the event of an encumbrance on the aircraft; (4) coverages and limits of liability; (5) pilot warranty; and (6) any other pertinent clauses and conditions.

THE POLICY LAYOUT

The insurance policy is a contract between the insured and the insurer. It defines the rights and duties of the contracting parties and while different policies are designed to cover various risks, they all have similar components: declarations, insuring agreements, definitions, exclusions, and conditions. Many aviation insurance policies also have endorsements.

Declarations

The *declarations* make up the first part of the insurance policy and include the descriptive material relating to the risk. The declarations identify the person(s) or organization(s) covered by the contract, period of coverage, policy coverage and limits, premium charged, description of the object of insurance, and any warranties or promises made by the insured regarding the nature and control of the insured risk.

Insuring Agreements

The *insuring agreements* broadly define the coverages afforded under the policy. For example, in most liability policies these agreements cover claims arising out of the insured's negligence or alleged negligence. They promise to defend any liability suit brought against the insured if the coverage applies.

Definitions

The *definitions* of important terms used in the policy are usually included under a separate section. Terms found in the hull and liability policy include "aircraft," "bodily injury," "property damage," "named insured," "passenger," "pilot-in-command," and "Federal Aviation Administration."

Exclusions

Exclusions reduce the broad coverage provided in the insuring agreements. The purpose of exclusions is to:
1. Eliminate duplicate coverage in other policies the insured may have such as workers' compensation coverage.
2. Eliminate coverage not needed by the typical insured even though it may be important to some insureds.
3. Eliminate specialized coverage that the insurer is not qualified to offer or that requires special underwriting and rating, such as air meet liability.

Conditions

The *conditions* provide the ground rules by enumerating the duties of the parties to the contract. Remember, the insurance policy is a conditional contract. Before the insurance company will pay a loss or defend an insured, the insured has certain duties to perform under the contract. Failure to do so may release the insurer from its obligations. Many conditions found in insurance policies are common to all. For example, all policies contain cancellation provisions as well as duties required by the insured in the event of loss, such as giving notice to the insurer within a certain time period and filing a proof of loss. There are also requirements with regard to protecting the property against further loss and cooperation of the insured.

Endorsements

Endorsements are used by an underwriter to make changes in the contract to which they are attached. They may increase or decrease the coverage, change the premium, correct a statement, or make any number of other changes to the contract. The pilot warranty might be amended to include a named pilot who does not meet the minimums or the territorial limits in the policy may be extended to include a particular trip. These types of situations would normally require an endorsement. See Appendix C for examples of aviation insurance endorsements.

KEY TERMS

Aleatory contracts	Implied authority
Conditional contract	Apparent authority
Unilateral contract	Agent
Bilateral contract	Broker
Personal contract	Waiver
Contract of adhesion	Estoppel

Utmost good faith   Application
Representation   Binder
Misrepresentation   Declarations
Promissory warranty   Insuring agreements
Affirmative warranty   Definitions
Parol (Oral) evidence rule   Exclusions
Concealment   Conditions
Fraud   Endorsements
Contractual authority

REVIEW QUESTIONS

1. Insurance policies are referred to as conditional contracts. What does that mean? Why are any ambiguities in the insurance policy generally interpreted in favor of the policyholder? Why can't an insured assign his policy to someone else if it covers the same aircraft?

2. What is a representation? How is the materiality of a misrepresentation determined? What is a warranty? Give an example of a "promissory" and an "affirmative" warranty. How are warranties distinguished from representations?

3. What is the significance of the parol (oral) evidence rule? Distinguish between concealment and fraud. Distinguish between concealment and a misrepresentation.

4. Describe the three different types of authority possessed by an agent or broker. Why do underwriters restrict or eliminate binding authority for agents and brokers on aviation risks? How is a broker different from an agent?

5. Define the terms "waiver" and "estoppel." How do they affect the powers of agents and brokers?

6. All insurance policies have similar components. Identify the five major components and discuss the purpose of each part. What are endorsements?

REFERENCES

Athern, James L., and S. Travis Pritchett. *Risk and Insurance* (5th ed.). West Publishing Company, St. Paul, Minnesota, 1984.

Bickelhaupt, David L. *General Insurance* (11th ed.). Richard D. Irwin, Inc. Homewood, Illinois, 1983.

Gordis, Philip. *Property and Casualty Insurance* (24th ed.). The Rough Notes Co., Inc., New York, New York, 1977.

Mehr, Robert I., and Emerson Commack. *Principles of Insurance* (7th ed.). Richard D. Irwin, Inc., Homewood, Illinois,, 1980.

Chapter 7

Aircraft Hull Insurance

OUTLINE

Introduction
Coverage
Exclusions
Limit of Liability - Total or Partial Loss
Conditions Applicable to the Hull Coverage
Newly Acquired Aircraft
Common Enorsements Related to the Hull Coverage
Conclusion

OBJECTIVES

At the end of this chapter you should be able to:
Distinguish between the two most common hull coverages offered.
Define the term "aircraft" as used in the hull and liability policy.
Explain how the insured value is determined.
Describe the purpose of deductibles and various types of deductibles used in aircraft hull insurance.
Summarize the common exclusions applicable to the hull coverage.
Distinguish between an "actual cash value" and a "valued basis" coverage.
Describe the difference between a partial loss repaired by the insured and one repaired by someone other than the insured.
Identify the insured's duties in the event of loss.
Explain the appraisal provisions.
Discuss some of the common endorsements related to the hull coverage.

INTRODUCTION

Aircraft hull is derived from the marine term "hull" and means insurance against physical damage to the aircraft itself. Coverage for physical damage to the airplane is similar to the physical damage coverage written for automobiles; however, there are several important differences. In the first place, the airplane is generally more susceptible to damage than an automobile. In the second place, the value of the aircraft is generally far higher than, that of an automobile. Third, depreciation and obsolescence are of greater importance in aviation physical damage. One of the reasons why rates for used aircraft are higher than those covering new aircraft is that in the event of partial loss, old parts are generally replaced with new parts without any deduction for depreciation.

COVERAGE

The two most common hull coverages are *all risks—ground and flight* and *all risks—not in motion*. Some companies still write *all risks—not in flight* which includes coverage while the aircraft is taxiing. Years ago underwriters even wrote hull coverage for specified perils such as fire, explosion, lightning, theft, vandalism, and so forth. Because of the moral hazard and the lack of spread in rates caused by a number of factors including competition and improved loss ratios, underwriters no longer offer such a wide variety of hull coverages. There is simply not enough credit in the rates to warrant the distinction in coverages.

All Risks—Ground and Flight

The broadest aircraft hull coverage, all risks—ground and flight, provides all risks protection whether or not the aircraft is in flight at the time of loss. This coverage further provides that if the aircraft disappears after takeoff and is not reported or located within 60 days, it is considered lost in flight and hence, is covered.

All Risks—Not in Motion

This coverage is applicable to physical loss or damage while the aircraft is on the ground and not moving under its power or resulting momentum. This coverage includes a loss occuring while the aircraft is being pushed into the hangar or towed by a tractor but does not insure against damage the aircraft may sustain while taxiing.

Hull Coverage Definitions

There are several important definitions applicable under the hull portion of an aircraft hull and liability policy. First of all is the *aircraft* itself which is defined as the aircraft or rotocraft described in the declarations including the propulsion system and equipment usually installed in the aircraft, such as any operating, navigating, or radio equipment, (1) while installed in the aircraft, (2) while temporarily removed from the aircraft, and (3) while removed from the aircraft for replacement until such time as replacement by a similar item is started. Also included are tools and equipment in the aircraft which have been specially designed for the aircraft in which they are ordinarily carried.

In flight means the time commencing with the actual takeoff run of the aircraft and continuing thereafter until it has completed its landing roll. Or, if the aircraft is a rotorcraft, from the time the rotors start to revolve under power for the purpose of flight until they subsequently cease to revolve.

In motion means while the aircraft is moving under its own power or the momentum generated therefrom or while it is in flight and, if the aircraft is a rotorcraft, any time that the rotors are rotating.

Insured Value

The *insured value* is that amount which is stated in the policy as the insured value. Usually, this amount represents the purchase price of the aircraft, if new, or the current market value, if used. The insured value must be the actual cash value of the aircraft because a moral risk may be created by insuring over value and insufficient premiums developed if under valued. This is particularly important because of the absence of a co-insurance clause in aviation policies. Co-insurance refers to a participation percentage in every loss by the insured. Years ago, co-insurance was quite prevalent in hull contracts. Under such provisions, the insured payed a specified proportion of any loss that occurred, and the insurance company paid the balance.

Another past practice which is very infrequently found today is a set depreciation figure (approximately 12 percent). Where this provision appeared, total losses were settled subject to the depreciation factor on a prorata basis.

Deductibles

Most aircraft hull coverages are written subject to a deductible. This is particularly true for single-engine aircraft flown for business and pleasure purposes and aircraft used for commercial purposes. The deductible means that the insured must bear a certain amount of damage in the loss. Deductible clauses excluding small losses are based on sound insurance principles. Deductibles reduce the price of insurance by eliminating numerous small claims that are relatively expensive to handle. Deductibles also decrease the moral hazard. An insured forced to pay a part of each loss may be more careful, thus encouraging loss prevention.

Types of Deductibles

The common type of deductible is the *straight deductible* found in single-engine, business and pleasure policies. It is generally expressed as a specified amount (e.g., $50, $100, $250, or more) or as a percentage of the insured value (e.g., 5 percent, 10 percent, or more). The standard deductible which most companies use for business and pleasure risks is $50 ground—no motion and $250 inflight and taxiing (in motion). Some companies apply a dollar deductible with respect to ground losses, and a percentage deductible with respect to flight losses. For example, one company applies a $50 deductible to ground losses and a 5 percent deductible to flight losses. Other combinations are possible and an insured may eliminate the deductibles for an additional premium. Similarly, a larger deductible with a commensurately lower premium is sometimes entertained if the larger deductible is not imposed at the underwriter's request.

Generally, the standard deductibles for commercial risks (aircraft used for flight instruction, rental, or charter) are higher than those for business and pleasure risks. A typical deductible for commercial operators aircraft would be $500 "across the board" ($500 ground—no motion and $500 in motion). Multiengine aircraft flown by corporations with professional pilots (industrial aid use) are generally subject to no deductibles. The reason being, even minor claims involving multiengine aircraft can run into thousands of dollars which would circumvent the purpose of a deductible and simply become a burden to the insured.

Deductibles generally do not apply to total or partial losses caused by theft, robbery, vandalism, fire, lightning, or explosion or while the aircraft is dismantled and being transported. These types of losses would also not be consistent with the primary purpose of deductibles which is to eliminate petty claims.

A *franchise deductible* is similar to a straight deductible except that once the amount of loss exceeds the franchise deductible, the entire loss is paid in full. This type of deductible is used on occasion in commercial risks, although it is generally stated as a percentage of the insured value rather than a dollar amount. Assume that an aircraft has an insured value of $20,000 subject to a 5 percent franchise. If a loss amounts to less than $1,000, the insurer is free of liability, but if the loss exceeds $1,000, the insurer is liable for the full amount.

The major disadvantage with the franchise deductible from the insurer's standpoint is the moral hazard that the insured may try to inflate the claim in an effort to collect the entire loss.

Very infrequently, aviation underwriters will offer a *disappearing deductible*. The disappearing deductible combines the franchise and straight deductibles. The typical version provides that no portion of loss less than a minimum amount will be paid. Alternately, the deductible does not apply at all if the loss exceeds a higher stated dollar limit. For losses falling between the minimum and the stated dollar limit, the insured receives a percentage of the amount by which the loss exceeds the minimum amount.

In the case of the scheduled air carriers, companies will occasionally write hull coverage with an aggregate deductible. Whereas a straight deductible applies to each loss, an *aggregate deductible* applies to losses during a specified period of time, such as a calendar year. A policy may provide that no losses will be paid during 19XX, for example, until the insured has incurred losses in the mount of $5 million.

EXCLUSIONS

Most aircraft hull coverages have a limited number of exclusions. The major ones are as follows.

1. *Wear and tear*. There is no coverage for loss or damage to the insured aircraft which is due and confined to *wear and tear*, deterioration, freezing, mechanical, structural, or electrical breakdown or failure, unless the loss is the direct result of other physical damage covered under the policy.

   For example, the company will not pay for cracked windshields caused by freezing, mechanical breakdowns, or blown tires; however, if these perils cause an accident resulting in damage to the aircraft, the company will pay including these items.

2. *Tires*. No coverage applies to loss or damage to tires unless caused by theft, vandalism, or malicious mischief; or directly by other physical damage covered under the policy.

3. *Embezzlement*. There is no coverage for loss or damage to the insured aircraft caused when someone with a legal right to possess the aircraft embezzles or converts it under a lease, rental agreement, conditional sale, mortgage, or other legal agreement regarding the use, sale, or lease of the aircraft.

4. *War Confiscation*. The hull coverage excludes any loss or damage to the aircraft caused by declared or undeclared war, invasion, rebellion, or by the seizure or detention of the aircraft by any government. Coverage is also excluded for any loss or damage done by or at the direction of any government.
Loss or damage arising out of a hijacking would normally be covered unless it was carried out by some governmental authority.

5. *Other Exclusions*. Some policies include additional exclusions pertaining to the types of aircraft and the airworthiness certificate applicable to it. If the aircraft has been converted from the type described in the declarations to any other type or if the air worthiness certificate has become void or has been converted or restricted or if the operations require a special permit or waiver by the FAA (even if such permit or waiver is granted), there is no coverage. Other policies specifically exclude coverage for wearing apparel and other personal effects.

LIMIT OF LIABILITY—TOTAL OR PARTIAL LOSS

Total Loss

In the event of a total loss, coverage can either be provided on what is referred to as an actual cash value (ACV) basis or on a valued basis. If a policy is written on a *valued basis*, it is presumed that the insured value shown on the declarations represents the reasonable market value of the aircraft at the time coverage was written. In case of a total loss, recovery is based on the amount of insurance purchased (insured value), regardless of market value at the time of loss. If the policy is written on an actual cash value basis, a total loss is settled on the basis of actual cash value at the time of loss which may be less than the insured value. In no event will a company pay more than the insured value, even if the aircraft has appreciated as happens with some older aircraft.

Actual cash value is considered to be replacement cost new less observed depreciation. Obviously, this is much more difficult to determine and consequently valued basis policies are preferred by insureds.

Some policies provide for a return of any *unearned hull premium* in the event of a total loss. In such a case, the company would compute what they have earned based on the percentage of the policy that has expired at the time the aircraft became a total loss and return the unearned portion to the insured.

Partial Loss

In the event of a partial loss there are two situations to be considered: (1) when repairs are made by the insured and (2) when they are made by someone other than the insured. In the first situation, the amount paid for a partial loss is the actual net cost for material and parts of like kind and quality plus the actual straight time wages (no allowance is made for overtime wages). In addition, a figure of 50 percent of the amount of wages is generally allowed for overhead and supervisory expenses and necessary and reasonable transportation costs. The amount of the deductible is then subtracted from this figure and the remainder is the liability of the company for a partial loss.

If repairs are made by someone other than the insured, the actual cost of repairs (excluding overtime wages) plus transportation expenses is paid. In other words, the bill of the repair organization will be paid, less the deductible, but the adjustor will eliminate overtime wages, if any, and, of course, satisfy himself of the fairness of the bill.

Note that in both instances regarding partial losses no specific mention is made of depreciation. This is unnecessary since the policy refers to materials of like kind and quality.

In no event can the liability of a company for a partial loss exceed the amount recoverable as computed for a total loss. This takes care of the situation of a constructive total loss, in which the cost of repairs would exceed the amount payable for a total loss of the insured aircraft. In some cases the cost of repairing an old aircraft for which parts are no longer available would exceed the value of a total loss. Therefore, policies generally contain a specific provision that in no event shall payment for a partial loss exceed what would be payable in the event of a total loss.

For a very old aircraft and those of relatively low value, it is customary to insert in the policy what is known as a *component parts schedule*. Such aircraft are often difficult or impossible to repair. The component parts provision limits the company's liability for each specified part of the aircraft to a stipulated percentage of the sum which would be paid in the event of a total loss. Thus a figure of 15 percent for the engine means that the company will not pay more than 15 percent of the total insured value of the aircraft in the event of a total loss to the aircraft's engine.

Many policies also contain a provision which states that the company, at its option, may replace the lost or damaged aircraft with another of like kind and quality. If the aircraft is replaced or if the insured is paid for a total loss, the policy provides that the company then is entitled to any remaining salvage value. However, the insured cannot abandon the aircraft to the company without the company's consent.

Transportation Costs

The reference to *transportation costs* under the settlement of partial losses is explained in the policy provision. The policy stipulates that when transportation is necessary, the least expensive means must be used whether this involves moving the damaged aircraft or securing parts or materials for repairs. Damaged parts or the damaged aircraft must be transported to the most practical place for repairs and new parts must be secured from the nearest available source. If the aircraft is transported to some location other than the place of the accident, the transportation expenses include the cost of taking it to the place of repair and returning it either to the place of the accident or the insured's home airport, whichever is nearer.

Under the hull coverage, if a loss results from theft, robbery, or pilferage the loss is considered fully paid if the stolen property is returned before payment is made by the company. Any physical damage is reimbursed.

Automatic Reinstatement

In the event of loss or damage to an insured aircraft, whether or not covered by the policy, the insurer will reduce the insured value of the aircraft by the amount of such loss. Once repairs have begun, the insured value is increased by the amount of such repairs completed until the insured value of the aircraft as shown in the declarations is fully restored or the policy terminates.

CONDITIONS APPLICABLE TO THE HULL COVERAGE

The conditions of the aircraft hull coverage are similar in most respects to those of other physical damage policies and indicate the rights and responsibilities of both the insured and the insurer in the event of loss. These conditions relate to the insured's duties in the event of a loss, appraisal, salvage, subrogation, assistance and cooperation of the insured, and action against the company.

Insured's Duties in the Event of Loss

In the event of a loss, the insured must do the following.

1. *Give notice* as soon as practicable to the company or any of its authorized

agents and also, in the event of theft, robbery, or pilferage, to the police. The insured cannot offer to pay any reward for recovery of the aircraft.

2. *Protect the aircraft* from further loss or damage. Any further loss or damage resulting from failure to protect it is not covered. All reasonable expenses incurred by the insured to prevent further damage or loss are recoverable under the terms of the policy except that any payment for security services or reward cannot be offered without written authorization of the insurer, and of course, the maximum policy limit cannot be exceeded.

3. *File a sworn proof of loss* with the company within 90 days (some companies require 60 days), unless the time is extended in writing by the company. The proof of loss must include the place, time, and cause of the accident; the interest of the insured or others in the aircraft; the current value; all encumbrances; all changes in title; and a schedule of any other insurance covering the aircraft in question. Most companies also require that the damaged aircraft and the log book or any other records be available for inspection upon request.

Appraisal Provisions

The *appraisal condition* provides that, in case the insured and insurer fail to agree on the amount of loss, each shall select a disinterested appraiser upon written demand by the other party. Some companies require that the selection of the appraiser must be given within a certain number of days (generally 20) after the demand is made and the appraisers then select a competent and disinterested umpire. If agreement as to an acceptable umpire cannot be reached, again within a certain time period (generally 15 days), a judge of a court of record in the state where the property is located selects one. The appraisers then appraise the separate damaged articles and submit estimates only on those articles where there are differences to the umpire. The written appraisal of any two then determines the amount of loss.

The insured and the company each pay for their own appraiser and equally share the expenses of the appraisal and the umpire.

Salvage

The value of all salvaged property shall inure to the benefit of the company; however, there can be no abandonment of the property without the consent of the company.

Subrogation

The company shall be subrogated to all of the insured's rights of recovery against other parties and the insured is required to do whatever is necessary to enforce such rights.

Assistance and Cooperation of the Insured

The policy requires that the insured must cooperate with the company and upon request will assist in making settlements, in the conduct of suits, and in enforcing any right of subrogation and shall attend hearings and trials and assist in securing and giving evidence and obtaining the attendance of witnesses.

Action Against the Company

No action shall lie against the company unless the insured has fully complied with all the terms of the policy. Generally companies require at least 60 days after proof of loss is filed and the amount of loss is determined.

Other conditions applicable to the hull and liability portion of the policy such as changes in the policy, assignment, cancellation, and territorial limits will be taken up after the discussion of liability in the next chapter.

NEWLY ACQUIRED AIRCRAFT

If an insured acquires an additional or replacement aircraft, he normally has automatic hull coverage provided the aircraft is reported within 30 days from the date of delivery. The same coverage and deductibles will apply and the insured value will be the actual cost of the aircraft to the insured.

COMMON ENDORSEMENTS RELATED TO THE HULL COVERAGE

An endorsement provides for additional provision(s) to a policy whereby the scope of its coverage is restricted or enlarged.

Loss Payable and Breach of Warranty

Since so many aircraft are currently being financed, underwriters do make coverage available for the financial protection of lienholders. This coverage takes the form of an endorsement (attachment) to the policy. Its purpose is to provide an inducement to lend monies, because protection of the collateral is provided for by a broadening of policy terms.

It provides that adjustment of loss shall be made with the named insured but that payment of such loss shall be to both the named insured and the lienholder as their respective interests may appear. It further provides that, with respect to the lienholder's interest only, the policy shall not be invalidated by any act or neglect of the named insured. In effect it is a contract between the company and the lienholder in the event the insured breaches his contract and thus jeopardizes the lienholder's interest. This latter protection is particularly important to the lienholder since there are several warranties made by the named insured relative to the use of the aircraft, its proper licensing, and the experience and qualifications of its pilots which if violated do void coverage.

Component Parts Schedule

Many makes of aircraft are in use today whose manufacturers have either ceased operations or have discontinued those particular types of aircraft. In many instances this presents a problem to the underwriters in that replacement parts are either very scarce or entirely unavailable. As a consequence, the cost to repair damage to, or replace, a part of the aircraft is out of proportion to the value of the entire plane. When insuring such risks, the component parts schedule is used. It limits the amount that will be paid for repairs to or replacement of certain important parts of the aircraft to specified percentages of the amount of insurance. For example, if the insured value is $20,000, the maximum amount the insured could collect for loss involving the propellers might be 10 percent of the total, or $2,000.

Loss of Use

A related hull coverage, generally added by endorsement, is loss of use. This coverage is designed to reimburse the insured for extra expense of obtaining another plane when his own business-used aircraft is out of service due to damage covered by the policy. Extra expense is generally defined as the actual cost of leasing or renting substitute aircraft, but does not include storage charges, service fees, salaries, maintenance, or operating costs. Reimbursement commences on the seventh or eighth day following the damage to the insured aircraft and cannot exceed 25 percent of the insured value on the damaged aircraft.

Generally, this coverage is only offered to those risks for which the use of aircraft is essential. Coverage does not apply if the insured has available another aircraft of similar type without charge. Also excluded are extra expenses for any period the aircraft is unavailable because work is being performed that is not necessitated by the damage to the insured aircraft.

CONCLUSION

For a clear understanding of the hull coverage under a typical hull and liability contract, please turn to the sample policies under Appendix B. While these contracts represent examples from several leading underwriters, you should request specimen copies from other companies for comparison purposes.

KEY TERMS

All risks—ground and flight	Disappearing deductible
All risks—not in motion	Aggregate deductible
All risks—not in flight	Wear and tear
Aircraft	Valued basis
In flight	Actual cash value
In motion	Unearned hull premium
Insured value	Component parts schedule
Straight deductible	Transportation costs
Franchise deductible	Appraisal condition

REVIEW QUESTIONS

1. What are the two most common hull coverages? Why do you think all risks—ground (including taxiing) is a less popular coverage from an underwriting standpoint?
2. Would engines temporarily removed from the aircraft for overhaul be included under the hull coverage? When is the aircraft deemed to be "in flight"?
3. How is the insured value determined? Is co-insurance common under the hull coverage? Do underwriters today use a fixed depreciation figure in determining values in the event of total losses?
4. What is the purpose of deductibles? Distinguish between the following deductibles: straight, franchise, disappearing, and aggregate.
5. List and briefly describe the common exclusions found under the hull coverage.
6. What is the difference between "actual cash value" and "valued basis" hull coverage?
7. What expenses will the company pay in the event of a partial loss repaired by someone other than the insured? By the insured?
8. Why do underwriters use a component parts schedule when insuring some older aircraft? What is meant by "reasonable transportation costs"?
9. List the insured's duties in the event of loss or damage to the aircraft.
10. What condition under the policy addresses the problem of the insured and insurer disagreeing with regard to the amount of loss? How is the amount of loss determined in such a case?
11. Does hull coverage apply to newly acquired aircraft? What is loss of use coverage?

Chapter 8

Aircraft Liability Insurance

OUTLINE

Introduction
Legal Liability Coverages
Limits of Legal Liability
Medical Payments
Guest Voluntary Settlement (Admitted Liability)
Definition of Insured
Exclusions
Special Coverage Features
Conditions Applicable to the Liability Coverages
Other Conditions Applicable to Hull and Liability
Common Endorsements Related to the Liability Coverage
Conclusion

OBJECTIVES

At the end of this chapter you should be able to:

Identify the three basic legal liability coverages.

Define single limit liability.

Explain how medical payments coverage works.

Describe the purpose of guest voluntary settlement coverage and how it operates.

Distinguish between those individuals and organizations covered and not covered under the definition of insured.

Summarize the major exclusions found under aircraft liability coverages.

Describe several of the special coverage features applicable to the liability portion of the contract.

Discuss the conditions applicable to the liability coverages.

Highlight the general conditions applicable to the hull and liability coverages found in the combined aircraft policy.

INTRODUCTION

As a general rule the liability of general aviation aircraft owners and operators for injury or damage to persons or property is in accordance with the same rules of law applicable to other damage suits arising out of accidents. There are no federal aircraft liability statutes and unlike automobile liability, aircraft liability coverage is a legal requirement in only a few states. The basic legal principles to be applied therefore are the common law rules of negligence—that is, the burden is on the person who has been damaged to prove fault as a proximate cause of the accident. A failure to exercise the requisite degree of legal care owned to the damaged plaintiff is required before the owner or operator owes him anything.

In these days of consumerism and free-and-easy lawsuits every owner and most pilots need liability coverage. Even if they are finally proven not at fault for the accident, the cost of legal defense can be devastating.

LEGAL LIABILITY COVERAGES

Aircraft liability insurance provides the policyholder with protection against third party claims involving bodily injury or property damage arising out of his ownership, maintenance, or use of aircraft. Three legal liability coverages are available to the insured, each of which is generally written subject to its own specific limits of liability.

Bodily Injury Excluding Passengers

This coverage protects the insured from the liabilities imposed upon him by law for damages for bodily injury, sickness, disease, mental anguish, or death suffered by any person or persons, other than passengers, due to an accident arising out of the ownership, maintenance, or use of any aircraft specifically described in the policy. Separate per person and per accident limits apply to this coverage.

Passenger Bodily Injury Liability

This coverage applies in the same manner as the coverage above but with respect only to passengers. *Passengers* are defined to include persons in, on, or boarding the aircraft for the purpose of flying therein or those alighting therefrom following a flight or an attempted flight. Again, separate per person and per accident limits apply.

Property Damage Liability

This coverage insures against the liability imposed upon the insured by law for damages because of injury to or destruction of property including the use thereof due to an accident arising out of the ownership, maintenance, or use of the aircraft insured. The limit for this coverage is a single limit expressed on a per accident basis.

The coverages noted above can be and are often written on an *occurrence* basis. This is defined in the policy as being an accident or a continuous or repeated exposure to conditions which result in damage or injury accidentally caused.

LIMITS OF LEGAL LIABILITY

The insurer's maximum limit of legal liability for bodily injury or property damage arising out of any occurrence is dictated by the specific limits of liability indicated in the declarations for each of the coverages which might be provided.

In a typical policy these limits might appear as follows:

Liability Coverages	Limits of Liability
a. Bodily injury excluding passengers	$100,000 each person
	300,000 each occurrence
b. Passenger bodily injury	$100,000 each person
	300,000 each occurrence
c. Property damage	$100,000 each occurrence

As an alternative to the separate limits for each coverage, *single limit legal liability* insurance can be written. As the name implies, this coverage provides one limit which represents the insurer's maximum liability for one claim or for any combination of claims which might arise from one accident. Generally, all three coverages are included but occasionally single limit legal liability will be written for coverages (a) and (c) alone. This is true where for some reason the insured has no need for passenger bodily injury coverage or where (b) is purchased as a separate coverage along with the single limit bodily injury and property damage excluding passengers.

Because of the catastrophe exposures faced by many large corporate, commercial, and airline operators, the acquisition of excess layers of liability coverage is a neccesity in order to protect their multimillion dollar assets. Often the arrangement of these excess layers of liability protection has a decided influence on the limits of liability and the method of expressing these limits in their primary policy or in any one given excess policy.

Limits might typically appear as follows:

Liability Coverage	Limit of Liability
Either:	
Single limit bodily injury and property damage including passengers	$1,000,000 each occurrence

Or:

Single limit bodily injury
and property damage
excluding passengers

$1,000,000 each occurrence

A typical corporate aircraft operator generally purchases a primary single limit of at least $20,000,000 and depending on the company's assets and philosophy with regard to insurance protection might purchase excess layers up to $50,000,000. A major air carrier will typically carry legal limits up to $200,000,000.

As in the case with the writing of separate limits for each coverage, single limit liability coverage can be written on either an accident or occurrence basis; occurrence, however, is considered to be a broader term.

MEDICAL PAYMENTS

Medical payments is a supporting coverage normally available to non-commercial insureds where passenger bodily injury liability is written. This coverage provides payment for all reasonable expense of medical, surgical, ambulance, hospital, nursing, and related services and, in the event of death, reasonable funeral expense on behalf of injured parties while riding in the insured aircraft. It may be written to specifically exclude or, for an additional premium, specifically include the pilot and other crew members. Payment is made regardless of legal liability and is limited to the specific per person and per occurrence limits appearing in the declarations for medical payments. From a practical standpoint the provision is valuable in that persons who have their medical bills paid in full are less likely to sue under the liability provision of the contract.

GUEST VOLUNTARY SETTLEMENT (ADMITTED LIABILITY)

Guest voluntary settlement, or as it is more commonly known, admitted liability, is a supporting coverage peculiar to aviation insurance and available to selected noncommercial corporate risks in conjunction with passenger bodily injury liability coverage. It provides that if a guest passenger (or crew member if included) suffers death or injury resulting in dismemberment or loss of sight, a sum up to but not exceeding a stated principal sum be offered the guest (or crew member) or his survivor. The payment is made provided that the offer is requested by the named insured and that a full release for all bodily injury is obtained from the recipient (except in an employee's case which is covered under a workers' compensation law). With few exceptions, an employee cannot sue his employer and as such, this coverage becomes a form of accident insurance for employees.

Admitted liability is designed to make it unnecessary for an insured's guest to resort to legal action to secure compensation for injury. This avoids the embarrassment of a "friendly suit" and the necessarily high cost of litigation. The named insured always has the choice of either permitting the offer of voluntary settlement or of relying upon the protection of his passenger bodily injury liability coverage and the determination of his legal liability by a court of law. The written release is necessary in order to make any voluntary settlement binding upon the recipient. A typical limit for admitted liability would be $200,000 each person. Higher or lower limits are available.

Weekly indemnity coverage can be included as part of guest voluntary settlement. It provides that in the event that a guest passenger is totally disabled from performing all duties pertaining to his occupation, the insurer will reimburse the named insured for payment made for loss of earnings up to a stated sum per week, not to exceed 80 percent of the recipient's average weekly wage, and for a period not to exceed a maximum stated number of weeks. Generally where weekly indemnity coverage is written for a period in excess of 52 weeks, coverage for that period extending beyond the 52nd week is contingent upon the party being totally disabled from performing the duties pertaining to any occupation.

Permanent and total disability coverge can be provided in conjunction with guest voluntary settlement whether weekly indemnity coverage is written or not. This coverage provides for the payment of a sum up to but not exceeding the stated principal sum (less any payment which might already have been made under weekly indemnity) in the event the injured party is determined to have been permanently and totally disabled. This coverage is contingent upon a full release being obtained from the recipient and again is offered only at the request of the named insured.

DEFINITION OF INSURED

The definition of *insured* not only includes the *named insured* (person or organization named in the declarations) but also any other person while using or riding in the aircraft described, and for any person or organization legally responsible for its use, provided such use is by or with the permission of the named insured. This is commonly referred to as the *omnibus clause* which picks up any liability incurred by passengers or another pilot, other than the named insured, who is flying the aircraft with the named insured's permission.

The extension of coverge does not apply, however, to bodily injury or death suffered by any person who is a named insured, or to any employee of an insured for bodily injury or death suffered by a fellow employee during the course of his employment. Further, to avoid covering those liabilities not normally contemplated by this coverage, the extension of coverage does not apply to persons or organizations engaged in the manufacture, maintenance, repair, or sale of aircraft, engines, or components, or in the operation of any airport or flight school. It is recognized that such individuals and organizations should have their own insurance.

EXCLUSIONS

The exclusions applicable to the aircraft liability coverages are similar to those found in other liability contracts. The major ones are:

1. *Bodily injury to any employee*. Bodily injury, sickness, disease, mental anguish or death of any employee of the insured while engaged in the duties of his employment. The coverage also excludes any obligation for which the insured or any company as his insurer may be held liable under any workers' compensation or similar law.
2. *Liability assumed*. To liability assumed by the insured under any contract or agreement.
3. *Property in the insured's care or custody*. Injury to or destruction of property owned, rented, occupied, or used by, or in the care, custody, or control of the insured, or carried in or on any aircraft of the insured.
4. *Other exclusions*. Additional liability exclusions are found in some policies pertaining to the safe operation of the aircraft. Because of the extreme importance of the use to which the aircraft is put, some policies exclude particular operations. For example, coverage might be excluded to any insured who operated or who permits the operation of the aircraft: in violation of its FAA airworthiness certificate or in violation of any FAA pilot certificate; in violation of any regulations of the FAA applicable to aerobatic flying, instrument flying, repairs, alterations and inspections, night flying, minimum safe altitudes, and student instruction; for any unlawful purpose, closed course racing, crop dusting, spraying, seeding, or any form of hunting.

If medical coverage is carried, another exclusion found in all policies states that any payment made under this coverage cannot be used to satisfy any claim under a workers' compensation or similar law.

SPECIAL COVERAGE FEATURES
Defense, Settlement, and Supplementary Payments

The company agrees to defend any suit against the insured and pay all expenses incurred by the company and all costs taxed against the insured; premiums on appeal bonds required to release attachments relating to lawsuits defended by the insurer; bail bond cost up to $250 per bond; expenses incurred by the insured for first aid at the time of the accident; and reimbursement to the insured for reasonable expenses incurred at the insurer's request in assisting the company in the investigation or defense of any claim or suit.

Temporary Use of Substitute Aircraft

In the event the named insured's aircraft is withdrawn from normal use because of its breakdown, repair, servicing, loss, or destruction, the liability insurance afforded by the policy with respect to the aircraft applies with respect to another aircraft not so owned while temporarily used as the substitute for the aircraft.

Use of Other Aircraft

The liability coverages provided under the policy apply to the named insured, if an individual and his spouse, with respect to the operation of any non-owned aircraft. This provision does not apply to any aircraft owned in full or in part by, licensed in the name of, hired aircraft by, or furnished for regular use to the named insured.

Newly Acquired Aircraft

If an insured acquires an additional or replacement aircraft he normally has automatic liability coverage provided the aircraft is reported within 30 days from the date of delivery. The same coverages and limits of liability apply to the new or replacement aircraft.

CONDITIONS APPLICABLE TO THE LIABILITY COVERAGES

The conditions applicable to the liability coverages are very similar to the hull coverage with several additional items. The conditions relate to the insured's duties in the event of an accident, financial responsibility laws, medical reports, subrogation, assistance and cooperation of the insured, and action against the company.

Insured's Duties in the Event of Loss

In addition to giving notice as soon as practicable, if a claim is made or suit is brought against the insured, the insured is required to immediately forward to the company every demand, notice, summons, or other process received by him or his representatives.

Financial Responsibility Laws

This condition states that when the policy is certified as proof of financial responsibility for the future under the provisions of any aircraft financial responsibility law, the insurance afforded under the policy for bodily injury liability and property damage liability shall comply with the provisions of such law. However, in no event can the limits of liability be in excess of liability limits stated in the policy. The insured must reimburse the company for any payment made by the company which it would not have been obligated to make except for the financial responsibility laws.

Medical Reports

As soon as practicable the injured person or someone on his behalf shall give the company written proof of claim and if requested from the company, execute authorization to enable the company to obtain medical reports and copies of records. The injured person is also required to submit to a physical examination by physicians selected by the company when and as often as they may require.

Subrogation

The company shall be subrogated to all of the insured's rights of recovery against other parties and the insured is required to do whatever is necessary to enforce such rights.

Assistance and Cooperation of the Insured

The insured must cooperate with the company and upon request will assist in making settlement, in the conduct of suits, and in enforcing any right of subrogation, contribution or indemnity against any person or organization who may be liable to the insured because of loss, injury, or damage. The insured is also required to attend hearings and trials and assist in securing and giving evidence and obtaining the attendance of witnesses.

Action Against the Company

No action shall be against the company unless the insured has fully complied with all the terms of the policy. In addition, with respect to the liability coverages, there can be no action against the company until the amount of the insured's obligation to pay shall have been finally determined either by judgment against the insured after actual trial or by written agreement of the insured, the claimant, and the company.

OTHER CONDITIONS APPLICABLE TO HULL AND LIABILITY

Some conditions apply to both the hull and liability portion of the contract and are found under all contracts.

1. *Two or more aircraft insured.* When two or more aircraft are insured under a policy, the terms of the policy apply separately to each.
2. *Policy period and territorial limits.* Every policy indicates that coverage applies during the policy period within a certain territorial limit. A fairly standard territorial limit includes the United States, Canada, and Mexico. An extension to these limits is often provided.
3. *Changes.* No changes to the policy are allowed without approval by the company and upon issuance of an endorsement to that effect. Further, this condition states that any notice to an agent or knowledge possessed by any agent or by any other person shall not waive or change any part of the policy or stop the company from asserting any right under the terms of the policy.
4. *Assignment.* The insurance policy is a personal contract, which means that the insurance company has a right to select its policyholders. Generally speaking, no insurance company can be compelled to issue insurance to anyone whom they do not wish to insure. As a result, there are practically no situations in which the policyholder can make the coverage of the policy apply to another person or organization without prior written consent of the company.
5. *Cancellation.* The policy may be cancelled at any time by the named insured by simply giving written notice to the company when the cancellation should take effect and subsequently returning the policy or having a lost policy receipt completed. The company may cancel the policy at any time by generally giving 10 days written notice. If the named insured cancels, the return premium is computed on a short rate basis which includes a penalty. If the company cancels, earned premium is computed on a pro rata basis. Both short rate and pro rata tables are generally included in the policy.
6. *Declarations.* The following clause is typical of those found in most aircraft hull and liability contracts:

    By acceptance of this policy, the Named Insured agrees that the statements in the declarations are his agreements and representations, that this policy is issued in reliance upon the truth of such representations and that this policy embodies all agreements existing between himself and the Company or any of its agents relating to this insurance.

    This statement simply means that the contract is issued upon the understanding that the statements contained in the application for insurance are correct. The legal effect is that if the insured's declarations are false and relate to some material fact, the insurer is under no obligation to make payment in the event of a loss. The latter portion of the above clause is the entire contract rule, which states that the entire agreement between the parties is embodied in the written contract and oral evidence cannot be introduced to vary the terms of the agreement.

COMMON ENDORSEMENTS RELATED TO THE LIABILITY COVERAGE

Aircraft Non-Ownership Liability

The aircraft liability coverages written for a business firm follow only aircraft described in the policy or while that aircraft is laid up for maintenance or repair, a temporary substitute aircraft. In addition, not every aircraft used as a temporary substitute may be covered. Some policies place restrictions on the size, seating capacity, and so forth. Unless the named insured is an individual, there is no coverage under the aircraft policy for liability arising out of any aircraft: (1) rented or chartered in the name of the firm or (2) rented, borrowed, or chartered by employees (known or unknown by their employers) and flown on company business.

The gap in protection for liability arising out of the use of non-owned aircraft can be remedied by attaching a *non-ownership liability* endorsement to the policy. Some insurers restrict the coverage to fixed-wing aircraft with a certain seating capacity. It is not designed for an insured who uses a non-owned aircraft on a regular basis such as a leased aircraft. Most non-ownership liability endorsements limit the consecutive number of days coverage will apply unless the insured notifies the company and pays an additional premium.

Use of Military Installations

For those insureds who deal with the government and have a need to fly into military airfields, the government requires that the insured waive their subrogation right and assume all liability for such flights. This endorsement is designed to amend the subrogation provision and assumed liability exclusion found in all policies to accommodate this requirement by the government.

CONCLUSION

For a clear understanding of the liability coverages under a typical hull and liability contract, please turn to the sample policies under Appendix B. While these contracts represent an example from several leading underwriters, you should request specimen copies from other companies for comparison purposes.

KEY TERMS

Aircraft liability insurance
Passengers
Occurrence
Single limit legal liability
Medical payments
Guest voluntary settlement

Weekly indemnity
Permanent and total disability
Insured
Named insured
Omnibus clause
Non-ownership liability

REVIEW QUESTIONS

1. What is aircraft liability insurance? Distinguish between the three basic coverages. Define "passengers." Why might an insured select a single-limit of liability coverage? What are the two ways a single-limit of liability can be written?
2. What is the purpose of medical payments coverage? Guest voluntary settlement? What are the two additional coverages that can be included under the GVS?
3. What is the omnibus clause under the definitions of insured? Who are not covered under the definition?
4. List the major exclusions found under the liability coverages. Some policies include additional exclusions. What are they?
5. Describe the following provisions: temporary use of substitute aircraft; use of other aircraft; and newly acquired aircraft.
6. Discuss some of the conditions applicable to the liability portion of the contract.
7. Describe the following conditions found under the combined aircraft hull and liability contract: two or more aircraft insured; policy period and territorial limits; changes; assignment; cancellation; and declarations.
8. What is the purpose of the aircraft non-ownership liability and use of military installations endorsements?

Chapter 9

Airport Premises, Products, HangarKeepers, and Other Aviation Liability Coverages

OUTLINE

Airport Premises Liability
Other Airport Liability Coverages
Other Aviation Liability Coverages

OBJECTIVES

At the end of this chapter you should be able to:

Recognize the purpose of the airport premises liability coverage and describe the basic information included under the declarations.

List the exclusions found in a typical airport premises liability policy and explain why they are included.

Discuss the unique conditions found in an airport premises liability policy.

Explain the coverage provided by the following endorsements:
medical payments, contractual liability, alterations and /or new construction liability, and elevator liability.

Identify the types of products and services sold by a fixed base operator. Describe the coverage provided under products and completed operations liability and hangarkeepers liability.

Explain why air meet liability is not covered under the basic airport premises liability policy.

Explain why an individual or company not owning an aircraft might want to purchase an aircraft non-ownership liability policy.

Highlight the coverage found under the following policies: manufacturers product liability, pilot accident insurance, loss of license insurance, and ultralight aircraft insurance.

AIRPORT PREMISES LIABILITY

The owner or operator of an airport or portions thereof such as a fixed base operator has the same general type and degree of liability exposure as the operator of most public premises. People sustain injuries and damage their clothing when they fall over obstructions or trip over concealed obstacles. Their automobiles get damaged when struck by airport service vehicles on the airport premises. Claims from such accidents can be for large amounts but claims stemming from aircraft accidents have even greater catastrophe potential. The occupants of aircraft may be killed or severely injured and expensive aircraft damaged or destroyed, not to mention injury to other persons or other types of property at or near an airport. Liability in such instances may stem from a defect in the surface of the runway, from the failure of the airport operator or owner to mark obstructions properly, or from failure to send out the necessary warnings and to close the airport when it is not in usable condition.

The purpose of *airport premises liability* coverage is to protect the owner or operator of an airport against loss because of legal liability for all activities carried on at the airport. If an insured is not the owner, but a tenant, his limited operations are also covered. For example, fixed base operators, aircraft sales agencies, and aircraft repair shops may occupy only a small part of an airport area, but accidents for which they may be held liable may occur anywhere on the airport.

Declarations

The declarations under the airport premises liability include the following.
1. Name and address of the insured and whether this is an individual, partnership, corporation, or joint venture.

2. The policy period—generally one or three years.
3. Coverages and limits of liability. Insurance is afforded only with respect to coverages for which a premium is indicated. In establishing the limits of liability, an insured normally considers the hull value and passenger liability of the largest aircraft using the airport.
4. Description of premises and purpose of use.
5. Whether the insured is conducting any other operations at the insured location or any other location.
6. Whether during the past three years any insurer has cancelled, declined, or refused to renew any liability insurance to the named insured except as stated.
7. A schedule of coverages including premium basis and advance premiums.
8. Whether the insured occupies the entire premises.
9. Whether the insured's interest in the premises is that of owner or general lessee or tenant.

Insuring Agreements

Coverage can be written for bodily injury liability and property damage arising out of the ownership, maintenance, or use of the airport premises described in the declarations. Both coverages are generally written on an occurrence basis. As in the aircraft liability policy, the coverages can be written with separate limits for the bodily injury and property damage, or a single-limit BI and PD.

Definition of Insured

The term "insured" includes the named insured and also any partner, executive officer, director, or stockholder while acting within the scope of his duties as such.

Exclusions

With respect to premises operations coverage, most airport liability contracts include the following exclusions:
1. Liability assumed by the insured under any contract or agreement except incidental contracts such as a lease of premises, easement agreement, side-track agreement, or elevator maintenance agreement.
2. Liability arising out of the maintenance or use of any aircraft owned by, hired by or for, or loaned to the insured, or any aircraft in flight by or for the account of the insured.
3. Any liability arising from the ownership or operation of automobiles or other vehicles away from the premises.
4. Any air meet, air race, demonstration, or show for which an admission charge or an automobile parking charge is made.
5. Any grandstand or group seating structure of any kind.
6. Watercraft while away from the premises, or power driven land vehicles and vehicles attached, including loading and unloading, while away from the premises or the ways immediately adjoining.
7. Any elevator, other than an elevator which is not operated, maintained, or controlled by the insured and is located in a building of which the insured is not the owner, general lessee, or sole tenant.
8. Operations on or from other premises which are owned, rented, or controlled by the insured.
9. Bodily injury liability coverage does not apply to injury of an employee of the insured or to any obligation for which the insured may be held liable under any workers' compensation law.
10. Property damage liability does not apply to injury to or destruction of any property owned, occupied, rented, or in the care, custody, or control of the insured.
11. Any sickness or injury incurred by employees which is not covered by state workers' compensation law.
12. Injury by products manufactured or sold by the insured or work which has been completed by the insured out of which the accident arises, unless specifically assumed.

13. Liability due to work of independent contractors or as a result of structural alterations, unless specifically assumed.
14. Contractual liability, unless specifically assumed.
15. Liability imposed as a result of liquor laws (so-called dram shop liability).
16. Intentional injury or damage.
17. Any war, civil insurrection, or rebellion.

Several of the exclusions are present because the risk is expected to be covered by other insurance policies, as in the case of 2, 3, 4, 6, 7, 9, 10, 12, 13, 14, and 15 above. The war hazard is excluded in all types of insurance contracts, as is intentionally caused injury or damage. Damage to property in the care, custody, or control of the insured is excluded in almost all liability policies, since it is considered to be in the same category as property which the insured himself owns.

Conditions

A number of the conditions in the airport premises liability contract are similar to those which have been previously noted in connection with the combined aircraft hull and liability policy. Specifically, most airport liability policies contain the following provisions:

1. Assignment. The policy cannot be assigned without the written consent of the company. 2. Subrogation. Upon payment of a loss, the company will be subrogated to all of the insured's rights of recovery against negligent third parties. 3. Changes. No change may be made in the policy without the written consent of the company. No agent may waive any provision of the policy. 4. Cancellation. The policy may be cancelled by giving 10 days written notice to the insured. The insured has the right to cancel his policy at any time, in which case the premium will be returned on a short-rate basis. 5. Notice of accident. The insured is expected to give written notice of accident to the company as soon as possible. 6. Other insurance. If the insured has other insurance, each company will pay only its pro rata share of any loss.

Other conditions relate to premium, inspection and audit, assistance and cooperation of the insured, and automatic coverage.

Premium

Airport premises liability policies generally contain a specific description of the method of which the premium for the policy will be computed. The following are among the most common methods: area of the premises; sales; number of admissions; and number of objects insured. The exact method used will vary with the nature of coverage. In some cases a uniform premium is applied. Here the premium is the same for all eligible insureds regardless of their personal characteristics. This is usually the case with smaller airports or tenants on an airport.

Inspection and Audit

The inspection and audit clause gives the company the right to inspect the insured's premises and to audit his books. The reason for the inspection privilege is to enable the company to determine the hazards present and to charge a correct premium. It is also to benefit the insured, since companies are often able to make recommendations which will enable the insured to reduce his accidents. The right to audit the insured's books is necessary because many airport liability contracts are written with only a deposit premium. The exact premium is determined after the expiration of the policy from an audit of the insured's books.

Assistance and Cooperation

This clause requires the insured's assistance and cooperation and is especially important in airport liability contracts. Often the company's only defense against a claim is the insured's testimony.

Automatic Coverage

Most airport liability contracts provide automatic coverage for new premises and operations for 30 days. Naturally, if an additional premium is due, the insured must notify the company within this 30-day period and pay such additional premium as is required.

OTHER AIRPORT LIABILITY COVERAGES

Additional coverages are included under the basic airport premises liability contract by checking the appropriate boxes under the schedule of coverages in the declarations and by the addition of coverage endorsements. These additional coverages include medical payments, contractual liability, alterations and/or new construction, elevator liability, products and completed operations, hangarkeepers liability, and air meet liability.

Medical Payments

Medical payments can be provided to cover all reasonable medical expenses incurred by the insured arising out of injuries to members of the public while on the premises. The medical payments coverage is applicable regardless of whether the insured is legally responsible for injuries which are sustained. Coverage applies only to members of the public. There is no coverage with respect to: the insured, his partners, or employees; any injury covered by a workers' compensation law; or any independent contractors employed by the insured.

Medical expenses are normally defined as all necessary medical, surgical, x-ray, and dental services, including prosthetic devices, and necessary ambulance, hospital, professional nursing, and funeral services. A separate limit of liability applies to each person and each accident.

Contractual Liability

As in other business concerns, the operator of an airport or fixed base operator may enter into an agreement with a concern such as a railroad, holding the railroad harmless for accidents. By endorsement, the assumed liability exclusion of the airport premises liability policy can be eliminated. Coverage is afforded the insured for the liability he assumes under the provisions of hold harmless agreements in leases or contracts with others such as the airport owner and/or lessor, the gasoline or oil supplier, fuel equipment supplier, and others.

Since contracts in the aviation field are so diversified and often involve such substantial liabilities, underwriters will normally only approve designated contracts and not offer the coverage on a blanket basis.

Alterations and/or New Construction Liability

Operations by independent contractors for the insured may be covered for the extension of runways, installation of new landing strips, demolition or alterations of existing structures, and the construction of hangars, administration buildings, or repair shops. Underwriters require information on the extent and duration of the contracted operation as well as contract costs.

Elevator Liability

Elevator liability coverage can also be obtained by adding an endorsement to the contract which protects the insured for all liability arising out of ownership, maintenance, or use of any designated elevator or escalator.

Products and Completed Operations

Liability coverage arising from the sale of products and completed operations hazard is available to the supplier of aircraft products and to the airport owner and fixed base operator in relation to the manufacture, sale, and distribution of products; repairs and modification to aircraft; and to the performance of services relating to aircraft products. Specifically, aircraft products coverage includes: (1) sale of new and used aircraft; (2) sale of aircraft parts and accessories; and (3) sale of fuel and oil. *Completed operations* is defined as aircraft repairs and servicing, including installation of parts and accessories.

Products liability protects the insured for liability incurred as a result of injury to members of the public which may result from defective products or from completed operations. In essence, the coverage is designed to pay for occurrences which result from mistakes in the manufacture or preparation of products or the rendering of service work.

Coverage

Products liability covers sums which the insured becomes legally obligated to pay as damages if the accident occurs: (1) away from the insured's premises and (2) after the insured has relinquished the product to others. Accidents which occur on the premises of the insured because of defective products would be covered by the basic airport premises liability contract. For example, suppose a customer had contaminated fuel pumped into his aircraft resulting in engine damage and inability to take off. The airport premises liability policy would cover such an accident, since the customer was still on the premises. If the accident took place after takeoff and was incurred while in flight away from the airport, the products liability coverage would come into play. The products coverage is basically an off-premises coverage since the basic airport premises liability policy provides protection for accidents occurring on the premises.

The coverage afforded by the products and completed operations sections of the policy is often considered to be two different types of coverages. It is in the sense that the coverage of each generally applies to a different type of insured. The products liability coverage is applicable to those who manufacture or market aircraft products and components to be sold to others. The completed operations section is applicable primarily to firms engaged in servicing, installation, and repair work, such as fixed base operations.

Products liability is also purchased by restaurants and fast food establishments located at airports. The coverage would protect an insured for claims arising out of such things as food poisoning and foreign substances in food products.

Limits of Liability

The products liability coverage contains three limits of liability: a per-person, a per-accident, and an *aggregate policy limit*. A major problem in the writing of products liability has been that of catastrophe losses. Products which are widely distributed may cause tremendous losses before a mistake is discovered. The very nature of the coverage lends itself to covering losses which may run into very large figures. This is true both with respect to bodily injury and also property damage. Companies have limited their liability for catastrophe losses by imposing an aggregate limit of liability with respect to BI and PD.

Products liability for the aircraft and engine manufacturers as well as the thousands of component parts manufacturers is a specialized line of aviation insurance and large volumes of it are written by only a few of the markets, most notably AAU, USAU, and Lloyd's of London. Because of the catastrophe exposure, most markets sell this coverage only after careful inspection of all the insured's operations.

Hangarkeepers Liability

Hangarkeepers liability protection, basically a form of bailee insurance, covers the insured's liability for loss or damage to aircraft which are the property of others and in the custody of the insured for safekeeping, storage, or repairs and while in or on the described premises. Basic hangarkeepers coverage excludes aircraft while in flight.

While this form of protection, like most aviation contracts, is not a standard form, it is written on approximately the same terms by most insurers who write it, usually as an endorsement to the airport premises liability policy. The need for Hangarkeepers liability coverage arises because of the airport liability policy exclusion of liability for property in the care, custody, or control of the insured. Airport owners and operators including FBO's who provide hangarage or operate a maintenance and repair facility need hangarkeepers coverage. Once a charge is made, a bailee-bailor relationship is established and the airport owner or FBO is responsible for a high degree of care of the property in his control. Hence, he can be held liable for damage caused by any neglect or failure to exercise this care by himself or his employees.

Coverage

The hangarkeepers liability coverage assumes the insured's legal obligations for injury or to or destruction of aircraft. Aircraft means any aircraft including component parts and tools and repair equipment, operating and navigation instruments, and radio equipment including parts temporarily detached and not replaced by other similar parts. Coverage applies only to property in or on the premises described in the policy.

The hangarkeepers liability endorsement contains a limited number of exclusions. The most noteworthy of these relates to the product hazard of the insured's operation. Damage to materials furnished or faulty work performed by the insured out of which the accident arises is not covered. Obviously the purpose of this exclusion is to keep the policy from covering the obligation of the insured to correct defective or unsatisfactory workmanship or to replace defective materials. For example, if the insured had repaired the electrical system of a customer's aircraft and because the work was done carelessly, the system failed and caused a fire, the exclusion would free the insurer of any responsibility for the cost of repairing the electrical system a second time. It would not affect the insured's liability for other damage to the aircraft.

There is no coverage of aircraft owned, rented, or loaned to the insured, a member of his family, or any of his employees. If the insured is a partnership or corporation the same exclusion applies to any partner, officer, or member of his family. Coverage in these situations is available, of course, through the hull coverage under a combined aircraft hull and liability policy.

Limits of Liability

Hangarkeepers liability coverage is written with a limit per aircraft and a limit per occurence for each location for which the insured has operations. Normally an insured will carry limits sufficient enough to protect him against loss or damage to an average aircraft and average total aircraft in his care, custody, or control at any one time.

The endorsement generally contains a deductible clause which requires at least $50 be deducted from every loss. The amount of deductible can vary up to $1,000 and generally does not apply to fire, lightning, or explosion losses.

Air meet Liability

The airport premises liability policy excludes liability for accidents occurring during air meets or aerial exhibitions for which an admissions charge is made. The reason for this exclusion is that the hazards during air meets and aerial exhibitions are much greater than those usually encountered in connection with the operation of an aircraft.

During the summer months in particular, many airports are the scene of an air meet that involves the serious additional hazards of grandstand or bleacher collapse and stunting or racing at high speeds and low altitudes near a crowd of assembled spectators. Although the show may be conducted with strict adherence to federal regulations, aircraft can go out of control with disastrous results. Consequently, this insurance requires extremely careful underwriting and inspection. When the risk is accepted, the air meet liability endorsement is attached to the airport premises liability policy.

The coverage, which is usually written for a very short term, protects only the sponsor; it does not cover the liability of participants; nor does it respond for injury to the participants. Premiums vary tremendously depending on the nature, size, and duration of the show.

One of the main attractions at many air meets in the past few years has been an aerobatic team from one of the branches of the armed services. Before such a team will perform, however, the U.S. government must be presented with a certificate of insurance showing that the sponsor is covered by the necessary liability insurance and that the contract has been endorsed to hold the service team and the U.S. government harmless from any liability arising out of the team's participation.

OTHER AVIATION LIABILITY COVERAGES

Aerial Application

An area of particular specialization and growing importance within the field of aviation insurance is aerial application. *Aerial application* is generally defined as those activities that involve the discharge of materials from aircraft in flight for food and fiber production and health control. This is an inherently dangerous activity requiring special techniques and approaches, but with the technological developments of recent years, one that is becoming more essential to the economy. Rapid advances in agricultural technology with more advanced techniques in manufacturing aircraft for this work have combined to make it a profitable insurance line. Growth of this business has made insurance coverage for these businesses a matter of more popular interest. National Aviation Underwriters is one of the leading domestic insurers of this line of insurance.

Coverage

Coverage of aerial application aircraft is divided into three distinct segments: third party liability coverage excluding chemical liability insurance; *chemical liability* coverage; and hull coverage. Hull coverage was discussed in Chapter 7 and is basically the same for aerial application aircraft.

Liability insurance needs of aerial applicators differ somewhat from those of the regular aircraft owner or operator. They are also very similar. There are basically two categories of liability insurance available for aerial operators: (1) third party liability coverage with no chemical damage coverage and (2) third party liability coverage plus liability protection for damage from chemicals.

Each liability form is written to cover both bodily injury and property damage. With the normal third party claims from operation of the aircraft there is not a large bodily injury exposure and even the property damage risk is not too great. The greatest hazard seems to be with power transmission lines, which, if broken, may cause substantial *consequential loss* (losses to power company customers as a result of the downed lines). Because this exposure is so great, some policies exclude any consequential loss. Additionally, liability coverage is written with a deductible which varies depending upon the type of operation, past experience, and even area of operation. For example, a firm involved only in seeding and fertilizing might have a smaller deductible than one involved in using chemicals in a truck farm area where the chemical could drift from the crop being treated and damage a neighboring crop.

Individual and Corporate Non-Ownership

By virtue of the definition of insured, the coverages provided an aircraft owner through his aircraft liability policy are generally available to those who are permitted to use the aircraft or in whose interest the aircraft is used. These parties, however, may be reluctant to rely upon the owner's insurance and therefore prefer to purchase their own coverage. Such coverage is available to them through an *aircraft non-ownership liability* policy.

The need for aircraft non-ownership liability protection is great because of the tremendous amount of travel by air today. Individual businessmen, salesmen, and executives of large corporations have found the utilization of an airplane enables them to cover a wider area of operation in less time, economically, and with a minimum amount of personal energy. These savings are accomplished by point-to-point travel in a rented or chartered airplane and by being able to designate the most convenient times of departure or arrival, not possible with scheduled means of transportation. The necessity for insurance in most lines is usually very apparent. With non-ownership liability, this is not always true. Corporate management is frequently unaware that some of its personnel are flying on company business. Furthermore the limits of liability carried under the owner's policy may not be adequate for the corporation.

An aircraft non-ownership liability policy can be written to cover the liabilities arising out of the use of a particular non-owned aircraft, or it may cover liabilities arising out of the use of any non-owned aircraft. In the case of a particular non-owned aircraft, underwriters will normally treat the risk similar to an owned aircraft for rating purposes. Most non-ownership exposures contemplate infrequent usage whether anticipated exposures are known or unknown. The coverage is always written as excess insurance over any other valid and collectible insurance available to the insured.

Up to this point stress has been placed on the need which a business may have for this coverage. Equally in need of such insurance is any individual who flies or charters aircraft which he does not own. If he flies a friend's aircraft, it may be uninsured or have inadequate limits of liability. If he flies an airplane rented from an FBO, the FBO's aircraft liability policy may not extend to cover the liability of a renter pilot. In any event, those who rent aircraft usually do not actually see the owner's liability policy and they are exposing themselves to uncertainty both as to coverage and amount.

Underwriters also make available coverage for damage to the non-owned aircraft being used by the insured. In effect, this is subrogation coverage which would respond in the event the owner's carrier comes after the negligent party following loss or damage to the owner's aircraft. This type of coverage is particularly important for a freelance flight instructor.

Hangarkeepers often buy a variation of this coverage called *hangarkeepers in-flight* coverage which protects them for loss or damage to non-owned aircraft while in-flight and in their care, custody, or control. Instead of a separate policy, the coverage is normally provided under his owned aircraft liability coverage by amending the care, custody, and control exclusion. Again, infrequent use is contemplated and if such exposure were a long term arrangement such as a leased aircraft, it would be treated similarly to an owned aircraft.

Manufacturer's Product Liability

Many different types of products are manufactured for the aviation industry. These products include airframe and component assemblies, engines and control surfaces, seating, food service equipment, and often non-operational comfort and convenience items. The number of airframe and engine manufacturers is quite limited; however, the number of suppliers of aircraft components runs into the thousands. While only a small likelihood exists that a product from one of the suppliers will fail, there is a good chance in today's legal climate that the supplier will be sued anyway whenever his product is involved in an aviation accident. Most product liability insurance policies exclude all aviation exposures. Consequently many suppliers of aircraft components turn to the aviation insurance market for a separate manufacturer's product liability policy. The major markets for this specialized coverage are AAU, USAU, and INA.

The policy provides coverage for damage arising out of the use of goods or products manufactured, sold, handled, or distributed by the insured. *Grounding coverage* can also be provided should, in the interests of safety, an aircraft be withdrawn from service because of the existence or alleged or suspected existence of a fault, defect, or condition in two or more such aircraft.

Substantial limits of liability for bodily injury and property damage are available subject to an annual aggregate limit and a sublimit with repsect to the grounding liability mentioned above.

Pilot Accident Insurance

Accident policies in today's insurance market are readily available; however, in many such policies protection for pilots and crew members is excluded. The pilot accident policy is a limited exposure, covering only those accidents resulting from exposure to aircraft. The policy provides protection for pilots and crew members while flying, servicing, or repairing any aircraft. Benefits provide for loss of life, limb or sight as well as total disability, payable weekly up to 52 weeks. Medical expense is also payable up to the limit purchased.

Loss of License Insurance

Many pilots who fly commercially and depend upon flying as a primary source of income purchase *loss of license* insurance. As the name implies, coverage is afforded in the event an accident or an illness causes a disabling physical condition which prevents a pilot from passing the medical requirements necessary to obtain his medical certificate. The policy will generally pay the pilot a predetermined amount per month, (usually anywhere from 90 to 120 days), until the pilot recovers and is able to receive his medical certificate which will permit him to go back to flying.

If after a predetermined number of months (usually 12 months) the pilot is still disabled and if it appears the condition will continue, the company will pay a lump sum settlement to the pilot.

Ultralight Aircraft Insurance

The tremendous growth in the number of ultralight aircraft over the past several years has prompted several companies to develop a policy specifically designed for the ultralight aircraft pilot. The primary market is Avemco.

The basic policy provides four different coverages. They may be purchased in any combination to meet the insurance needs of ultralight aircraft pilots and owners. Available coverages for most single place ultralight aircraft used for sport and recreation only are:

1. Liability insurance for an owned ultralight aircraft up to $100,000
2. Insurance for physical damage to an owned ultralight aircraft up to $10,000 (less $250 deductible)
3. Liability insurance for use of non-owned ultralight aircraft
4. Liability insurance for physical damage to a non-owned ultralight aircraft

KEY TERMS

Airport premises liability	Chemical liability
Medical payments	Consequential loss
Completed operations	Aircraft non-ownership liability
Products liability	Hangarkeepers in-flight
Aggregate policy limit	Grounding coverage
Hangarkeepers liability	Pilot accident policy
Aerial application	Loss of license

REVIEW QUESTIONS

1. What is the purpose of the aircraft premises liability policy? Give some examples of accidents which would be covered under this policy. Describe some of the basic items found under the declarations. List 10 exclusions found under the policy. What is the purpose of many of the exclusions?
2. Which conditions are found in most liability contracts? Which ones are unique to the airport premises liability policy?
3. What is the purpose of medical payments coverage? contractual liability? alterations and/or new construction liability? elevator liability?
4. What are the typical products and services sold by a fixed base operator? What is meant by completed operations? Why does an airport operator or FBO need products liability coverage? Why does the coverage apply away from the insured's premises? Why is products liability written with an aggregate limit?
5. A fixed base operator who has aircraft of others in his care, custody, or control for storage or repair should consider which coverage? What coverage is needed for airports who sponsor air shows? What is chemical liability? Consequential loss?
6. Should a large corporation with facilities throughout the country and no known aircraft exposure consider aircraft non-ownership liability? Why? If an individual

pilot is covered under the "omnibus" provisions of an owner's aircraft hull and liability policy, why would he consider an individual aircraft non-ownership liability policy?

7. Many small aircraft component suppliers purchase manufacturer's product liability coverage even though the likelihood of their being proven negligent in the event of an accident is very small. What is the reason for this?

8. Who would be the most likely candidates for loss of license insurance? How does this coverage work?

Chapter 10

Other Lines Of Insurance

OUTLINE

Introduction
Fire and Allied Lines
Business Automobile Insurance
Workers' Compensation Insurance
Crime, Fidelity, and Surety Coverage
Life and Health Insurance
Principles of Insurance Buying

OBJECTIVES

At the end of this chapter you should be able to:

Identify the perils covered under the standard fire policy; the extended coverage endorsement; and the vandalism and malicious mischief endorsement.

Describe the type of property covered under the standard fire policy.

Discuss the purpose of business-interruption and extra-expense insurance.

Describe several other allied fire lines of insurance.

List the coverage provided under the business automobile policy and describe the types of autos covered.

Summarize the coverages provided under the standard workers' compensation and employees liability policy.

Distinguish between fidelity and surety coverage.

Distinguish between term, endowment, and whole life insurance.

Highlight the features of group insurance.

Discuss the purpose and coverages provided under group life and health policies.

Describe the "large-loss" principle of insurance buying.

Distinguish between essential, desirable and available coverages.

Define "employee benefit plans."

Discuss the importance of loss prevention and safety.

INTRODUCTION

Providing coverage against aviation risks is just one aspect to an insured's overall need for insurance protection. Many non-aviation risks must be analyzed by FBO's, air carriers, and other firms engaged in the aviation industry. While aviation insurance is the major focus of this text, it is important to recognize that there are risks common to all individuals and businesses. These risks must be analyzed as part of the total package of insurance protection. Insurance buying involves integrating all coverages, both aviation and non-aviation.

This chapter includes a brief description of the other major lines of insurance which firms engaged in aviation must consider in analyzing their overall insurance needs.

FIRE AND ALLIED LINES

Fire Insurance

The *standard fire policy* with the general property form (GPF) attached is the basic form for insuring commercial buildings and contents. The perils covered are those listed in the standard fire policy — fire, lightning, and property removal from premises endangered by those perils. An *extended coverage endorsement* can be attached to cover the insured against seven additional perils: windstorm, hail, explosion, riot and civil commotion, damage by aircraft, damage by vehicle, and some types of smoke damage. Another endorsement, *vandalism and malicious mischief*, is available which covers willful and malicious damage to property, including damage to the building only when caused by burglars.

The first section of the GPF describes the covered property and the second section, property not covered by the form. This form may be used to cover buildings (hangars and administrative offices), personal property of the insured, and personal property of others (excluding aircraft and components which are covered under the hangar keepers liability). The building coverage includes not only the building and attached additions and extensions but also machinery and equipment that are permanent parts of the building and are used in its service. Non-permanent personal property used for the maintenance or service of the building such as fire extinguishing apparatus, outdoor furniture, floor coverings, refrigeration, and ventilating equipment is also covered.

Personal property owned by the insured such as furniture, fixtures, equipment and supplies is also covered. Coverage is provided in (or within 100 feet of) the described building for the insured's interest in personal property owned by others.

Other extensions cover property temporarily removed from the premises for purposes of cleaning, repairing, reconstruction, or restoration; newly acquired property up to 30 days; personal effects belonging to the insured's officers, partners, or employees; valuable papers and records; outdoor trees, shrubs, and plants. Each of these extensions of coverage is subject to limitations and exclusions.

The basic fire policy with the GPF covers primarily direct loss. However, one type of extra-expense coverage is provided. At no additional charge the general property form includes debris removal coverage to pay the cost of hauling away the debris of covered property damaged by fire or any other insured peril.

Business–interruption insurance

The standard fire policy only covers losses from the perils described. An indirect loss, such as loss of income while the damage is being repaired, must be covered by attaching the proper form to a standard fire policy. One of these is the *business–interruption form* which is designed to do for insureds what their business would have done had its operations not been interrupted. Payments made by business–interruption insurance covers gross earnings and those fixed charges that continue whether or not the business is operating. Gross earnings, in the case of aircraft and components manufacturing firms, are defined as the total net sales value of production less cost of raw materials and services and supplies associated with the raw materials.

Extra–expense form

Many aviation firms, if they expect to retain their goodwill as going concerns, must continue operations even though their facilities are completely destroyed by fire. A component parts manufacturer, for example, may have taken years to build up its revenues. If its facilities are destroyed by fire it will make every effort to continue operations, even at sharply increased costs. *Extra–expense insurance* will indemnify the firm for the added cost of doing business under the unfavorable conditions resulting from an insured peril.

Other Allied Lines

Contingent business–interruption insurance provides protection against the interruption of the insured's business through physical damage to the facilities of another. For example, this coverage may be important to an aircraft distributor or dealer whose business may suffer if the aircraft manufacturer's plant is closed as a result of damage by fire or another peril. Similarly, a firm making parts for the aircraft manufacturer would suffer a loss of earnings if the customer's plant burned.

A *tuition form of business–interruption insurance* is available for schools. If a building used by a flight school is damaged by fire, it may result in lost ground school revenue for a period of months until alternate accommodations can be found. This form reimburses the flight school for loss of tuition and other revenues less noncontinuing expenses.

Rent insurance is available to protect landlords if the property rented to tenants is destroyed by fire. *Rental value insurance* is available to protect a tenant whose lease requires rent payments even during a period in which the property is untenable.

Earthquake insurance is purchased quite frequently by insureds on the West Coast as an endorsement on a fire contract. Generally, elsewhere it is written as a separate earthquake and volcanic eruption policy.

Rain insurance is another allied line and is often written for sponsors of air meets. The limit of liability is generally 100 percent of the insured's share of the income from similar air meets in the past.

Direct damage caused by the discharge of water from an automatic sprinkler system can be covered by *sprinkler–leakage insurance. Water damage insurance* can be purchased to cover losses arising from the accidental discharge, leakage, or overflow of water or steam from plumbing, heating, refrigerating, and air–conditioning systems. This form of insurance also covers losses from rain or snow which enters a building through open or defective doors, windows, ventilators, transoms, and roofs.

BUSINESS AUTOMOBILE INSURANCE

Private passenger automobiles which are owned or leased by individuals (sole proprietors) may be insured under the personal automobile policy, while automobiles owned or leased by partnerships or corporations must be insured under the *business automobile policy.* The basic policy covers the insured's negligence for bodily injury and property damage to others as well as physical damage to the vehicle itself through comprehensive and collision coverage. Comprehensive coverage provides protection for losses from any cause other than collision with another object or its overturn.

The policy can be expanded to provide coverage for medical payments, uninsured motorist insurance, and any no–fault provisions required by law. The insured is able to purchase the desired scope of coverage (in terms of type autos covered) by selecting from the following list those autos for which coverage is to be bought.

1. Any auto
2. Owned autos only (includes trailers and private passenger autos)
3. Owned private passenger autos only
4. Owned autos other than private passenger autos only (trailers and other non–private passenger auto types)
5. Owned autos subject to no–fault
6. Owned autos subject to compulsory uninsured motorist law
7. Specifically described autos (for example, trucks and autos used as public or livery conveyance for passengers)
8. Hired autos only
9. Non–owned autos only

The numerical symbol for a classification of auto is shown opposite the desired coverage scheduled on the declarations page of the policy. More than one symbol can be used for any one coverage. While all nine classifications apply to the liability coverage, only five of the categories — 2, 3, 4, 7, and 8 — apply to the comprehensive and collision coverages.

Liability coverage for an insured's vehicles used exclusively on an airport are generally covered under the airport premises liability policy.

WORKERS' COMPENSATION INSURANCE

Every state has a system of *workers' compensation* requiring employers to compensate workers injured on the job. The benefits payable under the various state laws vary considerably; however, the underlying principle is that economic loss arising out of job–related accidents or death should not be borne by the employee or his beneficiaries. The state laws accomplish this by eliminating the question of negligence.

Insurers have developed a standard workers' compensation and employers' liability policy to protect employers under compensation acts. Under coverage A of the policy, the insurer promises to make all payments required by the state's compensation law. An *all states endorsement* can be attached to cover employees injured in other states and provide workers' compensation coverage for employees excluded by the law. Coverage B provides liability coverage for employers in the event of suits arising from illegal employment of minors, losses claimed by the injured worker's spouse, and in some states, accidents involving gross negligence. The basic limit of liability for coverage B is $100,000 per accident or disease, but this can be raised for an additional premium. Premiums are determined by applying a rate for each class of worker to the total payroll for each classification of worker.

CRIME, FIDELITY, AND SURETY COVERAGE

Crime coverage is written to protect the insured against loss by *burglary* (forcible entry, with visible marks of forcible entry, into a premises for the purpose of unlawfully taking property of another), *robbery*, (taking of property by unlawful means from a person by violence, force, or by putting the person in fear of injury), theft, forgery, embezzlement, and other dishonest acts.

Fidelity coverage is written to protect the employer from employee dishonesty. *Surety coverage* is written to guarantee the performance of some obligation assumed by the applicant. Fidelity coverage is a form of both crime and surety coverage.

Crime Insurance for Businesses

In general, crime insurance may be classified according to: (1) types of perils covered, for example, burglary only, robbery only, or all–inclusive peril of theft and (2) the type of property covered, for example, primarily merchandise and equipment, money and securities only, or securities only.

Crime policies exclude any loss unless records have been kept plus the following: manuscripts, records, or accounts; glass, lettering, or ornamentation; loss or damage occurring during fire or contributed to by fire; and loss caused by vandalism and malicious mischief, war, nuclear hazards, or any dishonest act of an associate or employee. Other policies are available to cover these exposures. A comprehensive crime policy, known as the 3D policy, is available to cover in a single form the crime exposures insurable under separate policies. A blanket crime policy is also available.

Fidelity and Surety Bonding

A *bond* is a contract under which one party is bound financially for the performance by another of an agreed upon obligation. Thus a contract of suretyship involves three parties: the principal, who promises to act in a certain way; the surety, who guarantees to be bound with the first party to fulfill the obligation; and a third party, the obligee, to whom these promises are made. If the principal does not perform as promised, the surety is forced to indemnify the obligee.

Bonds may be divided into two broad groups: (1) bonds that guarantee the honesty of the principal (fidelity bonds) and (2) bonds that guarantee that the principal will perform certain obligations (surety bonds). The surety, under either type of bond, is called upon only on the failure of the principal to live up to his or her agreement.

The *blanket fidelity bond*, which covers all workers including any hired after the bond goes into effect, is the most common type to protect firms from employee thefts. Requiring employees to be bonded often discourages stealing which might otherwise occur. The character investigation conducted by the bonding company sometimes discloses unfavorable facts about an employee's honesty, enabling the business to take steps to prevent potential losses.

LIFE AND HEALTH INSURANCE
Types of Life Insurance Policies

Basically, life insurance policies are the three basic types: (1) term insurance, (2) endowment insurance, and (3) whole life insurance.

Term Insurance

A *term insurance* policy is a contract between the insured and the insurer whereby the insurer promises to pay the amount of the policy to a third party (the beneficiary) should the insured die within a given period. If the insured does not die during the specified period, the contract expires. There are no survival benefits. The distinguishing feature of term insurance is that the contract is for a fixed period and that little or no cash value is accumulated as a savings or emergency fund for the policyholder.

A variety of term forms are available to the purchaser. *Straight term* is written for a year, or for a specified number of years, and terminates automatically at the end of the designated period.

Renewable term insurance is a contract under which the insured may renew the policy, before its expiration date, without taking another medical examination or otherwise proving to be still insurable. The premium rate charged on renewal will be higher than the rate charged originally since the person is older and the probability of dying within the next period will increase.

Convertible term policies, which are available from most life insurers, may be converted into whole life or endowment insurance (discussed below) at any time during a specified period without evidence of insurability.

Some insurers write a convertible term policy which provides that at the expiration of a stated period, the policy will automatically be converted into a whole life policy. This policy is called *automatically convertible term* insurance. Another form of term insurance is *decreasing term*, under which the face amount payable reduces each year that the policy is in force.

Because the probability of death increases with age, premiums for term insurance increase with the age of the applicant. At advanced ages the premium rate, reflecting the much higher death rate, rises at a sharply increasing pace. It is possible, however, to buy term insurance and pay a higher level premium each year throughout the life of the policy rather than pay increasing premiums each year.

Endowment Insurance

Endowment insurance is a type of life insurance contract under which the insurer promises to pay a stated amount of money either to the beneficiary, at once, if the insured dies during the life of the policy (the "endowment period"), or to the insured if he or she survives the endowment period. Thus a $10,000 endowment at age 65, issued to a person aged 25, promises to pay $10,000 to the designated beneficiary if the insured dies any time within the 40-year period. If the person lives to age 65, the $10,000 face amount is payable to that person.

Premiums for endowment policies are comparatively high and almost always are issued on an annual level premium basis. Endowment policies produce a large savings accumulation which is a useful way of building funds for retirement.

Whole Life Insurance

Whole life insurance is a type of life insurance contract under which the subject of the insurance is covered for an entire life regardless of the number of premiums scheduled to be paid.

Premiums on whole life policies may be paid under the single-premium, limited payment, or continuous-premium plan. The single-premium plan involves the payment of a relatively large sum at the issuance of the policy. The payment must be large enough so that it, together with interest to be earned on its investment, will be large enough for the insured to honor all obligations under the contract without the necessity of any further premium payments.

The limited payment plan is an arrangement whereby the insured continues to pay premiums for a period of years (or until death, if sooner), after which no further premium payments need be made. The most common of these types of payment plans are the 20-pay life and life paid-up at age 65.

The most common plan of whole life insurance is written on a continuous-premium basis and is variously known as an "ordinary life" policy or a "continuous premium whole life" policy. Under this plan the insured pays a flat amount (the same amount year after year) as long as the policy remains in force.

GROUP LIFE AND HEALTH COVERAGE

In group insurance the underwriting unit is the group, and not the individual in the group. Thus selection and rating are based on the group as a whole, and the policy is issued to the group. The insureds are not contracting parties. Individual members of the group are issued certificates of participation, and booklets are also provided describing the coverage included in the master policy.

Another feature of group insurance is the fact that members of the group do not bear the full cost of their insurance. Employers nearly always are required to assume part of the premium expense. In addition, individual employees who are members of the group usually have no choice as to the amounts of insurance that may be purchased for them. They are entitled only to the amounts set up by benefit formulas to eliminate adverse selection against the insurer, which could occur if those who are in poor health were allowed to take disproportionately large amounts of insurance.

Group Life Insurance

Group life insurance is life insurance that is usually written on a term basis without medical examination on a group of persons under a master policy. Only one policy is issued, but members of the insured group receive certificates of participation in the plan.

The model group life insurance definition was developed by the National Association of Insurance Commissioners in 1917. The original definition and standard provisions have been revised over time but it still forms the basis for group life insurance laws in many states.

The definition prescribes the minimum lives to be covered as 10 for employees of a single employer. No state has a minimum over 25 for single-employer groups and many have no minimum. the definition also specifies employees eligible for coverage and maximum limits. The model group law requires a number of standard provisions in the master contract involving method of premium payment, evidence of insurability, and termination of employees.

Group Health Insurance

Group health insurance is basically designed to cover employees for off-the-job accidents, sickness, and long-term disability. Workers' compensation insurance covers on-the-job accidents. Occupational sicknesses usually are not covered by group health if they are covered under the state workers' compensation law.

Coverages frequently written under group policies include accidental death and dismemberment, surgical expense, major medical expense, psychiatric expense, nursing care, and vision care. Other associated coverages which are available, but generally very expensive are dental insurance and disability income insurance. *Disability income insurance* provides coverage in the event an employee becomes disabled, which is usually defined in terms of ability to work. The benefits do not start until after a certain number of days have elapsed, and are payable for the length of time specified in the policy.

In the case of health insurance, there are generally no minimums with regard to participation in the group. The eligible groups are less restricted than those for group life insurance. Group health insurance is broad enough to include dependent's coverage; however in no group health policy can the employer or association be named as beneficiary.

PRINCIPLES OF INSURANCE BUYING

Aviation, Fire, and Casualty Insurance

Essential Coverages

Desirable Coverages

Available Coverages

The lines of insurance discussed in this chapter merely reflect the diversity of major coverages available for a typical firm in the aviation industry. It by no means is all inclusive and no attempt is made to explore each coverage in detail. The purpose, as stated at the outset, is merely to review the major lines of insurance to be considered by any firm in completing an insurance protection program.

Certain principles and practices should be considered before purchasing insurance.

A basic principle of insurance is the substitution of a small certain loss (premium) for a large uncertain one. This is commonly referred to as the *large-loss principle*. Many insurance buyers seem to avoid this principle and substitute small certain losses for small uncertain ones. A typical comment from an insured is, "Why not submit the claim–whatever the loss. That's what I have insurance for, isn't it?" True, but that is not the primary purpose of having insurance. For example, some FBO's will carry low deductibles under their hangarkeepers liability coverage at the expense of essential protection like higher limits. By keeping their deductibles low and submitting minor claims, they end up paying a higher premium which could very well have purchased higher limits with a higher deductible.

Small losses which can be financed from current income or possibly avoided or even eliminated through loss prevention techniques should not be submitted in order to keep premiums in line. In purchasing insurance, too much weight may be given to the probable chance or even the cause of loss and not enough to the possible size of loss.

An important consideration in buying insurance is to buy protection first against all losses which potentially are so large as to be financially disastrous. Insurance against these losses can be considered *essential coverages*. Aircraft liability and hull coverage (depending on the value of the aircraft) would certainly fall under this category, as would airport premises, products, and hangarkeepers liability.

Some other lines of insurance may be essential because they are required by contract; other types are required by law. For example, when property is leased or mortgaged to a bank, fire insurance is usually required by the leasor or mortgagee. Workers' compensation insurance is required by law as is auto liability in most states.

Some coverages, while not absolutely essential, are nevertheless highly desirable. For the business and pleasure aircraft operator or corporate insured, admitted liability, medical payments, and non-ownership liability are certainly important. For the FBO, it may include in-flight hangarkeepers liability or non-ownership liability coverage. Air carriers may wish to purchase excess limits of liability.

If the budget permits it, the risk manager may want to consider other coverages available from the insurance market. While few businesses can afford the luxury of insurance simply because it is available, there are coverages to consider depending upon the company's particular circumstances. The FBO or air carrier located on the West Coast may wish to consider the earthquake or business-interruption insurance discussed in this chapter. Crime insurance, also discussed in this chapter, would fall into this category. Numerous other specialty coverages under aviation, fire, and casualty are also available, including loss-of-use coverage for business and pleasure aircraft owners, loss-of-license insurance, and even personal property floaters covering mechanic's tools.

The dividing line between the categories is highly arbitrary. It depends on the insured's business, income, financial status, desires, and attitude toward loss assumption, avoidance, and prevention. Coverage that was essential last year may only be desirable this year. For example, an FBO who covered all of his single-engine aircraft for full commercial use (instruction, rental, and charter) last year may only need limited commercial coverage (instruction and rental) this year because virtually all charter work is now being done in his multiengine aircraft. It is now only desirable that he maintain full commercial usage and not essential as was the case during the previous year when extensive charter work was done in single-engine aircraft.

Life and Health Insurance

Both life and health insurance fall under the broad category of employee benefit programs which any business must consider. Other areas under employee benefit programs would include pension and investment programs which an employer must consider but are beyond the scope of our review.

Employee benefit plans may be defined as any type of plan, sponsored or initiated unilaterally or jointly by employers and employees, which provides benefits that stem from the employment relationship and is not underwritten or paid directly by government. The intent is to include plans that provide in an orderly, predetermined fashion for (1) income maintenance during periods when regular earnings are cut off because of death, accident, sickness, retirement, or unemployment and (2) benefits to meet expenses associated with illness or injury.

Three primary reasons for initiating private employee benefit plans are:
1. To improve employee-employer relations
2. To meet the demands of unions
3. To satisfy the desire of the employers and key employees to provide for their personal insurance and retirement needs at low cost

The relationship between employee benefit plans and the morale and productivity of employees is by no means clear. If alternative jobs offer the same conditions, these conditions cannot be a factor in influencing the decision to accept one job over another. Today, group life and health insurance and related employee benefit plans are so widespread that they offer little contrast. Whichever jobs employees choose, they will probably be covered under a group life and health plan. An employer's lack of an adequate plan may act as a "dissatisfier," but having a good group plan will not necessarily lead to greater employee satisfaction.

The demand by unions for life and health insurance benefits and pensions is one of the principal reasons why many firms have these plans. Some group insurance plans are established because the firm's officers look at group insurance as a way of getting life and health insurance coverage for premiums lower than those charged for indiviudal insurance. Furthermore, group insurance seems especially attractive to those officers who are otherwise uninsurable. An additional, and frequently the most important, incentive is the favorable tax treatment accorded employer-financed life, health, and retirement programs for employees.

Integrating Insurance Buying

Buying insurance is basically a budgeting problem. It has been stressed in this chapter that the insurance budget should be overall, not spearate for each coverage. Insurance planning and buying involves integrating all coverages: aviation, fire, casualty, life, and health as part of the broader process of risk management discussed in Chapter 4. The problem with non-integrated insurance buying is that policies are bought because they fill a particular need, without consideration of priorities. This can result in added expense, overlapping, or inadequate coverage in certain areas. An integrated approach to insurance buying also forces risk managers to consider alternatives to insurance as a risk management device.

Loss Prevention and Safety

Loss prevention and safety embraces all attempts to prevent losses and to minimize any damage should they occur. It is certainly more desirable than insurance, since insurance, in and of itself, does nothing to reduce losses. While insurance is economically desirable, it actually increases the total burden of losses because the administrative cost of providing insurance must be added to the cost of the losses. This added cost is offset, however, by the stimulus given to loss prevention and safety by insurance companies.

Loss prevention and safety is designed to eliminate possible causes of loss, either through the elimination of physical hazards or through the improvement of mental skills, performance, and attitudes such as pilot training programs. A distinction may be made between loss prevention and loss protection. Loss-protection methods have as their purpose the minimizing of loss once it has occurred. Firefighting equipment, for example, does nothing to reduce losses, but may greatly minimize the damage once a fire starts.

In order to stimulate loss prevention and safety, insurance companies have made reductions in premiums available in many lines of insurance. Corporate insureds whose pilots attend recurrent flight training programs such as those provided by Flight Safety, Inc., are afforded the most favorable rates under their aircraft hull and liability insurance. In fire insurance, the installation of an approved sprinkler system considerably reduces the insured's rates. In workers' compensation, the loss-prevention activities of the insureds and insurers often make possible a reduction in the number and extent of accidents, which is reflected in a lower rate for the insured. In many lines of insurance, which are "experience-rated," such as workers'-compensation, the reduction of losses will be directly reflected in a reduction in premium for the insured.

KEY TERMS

Standard fire policy
Extended coverage endorsement
Vandalism and malicious mischief
Business-interruption form
Extra-expense insurance
Contingent business-interruption insurance
Tuition form of business-interruption insurance
Rent insurance
Rental value insurance
Earthquake insurance
Rain insurance
Sprinkler-leakage insurance
Water damage insurance
Business automobile policy
Workers' compensation
All states endorsement
Crime coverage

Burglary
Robbery
Fidelity coverage
Surety coverage
Bond
Blanket fidelity bond
Term insurance
Straight term
Renewable term
Convertible term
Automatically convertible term
Decreasing Term
Endowment term
Whole life insurance
Group life insurance
Group health insurance
Disability income insurance
Large-loss principle
Essential coverages
Employee benefit plans
Loss prevention and safety

REVIEW QUESTIONS

1. What are the perils covered under the standard fire policy? Under the extended coverage endorsement? Briefly describe the property covered under the GPF.
2. Distinguish between "business-interruption" and "extra-expense" insurance. Describe the coverage provided by the following allied fire lines: contingent business-interruption insurance, tuition form of business-interruption insurance, rent insurance, rental value insurance, earthquake insurance, and rain insurance.
3. Identify the coverages provided under the business automobile policy. List five of the nine types of autos covered under the BAP.
4. What is the purpose of workers' compensation insurance? Describe coverage B under the standard workers' compensation and employers' liability policy. Are industrial-related diseases covered as well as accidents?
5. What are the normal exclusions under crime policies? what is the purpose of the 3D policy? Distinguish between fidelity and surety bonding. What is the purpose of the blanket fidelity bond?

6. Describe the differences between term, endowment, and whole life insurance. What is meant by "group insurance"? Describe some of its features. What are the basic coverages found under group health insurance? Why do you think dental insurance is so expensive?

7. What is meant by the "large-loss principle"? Why do some insureds avoid the principle? Describe several essential, desirable, and available coverages for business and pleasure aircraft owners and FBO's.

8. Why have employee benefit programs become so important in recent years? Describe two essential insurance coverages which employers must consider as part of the total employee benefit program.

9. Why is an integrated approach to insurance buying so important? What is the relationship of loss prevention and safety to insurance buying?

Chapter 11

Underwriting and Pricing Aviation Risks

OUTLINE

The Function of Underwriting
Evaluating the Aircraft Hull and Liability Risk
Evaluating the Airport Liability Risk
Pricing Aviation Risks
Reinsurance
Conclusion

OBJECTIVES

At the end of this chapter you should be able to:
Understand the purpose, function, and need for underwriting.
Describe the unique nature of aviation exposures faced by underwriters.
Define and discuss the underwriting processes of preselection and postselection.
Explain the conflict which may arise between the production and the underwriting staffs.
List the basic information needed by underwriters to provide an aircraft hull and liability quotation.
Discuss the importance of age, construction, and configuration in underwriting the type of aircraft.
Explain the importance of pilot requirements in underwriting the aircraft risk.
Describe the five purpose of use categories.
Summarize the major factors taken into consideration by underwriters in evaluating airport risks.
Give some examples of rating aviation risks.
Discuss the purpose of reinsurance.
Define prorata and excess reinsurance.

THE FUNCTION OF UNDERWRITING

Underwriting is the process of selecting and pricing risks (prospective insureds) which are presented to the insurer. The purpose of underwriting is to maximize profits by accepting a favorable distribution of risks. The process is based on selection, so this part of the definition of underwriting is discussed first. Pricing and reinsurance (the purchase of insurance by insurers), such significant parts of the total process, are explained in separate sections of this chapter.

The Need for Underwriting

Applicants for insurance are not selected randomly, neither do they have the same loss expectancies. A newly rated private pilot flying a high-performance single-engine aircraft presents a completely different risk than a private pilot with 1000 total hours including 100 hours in the particular model. Those applicants with loss expectancies substantially higher than are provided for in the premium charged for a particular class of risks should either be charged a higher premium or declined coverage.

If a company were to refrain from discriminating against applicants failing to meet underwriting standards comtemplated in the rate level, it would be forced to charge all insureds rates higher than those charged by competitors in order to remain profitable. This higher rate would cause a loss of attractive risks who would insure at the lower rates charged by competing companies practicing selective underwriting.

Only those not eligible for coverage by the selective underwriters would buy protection from the nonselective one. The result would be that the nonselective company would have to charge even higher rates, producing a vicious cycle of high rates that could not attract sufficient numbers or a spread of risks sufficient enough to enable the company to remain in business. There is an expression in the insurance business, "Select or be selected against."

Another need for underwriting is equity in the rate structure, which means that, within a broad range or classification of risks, an insured should be charged a premium commensurate with loss expectancy. Classifications that differentiate among exposures are used for rating purposes. Of necessity, these classifications must be broad enough to include an adequate number of exposure units so that the law of averages will work, yet not too broad so that substantially different risks are lumped together. On the other hand there will be a loss of credibility in the rates if there are too many classifications and not enough risks in each classification for the law of averages to work.

Insurers must have a workable selection process for assigning all acceptable exposures to their correct classification and for assuring that there will be a sufficient number of insureds with below-average loss expectancies to offset those with loss expectancies above the class average. A limit must be set for the amount by which an applicant's loss expectancy can exceed the class average without rejection or assignment to a different class.

As noted, the primary purpose of underwriting (risk selection) is to obtain a profitable distribution of risks. If underwriting is to produce a profitable distribution or risks, it must produce a safe distribution of them. A safe distribution of risks requires their diversification among many types of aircraft, purposes of use, pilots, coverages, and geographical areas. Overconcentration of exposures is poor underwriting practice.

The Nature of Aviation Exposures

Catastrophe Loss

Aircraft and the perils of flight present many unique problems for aviation underwriters but none is more fundamental than the constant exposure to *catastrophe loss*. The threat of this type of loss exists to some degree in every form of insurance but nowhere must it be given such positive consideration or be more carefully underwritten than where aircraft are involved.

Of the many reasons for this condition the most significant is the physical properties of aircraft themselves. Because of the environment in which they operate, they must be of relatively light construction and intricate design. Airplanes simply cannot be engineered in the same manner as trailer trucks or trains and made to accommodate the impacts of collision or the stresses and strains associated with other types of accidents to which they might become exposed. With specific design, weight, and speed requirements to be met, aircraft must be accepted by underwriters as being considerably more susceptible to substantial damage and total loss than any other type of vehicle.

Substantial damage or total loss alone, of course, does not necessarily constitute catastrophe loss but with aircraft there always exists the possibility of personal injury, property damage, and loss of life. A review of some of the more recent aircraft accidents shows how quickly these factors can turn airplane accidents into major disasters receiving front page headlines. As speeds, size of equipment, fuel load, and passenger capacities increase, the probability of this type of catastrophe will also increase.

Limited Spread

Complicating this exposure to catastrophe loss is a situation which provides the aviation underwriter with a very *limited spread of risks* . The combined fleets of all the certificated U.S. scheduled airlines include only about 3,000 aircraft. The total of all active U.S. civil aircraft is only approximately 225,000. The significance of these figures is twofold. In the first place there are fewer units at risk compared to other lines of insurance for as successful an operation of the law of large numbers, upon which insurers traditionally rely for ability to predict losses. Secondly, numbers for any one insurer are too few to permit the development of credible statistics upon which actuarially sound rating formulas can be based. This absence of credible statistics places the underwriter in the position of having to rely to a large extent upon personal judgment in selecting risks and determining rates. There is no industry rating bureau in aviation as there are in other fire and casualty fields which develop rating manuals based on statistics reported by the various member companies.

Diversification

Though spread is limited and catastrophe loss a threatening possibility, the aviation underwriter's task would not be nearly so difficult if each risk could be conveniently categorized, dealt with as a unit of a class, and underwritten in a manner similar to automobiles. Unfortunately, this treatment is not possible. Even aircraft of identical make and model present insuring problems which make it impossible to rate them by class. Their values, for example–and value is one factor which determines the size of possible loss and necessarily influences rate–can differ by thousands of dollars depending upon the radios, navigational aids, or other types of avionics equipment on board.

Even more important to the underwriters than the varying factors which determine the amount of possible loss are those which have a bearing on the probability of loss. Factors such as prevailing weather conditions, the use for which an aircraft is flown, and the experience and abilities of the pilots are as fundamental to this problem as are the number of hours flown and the quality of maintenance received. There exist so many variables vital to the proper analysis of every risk that underwriters must treat each case in accordance with its own particular merits. They cannot rely on broad identification with a class to justify insurability or to act as anything but the most general basis for their rating.

Rapidity of Change

Having to shoulder the burden of prudent risk selection, underwriters must be more than just able insurance people. Such individuals must be technically versed in the structural and aerodynamic problems associated with flight as well as the operational and physiological problems encountered by the pilot. They must have an understanding and appreciation of aircraft power plants and, most importantly, they must be able to keep abreast of the developments and changes which take place almost daily within the industry. Aviation is a dynamic field and underwriters cannot afford to find themselves lagging behind. They must be constantly aware of new hazards which arise as speeds increase and the state of the art of flying becomes more sophisticated. They must be equally aware of the declining importance of hazards which may have been serious at one time but which are reduced or eliminated by advancing technology or other change.

Selection of Risks

The agent or broker who sells the business generally makes a preliminary appraisal of the exposure. The major part of underwriting, however, is done by full-time underwriters in home or branch offices. To some extent, groups outside the company, such as engineering firms, auditing firms, and credit-rating organizations, supplement the underwriters by furnishing information and recommendations upon which underwriting decisions are based.

Methods of Selecting Insureds

In selecting new insureds, underwriters have two problems. One is how to select new insureds; that is, how to decide whether to accept or reject an application for insurance. This may be called *preselection*. The other problem is how to get rid of undersirable insureds. This is called *postselection*.

The rules governing the preselection of insureds begin with instructions to the agent, who will be instructed to refuse certain types of applicants. For example, agents for a particular company may be told to refuse applications from low-time private pilots in light twin-engine aircraft or experimental aircraft. Agents also will be instructed on the maximum insured value or limits of liability the company can entertain as well as their general underwriting practice with regard to amending pilot warranties, extending territorial limits, and so forth.

Rather than simply reject an application for insurance, underwriters may make a counter offer. We will agree to cover your twin-engine aircraft provided you use a co-pilot on all flights into high density traffic areas. The company is free to charge whatever rate it wishes and may accept or reject the risk at that rate, or make a counter offer at a higher rate. The underwriter might also offer insureds restricted coverage, or require them to use special protective measures or install specific loss prevention devices. For example, an underwriter might require an insured to install a burglar alarm on his aircraft if it is regularly tied down at a particular airport. The underwriter might require that an FBO's chief pilot check out each new renter pilot before letting him use the aircraft.

It is usually easier for underwriters to refuse an application than face the difficulty of dealing with an insured who is considered undesirable. However, a company can be too conservative, and literally underwrite themselves out of business. Also, in dealing with agents which represent a significant volume of business it is understandable that an underwriter is going to have accept some below average risks in order to attract the agent's better risks.

The easiest method of eliminating an undesirable risk is simply waiting until the expiration of the policy. Then the company notifies the agent that it does not wish to renew the contract. The circumstances, however, may be of a nature that the underwriter does not want to wait until the end of the policy term but must terminate the policy as soon as possible. If, for example, a followup inspection of an FBO's premises reveals undersirable physical conditions or unsound operational practices and procedures, the underwriter might recommend immediate cancellation of the policy.

Underwriting and Production

One of the unique problems faced by insurers compared to other businesses is the conflict which often arises between underwriting and production. The production (or marketing) people are charged with the responsibility of developing new business. The underwriters on the other hand must obtain a profitable distribution of exposure units. To the production people, however, the underwriters often appear to be interested only in keeping the greatest possible amount of insurance from being accepted either by offering uncompetitive rates and restrictive coverages or simply by rejecting the risks. This conflict becomes even more pronounced in a small branch office where the few individuals based there are charged with the responsibility of both production and underwriting.

EVALUATING THE AIRCRAFT HULL AND LIABILITY RISK

Agents or brokers who submit a completed application for hull and liability insurance (see Appendix A) generally include all the information needed by the underwriter to make a firm quotation. If an application is not available or time does not permit the completion of one, an underwriter will often give a quotation in writing or over the phone subject to his receiving a completed application within a stated period of time. The basic information needed to offer a quotation includes the following:

1. Name and address of owner and mortgagee, and the amount of mortgage.
2. Age of the prospect, if an individual and the pilot of the aircraft.
3. Business of the prospect.
4. Aircraft name, year, model, and license number, and whether landplane, seaplane, or amphibian.

5. Insured value.

6. The type of aircraft physical damage (hull) coverage desired and deductibles.

7. The type(s) and limit(s) of liability coverage desired.

8. Any coverage extensions beyond the standard policy provisions.

9. The purpose for which the aircraft will be used.

10. Pilot's name and age (if other than the insured).

11. Pilot rating, e.g., student, private, commercial, or ATP (air transport pilot).

12. Total logged flying hours and total logged hours as pilot in command.

13. Time as pilot in type of aircraft to be insured or in similar types; if the aircraft is multiengine, the insured must also give the number of pilot hours as first pilot in multiengine aircraft.

14. Name of the home airport.

15. Whether the aircraft is hangared or unhangared at the home airport.

16. The prospect's claim or loss experience history.

Certain commercial risks such as pilot instruction, aircraft rentals, and air taxi operations—as well as special types of aircraft (seaplanes, amphibians, and helicopters)—involve unusual exposures and require more detailed underwriting information.

Since so much depends upon the aviation underwriters' ability to carefully and knowingly select and rate risks, it will be helpful to discuss the major factors upon which they make their evaluation. Underwriters are concerned with four principal areas: (1) the type of aircraft to be insured, (2) the abilities of the pilot, (3) geographical considerations, and (4) the purpose for which the aircraft is to be used.

Type of Aircraft and Equipment

The specific aircraft to be flown determines the insured value which will be placed upon it and the number of crew members and passengers it can accommodate. This information provides the underwriters with the loss potential of the risk in terms of dollars by defining the top limit of loss to which the company is exposed with respect to physical damage to the aircraft and to some degree the maximum possible third party legal liability. They must consider this maximum loss potential before going onto the more important task of determining the probabilities of loss.

An aircraft's susceptibility to loss can be a function of any number of factors relative to its age, construction, and general configuration.

Age

The problem of age is largely one of gradual airframe deterioration and power plant weariness. After a period of time and after extensive exposure to the rigors of flight and the impact of numerous landings, all aircraft show signs of wear and tear. Often it is a decrease in performance by virtue of dents in the airfoils, corrosion of the skin, nicks in the propeller blades, or a dropping off of the rated horsepower of the engine. Most aircraft are designed with a sufficient margin built into their performance/weight ratio so that this decrease in performance has little effect on their airworthiness. With others, however, it is much more critical and any performance lag poses a serious problem.

Each type of airplane has its own effective lifespan ranging from a few years to several decades and many have inherent weaknesses which must be recognized. The underwriter must be aware of all of these characteristics and give them consideration in arriving at an underwriting decision. This consideration is particularly important since it has been estimated that about half of all active U.S. civil aircraft were manufactured more than 10 years ago.

Construction

Though an airplane's construction has a bearing upon frequency of loss, it is far more meaningful to the underwriter as a guide to how expensive repairs to the aircraft will be. With airplanes there is considerable variety in the complexity of construction and in the types of materials used, with the result that each presents its own peculiar repair problems. They are not like automobiles where a dented fender is a dented fender regardless of make or model. Older aircraft made of tubular steel or wood frame covered by doped fabric are particularly susceptible to the hazards of hail, windstorm, and general deterioration; but they are relatively easy to repair. Many maintenance facilities are available and rigged to recover or patch damaged skin and to repair or replace broken ribs and spars. These aircraft are quite different from aircraft of more traditional all-metal construction. Here, even most superficial damage requires the talents of an experienced sheet metal worker and the facilities of a specially equipped repair shop. With aircraft of particularly complex construction, underwriters must recognize that relatively minor damage can necessitate the replacement of an entire structural member at considerable expense. They must also be concerned with the possibility of a constructive total loss and face the inordinately high costs of repair.

Configuration

Aircraft *configuration* holds its own particular complications for the underwriter. For example, those airplanes having *conventional landing gear* (two main wheels mounted forward of the center of gravity with a balancing wheel in the rear) sit with a nose high attitude on the ground which detracts from the pilot's forward visibility and increases the hazards associated with ground operations. On the other hand, the more common *tricycle landing gear* aircraft (two main wheels aft of the center of gravity and a third wheel up under the nose) promotes better visibility on the ground but is considerably less forgiving of landings on rough or soft terrain or taxiing collisions with low obstacles. Seaplanes and amphibians face a full range of marine hazards as well as those of flight. Multiengine aircraft, though they enjoy the added reliability of multiple power plants, present an asymmetrical thrust and drag problem when one engine fails which requires more advanced pilot skills to handle properly. Virtually every type of aircraft has some characteristic basic to its configuration which creates its own particular set of problems.

One of the biggest problems facing corporate pilots in the last 20 years is the transition from prop to prop-jet and pure-jet aircraft. The principal problem here is that of pilot retraining and the added exposure presented during the period of transition. The prop-jet and pure-jet aircraft are not more difficult to fly but pilots do have to adjust their thinking and change some of their flying habits.

Pilots

The old adage, "Aviation, like the sea, is not inherently dangerous, just mercilessly unforgiving of human error," is a truism which indicates the importance to the underwriters of pilot experience and ability in the evaluation of an aircraft risk.

In this area the underwriters are fortunate to have operating in their behalf a rather intricate pilot licensing and rating system supervised by the Federal Aviation Administration. This system gives them at least some of the necessary assurances that the aircraft the company is insuring is operated by a qualified pilot. This assurance alone, however, is not enough. The FAA is not putting up thousands of dollars in protection against losses which the insured may incur. In addition, the underwriters must investigate the pilot's background, experience, and accident record to make sure the pilot's qualifications are adequate. Often, an underwriter will find it necessary to impose restrictions on the operation of an aircraft beyond those demanded by normal federal licensing regulations. Such restrictions may be imposed when a pilot first flies under the authority of a newly acquired rating or certificate or when he makes a transition from one type of aircraft to another. These restrictions are normally included in the wording of the pilot warranty in the policy and take the form of specific minimum flying hour requirements. Sometimes they are drafted to require that a pilot obtain so many additional hours of dual instruction before flying solo, or that he always be accompanied by a qualified co-pilot. Occasionally, they specify that flying be limited to fair weather and daylight hours.

The disturbing fact that over 70 percent of the non-airline accidents involve some degree of pilot error is evidence of the importance of the human factor in aviation. It justifies the utmost care taken by the underwriter in evaluating that aspect of each risk.

The following *minimum pilot requirements* are often used by underwriters; however, they are merely a guide and can be raised or lowered depending upon the limits of liability carried and other underwriting factors.

Aircraft	Certificate	Minimum Total Logged Hours		
		Total	In Type	In Model
SE – Fixed Gear	Student or better	None	None	None
SE – Retractible Gear	Private or better	200	50	10
ME – Light Twin	Private or better	500	100	10
ME – Heavy Twin	Private or better	1,000	200	10
Turbo-Prop or Jet	Commercial	2,000	500	10

Co-pilots having a commerical pilot's certificate are generally required for all turbo-prop or jet aircraft.

Geographic Considerations

The terrain, prevailing weather conditions, and other elements of the georgraphy of airports used and areas of most concentrated flying also have a decided effect upon an underwriter's evaluation of a risk.

Airport location is of particular significance for it has an important bearing on the safe operation of the aircraft insured. Every airplane has minimum required runway lengths determined by the distance necessary for its takeoff and landing rollout. Each minimum is predicated upon the airfield being at sea level and its runway temperature being a constant 59°F. As the elevation of the field and/or the temperature of the runway increases, the minimum also increases. An increase of 1000 feet of elevation or 15°F. of temperature, for example, increases the required minimum runway length by 10 percent. Clearly, one airport in the cool coastal areas of New England might be entirely adequate whereas its twin located 5000 feet above sea level near Denver, Colorado, or on the Mojave Desert of California, where runway temperatures reach 120°F., would be totally unacceptable from an underwriting standpoint.

Other concerns relative to airport location are the probability of exposure to hail and severe windstorm, or other local conditions which result in ususually frequent periods of restricted visibility. These factors increase the hazards associated with flight operations and must be considered by the underwriters.

Purpose of Use

Every aircraft risk is unique in its susceptibility to loss by virtue of the type of equipment flown, the attitude and aptitude of its pilots, and the geography of its particular part of the world. Still, each risk must be classified relative to some denominator common to a number of others to permit the insurer to make comparisons. In aviation insurance the purpose for which the aircraft is to be flown is employed as that common denominator. It permits risks exposed to the same general types of perils to be compared with one another and provides the starting point from which the underwriters can proceed in exercising their underwriting judgment.

Generally speaking, five *purpose of use categories* are used within the industry: (1) airline, (2) business and pleasure, (3) industrial aid, (4) commercial, and (5) special use.

Airline

The term *airline* refers to that class of business involving the operation of major, national, and regional air carriers. It is the most definitive of all the use categories and the only one which provides the underwriter with fairly credible statistics upon which to base a reasonable prediction of future losses. Many positive controls are imposed upon the operation of an airline which are nonexistent in other aviation activities. These controls assist in standardizing the quality of risks at a relatively high level. Many of the exposure variables which distort the experience figures in other use classifications are removed. Some of these exposure variables are: inexperienced pilots, poor maintenance, and inadequate airports. Although these controls provide a number of built-in protections against loss, they do not relieve the underwriter of any underwriting responsibilities. They effectively reduce the frequency of airline losses but do not alter the fact that those losses which do occur have an extraordinarily high degree of catastrophe.

Business and Pleasure

Business and pleasure applies to those risks which involve individually owned aircraft used for the owner's personal purposes and for which no charge is made or direct profit derived from use of the aircraft. A number of underwriting challenges are common to risks within this category; pilots of limited experience, flying clubs with multiple ownership of aircraft, aircraft which are of low value and marginally equipped, and the exposures associated with operation from airfields having limited facilities.

Industrial Aid

The term *industrial aid* applies to corporate-owned aircraft which are used for the transportation of employees, business associates, and executives and which are flown by professional pilots hired on a full-time basis specifically for that purpose. These pilots normally are well qualified, commercially rated, and at the controls many hours every month. Normally a considerable degree of control is exercised over the nature and conduct of the flights by either the corporate owner or a chief pilot. Consequently, industrial aid is considered a preferred type of business in aviation insurance and the rate structure is lower than business and pleasure. The accident record for this class compares favorably with that of the airlines.

Commercial Use

The term *commercial use* refers to charter operators, air taxi operators, and others who operate aircraft for general profit in transporting persons and cargo for hire, undertaking high altitude photography, and conducting similar operations not requiring a special waiver from the Federal Aviation Administration. This use category also includes the leasing of aircraft to renter pilots and giving flight instruction to student pilots and others. This latter category including rental and instruction is commonly referred to as *limited commercial use*.

In underwriting and rating risks in this category, two important factors must be considered. First, commercial aircraft are flown for many more hours a year than are business and pleasure or industrial aid aircraft and these extra hours increase the exposure at least proportionately. This is particularly true when we consider the number of pilots with varying levels of experience which may operate a particular aircraft. This can vary from an experienced pilot on a cross-country charter flight to a student pilot practicing touch and go's. This factor has an important bearing on the rates for the hull coverage.

Second, and more important, a very strong obligation exists on the part of the commercial operator to ensure the safety and well-being of the members of the public he serves. This obligation is recognized by the courts as being considerably higher than the obligation of a private owner to a guest and is reflected in the comparative size of awards granted in legal liability cases (see Chapter 5). For these two reasons, rates for commercial exposures are generally much higher than are rates for other noncommercial categories.

Special Use

Special use is reserved for the many uses to which aircraft are put, several of which require special waivers from the Federal Aviation Administration. Included within this class are crop dusting, low altitude photography, banner towing, pipeline patrol, flight testing, hunting, fire fighting, law enforcement, and many others. The only common denominator which exists between risks in this category is that each represents exposure to some of aviation's more serious perils. As a use classification it is of little assistance to the underwriter in providing much of a framework within which to develop rates, but it does serve to identify those risks to which very special and detailed underwriting attention must be given.

EVALUATING THE AIRPORT LIABILITY RISK

Owners and operators of airports are liable for all damage caused by their failure to exercise reasonable care. Their liability extends not only to lessees, airplane passengers, or other persons using the facilities of the airport, but also to spectators, visitors, and other members of the public who may be on or about the premises. Underwriters investigate all aspects of an airport's operation before entertaining the risk. All must show evidence of experienced personnel, careful maintenance, and adherance to regulations.

An airport liability policy is written subject to the careful completion and approval of a detailed application (see Appendix A). With respect to the basic premises coverage, underwriters look for the following basic information:

1. Name and address of the applicant
2. Name and location of the airport and the extent of the applicant's occupancy
3. Whether the airport has a control tower and the extent of the applicant's jurisdiction over airport traffic control
4. Type and length of runways
5. FAA classification (under National Airport System Plan)
6. Operations of the applicant including estimated annual gross receipts
7. Type of fueling and applicant's participation
8. Particulars concerning tiedown and hangaring of aircraft
9. Description of police, guard, and fire protection
10. Safety precautions to protect the public from accidents
11. Sub-lessees and their operations
12. List of hangars and other buildings on the airport occupied by the applicant
13. List of all airport vehicles, aircraft, and helicopters

Contractual liability requires attachment of a copy of each contract, lease agreement, or lease of gasoline equipment under which the applicant has assumed liability. Alterations insurance requires information relative to alterations or construction contemplated for the next 12 months. Elevator liability requires a listing of all elevators, escalators, and moving sidewalks.

Products liability requires an estimate of gross receipts for the next 12 months. Categories normally include fuel and lubricants, new and used aircraft, aircraft parts, aircraft repairs and servicing, and restaurants.

From an underwriting standpoint, acceptance of hangarkeepers liability coverage depends to a large extent upon the housekeeping practices of the insured. Fire is the greatest hazard and proper maintenance of hangars is vital. In line with good housekeeping, the underwriter wants to know if repairs are made and where. Since aircraft repairs generally require use of dopes, paints, washing of engines with inflammables, and welding of parts, it is necessary to know where these inflammables are stored and whether the repairs are made in the hangar where aircraft are stored. Of equal importance are the construction of hangars and repair shops and the location of repair shops in relation to storage hangars.

Underwriters must know the number of planes hangared or tied down and the average value of any one aircraft as well as the aggregate value of all aircraft. Tiedown facilities, if used, should be described in detail. Information concerning the average values of aircraft hangared or tied down is important in determining the limits of liability to be written. Ordinarily underwriters require that the limits of liability can not be less than the average value for each aircraft and the average aggregate value of all aircraft.

PRICING AVIATION RISKS

The pricing of insurance is called *ratemaking*. It is the calculation of the contribution that each policy holder shall make in order to bear his or her fair share of losses and expenses. The price a person pays for insurance is called a premium and is the rate per unit of coverage times the units purchased. The rate is the cost per unit of protection purchased. The unit of protection varies with the line of insurance. In hull insurance, the rate is for each $100 of protection; in workers' compensation, the unit of exposure is each $100 of payroll; and in products liability, it is for each $1,000 of gross receipts.

The pricing problem in insurance is complicated because rates have to be established before all costs are known. Ratemakers have to forecast the probable losses from a study of past experience. Thus an element of guesswork is involved. Furthermore, since insurance is a regulated industry, its rates are subject to a degree of state control, and companies may be frequently called upon to justify a certain rate.

Aviation Rates

In contrast to other property and casualty fields no rating schedule exists showing rates applicable to different classes of aviation risk. In the aviation field there is an open market. Rates, therefore, are not standard and are to a large degree based upon judgment. Some states require that companies file "rate spreads." Such a filing indicates a minimum and a maximum rate but leaves the actual rate for a specific risk to the judgment of the underwriter. The rates charged are influenced to a great extent by the company's own experience and the current economic cycle.

Some companies furnish rate sheets that provide an average rate for an average risk of a particular class. These rates are not firm, and the final rate quotation is made only after the underwriter has been given an opportunity to appraise the particular risk. Competition also influences rates.

Rates are ordinarily quoted on an annual basis. There are risks that do not lend themselves to annual quotations predicated upon the number of aircraft owned. FBO's that have an active turnover of owned aircraft may secure a policy requiring periodic reporting of aircraft. Premiums are determined from these reports which show the aircraft at risk during a particular time.

Hull and Liability Rates

Hull rates are generally annual and expressed either as a percentage of the insured value or as a dollar amount applicable to each $100 of insured value. A base rate is determined for the class of business largely based upon the value of the hull. To this premium are added debit or credit percentages because of usage, pilot experience, policy modifications, and numerous other items that enter into the negotiations of an aircraft premium under any rating scheme. For example:

Aircraft: Cessna 172; Insured Value: $30,000; Coverage: all risks ground and flight; Deductibles: $50 ground—No Motion and $250 In-flight and Taxiing; Use: Business and Pleasure; Pilot Warranty: Any Private Pilot or better.

Base Rate	Annual Premium
4% (or $4.00/$100 value)	$1,200

Debits and Credits

1. 15% credit off base for open pilot warranty with minimum of 300 hours.
2. 20% surcharge on base to include a named student pilot.
3. 10% credit off base for named private pilot with 150 hours.
4. For multiple ownership above basic two pilots add 5% for each additional private pilot and 10% for each additional student pilot.
5. Add 50¢ to base rate if aircraft is tieddown.

6. $40 credit off annual premium to increase in flight and taxiing deductible to $500.

Liability rates are usually expressed as an annual premium. For example, the premium for our Cessna 172 used in the above example may be as follows:

Coverage	Limits of Liability	Annual Base Premium
Bodily injury excluding passengers	$100,000 each person 300,000 each occurrence	$ 30
Passenger bodily injury	100,000 each person 300,000 each occurrence	150
Property damage	100,000 each occurrence	40

Similar to the hull coverage, debits and credits are added to the base premium depending upon a multitude of underwriting factors.

Medical payments coverage is generally written with a limit of $5,000 or $10,000 per seat and can include or exclude crew members. The premium per seat is quoted on flat annual basis.

Guest voluntary settlement coverage (admitted liability) which is generally only available to industrial aid accounts is quoted as a rate per $1,000 of coverage. Crew members can be included or excluded, and the coverage follows the number of seats on the aircraft. For example, a five-place aircraft on which $200,000 coverage is purchased for each seat might cost as follows:

Limits	Rate	Annual Premium
$200,000/1,000,000	$3.00/$1,000	$3,000

The admitted liability rate generally depends upon two factors: (1) the average number of passengers carried (load factor) and (2) the average mix of employees versus guests. Remember that employees cannot sue their employer and as such their only recourse would be to accept the admitted payment.

The premium for non-ownership liability coverage is generally very nominal and depends upon the known and unknown exposure anticipated by the insured. If there is no known exposure, the premium is generally around 50 percent of an owned aircraft liability premium.

Airport Liability Rates

Airports and the liability exposures they represent can vary considerably, from a Chicago O'Hare which is literally a city unto itself handling all types of aircraft activity, to a small grass strip on the outskirts of a rural town which serves as the base for several general aviation aircraft. Consequently, when the underwriter considers the factors which affect premises liability rates, the annual premium can vary from thousands of dollars to a couple of hundred dollars. Many larger airports will carry limits up to $100,000,000 while a $1,000,000 single limit of liability protection may suffice for the small grass strip.

Products liability rates vary according to the product classification. For example, based on limits of $100,000 each person and $300,000 each occurrence for bodily injury and $100,000 for property damage, the following rates would apply:

Classification	Rate per $1,000 of Gross Receipts
Sale of New Aircraft	$ 1.00
Sale of Aircraft Parts	2.50
Sale of Used Aircraft	3.50
Sale of Gas and Oil	4.35
Aircraft Servicing and Repair	15.78

Basic hangarkeepers liability rates largely depend upon whether or not the insured is simply storing aircraft or does repair and servicing work in the hangar facility. Rates can vary from 2 to 4 percent of the total limit of liability carried for one location. For example, a representative premium for limits of $100,000 any one aircraft and $500,000 all aircraft stored at any one time might be $10,000.

This brief discussion of aviation rates was merely intended to highlight some examples of rating used in the aviation insurance industry. A complete analysis would require a working knowledge of aviation underwriting and a complete review of a company's underwriting manuals which are continually revised and updated.

REINSURANCE

Even if underwriters were able to select the best risks to be covered, there are limitations on the amounts of insurance that could be sold by one insurer. The underwriters must find a safe distribution of exposure units. The financial condition and size of the insurer are important determinants of the volume of insurance it will underwrite. Top management must decide what is the largest single amount the company can afford to lose at one time.

Reinsurance is the insurance of insurance. When a company has received a large volume of insurance on a particular aircraft or airport in excess of the amount it wishes to retain, it can reinsure the contract. Furthermore, if the volume of business received by the company from all its agents is in excess of the amount that can be supported by the insurer's financial position, it can reinsure part of the business.

The great bulk of aircraft hull and liability premium is derived from risks which have a catastrophe potential far in excess of the retention capacity of any single insurer. In aviation, as in any other form of insurance where catastrophe exposure and capacity problems exist, reinsurance plays an important role. It is used by the independent insurer writing aviation on its own account outside of a group to provide a capacity in order to compete. It is also used by the groups to spread the loss potential of risks they have assumed. It would be difficult to imagine any sizable aviation risk where reinsurance is not involved.

Types of Reinsurance

Pro Rata Reinsurance

Under *pro rata reinsurance,* the originating (ceding) insurer and the reinsurer each receive a pro rata share of the premium and are responsible for a pro rata share of the claims. Aircraft hull insurance and other property lines are generally written on a pro rata basis when reinsurance is involved.

Reinsurance is further classified as *facultative* or *treaty.* In *facultative reinsurance,* an insurer with a contract to reinsure approaches other insurers. If a willing reinsurer can be found, the two insurers then negotiate the terms of the reinsurance. For example, suppose an insurer wanted to retain only $6 million on an aircraft hull insured for $10 million. The company would approach one or more other insurers and attempt to lay off $4 million of the risk. A more formalized approach is called *treaty reinsurance* under which an insurer enters into an agreement with the ceding insurer stating the terms on which reinsurance will be accepted. Under the treaty, all policies written in excess of a net retention limit are automatically ceded to the reinsurer.

Excess Reinsurance

Under *excess reinsurance,* the reinsurer is required to pay for losses in excess of the ceding insurer's retention limit as opposed to a pro rata settlement. For example, a company might write a single-limit of liability of $20 million and then lay off $10 million excess of $10 million. Each of the underwriters accepts a layer of the risk. The primary underwriter would pay for the entire amount of loss until the limit he has accepted is exhausted and then the next underwriter takes over payment of the loss until his limits are exhausted and so on. Excess reinsurance, like pro rata, can be written on a facultative or treaty basis.

CONCLUSION

Aviation insurance has expanded in direct ratio with the growth of the aviation industry itself. In the 80 plus years since the first flight of a heavier-than-air machine by the Wright brothers at Kitty Hawk, North Carolina, in 1903, aviation and airplanes have made enormous progress. What the next 80 years will hold, no one can tell. Risk will never be entirely eliminated in the age of flight and insurance will always be needed to bear the financial hazards of the men and the machines in which they fly.

KEY TERMS

Underwriting	Industrial aid
Catastrophe loss	Commercial use
Limited spread of risks	Limited commercial use
Preselection	Special use
Postselection	Ratemaking
Configuration	Hull rates
Conventional landing gear	Liability rates
Tricycle landing gear	Reinsurance
Minimum pilot requirements	Pro rata Reinsurance
Purpose of use categories	Facultative reinsurance
Airline	Treaty reinsurance
Business and pleasure	Excess Reinsurance

REVIEW QUESTIONS

1. What is the purpose of underwriting? How does underwriting serve to provide equity in the rating structure?
2. Discuss the unique nature of aviation exposures as distinguished from other lines of insurance. Why is the limited spread of risks such a difficult problem for underwriters? How does diversification of aircraft and rapidity of change complicate this problem?
3. Give some examples of how underwriters preselect risks. What is meant by postselection? Describe the conflict which often arises between production and underwriting.
4. Describe the basic information required by underwriters in order to offer an aircraft hull and liability quotation.
5. Discuss the major consideration taken by underwriters in reviewing the following areas: type of aircraft and equipment; pilots; geographical considerations; and purpose of use.
6. Distinguish between "business and pleasure" and "industrial aid." Why do you think hull rates for an aircraft used exclusively for charter operations are relatively low compared with an aircraft used for student instruction and rental (limited commercial)? On the other hand liability rates for an aircraft used exclusively for charter operations are relatively high compared to aircraft used for student instruction and rental purposes. Why? Describe what is meant by special use.
7. What is the basic information underwriters require in evaluating the airport liability risk? What underwriting information is needed for products and hangarkeepers liability?
8. What is the purpose of reinsurance? Distinguish between pro rata and excess reinsurance. What is the difference between facultative and treaty reinsurance?

Appendix A

Applications

1. USAIG All-Clear Aircraft Insurance Application

2. USAIG Non-Owned Aircraft Insurance Application

3. AAU Pilot Questionnaire

4. AAU Application for Airport/Fixed Base Operator's Liability Insurance

5. AAU Application for Helicopter Hull and Liability Insurance

6. AAU Turbo-Jet and Turbo-Prop Engine Aircraft Operation Questionnaire

7. USAIG Airport Insurance Application

8. USAIG Aviation Products Liability Insurance Application

USAIG All-Clear Aircraft Insurance Application

Name of Applicant_____

Address_____

You are ☐Individual ☐Corporation ☐Partnership ☐Other, explain_____

Your business is_____

Your present aircraft insurance company is_____Policy Expires_____

Aircraft Information

Year_____Make and Model_____FAA "N" No._____

Capacity: Pass._____ Crew_____ Standard Airworthiness Category ☐Yes ☐No

Is aircraft equipped with any modifications not provided by manufacturer (STOL Kit, performance devices, etc.) ☐No ☐Yes

Explain "Yes" answer_____

Aircraft is a landplane ☐Yes ☐No (describe)_____ It is usually hangared ☐Yes ☐No

Aircraft is usually based at_____

Purchase date_____ Purchase price (with equipment) $_____ Current Value $_____

Explain "Yes" answers on reverse side of application.

Will any charge (other than operating expenses) be made for the use of the aircraft?	☐No ☐Yes
Will the aircraft be used for anything other than transporting people?	☐No ☐Yes
Will the aircraft be used anyplace other than at paved runway airports?	☐No ☐Yes
Will the aircraft be used outside the continental United States?	☐No ☐Yes
Do you own any other aircraft?	☐No ☐Yes
Will the aircraft be used for student or pilot instruction?	☐No ☐Yes

Name of Instructor_____Flight School_____

Pilot Information
We require information on every pilot who will operate the aircraft. If there are more than two pilots, attach a separate sheet.

PILOT NO. 1

Name_____ Birth Date / Occupation _____ Yr. Learned to Fly

Mth. Day Yr.

Soc. Sec. No._____Date of Last Biennial Flight Review_____Last Medical_____

FAA Pilot Certificates: ☐Stu. ☐Pvt. ☐Com'l. ☐ATP ☐CFI ☐Other   Cert. No._____Issue Date_____

Ratings: ☐ASEL ☐AMEL ☐ASES ☐Instrument ☐Rotorcraft ☐Other_____

Flying Experience as Pilot-in-Command:

	All Aircraft		This Make & Model		S/E Retrac. Gear		Multi-Engine		Civilian Last 10 Yrs.			Military Last 10 Yrs.		
Total	Last 12 Mo.	Last 90 Da.	Total	Last 90 Da.	Total	Last 90 Da.	Total	Last 90 Da.	Jet	Turboprop	Prop	Jet	Turboprop	Prop

Describe and give dates of last Flight Refresher or Flight Transition Courses_____

Do you hold a current FSI Pro Card	☐No ☐Yes
Do you participate in FAA Pilot Proficiency Award Program	☐No ☐Yes
If "Yes" what phase have you completed?	☐I ☐II ☐III ☐IV
For what type aircraft?	_____

PILOT NO. 2

Name_____ Birth Date / Occupation _____ Yr. Learned to Fly

Mth. Day Yr.

Soc. Sec. No._____Date of Last Biennial Flight Review_____Last Medical_____

FAA Pilot Certificates: ☐Stu. ☐Pvt. ☐Com'l. ☐ATP ☐CFI Other   Cert. No._____Issue Date_____

Ratings: ☐ASEL ☐AMEL ☐ASES ☐Instrument ☐Rotorcraft ☐Other_____

Flying Experience as Pilot-in-Command:

	All Aircraft		This Make & Model		S/E Retrac. Gear		Multi-Engine		Civilian Last 10 Yrs.			Military Last 10 Yrs.		
Total	Last 12 Mo.	Last 90 Da.	Total	Last 90 Da.	Total	Last 90 Da.	Total	Last 90 Da.	Jet	Turboprop	Prop	Jet	Turboprop	Prop

Describe and give dates of last Flight Refresher or Flight Transition Courses_____

Do you hold a current FSI Pro Card	☐No ☐Yes
Do you participate in FAA Pilot Proficiency Award Program	☐No ☐Yes
If "Yes" what phase have you completed?	☐I ☐II ☐III ☐IV
For what type aircraft?	_____

EXPLAIN EACH "YES" ANSWER—With respect to each pilot...

As pilot, any accidents, any citations for FAR violations or license limitations?	☐No ☐Yes
Any physical impairments or limitations or waivers on Medical Certificate?	☐No ☐Yes
Any felony convictions or license suspensions arising out of operation of a motor vehicle?	☐No ☐Yes
Any arrests for operation of a motor vehicle recklessly or under influence of alcohol or drugs?	☐No ☐Yes
Will anyone, other than you or the pilots shown above, use your aircraft?	☐No ☐Yes

Aircraft Ownership

I do not own the aircraft by myself ☐   Names and addresses of: ☐ Co-owner(s) ☐ Mortgagee(s) ☐ Lessor(s)

_____   _____

_____   _____

_____   _____

Amount of any lien or loan, excluding interest and/or finance charges $_____
Does your lienholder require lienholder's interest insurance (Breach of Warranty)? ☐ No ☐ Yes

Indicate the coverages desired.

Coverage	Limits of Coverage				
Combined Liability Coverage for bodily injury and property damage	$	Each Occurrence			
Combined Liability Coverage for bodily injury (except to passengers) and property damage	$	Each Occurrence			
Liability Coverage for bodily injury to anyone but passengers	$	Each Person	$		Each Occurrence
Liability Coverage for bodily injury to passengers only	$	Each Person	$		Each Occurrence
Liability Coverage for property damage	$	Each Occurrence			
Medical Coverage	$	Each Person			
Aircraft Physical Damage Coverage $ _____ Not in-motion deductible	$ _____ In-motion deductible	$ _____ Limit			

Use this space for answering questions.

_____

_____

_____

_____

_____

_____

_____

_____

_____

Has any other insurer cancelled, declined or refused to write any aviation insurance for you or one of your pilots?
☐ No ☐ Yes

I/We authorize the following agent/broker to represent me/us in the placing of this insurance:

NAME AND ADDRESS OF AGENT/BROKER: _____

AGENT represents following Member Company(ies) of USAIG_____

I/We represent that all information provided in this application is true and complete to the best of my/our knowledge and that no relevant information has been withheld, I/We understand that no insurance is in force unless and until United States Aviation Underwriters, Incorporated (Managers of the USAIG) effects a binder of insurance or issues a policy. It is understood, however, that if insurance is ordered from and accepted by United States Aviation Underwriters, Incorporated, the full amount of premium becomes due and payable immediately. I/We authorize United States Aviation Underwriters, Incorporated to investigate all or any qualifications or statements contained herein.

Date _____ Signature of Applicant or Authorized Representative_____

NEW YORK • ANCHORAGE • ATLANTA • BOSTON • CHICAGO • DALLAS • DENVER
HOUSTON • LOS ANGELES • MEMPHIS • MINNEAPOLIS • ORLANDO • PHOENIX
PITTSBURGH • RICHMOND • SAN FRANCISCO • ST. LOUIS • SEATTLE • TOLEDO • WICHITA

390-AC Rev 4/83

USAIG   NON-OWNED AIRCRAFT INSURANCE APPLICATION

NAME OF APPLICANT _____

ADDRESS _____

☐ Quotation for the following insurance is requested for an annual period beginning _____ 19____

☐ The following insurance is requested for an annual period beginning _____ 19____

Present Insurance expires _____

APPLICANT IS: ☐ Individual ☐ Corporation ☐ Partnership (name each partner) ☐ _____

BUSINESS OF APPLICANT IS: _____

NON-OWNED AIRCRAFT — List year, make and model of aircraft which may be used by applicant in next 12 months

_____

PILOTS   Information required on an Individual applicant and on each pilot employee of a company applicant.   IF MORE THAN TWO PILOTS. ATTACH SEPARATE SHEET

NAME		AGE	OCCUPATION		YEAR LEARNED TO FLY	DATE OF LAST BIENNIAL	DATE OF LAST MEDICAL
FAA PILOT CERTIFICATE AND RATINGS NOW HELD	STU ☐ PVT ☐	COM'L ☐ ATR ☐	CFI ☐ OTHER ☐ _____	ASEL ☐ AMEL ☐	ASES ☐ AMES ☐	INSTRUMENT ☐ OTHER ☐ _____	CERT. NUMBER _____ DATE OF ISSUE _____

Pilot-in-Command Experience
by MAKE and MODEL of AIRCRAFT

	TOTAL HOURS	TOTAL HOURS LAST 12 MONTHS	TOTAL HOURS EST. NEXT 12 MONTHS	TOTAL HOURS LAST 90 DAYS	TOTAL HOURS INSTRUMENT
_____	_____	_____	_____	_____	_____
_____	_____	_____	_____	_____	_____
_____	_____	_____	_____	_____	_____

NAME		AGE	OCCUPATION		YEAR LEARNED TO FLY	DATE OF LAST BIENNIAL	DATE OF LAST MEDICAL
FAA PILOT CERTIFICATE AND RATINGS NOW HELD	STU ☐ PVT ☐	COM'L ☐ ATR ☐	CFI ☐ OTHER ☐ _____	ASEL ☐ AMEL ☐	ASES ☐ AMES ☐	INSTRUMENT ☐ OTHER ☐ _____	CERT. NUMBER _____ DATE OF ISSUE _____

Pilot-in-Command Experience
by MAKE and MODEL of AIRCRAFT

	TOTAL HOURS	TOTAL HOURS LAST 12 MONTHS	TOTAL HOURS EST. NEXT 12 MONTHS	TOTAL HOURS LAST 90 DAYS	TOTAL HOURS INSTRUMENT
_____	_____	_____	_____	_____	_____
_____	_____	_____	_____	_____	_____
_____	_____	_____	_____	_____	_____

With respect to each pilot: EXPLAIN EACH "YES" ANSWER

As pilot — any accidents, any citations for FAR violations or any license limitations? .... ☐ NO   ☐ YES

Any physical impairments or limitations or waivers on Medical Certificate? .... ☐ NO   ☐ YES

Any felony convictions or license suspensions arising out of the operation of a motor vehicle? .... ☐ NO   ☐ YES

Any arrests for operation of a motor vehicle recklessly or under the influence of alcohol or drugs? .... ☐ NO   ☐ YES

USES   EXPLAIN EACH "YES" ANSWER
Will applicant make any charge to others for use of the aircraft? .... ☐ NO   ☐ YES

_____

Will aircraft be used for other than transportation of persons (such as hunting, dusting, patrol, research, etc.)?.. ☐ NO   ☐ YES

_____

Will aircraft be operated at other than paved public airports or outside the continental U.S.? .... ☐ NO   ☐ YES

Where? _____ Purpose? _____ Frequency? _____

Will aircraft be used for student or pilot instruction? .... ☐ NO   ☐ YES

Name of trainee(s) _____ Instructor _____ Flight School _____

F-502

COMPANY applicants: State annual flying hours of Non-Owned aircraft used in business of applicant:

(a) Rented aircraft and use of employee owner aircraft—last year _____; estimated next year _____

(b) Chartered aircraft with non-employee pilots—last year _____; estimated next year _____

Average number of passengers each trip? _____; are passengers usually guests or employees? _____

Number of branch offices? _____. Total number of employees? _____

Number of employees who are pilots? _____; number employed in pilot capacity? _____

Number of employees who own aircraft? _____; number of these aircraft used on company business? ____

Number of aircraft owned by company? _____; makes and models: _____

Number of employees whose regular duties require aircraft travel? _____   Any charters or rentals for more than seven consecutive days? .... ☐ NO ☐ YES

Any use of jets, helicopters or aircraft over eight-place including crew? .... ☐ NO ☐ YES
EXPLAIN EACH "YES" ANSWER

_____

LIABILITY COVERAGE STATE LIMITS OF LIABILITY DESIRED	EACH PERSON	EACH OCCURRENCE
Bodily Injury Liability Excluding Passengers	$	$
Property Damage Liability	X X X	$
Passenger Bodily Injury Liability	$	$
SINGLE LIMIT BI, PD. Passengers Included ☐ Passengers Excluded ☐	X X X	$

LOSS HISTORY and PREVIOUS AVIATION INSURANCE   Explain each "YES" answer

Has any applicant had any aircraft/aviation losses/claims during last five years? .... ☐ NO ☐ YES

_____

Has any insurer canceled, declined or refused to renew any aviation insurance? .... ☐ NO ☐ YES

_____

Name of last or present aircraft insurance company: _____

_____

I/We authorize the following agent or broker to represent me/us in the placing of this insurance:

_____
name and address of agent or broker

I/We warrant that all information provided in this application is true and complete to the best of my/our knowledge and that no relevant information has been withheld. I/We understand that no insurance is in force unless and until United States Aviation Underwriters, Incorporated (Managers of the USAIG) effects a binder of insurance or issues a policy. It is understood, however, that if insurance is ordered from and accepted by United States Aviation Underwriters, Incorporated, the full amount of premium becomes immediately due and payable. I/We authorize United States Aviation Underwriters, Incorporated to investigate all or any qualifications or statements contained on this application.

Date _____ 19 _____   X _____
PERSONAL SIGNATURE OF APPLICANT OR AUTHORIZED EXECUTIVE IS REQUIRED

Agent represents following member company(ies) of USAIG: _____
Agent or broker — Please send to:

NEW YORK • ANCHORAGE • ATLANTA • BOSTON • CHICAGO • DALLAS • DENVER
HOUSTON • LOS ANGELES • MEMPHIS • MINNEAPOLIS • ORLANDO • PHOENIX
PITTSBURGH • RICHMOND • SAN FRANCISCO • ST. LOUIS • SEATTLE • TOLEDO • WICHITA

PILOT QUESTIONNAIRE
(BOTH SIDES MUST BE COMPLETED)

ASSOCIATED AVIATION UNDERWRITERS
90 JOHN STREET, NEW YORK, N.Y. 10038

3475 Lenox Road Atlanta, Georgia 30326	20 N. Wacker Drive Chicago, Illinois 60606	P.O. Box 740428 Dallas, Texas 75374-0428	3155 West Big Beaver Road Troy, Michigan 48084	9393 West 110th Street Overland Park, Kansas 66210
3435 Wilshire Boulevard Los Angeles, California 90010	90 John Street New York, New York 10038		2775 Mitchell Drive Walnut Creek, California 94598	18000 Pacific Highway South Seattle, Washington 98188

Name .... Age ....

Address .... Zip ....

Present Employer .... Date Employed ....

Address .... Position Held ....

Name of Insured (If Not Applicant) ....

Address ....

Policy number (if known) ....

Previous Employers	Position	Dates
....	....	....
....	....	....
....	....	....

Have you ever been discharged or asked to resign?........... If so, explain ....

PILOT CERTIFICATE AND RATINGS CURRENTLY HELD

☐ STUDENT	☐ SINGLE ENGINE LAND	☐ OTHER (Specify)	☐ MECHANIC AIRCRAFT
☐ PRIVATE	☐ SINGLE ENGINE SEA		☐ MECHANIC POWER PLANT
☐ COMMERCIAL	☐ MULTI-ENGINE LAND	☐ TYPE RATING (Specify aircraft)	☐ INSTRUMENT RATING, OBTAINED BY
☐ AIRLINE TRANSPORT	☐ MULTI-ENGINE SEA		☐ FAA FLIGHT CHECK
☐ INSTRUCTOR	☐ HELICOPTER		☐ MILITARY INSTRUMENT CARD

FAA Certificate No.   Date first certificated as pilot

If student, (a) name of instructor

           (b) airport at which instruction is given

Class of medical certificate held   Date of last FAA physical examination

Physical impairments, if any

Waivers, limitations, or conditions specified on medical certificate, if any

Date of last FAR Flight Review: Type of aircraft used: Date of last simulator flight

Flight Review conducted by: How often?

Make and model of aircraft on which approval is sought ....

Have you attended aircraft manufacturer's ground and flight training course or its equivalent ☐ Yes ☐ No

Name of training facility(ies) attended ....

Dates attended ....

FLYING EXPERIENCE IN LOGGED HOURS

	MAKE AND MODEL OF AIRCRAFT	DATES FLOWN (BY YEARS)	MILITARY PILOT	MILITARY CO-PILOT	AIRLINE PILOT	AIRLINE CO-PILOT	CIVILIAN PILOT	CIVILIAN CO-PILOT	TOTAL TIME	TOTAL LAST 12 MONTHS
SINGLE										
ENGINE										
AIRCRAFT										
Total S.E.										
MULTI-										
ENGINE										
& JET										
AIRCRAFT										
Total M.E.										
SEAPLANES										
AND										
HELICOPTERS									GRAND TOTAL	

AAU-8D (7/84)

SUMMARY OF FLYING EXPERIENCE—Show total pilot hours LOGGED

Total Time .... Cross Country .... Night .... Actual Instrument .... Hood Instruments ....

EDUCATION

Circle highest year completed: High School 1 2 3 4; College 1 2 3 4; Graduate School 1 2 3 4.

| | Name of School | Attended | | Did you graduate/complete course? (Indicate which, if no so state) |
		Form	To	
COLLEGE				
GRADUATE SCHOOL				
BUSINESS OR TECHNICAL SCHOOL				
AIRCRAFT REFRESHER OR TRANSITION COURSE				

AIRCRAFT ACCIDENTS

Have you ever been involved in any aircraft accident? ....If yes, explain all accidents.

Location	Date	Make and Model of Aircraft	License Number of Aircraft	Probable Cause and Remarks

Have you ever been grounded by FAA or military authorities? .... If so, explain.................
....

Has an FAA or military pilot certificate held by you ever been suspended or revoked by the authority having jurisdiction?
If so, explain...

Have you ever been cited for any violation of Federal Air Regulations? .... If so, explain all violations ....
....

Have you ever been convicted of or pleaded guilty to a felony of for drunken driving?........ If so, explain.......................

Has any Insurance Company or Underwriter at any time declined an application submitted by you or cancelled or refused to renew a policy held by you in regard to any type of insurance, whatsoever? .... If so, explain ....
....

PILOT MUST COMPLETE ALL STATEMENTS AND ANSWER ALL QUESTIONS
CONTAINED IN THIS QUESTIONNAIRE

PILOT'S STATEMENT

I hereby certify that all information given by me to the foregoing questions and statements is true and correct to the best of my knowledge. I hereby authorize this Company to investigate all or any qualifications or statements contained herein.

....
Signature of Pilot

Date ....

....
Signature of Chief Pilot of Corporate—Executive Fleet

THIS QUESTIONNAIRE SUBMITTED THROUGH:

APPLICATION FOR AIRPORT/FIXED BASE OPERATOR'S LIABILITY INSURANCE THROUGH

ASSOCIATED AVIATION UNDERWRITERS

HOME OFFICE • 90 JOHN STREET • NEW YORK, NEW YORK 10038

(Check Which is Desired) ☐ A QUOTATION ☐ INSURANCE ☐ SCHEDULED HAZARDS basis ☐ COMPREHENSIVE basis

Name of Applicant ....

....

Address ....
No.   Street   Town or City   County   State   Zip

Business of Applicant ....

Applicant is: ☐ Individual(s)   ☐ Corporation   ☐ Partnership   ☐ Other ....

Insurance is requested from ....19.....to 12:01 A.M. ....19......
Standard Time at the address of the Applicant

Applicant's interest in the premises is: ☐ Owner   ☐ Trustee   ☐ Lessee   ☐ Sub-Tenant

Audit period desired if applicable: ☐ Annual   ☐ Semi-Annual

COVERAGE, LIMITS OF LIABILITY AND SURVEY OF HAZARDS

COVERAGE	LIMITS OF LIABILITY DESIRED FOR HAZARDS A, B & C		(Co. use only)
	Each Person	Each Occurrence	
☐ A. BODILY INJURY LIABILITY	$,000.	$,000.	
☐ B. PROPERTY DAMAGE LIABILITY	x x x x	$,000.	
☐ C. SINGLE LIMIT BODILY INJURY AND PROPERTY DAMAGE LIABILITY	x x x x	$,000.	

(Check Hazard for Which Coverage is Desired)

☐ A. AIRPORT LIABILITY

1. Name and location of airport(s) ....

2. Applicant's occupancy   ☐ Entire   ☐ Part

3. Give the square footage of:

    (a) Terminal area occupied and used by: (1) applicant .... (2) all lessees ....

    (b) Parking lots operated by: (1) applicant .... (2) concessionaires ....

    (c) All other areas open to the public (name them) ....

    ....

4. Give the mileage, within the airport, of all (a) roads .... (b) sidewalks ....

5. Does applicant (a) have jurisdiction over airport traffic control? ☐ Yes ☐ No   (b) operate control tower? ☐ Yes ☐ No

6. Type and length of runways ....

7. Airline traffic? ☐ Yes   ☐ No   Estimate annual number of (a) passenger departures ...... (b) passengers enplaned ......

8. Describe non-aviation activities on airport premises: ....

    ....

APL-3A (4/83)   **IMPORTANT: COMPLETE ALL ITEMS ON ALL SIDES**

9. Describe fire protection: ....
   ....

10. Elevators, escalators, moving sidewalks. Give type and number of each ....
    ....
    ....

□ B. CONTRACTUAL LIABILITY — (Hold Harmless Agreements, Indemnification Clauses)

   11. If applicant has assumed liability under contract, lease agreement, lease of gasoline equipment, etc., enclose copy of such agreement for analysis.

□ C. OWNERS' AND CONTRACTORS' PROTECTIVE LIABILITY

   12. Contemplated alterations or new construction for next 12 months ....
       .... Cost $ ....

COVERAGE	LIMITS OF LIABILITY DESIRED FOR HAZARDS D & E			(Co. use only)
	Each Person	Each Occurrence	Annual Aggregate	
□ A. BODILY INJURY LIABILITY	$,000.	$,000.	$,000.	
□ B. PROPERTY DAMAGE LIABILITY	x x x x	$,000.	$,000.	
□ C. SINGLE LIMIT BODILY INJURY AND PROPERTY DAMAGE LIABILITY	x x x x	$,000.	$,000.	

□ D. COMPLETED OPERATIONS LIABILITY

   13. Estimated receipts for the next 12 months on Repairs, Parts and Services $ ....

□ E. PRODUCTS LIABILITY

   14. Estimated sales for next 12 months of:

       Gasoline and Oil (Gallons) ....Aircraft — New $....................Aircraft — Used $....................

       Foods and Beverages $....................... Miscellaneous $......................

□ F. HANGAR KEEPER'S LIABILITY

   15. Schedule of Locations and Limits of Liability Desired:

Name of Airport	City or Town Where Located	Limit of Liability Any One Aircraft	Limit of Liability Any One Loss	(Co. use only)
_____	_____	_____	_____	_____
_____	_____	_____	_____	_____

   16. Describe hangar structure ....
       ....
       ....

   17. Hangar(s) sprinklered?   □ Yes   □ No

   18. Does applicant engage in the repair of aircraft?   □ Yes   □ No

   19. Number of aircraft hangared .... Number of aircraft tied down outside ....

       Describe tie down method: ....

20. Highest valued aircraft in applicant's care, custody or control at any time $. . . . .

21. Maximum value of all aircraft in applicant's care, custody or control at any one time $. . . . .

What accidents or losses, by coverage, have occurred or have been reported to insurance carriers for the following periods.

a) Last 12 months . . . .

. . . .

b) Previous 24 months . . . .

. . . .

PLEASE COMPLETE THE FOLLOWING ON THE INSURANCE NOW IN EFFECT:

COVERAGE	NAME OF COMPANY	EXPIRATION DATE
Aircraft Liability		
Aircraft Hull		
Airport Liability		
Products Liability		

Date . . . .   Agent's or Applicant's Signature . . . .

This Application does not commit the Company to any liability nor make the Applicant liable for any premium unless and until the Company agrees to effect this insurance.

THE FOLLOWING MUST BE COMPLETED BY AGENT OR BROKER BEFORE POLICY CAN BE ISSUED

Name of Agent or Broker . . . .

Street Address . . . . City . . . .

☐ Broker   ☐ Agent   State . . . . Zip . . . .

☐ General Agent, if so, indicate name of Company . . . .

MEMBER COMPANIES

Checkbox signifies policy available. Please indicate clearly the Company of issue for this policy:

☐ ALLIANCE ASSURANCE COMPANY, LTD.
☐ ALLIANZ INSURANCE COMPANY
☐ THE AMERICAN INSURANCE COMPANY
☐ AMERICAN MOTORISTS INSURANCE COMPANY
☐ THE BUCKEYE UNION INSURANCE COMPANY
☐ CENTENNIAL INSURANCE COMPANY
☐ THE CONTINENTAL INSURANCE COMPANY
☐ FEDERAL INSURANCE COMPANY
☐ THE FIDELITY AND CASUALTY COMPANY OF NEW YORK

☐ FIREMAN'S FUND INSURANCE COMPANY
☐ FIREMEN'S INSURANCE COMPANY OF NEWARK, NEW JERSEY
☐ GLENS FALLS INSURANCE COMPANY
☐ THE HANOVER INSURANCE COMPANY
☐ LONDON ASSURANCE
☐ NATIONAL SURETY CORPORATION
☐ PHOENIX ASSURANCE COMPANY OF NEW YORK
☐ SEA INSURANCE COMPANY, LTD.
☐ PUERTO RICAN-AMERICAN INSURANCE COMPANY

Are you licensed by the company of issue? . . . .

An application from a state serviced by one of the following Branch Offices should be sent directly to that office

ATLANTA
P.O. Box 56406
Atlanta, Georgia 30343
404 688-1627

CHICAGO
20 N. Wacker Drive
Chicago, Illinois 60606
312 641-2929

DALLAS
9330 Amberton Pkwy., Suite 109
Dallas, Texas 75243
214 231-4341

DENVER
6 Parker Place
2600 S. Parker Rd., Suite 162
Aurora, Colorado 80014
303 750-8560

DETROIT
3155 West Big Beaver Road
Troy, Michigan 48084
313 643-4848

KANSAS CITY
9393 West 110th Street
Overland Park, Kansas 66210
913 341-9660

LOS ANGELES
3435 Wilshire Boulevard
Los Angeles, California 90010
213 388-1241

NEW YORK
90 John Street
New York, New York 10038
212 766-1600

SAN FRANCISCO
2775 Mitchell Drive, Suite 102
Walnut Creek, California 94598
415 945-7400

SEATTLE
18000 Pacific Highway South, Suite 601
Seattle, Washington 98188
206 241-0855

APPLICATION FOR HELICOPTER HULL AND LIABILITY INSURANCE THROUGH

 ## ASSOCIATED AVIATION UNDERWRITERS

HOME OFFICE • 90 JOHN STREET • NEW YORK, NEW YORK 10038

(CHECK WHICH IS DESIRED) ☐ A QUOTATION ☐ INSURANCE ☐ RENEWAL POLICY

Name of Applicant _____

Address _____
No.　　　　　Street　　　　　Town or City　　　　County　　　　State　　　　Zip

Business of Applicant _____

Applicant is: ☐ Individual(s) ☐ Corporation ☐ Partnership ☐ Other _____

Insurance is requested from _____ 19____ to _____ 19____

COVERAGES

	LIABILITY — LIMITS		HULL COVERAGE
	EACH PERSON	EACH OCCURRENCE	
A. BODILY INJURY LIABILITY Excluding Passengers	$	$	☐ ALL RISK BASIS
B. PASSENGER BODILY INJURY LIABILITY	$	$	☐ ALL RISK BASIS — ROTORS NOT IN MOTION
C. PROPERTY DAMAGE LIABILITY	x x x x x x	$	AMOUNT OF INSURANCE:
D. SINGLE LIMIT BODILY INJURY AND PROPERTY DAMAGE LIABILITY: Passengers — ☐ included ☐ excluded	$		$ _____ (must be equal to purchase price or current market value)
E. MEDICAL PAYMENTS Pilot — ☐ included ☐ excluded	$	$	DEDUCTIBLES:
☐ OTHER LIABILITY	$	$	ROTORS NOT IN MOTION: _____ ROTORS IN MOTION: _____

AIRCRAFT

YEAR, MAKE AND MODEL	LICENSE NUMBER	SEATING CAPACITY		LAND (L) SEA (S) AMP (A)	PURCHASED		PRICE PAID BY APPLICANT (INCL. EXTRAS)	PRESENT ESTIMATED VALUE (INC. EXTRAS)	ENGINE HRS. SINCE NEW OR SINCE LAST MAJOR OVERHAUL	NO. OF HOURS FLOWN LAST 12 MOS.
		CREW	PASS.		NEW OR USED	DATE				
1.										
2.										

Aircraft usually based at _____ ☐ Hangared ☐ Tied down
(Name of Home Airport)

IF TIED DOWN, DESCRIBE METHOD OF SECURING HELICOPTER: _____

APPLICANT IS: ☐ Sole Owner ☐ Owner subject to mortgage or conditional sales contract
☐ Other — explain _____

If aircraft is encumbered, name and address of lienholder _____

Amount of encumbrance (excluding interest and finance charges) $_____ Number of payments _____ Amount of each $_____
Date of final installment _____ Will Breach of Warranty Coverage be required by lienholder? _____

AIRCRAFT USE — CHECK ALL APPLICABLE USES:

☐ PLEASURE　(NON-PRO PILOTS)　　　　☐ AIR AMBULANCE　　　☐ FIRE CONTROL

☐ BUSINESS　(NON-PRO PILOTS)　　　　☐ AIR HEARSE　　　　☐ PARACHUTE DROPPING

☐ CORPORATE — EXECUTIVE (FLOWN BY PROFESSIONAL　☐ POLICE OPERATIONS　　☐ LOW ALTITUDE PHOTOGRAPHY
　　PILOTS HIRED FOR THIS PURPOSE)　　　☐ TRAFFIC CONTROL　　☐ CROP DUSTING

☐ INSTRUCTION　PILOT UPGRADE/CHECK OUT　☐ SEARCH AND RESCUE　☐ EXTERNAL LOAD — SLUNG CARGO

☐ CHARTER ☐ PASSENGER ☐ CARGO ☐ AIRLINE　☐ PATROL FLIGHTS (describe below)　☐ POLE/INFLIGHT PICK UP AND DEL.

☐ OTHER USES NOT LISTED: _____

ARE NON-FAA APPROVED LANDING SITES USED? _____ IF YES, HOW OFTEN? _____ DESCRIBE SITES _____

ARE BUILDING TOP LANDING PADS USED? _____ IF YES, HOW OFTEN? _____ GIVE LOCATION AND DESCRIPTION _____

IMPORTANT: COMPLETE ALL ITEMS ON BOTH SIDES

AAU31F (3/80)

Are overwater flights contemplated? _____ If yes, where and how often? _____

_____ Are floats installed? _____

Are flights at night contemplated? _____ How frequently? _____ Are landing sites lighted? _____

Is factory recommended maintenance program being followed? _____

PILOTS:

	AGE	HELICOPTER CERTIFICATE AND RATINGS					MEDICAL CERTIFICATE		TOTAL ALL AIRCRAFT	PILOT IN COMMAND HOURS — LOGGED HELICOPTER			
		PVT	CM'L	IFR	ATP	TYPE RATINGS (LIST)	DATE OF LAST PHYSICAL	CLASS		TOTAL RECIP.	TOTAL TURBINE	IN MODEL TO BE INSURED	TOTAL LAST 12 MONTHS
1.													
2.													
3.													
4.													

PILOT	1	2	3	4

1. HAVE YOU SUCCESSFULLY COMPLETED THE MANUFACTURER'S APPROVED PILOTS' GROUND AND FLIGHT TRAINING SCHOOL FOR THIS MAKE AND MODEL HELICOPTER? (YES OR NO)

2. DO YOU PARTICIPATE IN A FORMAL RECURRENT TRAINING PROGRAM? (YES OR NO) (IF YES, ATTACH BRIEF SUMMARY)

3. WAS YOUR ORIGINAL ROTOCRAFT RATING OBTAINED THROUGH THE MILITARY? (YES OR NO)

4. DO YOU HAVE ANY PHYSICAL IMPAIRMENTS? (YES OR NO)*

5. DO YOU HAVE ANY WAIVERS, RESTRICTIONS, LIMITATIONS OR CONDITIONS ATTACHED TO YOUR MEDICAL CERTIFICATE? (YES OR NO)*

6. HAS YOUR FAA OR MILITARY PILOT CERTIFICATE EVER BEEN SUSPENDED OR REVOKED? (YES OR NO)*

7. HAVE YOU EVER BEEN CITED FOR ANY VIOLATION OF FEDERAL AIR REGULATIONS? (YES OR NO)*

8. HAVE YOU EVER BEEN INVOLVED IN AN AIRCRAFT ACCIDENT? (YES OR NO)*

9. HAVE YOU EVER BEEN CONVICTED OR PLEADED GUILTY TO A FELONY OR DRUNK DRIVING CHARGE? (YES OR NO)*

* EXPLAIN ALL YES ANSWERS TO THESE QUESTIONS: _____

_____

_____

_____

_____

_____

NAME OF LAST AVIATION INSURANCE CARRIER (IF NONE, SO STATE) _____

TO THE APPLICANT'S KNOWLEDGE NO DAMAGE HAS BEEN SUSTAINED TO, NOR CLAIMS BY OTHERS HAVE ARISEN OUT OF THE OPERATION OF ANY AIRCRAFT OWNED BY OR IN THE CUSTODY OF THE APPLICANT EXCEPT: _____

_____

HAS ANY INSURANCE COMPANY OR UNDERWRITER AT ANY TIME DECLINED AN APPLICATION SUBMITTED BY, OR CANCELLED OR REFUSED TO RENEW A POLICY HELD BY THE APPLICANT OR ANY OF THE PILOTS NAMED HEREIN IN REGARD TO ANY TYPE OF INSURANCE WHATSOEVER? _____

IF SO, EXPLAIN _____

ALL PARTICULARS HEREIN ARE DECLARED TO BE TRUE AND COMPLETE TO THE BEST OF MY/OUR KNOWLEDGE AND NO INFORMATION HAS BEEN WITHHELD OR SUPPRESSED AND I/WE AGREE THAT THIS APPLICATION AND THE TERMS AND CONDITIONS OF THE POLICY IN USE BY THE INSURER SHALL BE THE BASIS OF ANY CONTRACT BETWEEN ME/US AND THE INSURER. I HEREBY AUTHORIZE THIS COMPANY TO INVESTIGATE ALL OR ANY QUALIFICATIONS OR STATEMENTS CONTAINED HEREIN.

DATE _____   **APPLICANT'S SIGNATURE** _____

THE APPLICATION DOES NOT COMMIT THE COMPANY TO ANY LIABILITY NOR MAKE THE APPLICANT LIABLE FOR ANY PREMIUM UNLESS AND UNTIL THE COMPANY AGREES TO EFFECT THIS INSURANCE.

_____

NAME OF AGENT OR BROKER _____

STREET ADDRESS _____ CITY _____

☐ BROKER   ☐ AGENT   STATE _____ ZIP _____

☐ GENERAL AGENT. (IF SO, INDICATE NAME OF COMPANY) _____

MEMBER INSURANCE COMPANY IN WHICH AGENCY LICENSE HELD _____

AN APPLICATION FROM A STATE SERVICED BY ONE OF THE FOLLOWING BRANCH OFFICES SHOULD BE DIRECTED TO THAT OFFICE

3375 LENOX ROAD ATLANTA, GA 30326	20 N. WACKER DR. CHICAGO, ILLINOIS 60606	9330 AMBERTON PARKWAY SUITE 109 DALLAS, TEXAS 75243	3155 WEST BIG BEAVER ROAD DETROIT, MICHIGAN 48084	9393 WEST 110th ST. OVERLAND PARK, KANSAS 66210
3435 WILSHIRE BOULEVARD LOS ANGELES, CALIFORNIA 90010	90 JOHN STREET NEW YORK, NEW YORK 10038	2775 MITCHELL DRIVE SUITE 102 WALNUT CREEK, CALIFORNIA 94598		18000 PACIFIC HIGHWAY SOUTH SUITE 601 SEATTLE, WASHINGTON 98188

TURBO-JET AND TURBO-PROP ENGINE AIRCRAFT OPERATION QUESTIONNAIRE

 **ASSOCIATED AVIATION UNDERWRITERS**

ATLANTA	CHICAGO	DALLAS	DENVER	DETROIT
P.O. Box 56406	20 N. Wacker Drive	9330 Amberton Pkwy., Suite 109	6 Parker Place	3155 West Big Beaver Road
Atlanta, Georgia 30343	Chicago, Illinois 60606	Dallas, Texas 75243	2600 S. Parker Rd., Suite 162	Troy, Michigan 48084
404 688-1627	312 641-2929	214 231-4341	Aurora, Colorado 80014	313 643-4848
			303 750-8560	

KANSAS CITY	LOS ANGELES	NEW YORK	SAN FRANCISCO	SEATTLE
9393 West 110th Street	3435 Wilshire Boulevard	90 John Street	2775 Mitchell Drive, Suite 102	18000 Pacific Highway South, Suite 601
Overland Park, Kansas 66210	Los Angeles, California 90010	New York, New York 10038	Walnut Creek, California 94598	Seattle, Washington 98188
913 341-9660	213 388-1241	212 766-1600	415 945-7400	206 241-0855

Name of Aircraft Owners . . . .

Address . . . .
      No.   Street   Town or City   County   State   Zip

Name of aircraft operator (if other than owner) . . . .

Address . . . .
      No.   Street   Town or City   County   State   Zip

AIRCRAFT: Year, Make and Model	FAA Identification Number	Initial Value (Excl. Extras)	Final Value (Excl. Extras)	Acceptance Date	Estimated Initial Operation Date	Estimated Hours to be Flown Annually
1.						
2.						

Aircraft usually based at . . . . ☐ Hangared;   ☐ Tied-down
(Name of Home Airport. If Private Airport, give detailed location.)

Home Airport: Length of longest runway . . . . Fuel and service ☐ own ☐ other ☐ none

Alternate Airport: (name, longest runway length. Are hangar, fuel and service available?

. . . .

Name and address of facility servicing aircraft at home airport:

. . . .

. . . .

Name and address of facility performing the following maintenance:

(a) Pre-flight . . . .

(b) 100 hour or progressive check . . . .

(c) Annual . . . .

(d) Repairs . . . .

Have the maintenance personnel of the above named facilities, who will service the aircraft, successfully completed the aircraft manufacturer's maintenance school?

. . . .

. . . .

. . . .

Name and address of equipment and/or modification installing facility (electronics, interior, etc.):

. . . .

. . . .

IMPORTANT: COMPLETE ALL ITEMS ON BOTH SIDES

AAU 87 A—(2/83)

PILOTS: This information is required for each pilot and co-pilot who will operate the aircraft.

NAME	Date of Birth m/d/y	Pilot Certificate and Ratings							First Pilot Hours Logged		Total Pilot Hours—Logged			Make and Model of Turbo Engine Aircraft Flown
		Pvt.	Cm'l	ASEL	AMEL	Instrum.	ATR	Other	Multi-Engine	ME In Com'd. over 12.500#	Turbo Prop	Turbo Jet	Total	Model of
1.														
2.														
3.														
4.														

Furnish the following physical information concerning pilots named above.

	1	2	3	4

Completed aircraft manufacturer's ground and flight training course (write yes or no) ...... Date.......

Upon completion of manufacturer's flight training course received/will receive following flight hours:

Completed aircraft manufacturer's maintenance course: (write yes or no)

If manufacturer's course not attended, name school and date at which similar course for the aircraft was completed: (If employer's course so state)

....

Has received or will receive aircraft type rating or competence check from: (if no so state)

1 ....

2 ....

3 ....

4 ....

Participate in formal flight training program ☐ Yes ☐ No How often .... Date Last Completed:.............

Name of school ....

If training by employer, give name and qualifications or instructor ....

....

Flight simulators used ☐ Yes ☐ No How often ....

Discuss briefly the present and future turbo engine operation (touch upon area of operation, operation procedure, minimum runway length to be used, landing visibility and ceiling minimums to be used during initial operation [if this is a new operation] and for how long, previous experience in operating such aircraft, current and proposed crew flight training):

....

....

....

....

....

....

....

I hereby certify that all information given by me to the foregoing questions and statements is true and correct to the best of my knowledge. I hereby authorize this Company to investigate all or any qualifications or statements contained herein.

Date ....   Signed by:...

                                                     Name & Title

THIS QUESTIONNAIRE SUBMITTED THROUGH:

USAIG — AIRPORT INSURANCE APPLICATION

NAME OF APPLICANT_____

ADDRESS_____

APPLICANT IS: ☐ Individual ☐ Corporation ☐ Partnership (name each partner)_____

whose business is:_____

Quotation for Airport Liability insurance is requested for an annual period beginning_____ 19____

Name of airport_____ located____ miles_____ of_____

(north, east, south, west)   (city)

APPLICANT IS: ☐ Tenant ☐ General Lessee ☐ Airport owner Present Insurance expires_____

OPERATIONS of APPLICANT — Indicate all operations and estimated annual gross receipts.

List all other sources and receipts below. Use separate sheet if necessary.

Fuel & Lubricants	$_____	Aircraft Repair	$_____	_____	$_____
Tiedowns & Hangaring	$_____	Aircraft Charter	$_____	_____	$_____
Landing Fees	$_____	Rental & Instruction	$_____	_____	$_____
New Aircraft	$_____	Helicopter Repairs	$_____	_____	$_____
Used Aircraft	$_____	Restaurant	$_____	_____	$_____
Aircraft Parts	$_____	Auto Parking	$_____	Total —	$_____

FUELING:
On premises ☐ YES ☐ NO Done by applicant ☐ YES ☐ NO

FUELING is by: ☐ Truck ☐ Hydrant ☐ Gas pump ☐ Gas pit ☐ _____

(other)

Annual Gallonage: Airline_____ gallons; General Aviation_____ gallons; Military_____ gallons.

Type of fuel sold: AVGAS ☐ JET FUEL ☐

Fuel Storage Facilities: Underground_____ gallons; Above ground_____ gallons.

Annual Gallonage of Turbine Engine Fuel:_____ gallons.

TIE DOWN & HANGARING by APPLICANT—are aircraft of others taxied, towed or moved by applicant? ☐ NO ☐ YES

Number of: tiedown spaces_____; T-hangars_____; multiple aircraft hangars_____

Number of aircraft: tied down_____; in T-hangars_____; in multiple aircraft hangars_____

Highest value a/c: tied down $_____; in T-hangars $_____; in multiple aircraft hangars $_____

Total value all a/c: tied down $_____; in T-hangars $_____; in multiple aircraft hangars $_____

APPLICANTS VEHICLES-ELEVATORS and AIRCRAFT

Indicate the number and type of vehicles maintained for use exclusively on the airport premises:

Fuel Trucks_____, Sweepers_____, Snow Removal_____, Fire Engines_____, Tugs_____

Hydrant Carts_____, Pickup Trucks_____, Passenger Cars_____, Other_____

State number of: Elevators_____, Escalators_____, Moving Sidewalks_____

State number of Aircraft owned or operated by applicant_____; number of Helicopters_____

CONTRACTS—Has applicant entered into any written agreements assuming the liability of others,

such as lease of premises, fuel supplier, equipment lease, etc? _____ ☐ NO ☐ YES (attach copies)

Does applicant use uniform customer contracts for hangaring, service, etc? ☐ NO ☐ YES (attach sample)

CONSTRUCTION by Independent Contractors—show estimated cost by type of construction—

Runways & taxiways..........	$_____ next year; $_____	next three years.
All others (describe)_____	$_____ next year; $_____	next three years.

F-137 3/77

AIRPORT DESCRIPTION—Elevation is_____ft.; Longest runway is_____ft.

Number of aircraft based at airport: Airline_____, General Aviation_____, Military_____

Runway Construction: ☐ Concrete ☐ Turf ☐ Gravel ☐ Blacktop ☐ Other_____; Are runways Lighted? ☐ NO ☐ YES

Aircraft traffic is controlled—_____ ☐ NO ☐ YES—by ☐ Tower ☐ Unicom—Operated by:_____

Is there an airport manager?_____ ☐ NO ☐ YES Employed by:_____

Is manager on premises during hours of operation?_____ ☐ YES ☐ NO Hours of operation_____to_____

Fire station located at airport_____ ☐ YES ☐ NO It is_____miles from the airport.

Is airport fenced?_____ ☐ NO ☐ YES Who maintains the airport?_____

Does the insured own, operate or maintain any aids to navigation? ☐ NO ☐ YES (describe)

If applicant is Owner or General Lessee—complete the following and enclose a map or FAA Form 5010-1

Airport manager is: ☐ Employee of applicant; ☐ Independent Contractor (furnish copy of contract)

Any Recreational or other Non-Aviation facilities or use of Airport premises? ☐ NO ☐ YES (describe)

List Airlines and Scheduled Air Taxis that will serve this airport during next three years:

Total Estimated Arrivals & Departures:	PRESENT YEAR	NEXT YEAR (EST.)	FOLLOWING YEAR (EST.)
Revenue Passengers			
Airline Aircraft			
General Aviation Aircraft			
Military Aircraft			

LIABILITY COVERAGE—state limits of liability desired

	EACH PERSON	EACH OCCURRENCE
Bodily Injury Liability	$ X X X	$
Property Damage Liability	X X X	$
Single Limit Bodily Injury and Property Damage	X X X	$
	EACH AIRCRAFT	
Ground Hangarkeepers Liability	$	$

LOSS HISTORY and PREVIOUS AVIATION INSURANCE   Explain each "YES" answer

Has applicant had any airport/aviation losses/claims during last five years?_____ ☐ NO ☐ YES

Has any insurer canceled, declined or refused to renew any airport/aviation insurance?_____ ☐ NO ☐ YES

Name of last or present airport/aviation insurance company:_____

I/We authorize the following agent or broker to represent me/us in the placing of this insurance:

_____
name and address of agent or broker

I/We warrant that all information provided in this application is true and complete to the best of my/our knowledge and that no relevant information has been withheld. I/We understand that no insurance is in force unless and until United States Aviation Underwriters, Incorporated (Managers of the USAIG) effects a binder of insurance or issues a policy. It is understood, however, that if insurance is ordered from and accepted by the United States Aviation Underwriters, Incorporated, the full amount of premium becomes immediately due and payable. I/We authorize the United States Aviation Underwriters, Incorporated to investigate all or any qualifications or statements contained herein.

Date_____19_____ X_____
PERSONAL SIGNATURE OF APPLICANT OR AUTHORIZED EXECUTIVE IS REQUIRED

Agent represents following member company(ies) of USAIG:_____

Agent or broker — Please send to:

NEW YORK • ANCHORAGE • ATLANTA • BOSTON • CHICAGO • DALLAS • DENVER
HOUSTON • LOS ANGELES • MEMPHIS • MINNEAPOLIS • ORLANDO • PHOENIX
PITTSBURGH • RICHMOND • SAN FRANCISCO • ST. LOUIS • SEATTLE • TOLEDO • WICHITA

USAIG   AVIATION PRODUCTS LIABILITY INSURANCE APPLICATION

Name of applicant_____

Address_____

Applicant is: ☐ Individual ☐ Corporation ☐ Partnership (Name each partner) ☐ Other (Describe below)

_____

_____

Quotation for the following insurance is requested for an annual period beginning_____19_____

  ☐ AVIATION PRODUCTS LIABILITY only ☐ AVIATION PRODUCTS LIABILITY/GROUNDING combined

How long has applicant been in the business of manufacturing aviation products?_____years,

EXPLAIN EACH "YES" ANSWER ON A SEPARATE SHEET

  Have any of applicant's products been discontinued during past three years? ☐ YES ☐ NO

  Are any of the products manufactured by the applicant currently the

  subject of any Federal Aviation Administration (FAA) Airworthiness Directive? ☐ YES ☐ NO

SECTION I: AVIATION PRODUCTS MANUFACTURED BY APPLICANT

PRODUCTS FOR FIXED WING AIRCRAFT (CIVILIAN AND MILITARY)

DESCRIPTION OF PRODUCT	TYPES OF AIRCRAFT WHICH UTILIZE PRODUCT	AIRCRAFT SYSTEM(S) IN WHICH PRODUCT IS UTILIZED

PRODUCTS FOR ROTARY WING AIRCRAFT (CIVILIAN AND MILITARY)

DESCRIPTION OF PRODUCT	TYPES OF AIRCRAFT WHICH UTILIZE PRODUCT	AIRCRAFT SYSTEM(S) IN WHICH PRODUCT IS UTILIZED

PRODUCTS FOR MISSILES OR SPACECRAFT

DESCRIPTION OF PRODUCT	TYPES OF CRAFT WHICH UTILIZE PRODUCT	SYSTEM(S) IN WHICH PRODUCT IS UTILIZED

Are any of the above listed products made exclusively to the specifications of applicant's customers? ☐ YES ☐ NO

If "yes", please identify the product with an asterisk.

Circle each of the above listed products which are made from material supplied by customer(s).

SECTION II: AVIATION SALES

Are any products manufactured by the applicant used in any of the models of aircraft listed below? ☐ YES ☐ NO

If "yes", complete the following:

MAKES AND MODELS	BOEING 747	BOEING SST	LOCKHEED 1011	LOCKHEED C-5A	DOUGLAS DC-10	CONCORDE SST
sales to date	$	$	$	$	$	$
next year (Est.)	$	$	$	$	$	$

GROSS AVIATION SALES INCLUDING ABOVE		NEXT YEAR 19	CURRENT YEAR 19	PRIOR YEAR 19	2nd PRIOR YEAR 19
FIXED	Airline	$	$	$	$
WING	Private	$	$	$	$
AIRCRAFT	Military	$	$	$	$
ROTARY	Airline	$	$	$	$
WING	Private	$	$	$	$
AIRCRAFT	Military	$	$	$	$
MISSILES		$	$	$	$

SECTION III: INSPECTION PROCEDURES

Describe inspection procedures:

By whom carried out:
government ☐
applicant ☐
customer ☐

SECTION IV: CUSTOMERS   List principal customers and percentages of gross sales to each:

CUSTOMER	% OF SALES	CUSTOMER	% OF SALES

SECTION V: LOSS HISTORY AND PREVIOUS INSURANCE   EXPLAIN EACH "YES" ANSWER ON A SEPARATE SHEET

Has applicant had any aviation products claims/losses? ☐ YES ☐ NO

Has any insurer cancelled, declined or refused to renew any aviation products liability insurance? ☐ YES ☐ NO

Name of last or present aviation products liability insurer:

Expiration date of policy:

Name of last or present general liability insurer:

Expiration date of policy:

LIMITS OF LIABILITY REQUIRED:

I/We authorize the following agent or broker to represent me/us in the placing of this insurance:

.... name and address of agent or broker ....

I/We warrant that all information provided in this application is true and complete to the best of my/our knowledge and that no relevant information has been withheld. I/We understand that no insurance is in force unless and until United States Aviation Underwriters, Incorporated (Managers of the USAIG) effects a binder of insurance or issues a policy. It is understood, however, that if insurance is ordered from and accepted by the United States Aviation Underwriters, Incorporated, the full amount of premium becomes immediately due and payable. I/We authorize the United States Aviation Underwriters, Incorporated to investigate all or any qualifications or statements contained herein.

Date _____ 19 ___   X..

Personal Signature of Applicant or Authorized Executive Is Required

Appendix B

Policies

1. USAIG All-Clear 360° Aircraft Policy

2. AAU Golden Wing Aircraft Insurance Policy

3. AVEMCO Aircraft Policy

4. AVEMCO Ultralight Aircraft Insurance Policy

5. AAU Airport/Fixed Base Operator's Liability Policy

ALL-CLEAR
360° AIRCRAFT POLICY

The Aetna Casualty and Surety Company
Hartford, Connecticut

Continental Casualty Company
Chicago, Illinois

**Employers Insurance of Wausau
A Mutual Company**
Wausau, Wisconsin

Hartford Fire Insurance Company
Hartford, Connecticut

Liberty Mutual Insurance Company
Boston, Massachusetts

Maryland Casualty Company
Baltimore, Maryland

Reliance Insurance Company
Philadelphia, Pennsylvania

Royal Indemnity Company
New York, New York

St. Paul Fire and Marine Insurance Company
St. Paul, Minnesota

State Farm Fire and Casualty Company
Bloomington, Illinois

The Travelers Indemnity Company
Hartford, Connecticut

United States Fidelity and Guaranty Company
Baltimore, Maryland

Zurich Insurance Company
Schaumburg, Illinois

USAIG
UNITED STATES AIRCRAFT INSURANCE GROUP

*is managed by United States Aviation Underwriters, Inc.
Home Office: One Seaport Plaza, 199 Water St., New York, NY 10038*

January 1, 1984

USAIG All-Clear Policy
Coverage Summary Page

Policy No. 360AC—

Former Policy No.

Name and Address of Policyholder

Your Coverage Summary Page gives you a complete rundown of the insurance you have under your All-Clear Policy. It, along with your policy and any endorsements you have, forms your complete insurance policy.

Your Policy Period is from

to

beginning and ending at   local

Standard Time at the address shown above.

( ) You own the aircraft by yourself

Policyholder is ( ) A. Individual   B. Corporation   C. Partnership

D.

Your business is

( ) You don't own the aircraft by yourself

Aircraft Use. You agree not to charge anyone for using your aircraft. They can, however, reimburse you for operating expenses.

Aircraft. Year. Make, Model and Type.	Airworthiness Category	FAA Identification	Passenger Capacity Excluding Crew
	Standard		

You keep your aircraft principally in the state of
Pilots.

Whom We'll Pay. Payments for loss covered under your Aircraft Physical Damage Coverage will be made to you and:

Limits of Your Coverage. You are insured up to the limits shown below for those coverages for which a dollar amount has been filled in. If no dollar amount appears, you don't have that coverage. These limits may be altered by the policy or by any attached endorsements.

Coverage	Limits of Coverage		
Combined Liability Coverage for bodily injury and property damage	$	Each Occurrence	
Combined Liability Coverage for bodily injury (except to passengers) and property damage	$	Each Occurrence	
Liability Coverage for bodily injury to anyone but passengers	$	Each Person $	Each Occurrence
Liability Coverage for bodily injury to passengers only	$	Each Person $	Each Occurrence
Liability Coverage for property damage	$	Each Occurrence	
Medical Coverage	$	Each Person	
Aircraft Physical Damage Coverage $ Not in-motion deductible	$ In-motion deductible	$ Limit	

Endorsements: The following endorsements have been added to your policy:

Premium . . . . $

Endorsement
Premium . . . . $

Total Premium . . . . $

This policy is written through the Aviation Managers on

Approved by United States Aviation Underwriters, Inc., Aviation Managers

---

Countersignature of Authorized Representative   Place of signing

360-AC CSP

Table of Contents

Your All-Clear Aircraft Policy

Because people use aircraft for a wide variety of purposes—business, recreational or a combination of both—your All-Clear Aircraft Policy has been designed to allow you to tailor your coverage to meet your individual flying needs. Your All-Clear Aircraft Policy can provide you with Liability Coverage, Medical Coverage and Aircraft Physical Damage Coverage. The coverage you currently have is indicated on the Coverage Summary page.

We want you to understand your coverage. So, we've written this policy in clear, easy-to-understand language.

Throughout this policy the words *you* and *your* refer to the person or organization named on the Coverage Summary page. *We, our* and *us* mean the insurance companies listed on the front page of your policy who are individually and together responsible under this policy. *Aviation Managers* means United States Aviation Underwriters, Inc.

Policy period. This policy will begin and end at the time and on the dates shown on the Coverage Summary page.

When and where you are covered. You are covered for occurrences that take place during the policy period while your aircraft described on the Coverage Summary page is in the United States and its territories and possessions, Canada, Mexico, the Bahama Islands, or while enroute between these places.

Policy Limits. The limits of your coverage are shown on the Coverage Summary page. These limits are the most we'll pay for: (1) Damage or loss of your aircraft; (2) bodily injury caused by your aircraft, including sickness, disease, mental anguish or death; (3) property damage caused by your aircraft, including the loss of use of the property. If two or more aircraft are protected under this policy, the limits of coverage apply separately to each aircraft.

What is an aircraft? Your aircraft includes your airplane or rotorcraft and any operating, navigating or radio equipment that's usually attached to the aircraft. Parts of your aircraft that are temporarily removed are also included as long as they're not replaced by other parts. Any tools and repair equipment standard for your type of aircraft are also included.

If you have a loss. If an occurrence happens, you should notify the Aviation Managers in writing as soon as reasonably possible. Include the time and place of the occurrence and the names and addresses of any injured people and witnesses. By an occurrence we mean any accident or continuous or repeated exposure to conditions which you don't expect to happen resulting in bodily injury or property damage. All injury or damage resulting from generally the same conditions will be considered one occurrence.

You agree to notify the police if your aircraft or any of its parts is stolen. You will also send us copies of all legal documents if you're sued or someone files a claim against you.

You agree to help us in obtaining and giving evidence, attending hearings and trials, and getting witnesses to testify. And you won't make any statements without our permission, except to government officials.

What's more, you agree not to voluntarily make any payments or take on any other legal responsibility without our permission. If you do, we may not reimburse you even if the loss or expense may have been covered by this policy. Of course, we will reimburse you for money spent for emergency first aid to others at the time of an accident.

Assignment-transfer. Neither you nor any other person or organization covered under this policy can transfer your interest under the policy without the written consent of the Aviation Managers.

If you die during the policy period, your legal representatives are covered while settling your estate provided the Aviation Managers are notified within 60 days of your death.

Changing this policy. You can change your coverage by having the Aviation Managers add an endorsement to this policy. Notice to your agent will not change the terms of this policy nor stop us or the Aviation Managers from enforcing any of our rights under it.

Cancelling this policy. You can cancel this policy at any time. We or the Aviation Managers have the same right.

You can cancel this policy by telling us in writing when in the future you want your coverage to end. We will compute the premium we've earned using the customary short rate table and procedure. Any premium we have not yet earned will be returned to you.

We or the Aviation Managers can cancel this policy by mailing or delivering notice to you at the address shown on the Coverage Summary page at least 30 days before the cancellation date. If, however, this policy is being cancelled because you didn't pay a premium, only 10 days notice will be provided. The mailing or delivery of the notice will be sufficient proof that you were notified.

We will compute the premium we've earned based on the percentage of the policy period that has been used at the time of cancellation. Any premium we have not yet earned will be returned to you.

Legal actions. Each of us named on the front cover of this policy, or the Aviation Managers, can bring a suit against you if you fail to pay a premium when it's due, or fail to live up to the terms of this policy in any other way. Any judgment involving one of us or the Aviation Managers will be binding on all.

State laws. If any terms of this policy conflict with state law, we'll comply with that law.

Limitations on use. To be covered under this policy the aircraft must be owned, maintained or used only for the purpose described on the Coverage Summary page and flown only by a pilot or pilots described there. The aircraft must also be registered under a "Standard" Category Airworthiness Certificate issued by the Federal Aviation Administration (FAA), or its foreign equivalent.

If you have other insurance. If you have other insurance covering a loss that's also covered by this policy, we'll pay only our share of any claim. We will figure what percentage the applicable limit of coverage for this policy is of the total amount of all valid and collectible insurance covering the loss. We will pay this percentage. For example, if you have a $5,000 limit under your Coverage for Property Damage and the total amount of all insurance against the loss is $10,000, we'll pay 50% of the loss.

This section does not apply to any insurance purchased as excess insurance. Excess insurance is insurance which becomes effective only when all other valid and collectible insurance covering the loss has been exhausted.

Similarly, coverage for Other Aircraft, Substitute Aircraft or for Newly Acquired Aircraft will be considered excess insurance and won't be affected by this section.

However, if any other insurance covering the loss was written through the Aviation Managers, the limit of coverage that applies under this policy will be reduced by the limit of coverage under the other insurance.

Our right of recovery. If we pay a claim under this policy, we will take over your right to recover that amount from any other person or organization. You agree not to do anything that will interfere with our chances of recovery and agree to cooperate with us.

Your Liability Coverage

Following is a description of your coverage under this policy for liability claims made against you. Check your Coverage Summary page to see which coverage you have.

Combined coverage for bodily injury and property damage. If you have this coverage we'll pay claims for bodily injury, mental anguish and damage to someone else's property resulting from the ownership, maintenance or use of the aircraft.

We will also pay claims for bodily injury, mental anguish, and damage to someone else's property resulting from your use or maintenance of a parking or storage area where you keep your aircraft, provided the parking or storage area isn't owned by you or leased to you for more than 30 days. But we won't pay more for all injury and damage in any one occurrence than the limit of coverage shown on the Coverage Summary page.

Combined coverage for bodily injury (except to passengers) and property damage. If you have this coverage we'll pay claims for bodily injury and mental anguish and damage to someone else's property resulting from the ownership, maintenance or use of the aircraft, except bodily injury and mental anguish claims by a passenger in your aircraft. A passenger is anyone who enters your aircraft to ride in or operate it.

We will also pay claims for bodily injury, mental anguish, and damage to someone else's property resulting from your use or maintenance of a parking or storage area where you keep your aircraft, provided the parking or storage area isn't owned by you or leased to you for more than 30 days. But we won't pay more for all injury and damage in any one occurrence than the limit of coverage shown on the Coverage Summary page.

Coverage for bodily injury to anyone but passengers. If you have this coverage, we'll pay claims for bodily injury and mental anguish to anyone—except a passenger—who is injured resulting from the ownership, maintenance or use of your aircraft. A passenger is anyone who enters your aircraft to ride in or operate it.

We will also pay for claims for bodily injury and mental anguish resulting from your use or maintenance of a parking and storage area where you keep your aircraft, provided you don't own or lease the parking or storage area for more than 30 days.

Two limits apply to this coverage. The "each person" limit, which is the most we'll pay for injury to any one person resulting from any one occurrence including damages for care and loss of services. And the "each occurrence" limit, which is the most we'll pay in any one occurrence no matter how many people or organizations are involved.

Coverage for bodily injury to passengers only. If you have this coverage we'll pay claims for bodily injury and mental anguish to any passenger in your aircraft who is injured resulting from the ownership, maintenance or use of the aircraft. A passenger is anyone who enters your aircraft to ride in or operate it.

Two limits apply to this coverage. The "each person" limit, which is the most we'll pay for injury to any one passenger resulting from any one occurrence including damages for care and loss of services. And the "each occurrence" limit, which is the most we'll pay in any one occurrence no matter how many people are involved.

Coverage for property damage. If you have this coverage we'll pay claims for damage to someone else's property resulting from the ownership, maintenance or use of the aircraft.

We will also pay claims for damage to someone else's property resulting from your use or maintenance of a parking or storage area where you keep your aircraft, provided you don't own or lease the parking or storage area for more than 30 days. But we won't pay more for damage in any one occurrence than the limit of coverage shown on the Coverage Summary page.

Who's covered

Besides you, certain other people and organizations are also covered under Your Liability Coverage. The words *you* and *your*, throughout this section, also include these other people and organizations.

They are:

• Anyone who is using or riding in your aircraft with your permission.

• Any person or organization that is legally responsible for the aircraft that you are using or that is being used with your permission.

Each person or organization is covered separately. But we won't pay more for all injury and damage in any one occurrence than the limit of coverage shown on the Coverage Summary page.

Who's not covered

Although the person or organization named on the Coverage Summary page is covered, we won't cover any liability claim against:

• Any other person or organization or their agents or employees that manufacture or sell aircraft, aircraft engines or aircraft accessories. Nor will we cover people or organizations that operate an aircraft repair shop, aircraft sales agency, aircraft rental service, commercial flying service or flying school or any person engaged in commercial aviation. Your employees, however, are covered against claims while performing any of these duties as part of their work for you.

• Any employee who, while working within the scope of his or her job duties, injures someone who works for the same employer.

Additional liability coverage

All payments described in this section are in addition to the applicable limit of liability coverage shown on the Coverage Summary page.

Defending suits. We will defend any liability suit brought against you for bodily injury or damage to property, even if the suit is groundless. We will also pay all costs of your defense, including investigation and court costs. We may investigate, negotiate and settle any claim or suit if we decide this is appropriate.

Bonds. We will pay premiums for appeal bonds and bonds to release any property and personal belongings that are being held as security. Any bail bond you may require because you violated a law or regulation during this policy period will also be paid for—up to $250 for each bond. However, we are not under any obligation to apply for or furnish these bonds.

Interest. We will also pay any interest on any part of a judgment we are paying.

Expenses. We will also reimburse you for all reasonable expenses you incur while helping us at our request. We won't, however, pay for the loss of earnings or salaries of you or your employees.

And we'll pay all medical and surgical expenses you incur while providing immediate medical treatment at the time of an accident or occurrence.

Suits for liability payment

No suit or other legal action to recover payment under this policy can be brought unless you have complied with all of its terms and a court has entered a judgment against you.

Liability claims we won't cover

Although your All-Clear Aircraft Policy provides you with broad liability coverage there are a few claims it will not cover.

• **Aircraft.** We won't cover claims for damage to your aircraft covered under Your Liability Coverage section of this policy.

• **Assumed liability.** We won't cover any liability you assume under a contract or agreement other than an airport contract you sign with a governmental body so you may use an airport.

• **Intentional injury.** We won't cover claims for intentional injury or property damage caused by you or at your direction, except to prevent a highjacking or other dangerous interference with the operation of an aircraft.

• **Workers' compensation.** We won't cover any liability claim that's covered under a workers' compensation, unemployment compensation, disability benefits law or similar law. Nor will we cover claims for injury to your employees while they're actually doing work for you, except for liability you assume under a contract or agreement you sign with a governmental body so you may use an airport. But we will cover claims brought by those domestics that you are not required to cover under workers' compensation.

• **Property damage.** We won't cover damage to any property you own, rent, control or transport. But we will cover the personal effects and baggage of each passenger in any one occurrence for up to $500. We will also pay up to $10,000 during the policy period for damage to hangars and their contents you don't own.

Financial Responsibility Laws

If this policy is certified as proof of insurance under any aircraft financial responsibility law, we will pay up to the limits of liability required by such law. But we won't pay more than the limit of coverage that would apply under this policy. You agree to reimburse us for any amount we are required to pay under the law that is in excess of what we would otherwise have paid under this policy.

Please note:

Attach Coverage Summary page and any endorsements.

This policy is not valid or complete unless a Coverage Summary page, approved by the Aviation Managers and countersigned by an Authorized Representative, is attached.

Notice of Annual Meetings

As a policyholder you are automatically a member of Employers Insurance of Wausau A Mutual Company, and Liberty Mutual Insurance Company.

This means you will receive dividends if they are declared by their Boards of Directors.

You may vote in person or by proxy at any meeting of these companies.

The Companies' Annual Meetings are as follows:

Employers Insurance of Wausau A Mutual Company: 10:00 a.m. on the 4th Friday of each May at the home office in Wausau, Wisconsin.

Liberty Mutual Insurance Company: 10:00 a.m. on the 3rd Wednesday of each April at the home office in Boston, Massachusetts.

Your Aircraft Physical Damage Coverage

You may also be protected against physical damage to your aircraft. If you have this coverage, we'll cover you against risk of physical loss or damage to your aircraft both while it's on the ground and while it's in flight. A fixed wing aircraft is in flight from the time it moves forward for takeoff and until it completes its landing run. A rotorcraft is in flight while its rotors are in motion as a result of engine power or autorotation.

We will consider an aircraft to be lost in flight if it disappears after take-off and isn't located or its whereabouts reported within 60 days.

What we'll pay

Total loss. If your aircraft is a total loss we'll pay you the amount shown on the Coverage Summary page for your Aircraft Physical Damage Limit, less any deductible that applies.

We will also return any unearned Aircraft Physical Damage premium to you. We will compute what we've earned based on the percentage of the policy period that has expired at the time the aircraft became a total loss. All your Aircraft Physical Damage coverage will end as soon as we make the payment, unless another aircraft is also insured for physical damage under this policy.

Partial loss—you make repairs. If the aircraft is only partially damaged and *you make repairs*, we'll reimburse you for the following items less any deductible that applies:
1. The cost of necessary material and parts of a similar kind and quality.
2. Wages paid at the current straight-time rate at the place of repair plus 150% of this amount to cover supervision and overhead.
3. The cost of transporting by the least expensive reasonable means: (A) The cost of transporting damaged parts from the site of the loss to the most practical place where they can be repaired; (B) the cost of transporting replacement parts from the place nearest the site of the loss; or (C) cost of transporting the aircraft to the most practical place where it can be repaired and then back to the place of the loss or your home airport, whichever is closer.

Partial loss—someone else makes repairs. If your aircraft is damaged *and the repairs are made by someone else*, we'll pay you the following, less any deductible that applies:
1. The net cost to you of repairing your aircraft with material and parts of a similar kind and quality. But we won't pay any overtime charges.
2. The cost of transporting by the least expensive reasonable means: (A) The cost of transporting damaged parts from the site of the loss to the most practical place where they can be repaired; (B) the cost of transporting replacement parts from the place nearest the site of the loss; or (C) the cost of transporting the aircraft to the most practical place where it can be repaired and then back to the place of the loss or your home airport, whichever is closer.

Your In-motion deductible. The In-motion deductible shown on the Coverage Summary page will apply to any loss to your aircraft while it is moving. This means you'll first pay an amount equal to the In-motion deductible. We will then pay the remainder of your loss up to the limit of your Aircraft Physical Damage coverage. An aircraft is in motion whenever it is moving on the ground or in flight as a result of engine power or autorotation.

No deductible, however, will apply to losses to your aircraft caused by an accident with another aircraft that we insure but which is owned by someone else.

Your Not in-motion deductible. The Not in-motion deductible shown on the Coverage Summary page will apply to each loss to your aircraft while it's not in-motion.

No deductible will apply, however, to any loss to your aircraft caused by: (1) fire, explosion, lightning, theft, robbery, vandalism; (2) an accident involving an aircraft we insure that's owned by someone else; (3) accidental damage to your aircraft while it's being transported after being dismantled. For example, while being transported on a flatbed truck.

What you must do. You agree to give us a sworn Proof of Loss Statement within 90 days of the loss. You also agree to allow us or anyone we designate to question you under oath and to show us the damaged property and any records you have to prove the loss.

When we'll pay. We will pay for a loss to your aircraft within 30 days from the time the agreement is reached on the amount of the loss. But you must have complied with the requirements of this policy. And we'll deduct any premiums you owe and any other debts you have with us.

Suits for aircraft physical damage payments. No suit or other legal action to recover payment can be brought under this policy unless you have complied with all of its terms and the action is brought within one year after the occurrence which led to the loss or damage.

Rights against third parties. This insurance is for your benefit alone and not for any other person or organization. Except for what you agree to do under an Airport Contract, you promise not to do anything that will take away our right to collect for damages caused by others.

Automatic reinstatement. If an aircraft is damaged we'll reduce the amount of insurance you have on the aircraft by the amount of damage. Once repairs are begun, we'll increase your insurance by the value of the completed repairs, until the original amount of coverage on the aircraft is restored or this policy expires.

Arbitration of disputes. If we can't agree with you on the amount of loss to your aircraft the following procedure will be used to settle the dispute:
1. You can request in writing that the dispute be submitted for arbitration. We can do the same.
2. Each will then select an appraiser and will inform the other of that choice within 20 days of the initial notification.
3. The appraisers will select a competent and impartial umpire. If the appraisers can't agree on an umpire within 15 days, a judge of the state in which the property is located can appoint an impartial umpire if asked to do so by you or us.
4. Each appraiser will appraise the loss for each item. If they don't agree, they'll submit their differences to the umpire. Agreement by two of the three will decide the amount of the loss.

You will then pay your appraiser and we'll pay ours. Any other costs of the appraisal and the umpire will be divided equally.

Salvage. If an aircraft covered under Aircraft Physical Damage Coverage is damaged you must do all you can to protect it from further loss. If you don't, we won't be responsible for further loss to the aircraft.

We will pay all reasonable expenses you incur in protecting your aircraft from further loss.

If your aircraft is destroyed and we pay for the total loss, we can elect to take over the salvage as our property. You cannot, however, merely abandon the damaged property to us. If we decide to take the salvage, we can sell it or do whatever else we want with it.

Aircraft damage we won't cover.

Although your All-Clear Aircraft Policy provides you with coverage against risk of damage or loss to your aircraft, there are a few things it will not cover.

Tires. We won't cover loss or damage to the tires of your aircraft unless caused by theft, vandalism or malicious mischief; or directly by other physical damage covered by this policy.

Wear-tear. We won't cover loss or damage to your aircraft caused by and confined to wear and tear, deterioration, freezing, mechanical or electrical breakdown or failure unless the loss is the direct result of other physical damage covered under this policy.

For example, if the windshield of your aircraft cracked by freezing, we won't pay for the windshield. However, if the cracked windshield is responsible for you having an accident, we'll pay for the resulting damage to your aircraft.

Embezzlement. We won't cover loss or damage to your aircraft caused when someone with a legal right to possess the aircraft embezzles or converts it under a lease, rental agreement, conditional sale, mortgage or other legal agreement governing the use, sale or lease of property.

War-confiscation. We won't cover loss or damage to your aircraft caused by declared or undeclared war, invasion, rebellion or by the seizure or detention of the aircraft by any government. Nor will we cover damage to your aircraft done by or at the direction of any government.

Ownership. We won't cover loss or damage to your aircraft if your position of ownership changes from that stated on the Coverage Summary page. For example, if you sell or mortgage your aircraft.

Your Medical Coverage

We will pay all reasonable medical expenses that passengers, pilots and crew members, including you, incur within one year from the date of an accident. But the aircraft must have been used by you or with your permission when the accident occurred. Reasonable medical expenses include the necessary cost of medical, surgical, dental, ambulance, hospital, professional nursing and funeral services.

What we'll pay. The amount shown on the Coverage Summary page for "each person" is the most we'll pay for all medical expenses for one person in any one accident. We won't, however, provide medical services to anyone or their employees until any medical benefits covered under workers' compensation have been deducted.

Whom we'll pay. We can pay each injured person directly or we can pay the hospital or any other organization that provided service. Any payment we make will be applied against the limits of your medical coverage and won't be an admission of legal responsibility by us.

Proof of loss. As soon as reasonably possible after the accident an injured person or someone representing him or her must give us written proof of the claim. An injured person must also submit to physical examination by any doctor we select whenever we reasonably ask. You will also help us obtain medical reports and copies of records.

Suits for medical payment. No suit or other legal action to recover payment can be brought under this policy unless you have complied with all its terms and at least 30 days have elapsed since the required proof of claim has been given to the Aviation Managers.

Your Coverage For Other Aircraft

Other aircraft. If you own the aircraft described on the Coverage Summary page alone or as a co-owner with your spouse, your Liability or Medical Coverage under this policy will also cover you and the following people while you or they are lawfully using another aircraft with your permission:

• Your spouse living in the same household.

• If you are a corporation, any of your executive officers, while they are using another aircraft on your behalf for business purposes.

We won't, however, cover the use of the other aircraft if the Coverage Summary page allows you to charge people for using your own aircraft. We also won't cover any aircraft that is owned or used on a regular or frequent basis by any of the people listed above or their employers, or members of their household or by an executive officer if you are a corporation. Nor will we cover you if you are leasing the aircraft described on the Coverage Summary page to someone else.

Substitute aircraft. If you are temporarily using another aircraft because your own has broken down, is damaged or needs servicing or repair, we'll continue to provide you with the same Liability and Medical Coverage as you have under this policy. But we won't cover the legal responsibility of anyone insured under this policy who owns the substitute aircraft. Nor will we cover the legal responsibility of any agent or employee of the owner of the aircraft.

Newly acquired aircraft. If you become the owner of another aircraft during the policy period, we'll cover it under this policy provided you notify the Aviation Managers within 30 days after you get it, pay an additional premium, and:

1. The aircraft replaces an aircraft described on the Coverage Summary page.
2. Or it is an additional aircraft and we insure all the aircraft you own at the time you buy it.

Unless you and the Aviation Managers agree differently in writing, new aircraft are covered up to the following amounts:

Liability & Medical Coverage:

Replacement Aircraft. Same Coverage and Limits of Coverage as on replaced aircraft.

Additional Aircraft. Same Coverage and Limits of Coverage as on your aircraft having the most similar passenger capacity, not counting the crew.

Aircraft Physical Damage Coverage:

Replacement Aircraft. Same Coverage and deductibles as on replaced aircraft. We'll pay the actual amount you paid for the aircraft.

Additional Aircraft. Same Coverage and deductibles as on aircraft having the most similar Limit of Coverage. We'll pay the actual amount you paid for the aircraft.

United States Aviation Underwriters, Incorporated
Aviation Managers

John V. Brennan

John V. Brennan
President

5

GOLDEN WING

Aircraft Insurance Policy

ASSOCIATED AVIATION UNDERWRITERS

GUIDE TO THE MORE IMPORTANT PROVISIONS

OF YOUR GOLDEN WING POLICY

This guide has been prepared to help you in reading your policy. It is not a part of the policy nor does it make reference to all of the provisions which might affect your insurance. You are therefore urged to read the entire policy carefully paying particular attention to any endorsements attached thereto.

Issued By		A STOCK COMPANY	Policy No. **GW**

Producer's Name and Address	. . .		Renewal of:

Item 1.
Named Insured and Address (Number and Street, Town or City, County and State)

.
.
.
.
.

DECLARATIONS

2. Policy Period:

From

to

12:01 A.M., standard time at the address of the insured as stated herein.

3. Insurance is provided only with respect to the following Coverages for which a limit of liability is specified, subject to all conditions of this policy.

	LIABILITY COVERAGES	LIMITS OF LIABILITY		PREMIUM
A	BODILY INJURY EXCLUDING PASSENGERS	$ Each Person $	Each Occurrence	$
B	PASSENGER BODILY INJURY	$ Each Person $	Each Occurrence	$
C	PROPERTY DAMAGE	$	Each Occurrence	$
D	SINGLE LIMIT BODILY INJURY AND PROPERTY DAMAGE Passengers	$	Each Occurrence	$
E	MEDICAL EXPENSE COVERAGE Crew	$ Each Person		$
	PHYSICAL DAMAGE COVERAGES	The Insured Value of the aircraft subject to the following deductibles:		
F	ALL RISK BASIS	While the aircraft is in motion $		$
G	ALL RISK BASIS NOT IN FLIGHT	While the aircraft is not in motion $		$
H	ALL RISK BASIS NOT IN MOTION			$

Total of above premiums	$
Plus premium endorsements	$
TOTAL PREMIUM	$

4. DESCRIPTION OF AIRCRAFT

Year, Make and Model	FAA Identification Number	Seating Capacity		Land Sea Amph.	Insured Value
		Crew	Other		
					$
					$
					$
					$

5. OWNERSHIP AND ENCUMBRANCES. The Named Insured is, and shall remain, the sole and unconditional owner of the aircraft described in Item 4, unless otherwise indicated herein.

6. AIRCRAFT USE. The Policy shall not apply to any Insured while the aircraft is being used with the knowledge and consent of such Insured for any purpose involving a charge intended to result in financial profit to such Insured unless otherwise indicated herein.

7. PILOTS. The policy shall not apply while the aircraft is in flight unless the pilot in command

_____
GW (1)   Authorized Representative   for Associated Aviation Underwriters

In consideration of the payment of the premium, in reliance upon the statements in the Declarations made a part hereof, subject to all of the terms of this policy including the applicable limits of liability, the Company agrees with the **Named Insured** with respect to those coverages indicated in Item 3 of the Declarations:

INSURING AGREEMENTS

I. LIABILITY COVERAGES

Coverage A—Bodily Injury Liability Excluding Passengers To pay on behalf of the **Insured** all sums which the **Insured** shall become legally obligated to pay as damages because of **bodily injury** sustained by any person excluding any **passenger,**

Coverage B—Passenger Bodily Injury Liability To pay on behalf of the **Insured** all sums which the **Insured** shall become legally obligated to pay as damages because of **bodily injury** sustained by any **passenger,**

Coverage C—Property Damage Liability To pay on behalf of the **Insured** all sums which the **Insured** shall become legally obligated to pay as damages because of **property damage,**

Coverage D—Single Limit Bodily Injury and Property Damage Liability To pay on behalf of the **Insured** all sums which the **Insured** shall become legally obligated to pay as damages because of **bodily injury** sustained by any person (excluding any **passenger** unless the words "including **passengers**" appear in Item 3 of the Declarations) and **property damage,**

caused by an **occurrence** and arising out of the ownership, maintenance or use of the **aircraft**; or, only with respect to Coverages A, C and D, caused by an **occurrence** and arising out of the maintenance or use of the **premises** in or upon which the **aircraft** is stored.

II. MEDICAL EXPENSE COVERAGE

Coverage E—Medical Expenses To pay all reasonable **medical expenses** incurred within one year from the date of injury, to or for each **passenger** (excluding any crew member unless the words "including crew" appear in Item 3 of the Declarations) who sustains **bodily injury** caused by an **occurrence**, provided the **aircraft** is being used by or with the permission of the **Named Insured.**

III. PHYSICAL DAMAGE COVERAGES

Coverage F—All Risk Basis To pay for any **physical damage** loss to the **aircraft**, including **disappearance** of the **aircraft.**

Coverage G—All Risk Basis Not in Flight To pay for any **physical damage** loss to the **aircraft** sustained while the **aircraft** is not in **flight** and which is not the result of fire or explosion following crash or collision while the **aircraft** was in **flight.**

Coverage H—All Risk Basis Not In Motion To pay for any **physical damage** loss to the **aircraft** sustained while the **aircraft** is not in **motion** and which is not the result of fire or explosion following crash or collision while the **aircraft** was in **motion.**

IV. DEFENSE, SETTLEMENT AND SUPPLEMENTARY PAYMENTS
Coverages A, B, C and D

The Company shall have the right and duty to defend any suit against the **Insured** seeking damages on account of such **bodily injury** or **property damage**, even if any of the allegations of the suit are groundless, false or fraudulent, and may make such investigation and settlement of any claim or suit as it deems expedient, but the Company shall not be obligated to pay any claim or judgment or to defend any suit after the applicable limit of the Company's liability has been exhausted by payment of judgments or settlements.

During such time as the Company is obligated to defend a claim or claims under the provisions of the preceding paragraph, the Company will pay with respect to such claim, in addition to the applicable limit of liability:

(a) all expenses incurred by the Company, all costs taxed against the **Insured** in any suit defended by the Company and all interest on the entire amount of any judgment therein which accrues after entry of the judgment and before the Company has paid or tendered or deposited in court that part of the judgment which does not exceed the limit of the Company's liability thereon;

(b) premiums on appeal bonds required in any such suit, premiums on bonds to release attachments in any such suit for an amount not in excess of the applicable limit of liability of this policy, and the cost of bail bonds required of the **Insured** because of an **occurrence** or violation of law or a regulation for civil aviation arising out of the use of the **aircraft**, not to exceed $250 per bail bond, but the Company shall have no obligation to apply for or furnish any such bonds;

(c) expenses incurred by the **Insured** for first aid to others at the time of an accident, for **bodily injury** to which this policy applies;

(d) all reasonable expenses incurred by the **Insured** at the Company's request, other than for loss of earnings or for wages or salaries of employees of the **Insured.**

V. TEMPORARY USE OF SUBSTITUTE AIRCRAFT
Coverages A, B, C, D and E

While an **aircraft** described in Item 4 of the Declarations is withdrawn from normal use because of its breakdown, repair, servicing, loss or destruction, such insurance as is afforded under Coverages A, B, C, D and E is extended to apply with respect to the use, by or on behalf of the **Named Insured** of any other **aircraft** not owned in whole or in part by the **Named Insured**, while temporarily used as a substitute therefor.

VI. SPECIAL NON-OWNERSHIP COVERAGE
Coverages A, B, C, D and E

The coverage provided by this Agreement applies only if the **Named Insured** is one individual or one individual and spouse. Such insurance as is afforded under Coverages A, B, C, D and E with respect to the **aircraft** described in Item 4 of the Declarations, is extended to apply with respect to the use, by or on behalf of the **Named Insured**, of any other aircraft not owned in whole or in part by, or furnished for regular use to, such **Named Insured** or spouse. The insurance provided by this Agreement shall apply only to the **Named Insured** and spouse, if any, and their employers, if any.

VII. AUTOMATIC INSURANCE FOR NEWLY ACQUIRED AIRCRAFT
All Coverages

If the **Named Insured** acquires ownership of an **aircraft** in addition to the **aircraft** described in Item 4 of the Declarations and within thirty days thereafter reports such acquisition to the Company, then the insurance afforded by this policy shall apply to such additional **aircraft** as of the time of such acquisition, provided that the Company insured all other **aircraft** owned in whole or in part by the **Named Insured** on such acquisition date. Unless the **Named Insured** and the Company agree otherwise, the Coverages and limits of liability pertaining to said additional **aircraft** shall be the same as is provided for that **aircraft** which is described in Item 4 of the Declarations as having the greatest **passenger** carrying capacity and, the Insured Value of the additional **aircraft** shall be the actual cost of the **aircraft** to the **Named Insured** but not exceeding 150% of the highest Insured Value of any **aircraft** described in Item 4 of the Declarations. The **Named Insured** shall pay any additional premium required because of the application of the insurance to such other **aircraft.**

VIII. UNITED STATES NAVY AND AIR FORCE INSURANCE REQUIREMENTS
Coverages A, B, C and D

If Associated Aviation Underwriters issues a certificate of insurance as required by United States Navy OPNAV Form 3770 or United States Air Force Regulation 55-20 or any replacement of either, then the insurance policy provisions required by such regulation shall be deemed to be incorporated herein and substituted for any policy provisions inconsistent therewith.

1

IX. TWO OR MORE AIRCRAFT
All Coverages

When two or more **aircraft** are insured under this policy, the terms of this policy shall apply separately to each.

X. POLICY PERIOD, TERRITORY
All Coverages

This policy applies only to **bodily injury** or **property damage** which occurs, and to **physical damage** losses to the **aircraft** which are sustained during the policy period, while the **aircraft** is within the United States of America, Canada, Mexico or the Bahama Islands or while enroute between points therein.

EXCLUSIONS
(See also Items 5, 6 and 7 of the Declarations)

This policy does not apply:

(a) Under Coverages A, B, C and D, to liability assumed by the **Insured** under any contract or agreement, but this exclusion (a) does not apply to the assumption by the **Named Insured** of the liability of others for **bodily injury** or **property damage** in any written hold harmless agreement required by a military or governmental authority as a prerequisite to the use of an airport or an airport facility;

(b) Under Coverages A, B and D, to any obligation for which the **Insured** or any carrier as his insurer may be held liable under any worker's compensation, unemployment compensation or disability benefits law, or under any similar law;

(c) Under Coverages A, B and D, to **bodily injury** to any employee of the **Insured** arising out of and in the course of his employment by such **Insured**; but this exclusion (c) does not apply to liability assumed by the **Named Insured** under any military or governmental agreement referred to in Exclusion (a) above;

(d) Under Coverages C and D, to **property damage** to property owned, occupied, rented or used by the **Insured** or in the care, custody or control of the **Insured** or as to which the **Insured** is for any purpose exercising physical control, but this exclusion (d) shall not apply to:

(i) personal effects of **passengers,** but not exceeding $250 for each **passenger** in each **occurrence,** or

(ii) an aircraft hanger or contents thereof but not exceeding $5,000 in any one **occurrence;**

(e) Under Coverage E, to **medical expense** incurred by or for any employee of the **Insured** to the extent that such expense is payable under any worker's compensation law or under any similar law;

(f) Under Coverages F, G and H, to **physical damage**
(i) to tires other than by fire, theft, vandalism or malicious mischief, or
(ii) caused by and confined to (a) wear and tear, (b) deterioration or (c) mechanical or electrical breakdown or failure of equipment, components or accessories installed in the **aircraft**

unless such **physical damage** be coincident with and from the same cause as other loss covered by this policy;

(g) Under Coverages F, G and H, to **physical damage** resulting from (1) capture, seizure, arrest, restraint or detention or the consequence thereof or of any attempt thereat, or any taking of the property insured or damage to or destruction thereof by any government or governmental authority or agent (whether secret or otherwise) or by any military, naval or usurped power, whether any of the foregoing be done by way of requisition or otherwise and whether in time of peace or war and whether lawful or unlawful; (2) war, invasion, civil war, revolution, rebellion, insurrection or warlike operations, whether there be a declaration of war or not.

LIMIT OF THE COMPANY'S LIABILITY

ALL COVERAGES
(Other Insurance)

Except with respect to insurance afforded by Insuring Agreements V and VI and to insurance specifically purchased by the **Named Insured** to apply in excess of this policy, if there is other insurance in the **Insured's** name or otherwise, against loss, liability or expense covered by this policy, the Company shall not be liable under this policy for a greater proportion of such loss, liability or expense than the applicable limit of the Company's liability bears to the total applicable limit of liability of all valid and collectible insurance against such loss, liability or expense. Insurance afforded by Insuring Agreements V and VI shall be excess insurance over any other valid and collectible insurance available to the **Insured**, either as an insured under a policy applicable to the aircraft or otherwise and if such other insurance shall have been written through Associated Aviation Underwriters as primary insurance then the Company's limits of liability under this policy shall be reduced by the applicable limits of such other policy.

COVERAGES A, B, C and D
(Total Liability)

Regardless of the number of (1) **Insureds** under this policy, (2) persons or organizations who sustain **bodily injury** or **property damage**, (3) claims made or suits brought on account of **bodily injury** or **property damage**, or (4) **aircraft** to which this policy applies, the Company's liability is limited as follows:

Coverages A and B. The total liability of the Company for all damages, including damages for care and loss of services, because of **bodily injury** sustained by any one person as the result of any one **occurrence** shall not exceed the limit of liability stated in the Declarations as applicable to "each person". Subject to the above provision respecting "each person", the total liability of the Company for all damages, including damages for care and loss of services, because of **bodily injury** sustained by two or more persons as the result of any one **occurrence** shall not exceed the limit of liability stated in the Declarations as applicable to "each **occurrence**".

Coverage C. The total liability of the Company for all damages because of all **property damage** sustained by one or more persons or organizations as the result of any one **occurrence** shall not exceed the limit of liability stated in the Declarations as applicable to "each **occurrence**".

Coverage D. The total liability of the Company for all damages, including damages for care and loss of services, because of **bodily injury** or **property damage** sustained by one or more persons or organizations as the result of any one **occurrence** shall not exceed the limit of liability stated in the Declarations as applicable to "each **occurrence**".

For the purpose of determining the limit of the Company's liability, all **bodily injury** and **property damage** arising out of continuous or repeated exposure to substantially the same general conditions shall be considered as arising out of one **occurrence.**

COVERAGES A, B, C and D
(Severability of Interests)

The insurance afforded applies separately to each **Insured** against whom claim is made or suit is brought, except with respect to the limits of the Company's liability.

COVERAGE E
(Total Liability)

The total liability of the Company for all **medical expenses** incurred by or on behalf of each **passenger** who sustains **bodily injury** as the result of any one **occurrence** shall not exceed the limit of liability stated in the Declarations as applicable to "each person".

COVERAGES F, G and H
(Total Liability)

In the event of a **total loss** the Company shall pay the Insured Value of the **aircraft** less any applicable deductible whereupon the Company's liability with respect to such **aircraft** shall terminate. In addition, the Company shall refund the pro rata unearned premium for such **aircraft.**

2

In the event of a **partial loss** the Company's liability shall not exceed the "cost to repair" the **aircraft** as specified herein, less any applicable deductible, but in no event shall the Company's liability for a **partial loss** exceed the amount for which the Company would be liable if the **aircraft** were a **total loss.**

The "cost to repair" shall consist of (a) transportation charges as specified herein and (b) the actual cost to repair the damaged property with materials and parts of like kind and quality with charges for labor at straight time rates. Transportation charges shall consist of the cost, where necessary, of transporting new or damaged parts or of transporting the damaged **aircraft** to the place of repair and return to the place of accident or home airport, whichever is nearer, by the least expensive reasonable means.

The Company shall have the right to return stolen property anytime before the loss is paid with payment for any resultant **physical damage.**

The amount specified as a deductible does not apply to losses caused by fire, lightning, explosion, transportation, theft, robbery or pilferage; however, loss caused by fire or explosion resulting directly or indirectly from collision of the **aircraft** while **in motion** shall be subject to the **"in motion"** deductible, if any.

In the event that two or more **aircraft** are insured hereunder, the applicable deductible shall apply separately to each.

DEFINITIONS

When appearing in this policy in **bold face** print:

"Aircraft" means the aircraft described in Item 4 of the Declarations (and when appropriate any aircraft qualifying under the provisions of Insuring Agreements V, VI or VII) including the propulsion system and equipment usually installed in the aircraft (1) while installed in the aircraft, (2) while temporarily removed from the aircraft and (3) while removed from the aircraft for replacement until such time as replacement by a similar item has commenced; also tools and equipment in the aircraft which have been specially designed for the aircraft and which are ordinarily carried therein;

"Bodily Injury" means bodily injury, sickness, disease or mental anguish sustained by any person which occurs during the policy period, including death at any time resulting therefrom;

"Disappearance" means missing and not reported for sixty days after commencing a **flight;**

"Federal Aviation Administration" means the duly constituted authority of the United States of America having jurisdiction over civil aviation, or its duly constituted equivalent in any other country;

"Flight" means the time commencing with the actual take-off run of the **aircraft** and continuing thereafter until it has completed its landing roll or, if the **aircraft** is a rotorcraft, from the time the rotors start to revolve under power for the purpose of **flight** until they subsequently cease to revolve;

"In Motion" means while the **aircraft** is moving under its own power or the momentum generated therefrom or while it is in **flight** and, if the **aircraft** is a rotorcraft, any time that the rotors are rotating;

"Insured" The unqualified word "Insured" means, (1) with respect to all Coverages, the **Named Insured** and (2) with respect to Coverages A, B, C and D only (a) any person while using the **aircraft** with the permission of the **Named Insured** provided the actual use is within the scope of such permission and (b) any other person or organization, but only with respect to his or its liability because of acts or omissions of the **Named Insured** or of an Insured under (a) above, provided, however, that the insurance afforded under this subsection (2) does not apply to

   (i) any person or organization, or agent or employee thereof (other than employees of the **Named Insured**) engaged in the manufacture, maintenance, repair, or sale of aircraft, aircraft engines, components or accessories, or in the operation of any airport, hangar, flying school, flight service, or aircraft or piloting service, with respect to any **occurrence** arising out of such activity, or

   (ii) any employee with respect to injury or death of another employee of the same employer injured in the course of such employment in an **occurrence** arising out of the maintenance or use of the **aircraft** or **premises** in the business of such employer, or

   (iii) the owner or lessor, or any agent or employee thereof, of any **aircraft** which is the subject of the extended insurance provisions of Insuring Agreements V or VI;

"Medical Expenses" means expenses for necessary medical, surgical, x-ray and dental services, including prosthetic devices, and necessary ambulance, hospital, professional nursing and funeral services;

"Named Insured" means the person or organization named in Item 1 of the Declarations;

"Occurrence" means an accident, including continuous or repeated exposure to conditions, which results in **bodily injury** or **property damage** neither expected nor intended from the standpoint of the **Insured,** but this definition shall not be construed so as to preclude coverage for **bodily injury** or **property damage** resulting from efforts to prevent dangerous interference with the operation of the **aircraft;**

"Partial Loss" means any **physical damage** loss which is not a **total loss;**

"Passenger" means any person in, on or boarding the **aircraft** for the purpose of riding or flying therein, or alighting therefrom after a ride, **flight** or attempted **flight** therein;

"Physical Damage" means direct and accidental physical loss of or damage to the **aircraft,** hereinafter called loss, but does not include loss of use or any residual depreciation in value, if any, after repairs have been made;

"Pilot in Command" means the pilot responsible for the operation and safety of the **aircraft** during **flight;**

"Premises" means such portions of airports as are designated and used for the parking or storage of **aircraft** exclusive of premises owned by, or leased for more than thirty days to, the **Insured;**

"Property Damage" means (a) physical injury to or destruction of tangible property which occurs during the policy period, including loss of use thereof at any time resulting therefrom, or (b) loss of use of tangible property which has not been physically injured or destroyed provided such loss of use is caused by an **occurrence** during the policy period;

"Total Loss" means any **physical damage** loss for which the "cost to repair" will equal or exceed the Insured Value of the **aircraft** as set forth in Item 4 of the Declarations. **Disappearance** or theft of the entire **aircraft** shall be considered as a **total loss.**

CONDITIONS
(Applicable to all Coverages unless otherwise indicated)

1. INSURED'S DUTIES IN THE EVENT OF OCCURRENCE OR LOSS

(a) In the event of an **occurrence** or loss, notice containing particulars sufficient to identify the **Insured** and also reasonably obtainable information with respect to the time, place and circumstances thereof, and the names and addresses of the injured and of available witnesses, shall be given by or for the **Insured** to the Company or to Associated Aviation Underwriters at any of the offices listed on the policy jacket as soon as reasonably possible. In the event of theft, robbery or pilferage the **Named Insured** shall also promptly give notice to the police.

(b) If claim is made or suit is brought against the **Insured**, the **Insured** shall immediately forward to the Company every demand, notice, summons or other process received by him or his representatives.

(c) The **Insured** shall cooperate with the Company and upon request will assist in making settlements, in the conduct of suits and in enforcing any right of subrogation, contribution or indemnity against any person or organization who may be liable to the **Insured** because of loss, injury or damage with respect to which insurance is afforded under this policy; and the **Insured** shall attend hearings and trials and assist in securing and giving evidence and obtaining the attendance of witnesses. The **Insured** shall not, except at his own cost, voluntarily make any payment, assume any obligation or incur any expenses other than for first aid to others at the time of accident.

2. FINANCIAL RESPONSIBILITY LAWS
Coverages A, B, C and D

When this policy is certified as proof of financial responsibility for the future under the provisions of any aircraft financial responsibility law, such insurance as is afforded by this policy for **bodily injury** liability and **property damage** liability shall comply with the provisions of such law to the extent of the coverage and limits of liability required by such law, but in no event in excess of liability stated in this policy. The **Insured** agrees to reimburse the Company for any payment made by the Company which it would not have been obligated to make under the terms of this policy except for the agreement contained in this paragraph.

3. MEDICAL REPORTS: PROOF AND PAYMENT OF CLAIM
Coverage E

As soon as practicable the injured person or someone on his behalf shall give to the Company written proof of claim, under oath if required, and shall, after each request from the Company, execute authorization to enable the Company to obtain medical reports and copies of records. The injured person shall submit to physical examination by physicians selected by the Company when and as often as they may reasonably require.

The Company may pay the injured person or any person or organization rendering the services and such payment shall reduce the amount payable hereunder for such injury. Payment hereunder shall not constitute an admission of liability of any person or organization or of the Company.

4. ADDITIONAL DUTIES OF NAMED INSURED
Coverages F, G and H

In the event of loss, the **Named Insured** shall

(a) protect the **aircraft**, whether or not the loss is covered by this policy and any further loss due to the **Named Insured's** failure to protect shall not be recoverable under this policy; reasonable expenses incurred in affording such protection shall be deemed incurred at the Company's request;

(b) file with the Company within 91 days after loss, sworn proof of loss in such form and including such information as the Company may reasonably require and shall, upon the Company's request, submit to examination under oath, exhibit the damaged property and produce for the Company's examination all pertinent records and invoices, permitting copies thereof to be made, all at such reasonable times and places as the Company shall designate;

(c) do all things necessary to transfer title to any salvage, including the insured **aircraft** if it is a **total loss,** to the Company or its nominee.

5. APPRAISAL
Coverages F, G and H

If the **Named Insured** and the Company fail to agree as to the amount of loss, either may, within 60 days after proof of loss is filed, demand an appraisal of the loss. In such event, the **Named Insured** and the Company shall each select a competent appraiser, and the appraisers shall select a competent and disinterested umpire. The appraisers shall appraise the amount of the loss and failing to agree shall submit their differences to the umpire. An award in writing of any two shall determine the amount of loss. The **Named Insured** and the Company shall each pay his chosen appraiser and shall bear equally the other expenses of the appraisal and the umpire. The Company shall not be held to have waived any of its rights by any act relating to appraisal.

6. SALVAGE
Coverages F, G and H

The value of all salvaged property shall inure to the benefit of the Company, however, there shall be no abandonment without the consent of the Company.

7. AUTOMATIC REINSTATEMENT
Coverages F, G and H

In the event of a **partial loss**, whether or not such loss is covered by this policy, the Insured Value of the **aircraft** as shown in Item 4 of the Declarations shall be reduced as of the time of loss by the amount of such loss. Upon the commencement of repairs the Insured Value shall be increased by the value of the completed repairs until the Insured Value of the **aircraft** as shown in Item 4 of the Declarations is fully restored or this policy terminates whichever shall first occur.

8. NO BENEFIT TO OTHERS
Coverages F, G and H

The insurance afforded by this policy shall not inure directly or indirectly to the benefit of any carrier or bailee liable for loss to the insured **aircraft.**

9. SUBROGATION
Coverages A, B, C, D, F, G and H

In the event of any payment under this policy the Company shall be subrogated to all of the **Insured's** rights of recovery therefor against any person or organization and the **Insured** shall execute and deliver instruments and papers and do whatever else is necessary to enforce such rights. The **Insured** shall do nothing after loss to prejudice such rights.

10. ACTION AGAINST THE COMPANY

No action shall lie against the Company unless, as a condition precedent thereto, the **Insured** shall have fully complied with all of the terms of this policy.

With respect to Coverages A, B, C and D, no action shall lie against the Company until the amount of the **Insured's** obligation to pay shall have been finally determined either by judgment against the **Insured** after actual trial or by written agreement of the **Insured**, the claimant and the Company.

Any person or organization or the legal representative thereof who has secured such judgment or written agreement shall thereafter be entitled to recover under this policy to the extent of the insurance afforded by this policy. No person or organization shall have any right under this policy to join the Company as a party to any action against the **Insured** to determine the **Insured's** liability, nor shall the Company be impleaded by the **Insured** or his legal representative. Bankruptcy or insolvency of the **Insured** or of the **Insured's** estate shall not relieve the Company of any of its obligations hereunder.

With respect to Coverages F, G and H, no action shall lie against the Company until sixty days after proof of loss is filed and the amount of loss is determined as provided in this policy.

11. CHANGES

Notice to any agent or knowledge possessed by any agent or by any other person shall not effect a waiver or a change in any part of this policy or estop the Company from asserting any right under the terms of this policy; nor shall the terms of this policy be waived or changed, except by endorsement issued to form a part of this policy signed by Associated Aviation Underwriters.

12. ASSIGNMENT

Assignment of interest under this policy shall not bind the Company until its consent is endorsed hereon; if, however, the **Named Insured** shall die or be adjudged bankrupt or insolvent within the policy period, the policy unless cancelled, shall, if written notice be given to the Company within 60 days after the date of such death or adjudication, cover (1) the **Named Insured's** legal representative as **Named Insured** but only while acting within the scope of his duties as such, and (2) under Coverages A, B, C and D, any person having proper temporary custody of the **aircraft** as an **Insured**, until the appointment and qualification of such legal representative but in no event for a period of more than 60 days after the date of such death or adjudication.

13. CANCELATION

This policy may be canceled by any **Named Insured** by mailing to the Company or to Associated Aviation Underwriters at any of the offices listed on the policy jacket, written notice stating when thereafter the cancelation shall be effective. This policy may be canceled by the Company by mailing to the **Named Insured** at the first address shown

GW-JI (1/78)

in Item 1 of the Declarations, notice stating when, not less than thirty days thereafter, such cancelation shall be effective. The mailing of notice as aforesaid shall be sufficient proof of notice. The effective date and hour of cancelation stated in the notice shall become the end of the policy period.

If the **Named Insured** cancels, earned premium shall be computed in accordance with the Company's short rate table and procedure. If the Company cancels, earned premium shall be computed pro-rata. Premium adjustment may be made either at the time cancelation is effective or as soon as practicable after cancelation becomes effective, but payment or tender of unearned premium is not a condition of cancelation.

14. DECLARATIONS

By acceptance of this policy, the **Named Insured** agrees that the statements in the Declarations are his agreements and representations, that this policy is issued in reliance upon the truth of such representations and that this policy embodies all agreements existing between himself and the Company or any of its agents relating to this insurance.

SHORT RATE CANCELATION TABLES

Percent of one and three year premiums earned if policy is canceled during the first year.

Days Policy in Force	One Year	Three Years	Days Policy in Force	One Year	Three Years	Days Policy in Force	One Year	Three Years	Days Policy in Force	One Year	Three Years	Days Policy in Force	One Year	Three Years	Days Policy in Force	One Year	Three Years
1	5	2.	37-40	21	8.4	95-98	37	14.8	154-156	53	21.2	219-223	69	27.6	292-296	85	34.
2	6	2.4	41-43	22	8.8	99-102	38	15.2	157-160	54	21.6	224-228	70	28.	297-301	86	34.4
3-4	7	2.8	44-47	23	9.2	103-105	39	15.6	161-164	55	22.	229-232	71	28.4	302-305	87	34.8
5-6	8	3.2	48-51	24	9.6	106-109	40	16.	165-167	56	22.4	233-237	72	28.8	306-310	88	35.2
7-8	9	3.6	52-54	25	10.	110-113	41	16.4	168-171	57	22.8	238-241	73	29.2	311-314	89	35.6
9-10	10	4.	55-58	26	10.4	114-116	42	16.8	172-175	58	23.2	242-246	74	29.6	315-319	90	36.
11-12	11	4.4	59-62	27	10.8	117-120	43	17.2	176-178	59	23.6	247-250	75	30.	320-323	91	36.4
13-14	12	4.8	63-65	28	11.2	121-124	44	17.6	179-182	60	24	251-255	76	30.4	324-328	92	36.8
15-16	13	5.2	66-69	29	11.6	125-127	45	18.	183-187	61	24.4	256-260	77	30.8	329-332	93	37.2
17-18	14	5.6	70-73	30	12.	128-131	46	18.4	188-191	62	24.8	261-264	78	31.2	333-337	94	37.6
19-20	15	6.	74-76	31	12.4	132-135	47	18.8	192-196	63	25.2	265-269	79	31.6	338-342	95	38.
21-22	16	6.4	77-80	32	12.8	136-138	48	19.2	197-200	64	25.6	270-273	80	32.	343-346	96	38.4
23-25	17	6.8	81-83	33	13.2	139-142	49	19.6	201-205	65	26.	274-278	81	32.4	347-351	97	38.8
26-29	18	7.2	84-87	34	13.6	143-146	50	20.	206-209	66	26.4	279-282	82	32.8	352-355	98	39.2
30-32	19	7.6	88-91	35	14.	147-149	51	20.4	210-214	67	26.8	283-287	83	33.2	356-360	99	39.6
33-36	20	8	92-94	36	14.4	150-153	52	20.8	215-218	68	27.2	288-291	84	33.6	361-365	100	40.

Percent of three year premium earned if a three year policy is canceled during the second or third year.

Policy in Force One Year Plus Days	Percent Earned	Policy in Force One Year Plus Days	Percent Earned	Policy in Force One Year Plus Days	Percent Earned	Policy in Force Two Years Plus Days	Percent Earned	Policy in Force Two Years Plus Days	Percent Earned	Policy in Force Two Years Plus Days	Percent Earned
1-5	40.4	126-130	50.7	251-255	61.	1-5	70.4	126-130	80.7	251-255	91.
6-10	40.8	131-135	51.1	256-260	61.4	6-10	70.8	131-135	81.1	256-260	91.4
11-15	41.2	136-140	51.5	261-265	61.8	11-15	71.2	136-140	81.5	261-265	91.8
16-20	41.6	141-145	51.9	266-270	62.2	16-20	71.6	141-145	81.9	266-270	92.2
21-25	42.1	146-150	52.3	271-275	62.6	21-25	72.1	146-150	82.3	271-275	92.6
26-30	42.5	151-155	52.7	276-280	63.	26-30	72.5	151-155	82.7	276-280	93.
31-35	42.9	156-160	53.2	281-285	63.4	31-35	72.9	156-160	83.2	281-285	93.4
36-40	43.3	161-165	53.6	286-290	63.8	36-40	73.3	161-165	83.6	286-290	93.8
41-45	43.7	166-170	54.	291-295	64.2	41-45	73.7	166-170	84.	291-295	94.2
46-50	44.1	171-175	54.4	296-300	64.7	46-50	74.1	171-175	84.4	296-300	94.7
51-55	44.5	176-180	54.8	301-305	65.1	51-55	74.5	176-180	84.8	301-305	95.1
56-60	44.9	181-185	55.2	306-310	65.5	56-60	74.9	181-185	85.2	306-310	95.5
61-65	45.3	186-190	55.6	311-315	65.9	61-65	75.3	186-190	85.6	311-315	95.9
66-70	45.8	191-195	56.	316-320	66.3	66-70	75.8	191-195	86.	316-320	96.3
71-75	46.2	196-200	56.4	321-325	66.7	71-75	76.2	196-200	86.4	321-325	96.7
76-80	46.6	201-205	56.9	326-330	67.1	76-80	76.6	201-205	86.9	326-330	97.1
81-85	47.	206-210	57.3	331-335	67.5	81-85	77.	206-210	87.3	331-335	97.5
86-90	47.4	211-215	57.7	336-340	67.9	86-90	77.4	211-215	87.7	336-340	97.9
91-95	47.8	216-220	58.1	341-345	68.4	91-95	77.8	216-220	88.1	341-345	98.4
96-100	48.2	221-225	58.5	346-350	68.8	96-100	78.2	221-225	88.5	346-350	98.8
101-105	48.6	226-230	58.9	351-355	69.2	101-105	78.6	226-230	88.9	351-355	99.2
106-110	49.	231-235	59.3	356-360	69.6	106-110	79.	231-235	89.3	356-360	99.6
111-115	49.5	236-240	59.7	361-365	70.	111-115	79.5	236-240	89.7	361-365	100.
116-120	49.9	241-245	60.1			116-120	79.9	241-245	90.1		
121-125	50.3	246-250	60.6			121-125	80.3	246-250	90.5		

5

ASSOCIATED AVIATION UNDERWRITERS

Organized in 1929 by

CHUBB & SON INC. AND MARINE OFFICE OF AMERICA CORPORATION

For the convenience of handling aviation insurance matters, the Company maintains specialized facilities at:

HOME OFFICE AND EASTERN BRANCH

90 John Street
New York, New York 10038
212-766-1600

ATLANTA
P.O. Box 56406
Atlanta, Georgia 30343
404 688-1627

CHICAGO
20 N. Wacker Drive
Chicago, Illinois 60606
312 641-2929

DALLAS
9330 Amberton Pkwy., Suite 109
Dallas, Texas 75243
214 231-4341

DENVER
6 Parker Place
2600 S. Parker Rd., Suite 162
Aurora, Colorado 80014
303 750-8560

DETROIT
3155 West Big Beaver Road
Troy, Michigan 48084
313 643-4848

KANSAS CITY
9393 West 110th Street
Overland Park, Kansas 66210
913 341-9660

LOS ANGELES
3435 Wilshire Boulevard
Los Angeles, California 90010
213 388-1241

SAN FRANCISCO
2775 Mitchell Drive
Suite 102
Walnut Creek, California 94598
415 945-7400

SEATTLE
18000 Pacific Highway South
Suite 601
Seattle, Washington 98188
206 241-0855

AVEMCO INSURANCE COMPANY

FOR AVIATION PEOPLE... BY AVIATION PEOPLE

AIRCRAFT POLICY

PLEASE READ YOUR POLICY

AVEMCO INSURANCE COMPANY
FREDERICK, MARYLAND

A capital stock insurance company incorporated under the laws of the State of Maryland, herein called the company, agrees with the insured named in the declarations made a part hereof, in consideration of the payment of the premium and in reliance upon the statements in the declarations and subject to all of the terms of this policy:

INSURING AGREEMENTS

I Coverage A — Liability (Including or Excluding Occupants) — Bodily Injury and Property Damage. To pay on behalf of the insured all sums which the insured shall become legally obligated to pay as damages because of bodily injury, sickness or disease, including mental anguish or death resulting therefrom, sustained by any person, excluding any occupant unless specified as "including occupants" in the declarations, or injury to or destruction of property, including the loss of use thereof, caused by an occurrence and arising out of the ownership, maintenance or use of the aircraft.

Coverage B — Medical Payments. To pay all reasonable expenses incurred within one year from the date of accident for necessary medical, surgical, x-ray and dental services, including prosthetic devices, and necessary ambulance, hospital and professional nursing services, (1) to or for each occupant, who sustains bodily injury, sickness or disease, caused by accident, if the aircraft is being used by the named insured or with his permission, and (2) to or for the named insured, if one individual, who sustains bodily injury, sickness or disease, caused by accident while in or entering any aircraft bearing a "Standard" Airworthiness Category Certificate or alighting therefrom following a flight or attempted flight therein or through being struck by any aircraft. If such bodily injury, sickness or disease shall, within one year from the date of the accident, result in death, the company will pay to the husband or wife of the deceased, if surviving, otherwise to the estate of the deceased, the sum of $2,500 less any amount for which the company may be liable for services specified above, but not more in the aggregate than the limit of liability stated in the declarations as applicable to "each person."

Coverage C — All Risks (Including or Excluding In Flight). To pay for all loss of or damage to the aircraft (a) while not in flight and (b) if specified as "Including In Flight" in the declarations, while in flight, including disappearance in the event the aircraft is not reported or located within sixty (60) days after take-off.

II Defense, Settlement, Supplementary Payments. With respect to such insurance as is afforded by this policy under Coverage A, the company shall:
(a)   defend any suit against the insured alleging such injury, sickness, disease or destruction and seeking damages on account thereof, even if such suit is groundless, false or fraudulent; but the company may make such investigation, negotiation and settlement of any claim or suit as it deems expedient;

(b) (1) pay all premiums on bonds to release attachments for an amount not in excess of the applicable limit of liability of this policy, all premiums on appeal bonds required in any such defended suit, the cost of bail bonds required of the insured in the event of an occurrence or violation of a law or regulation for civil aviation during the policy period, not to exceed $100 per bail bond, but without any obligation to apply for or furnish any such bonds;

(2) pay all expenses incurred by the company, all costs taxed against the insured in any such suit and all interest accruing after entry of judgment until the company has paid, tendered or deposited in court such part of such judgment as does not exceed the limit of the company's liability thereon;

(3) pay expenses incurred by the insured for such immediate medical and surgical relief to others as shall be imperative at the time of the accident;

(4) reimburse the insured for all reasonable expenses, other than loss of earnings, incurred at the company's request;

and the amounts so incurred, except settlements of claims and suits, are payable by the company in addition to the applicable limit of liability.

III Definition of Insured. With respect to the insurance for coverage A, the unqualified word "insured" includes the named insured and also includes any person while using the aircraft and any person or organization legally responsible for the use thereof, provided the actual use of the aircraft is by the named insured or with his permission. The insurance with respect to any person or organization other than the named insured does not apply:
(a) to any person or organization, or to any agent or employee thereof, engaged in the manufacturing of aircraft, aircraft engines or aircraft accessories, or operating an aircraft repair shop, airport, hanger or aircraft sales agency, with respect to any occurrence arising out of the manufacture or the operation thereof;
(b) to any employee with respect to bodily injury, sickness, disease or death of another employee of the same employer, injured in the course of such employment;
(c) with respect to bodily injury, sickness, disease or death of (1) a spouse, parent or child of such person or (2) a named insured;
(d) to any person receiving instruction, either dual or solo, unless specified in Item 7(a), of the declarations.

IV Use of Other Aircraft. If the named insured is one individual who owns the aircraft described in the declarations, such insurance as is afforded by this policy under Coverages A and B applies with respect to any other fixed-wing aircraft subject to the following provisions:

(a) With respect to the insurance afforded under Coverage A, the unqualified word "insured" includes (1) such named insured, and (2) any other person or organization legally responsible for the use by such named insured of an aircraft not owned or hired by such other person or organization. Insuring Agreement III does not apply to this insurance;

(b) Under Coverage B this insurance applies only if the injury results from the operation of such other aircraft by such named insured or on behalf of him by a pilot in his employ.

This Insuring Agreement does not apply:

(a) to any aircraft owned in whole or in part by or furnished for regular use to the named insured;

(b) to any occurrence arising out of the manufacture of aircraft, aircraft engines or aircraft accessories or the operation of an aircraft repair shop, airport, hangar or aircraft sales agency.

V Temporary Use of Substitute Aircraft. While the aircraft described in the declarations is withdrawn from normal use because of its breakdown, repair, servicing, loss or destruction, such insurance as is afforded by this policy under Coverages A and B with respect to such aircraft applies also with respect to a fixed-wing aircraft not owned by the named insured while temporarily used as the substitute for the described aircraft. This insuring Agreement does not cover as an insured the owner of the substitute aircraft or any agent or employee of such owner.

VI Automatic Insurance for Newly Acquired Aircraft. If the named insured who is owner of the aircraft, shall acquire ownership of another fixed-wing aircraft and so notifies the company within thirty (30) days following the date of its delivery to him and if the company insures all aircraft owned by the named insured at such delivery date, such insurance as is afforded by this policy also applies to such other aircraft as of such delivery date (a) with respect to Coverages A and B, only to the extent of the lowest limit of liability provided for each coverage and (b) with respect to Coverage C, only to the extent of the actual cost of the aircraft to the named insured, but not exceeding the highest limit of liability provided for any described aircraft.

In the event a particular coverage is not provided for any other owned aircraft, the company shall not be deemed to insure all aircraft owned by the named insured in respect to said coverage. The insurance with respect to the newly acquired aircraft does not apply to any loss against which the named insured has other valid and collectible insurance. The named insured shall pay any additional premium required because of the application of the insurance to such newly acquired aircraft.

VII Two Or More Aircraft. When two or more aircraft are insured hereunder, the terms of this policy shall apply separately to each.

VIII Policy Period, Territory. This policy applies only to occurrences, accidents and losses which happen during the policy period while the aircraft is within the Western Hemisphere, north of 16° North Latitude (excluding Cuba), but not during or in connection with a flight which involves flying outside such territorial limits or flying (a) more than one hundred (100) nautical miles from land with respect to single-engine aircraft or (b) more than two hundred (200) nautical miles from land with respect to multi-engine aircraft.

EXCLUSIONS

This policy does not apply:

(a) Under Coverage A, to liability assumed by any insured under any contract or agreement except liability assumed by the named insured under an Airport Contract;

(b) Under Coverage A, to injury to or destruction of property owned or transported by the insured or property rented to or in charge of the insured, but this exclusion (b) does not apply, as respects the named insured, to damages for injury to or destruction of

(1) personal effects of passengers, but not exceeding $200 for personal effects of any one passenger in any one occurence, or

(2) a hanger or contents thereof not owned by the insured, but not exceeding $2,000 during the policy period;

(c) Under Coverage A, to injury, sickness, disease, death or destruction with respect to which an insured under this policy is also an insured under a nuclear energy liability policy issued by Nuclear Energy Liability Insurance Association, Mutual Atomic Energy Liability Underwriters or Nuclear Insurance Association of Canada, or would be an insured under any such policy but for its termination upon exhaustion of its limit of liability;

(d) Under Coverage A, to bodily injury to or sickness, disease or death of (1) a spouse, parent or child of a named insured or (2) a named insured;

(e) Under Coverages A and B, to bodily injury to or sickness, disease or death of any employee of the insured arising out of and in the course of employment by the insured, or to any obligation for which the insured or any carrier as his insurer may be held liable under any workmen's compensation, unemployment compensation or disability benefits law, or under any similar law;

(f) Under Coverage C, to loss or damage

(1) to the aircraft which is due and confined to wear and tear, deterioration, freezing, mechanical or electrical breakdown or failure,

unless such loss or damage is the result of other loss or damage covered by this policy, or

(2) while the aircraft is subject to any bailment lease, conditional sale, mortgage or other encumbrance not specifically declared and described in this policy, or if the interest of the named insured becomes other than owner, or as stated in the declarations, or

(3) due to conversion, embezzlement or secretion by any person in possession of the aircraft under a bailment lease, conditional sale, purchase agreement, mortgage or other encumbrance;

(g) Under Coverages A, B and C, to any aircraft while in flight

(1) not bearing a valid and currently effective "Standard" Airworthiness Category Certificate issued by the Federal Aviation Agency, or

(2) being operated by a Student Pilot carrying passenger(s), or

(3) being operated by a pilot not meeting the requirements set forth in Item 7 of the declarations, or

(4) unless the aircraft is being used in accordance with the "Purposes" provisions of Item 6 of the declarations;

(h) Under Coverages A, B and C, to occurrences, accidents or losses

(1) during or in connection with a flight involving any trafficking in narcotics, drugs or hallucinogenics or involving the unlawful importation or exportation of property or persons, or

(2) due to (a) capture, seizure, arrest, restraint or detention, or the consequences thereof or any attempt thereat, or any taking of the aircraft or any loss or damage thereof by any Government or governmental authority or agent (whether secret or otherwise) or by any military, naval, or usurped power, whether any of the foregoing be done by way of requisition or otherwise and whether in time of peace or war, and whether lawful or unlawful, (b) war, invasion, civil war, revolution, rebellion, insurrection or warlike operation, whether there be a declaration of war or not.

DEFINITIONS

1. **Occupant.** The word "occupant" means any person in or entering the aircraft for the purpose of riding therein or alighting therefrom following a flight or attempted flight therein.

2. **Occurrence.** The word "occurrence" means an accident, or a continuous or repeated exposure to conditions, which results in injury during the policy period, provided the injury is accidentally caused. All damages arising out of such exposure to substantially the same general conditions shall be deemed to arise out of one occurrence.

3. **In Flight.** The term "in flight" means the time commencing when the aircraft moves forward in attempting to take-off and continuing thereafter until it has completed its landing run.

4. **In Motion.** The term "in motion" means all times when the aircraft is moving under its own power or the momentum generated therefrom.

5. **AIRCRAFT.** The word "aircraft" means the aircraft described in this policy including operating, communication and navigation equipment and instruments usually attached thereto, including parts temporarily detached from the aircraft and not replaced by similar parts.

6. **Airport Contract.** The term "Airport Contract" means a written agreement required by statute or ordinance or by any rule or regulation promulgated by any Federal, State, County or Municipal Authority as a condition to the use of an airport or airport facility.

CONDITIONS

1. Limits of Liability — Coverage A

The limit of liability stated in the declarations as applicable to "each person" is the limit of the company's liability for damages, including damages for care and loss of services, arising out of bodily injury, sickness or disease, including mental anguish or death at any time resulting therefrom, sustained by one person in any one occurrence; the limit of liability stated in the declarations as applicable to "property damage" is the limit of the company's liability for all damages arising out of injury to or destruction of property of one or more persons or organizations, including loss of use thereof, as a result of any one occurrence; the limit of such liability stated in the declarations as applicable to "each occurrence" is, subject to the above provisions respecting "each person" and "property damage", the total limit of the company's liability for all damages, including damages for care and loss of services, arising out of bodily injury, sickness or disease, including mental anguish or death at any time resulting therefrom, sustained by one or more persons in any one occurrence and for all damages arising out of injury to or destruction of property of one or more persons or organizations, including loss of use thereof, as a result of any one occurrence.

Coverage B

The limit of liability stated in the declarations as applicable to "each person" is the limit of the company's liability for all expenses incurred by or on behalf of each person who sustains bodily injury, sickness or disease, including death resulting therefrom, in any one accident.

2. Severability of Interest — Coverage A

The insurance afforded applies to each insured against whom claim is made or suit is brought, but the inclusion herein of more than one insured shall not operate to increase the limits of the company's liability.

3. Action Against Company — Coverage A

No action shall lie against the company unless, as a condition precedent thereto, the insured shall have fully complied with all of the terms of this policy, nor until the amount of the insured's obligation to pay shall have been finally determined either by judgment against the insured after actual trial or by written agreement of the insured, the claimant and the company. Any person or organization or the legal representative thereof who has secured such judgment or written agreement shall thereafter be entitled to recover under this policy to the extent of the insurance afforded by this policy. No person or organization shall have any right under this policy to join the company as a party to any action against the insured to determine the insured's liability, nor shall the company be impleaded by the insured or his legal representative. Bankruptcy or insolvency of the insured or of the insured's estate shall not relieve the company of any of its obligations hereunder.

Coverage B

No action shall lie against the company unless, as a condition precedent thereto, there shall have been full compliance with all the terms of this policy, nor until thirty (30) days after the required proofs of claim have been filed with the company.

4. Financial Responsibility Laws — Coverage A

When this policy is certified as proof of financial responsibility for the future under the provisions of any financial responsibility law, such insurance as afforded by this policy shall comply with the provision of such law, to the extent of the coverage and limits of liability required by such law, but in no event in excess of the limits of liability stated in this policy. The insured agrees to reimburse the company for any payment made by the company which it would not have been obligated to make under the terms of this policy except for the agreement contained in this paragraph.

5. Assault and Battery — Coverage A

Assault and battery shall be deemed an occurrence, but when committed by or at the direction of the insured it shall not be deemed an occurrence unless committed for the purpose of preventing dangerous interference with the operation of the aircraft.

6. Medical Reports; Proof and Payment of Claim — Coverage B

As soon as practicable the injured person or someone on his behalf shall give to the company written proof of claim, under oath if required, and shall, after each request from the company execute authorization to enable the company to obtain medical reports and copies of records. The injured person shall submit to physical examination by physicians selected by the company when and as often as the company may reasonably require.

The company may pay the injured person or any person or organization rendering the services and such payment shall reduce the amount payable hereunder for such injury. Payment hereunder shall not constitute admission of liability of any person or, except hereunder, of the company.

7. Limit of Liability; Settlement Options; No Abandonment — Coverage C

The limit of the company's liability for loss shall not exceed the applicable limit of liability stated in the declarations, or, in the case of partial loss or damage to the aircraft, what it would cost to repair the aircraft or replace parts thereof with others of like kind and quality. The cost of repair shall consist of (a) transportation charges as specified herein and (b) net cost to the insured (excluding premium charges for overtime) to repair with material and parts of like kind and quality.

Transportation charges shall consist of the cost, where necessary, of transporting new or damaged parts or of transporting the damaged aircraft to the place of repair and return to the place of accident or home airport, whichever is nearer, by the least expensive reasonable means. In the case of loss occurring outside the contiguous United States, transportation charges shall in no event exceed fifteen (15) percent of the amount of the determined loss exclusive of such transportation charges.

The company may pay for the loss in money or may repair the aircraft or replace parts thereof, as aforesaid, or may return any stolen property with payment for any resultant loss thereto at any time before the loss is paid or the property is so replaced. In the event of loss for which the company is liable hereunder, the value of any salvage remaining shall inure to the benefit of the company, and there shall be no abandonment without the consent of the company.

The "in motion deductible" specified in the declarations shall not apply to loss caused by collision with another aircraft insured by the company.

8. Insured's Duties When Loss Occurs — Coverage C

When loss occurs, the insured shall:

(a) protect the aircraft, whether or not the loss is covered by this policy, and any further loss due to the insured's failure to protect shall not be recoverable under this policy; reasonable expense incurred in affording such protection, provided loss is covered by this policy, shall be deemed incurred at the company's request;

(b) give notice thereof as soon as practicable to the company, and also, in the event of theft, larceny, robbery or pilferage, to the police but shall not, except at his own cost, offer to pay any reward for recovery of the aircraft;

(c) file proof of loss with the company within ninety (90) days after the occurrence of loss, unless such time is extended in writing by the company, in the form of a sworn statement of the insured setting forth the interest of the insured and of all others in the property affected, any encumbrances thereon, the actual cash value thereof at time of loss, the amount, place, time and cause of such loss, and the description and amounts of all other insurance covering such property.

Upon the company's request, the insured shall exhibit the damaged property to the company and submit to examinations under oath by anyone designated by the company, subscribe the same and produce for the company's examination all pertinent records and sales invoices, or certified copies if originals be lost, permitting copies thereof to be made, all at such reasonable times and places as the company shall designate.

9. Appraisal — Coverage C

If the insured and the company fail to agree as to the amount of loss, either may, within 60 days after proof of loss is filed, demand an appraisal of the loss. In such event the insured and the company shall each select a competent appraiser and the appraisers shall select a competent and disinterested umpire. The appraisers shall state separately the amount of loss and failing to agree shall submit their differences to the umpire. An award in writing of any two shall determine the amount of loss. The insured and the company shall each pay his chosen appraiser and shall bear equally the other expenses of the appraisal and umpire. The company shall not be held to have waived any of its rights by any act relating to appraisal.

10. Payment of Loss; Action Against Company — Coverage C

Payment for loss may not be required nor shall action lie against the company unless, as a condition precedent thereto, the insured shall have fully complied with all the terms of this policy nor until thirty (30) days after proof of loss is filed and the amount of loss is determined as provided in this policy.

11. Rights Against Third Parties — Coverage C

The insurance afforded by this policy shall not enure directly or indirectly to the benefit of any third party. Any act or agreement by the insured, prior or subsequent hereto, whereby any right of the insured, to recover the full value of, or amount of damage to, any property lost or damaged and insured hereunder, from any third party liable therefor, is released, impaired or lost, shall relieve the company from any liability under this policy for or on account of any such loss or damage, but the company's right to retain or recover the premium shall not be affected. This condition shall not apply to an airport contract.

12. Automatic Reinstatement — Coverage C

When the aircraft is damaged, whether or not such damage is covered under this policy, the liability of the company in respect to the aircraft shall be reduced by the amount of such damage and such reduced liability shall continue until repairs are commenced when the liability shall automatically be increased by the value of the completed repairs until the limit of liability is fully reinstated or the policy has expired.

13. Assistance and Cooperation of the Insured — Coverages A and C

The insured shall cooperate with the company and, upon the company's request, assist in making settlements, in the conduct of suits and in enforcing any right of contribution or indemnity against any person or organization who may be liable to the insured because of bodily injury, property damage or loss with respect to which insurance is afforded under this policy, attend hearings and trials and assist in securing and giving evidence and obtaining the attendance of witnesses. The insured shall not, except at his own cost, voluntarily make any payment, assume any obligation or incur any expense other than for such immediate medical and surgical relief to others as shall be imperative at the time of accident.

14. Subrogation — Coverages A and C

In the event of any payment under this policy, the company shall be subrogated to all the insured's rights of recovery therefor against any person or organization and the insured shall execute and deliver instruments and papers and do whatever else is necessary to secure such rights. The insured shall do nothing after loss to prejudice such rights.

15. Other Insurance — Coverages A and C

If the insured has other insurance against a loss covered by this policy, the company shall not be liable under this policy for a greater portion of such loss than the applicable limit of liability stated in the declarations bears to the total applicable limit of liability for all valid and collectible insurance against such loss; provided, however, that under Coverage A the insurance under Insuring Agreements IV and V shall be excess insurance over any other valid and collectible insurance.

Coverage B

The insurance under Insuring Agreements IV and V shall be excess insurance over any other valid and collectible aircraft medical payments insurance.

16. Notice — All Coverages

In the event of an accident, occurrence or loss, written notice containing particulars sufficient to identify the insured and also reasonably obtainable information with respect to the time, place and circumstances thereof, and the names and addresses of the injured and of available witnesses, shall be given by or for the insured to the company or any of its authorized agents as soon as practicable. In the event of theft the insured shall also promptly notify the police. If claim is made or suit is brought against the insured, he shall immediately forward to the company every demand, notice, summons or other process received by him or his representative.

17. Changes — All Coverages

Notice to any agent or knowledge possessed by any agent or by any other person shall not effect a waiver or a change in any part of this policy or estop the company from asserting any right under the terms of this policy; nor shall the terms of this policy be waived or changed, except by endorsement issued to form a part of this policy, signed by a duly authorized representative of the company.

18. Assignment — All Coverages

Assignment of interest under this policy shall not bind the company until its consent is endorsed hereon; if, however, the named insured shall die, this policy shall cover (a) his legal representative as named insured but only while acting within the scope of his duties as such, and (b) any person having proper temporary custody of the aircraft, as an insured, until the appointment and qualification of such legal representative; provided, the notice of cancellation addressed to the insured named in the declarations and mailed to the address shown in this policy shall be sufficient notice to effect cancelation of this policy.

19. Cancellation — All Coverages

This policy may be cancelled by any named insured by surrender thereof to the company or by mailing to the company written notice stating when thereafter the cancellation shall be effective. This policy may be cancelled by the company by mailing to the named insured at the address shown in this policy written notice stating when not less than thirty (30) days thereafter such cancellation shall be effective. The mailing of notice as aforesaid shall be sufficient proof of notice. The time of surrender or the effective date and hour of cancellation stated in the notice shall become the end of the policy period. Delivery of such written notice either by the named insured or by the company shall be equivalent to mailing.

If the named insured cancels, earned premium shall be computed in accordance with the customary short rate table and procedure. If the company cancels, earned premium shall be computed pro rata. Premium adjustment may be made either at the time cancellation is effected or as soon as practicable after cancellation becomes effective, but payment or tender of unearned premium is not a condition of cancellation.

20. Cancellation for Non-Payment of Installment Premium— All Coverages

Upon the failure of the named insured to pay any installment of the premium, the insurance shall cease and terminate, provided at least ten (10) days notice is mailed by the company to the named insured at the address shown in this policy stating when thereafter such cancellation shall become effective. Such cancellation shall be deemed to have been made at the request of the named insured and shall be on a short rate basis.

21 Terms of Policy Conformed to Statute — All Coverages

Terms of this policy which are in conflict with the statutes of the state wherein this policy is issued are hereby amended to conform to such satutes.

22. Declarations — All Coverages

By acceptance of this policy the named insured agrees that the statements in the application and declarations are his representations and agreements, that this policy is issued in reliance upon the truth of such representations and that this policy embodies all agreements existing between himself and the company or any of its representatives relating to this insurance.

IN WITNESS WHEREOF, the AVEMCO Insurance Company has caused this policy to be signed by its President and Secretary and countersigned on the declarations page by a duly authorized representative of the Company.

John H. Ballard   Secretary   _David E. Jensen_   President

Short Rate Cancelation Table For Term of One Year																																																		
Per Cent of One Year Premium	53	54	55	56	57	58	59	60	61	62	63	64	65	66	67	68	69	70	71	72	73	74	75	76	77	78	79	80	81	82	83	84	85	86	87	88	89	90	91	92	93	94	95	96	97	98	99	100
Days Policy in Force	154-156	157-160	161-164	165-167	168-171	172-175	176-178	179-182	183-187	188-191	192-196	197-200	201-205	206-209	210-214	215-218	219-223	224-228	229-232	233-237	238-241	242-246	247-250	251-255	256-260	261-264	265-269	270-273	274-278	279-282	283-287	288-291	292-296	297-301	302-305	306-310	311-314	315-319	320-323	324-328	329-332	333-337	338-342	343-346	347-351	352-355	356-360	361-365
Per Cent of One Year Premium	5	6	7	8	9	10	11	12	13	14	15	16	17	18	19	20	21	22	23	24	25	26	27	28	29	30	31	32	33	34	35	36	37	38	39	40	41	42	43	44	45	46	47	48	49	50	51	52
Days Policy in Force	1	2	3-4	5-6	7-8	9-10	11-12	13-14	15-16	17-18	19-22	21-22	23-25	26-29	30-32	33-36	37-40	41-43	44-47	48-51	52-54	55-58	59-62	63-65	66-69	70-73	74-76	77-80	81-83	84-87	88-91	92-94	95-98	99-102	103-105	106-109	110-113	114-116	117-120	121-124	125-127	128-131	132-135	136-138	139-142	143-146	147-149	150-153

AIRCRAFT POLICY

AVEMCO INSURANCE COMPANY

FREDERICK, MARYLAND 21701

(A CAPITAL STOCK INSURANCE COMPANY)

No. AV ☐ [_____]

DECLARATIONS

Item 1. Named Insured and Address

Item 2. Policy Period.
(MO DAY YR) (MO DAY YR)
To

COMPANY USE ONLY

12 01 A.M. standard time at the named insured's address stated herein.

Item 3. The insurance afforded is only with respect to such and so many of the following coverages as are indicated by specific premium charge or charges. The limit of the company's liability against each such coverage shall be as stated herein, subject to all of the terms of the policy having reference thereto.

	COVERAGES	LIMITS OF LIABILITY			COMPANY USE	PREMIUMS
A	Liability (cluding Occupants) Bodily Injury & Property Damage	$ each person	$ property damage	$ each occurrence		.00
B	Medical Payments	$ each person				.00
C	All Risks(cluding In Flight)	$ less $		deductible		.00
						.00
ENDORSEMENTS						.00
				Installment Service Fee		.00
				TOTAL POLICY PREMIUM	$	.00

Item 4. The named insured is a (n) ✳( ) whose business is
✳(I) Individual, (C) Corporation, (P) Partnership, (O) Other

Item 5. AIRCRAFT - FAA Number - Year - Make and Model   Usually Based In
N-

Item 6. PURPOSES: This policy applies to any use of the aircraft except (a) instruction of any person not specified in Item 7(A) below or (b) any use for which a charge is made to others or while the aircraft is rented or leased for a consideration.

Item 7. PILOTS: This policy applies when the aircraft is in flight, only while being operated by one of the following pilots (indicated by X below) who, (1) holds a valid and effective Pilot and Medical Certificate, (2) has a current biennial flight review and (3) if carrying passengers, has completed at least three Take-Offs and Landings within the preceding 90 days in an aircraft of the same make and model as the insured aircraft:

Item 8. Any loss under Coverage C is payable as interest may appear to the named insured and (name & address)

The aircraft is unencumbered unless an amount of encumbrance is stated herein. $

Item 9. The named insured is the sole and unconditional owner of the aircraft unless otherwise stated

SPECIMEN

COUNTERSIGNED _____ 19____
AT _____   BY _____
                              AUTHORIZED REPRESENTATIVE

FORM AEP 3 82-1

Ultralight Aircraft Insurance Policy

SPECIMEN

Please Read Your Policy Carefully

UP (10-82)-1

AVEMCO Insurance Company

411 Aviation Way, Frederick, Maryland 21701

A capital stock insurance company incorporated under the laws of the State of Maryland.

AGREEMENT

We agree to provide insurance for the Coverages which **you** have purchased. The insurance is subject to the terms of this Policy. It is based on **your** statements in the Application.

DEFINITIONS USED IN THIS POLICY

(These defined terms are printed in bold type in this Policy.)

(1) **"Accident"** means a sudden event, or continued or repeated contact with the same conditions that results in **bodily injury, property damage** or **non-owned ultralight damage** during the Policy Period.

(2) **"Airport contract"** means an agreement an **insured person** signs with a federal, state or municipal body so they may use its airport.

(3) **"Bodily injury"** means physical injury to or death of a person.

(4) **"Insured person"** means:
 (a) **you**;
 (b) a person shown in Item 6 of the Data Page.

(5) **"Loss"** means direct physical loss of or damage to **your ultralight** during the Policy Period. **Loss** does not include depreciation or loss of its use. It also does not include loss of or damage to:
 (a) communication or sound reproduction equipment;
 (b) floats while detached from **your ultralight**.

(6) **"Non-owned ultralight"** means an **ultralight you** do not own in whole or in part and which is furnished or leased to **you** for not more than 30 consecutive days. Its use must be with the owner's permission.

(7) **"Non-owned ultralight damage"** means direct physical loss of or damage to a **non-owned ultralight**. This includes loss of its use. It does not include loss of or damage to communication or sound reproduction equipment.

(8) **"Policy territory"** means the United States of America, except Alaska and Hawaii.

(9) **"Prohibited use"** means use of an **ultralight**:
 (a) during the hours of sunset to sunrise, except as allowed by the Federal Aviation Regulations;
 (b) with more than one occupant, including the pilot;
 (c) for which an **insured person** gets money or other benefits;
 (d) to unlawfully traffic in or carry drugs, narcotics or other property;
 (e) for aerial towing;
 (f) for a purpose other than recreation or sport.

(10) **"Property damage"** means loss of or damage to property of others. This includes loss of its use. It does not include loss of or damage to:
 (a) a **non-owned ultralight**;
 (b) property owned in whole or in part by an **insured person**;

 (c) property carried in an **ultralight**;
 (d) property rented to or in the charge of an **insured person**.

(11) **"Ultralight"** means a fixed-wing, engine-powered aircraft which meets all of the following requirements:
 (a) It must not be certificated or required to be certificated by the Federal Aviation Administration.
 (b) It must weigh less than 254 pounds empty weight without floats and emergency safety devices.
 (c) It must have a fuel capacity of less than 5 U.S. gallons.
 (d) It must not be capable of more than 55 knots calibrated airspeed at full power in level flight.
 (e) It must have a power-off stall speed which does not exceed 24 knots calibrated airspeed.

(12) **"We"**, **"us"** and **"our"** mean AVEMCO Insurance Company.

(13) **"You"** and **"your"** mean the Policyholder named in Item 1 of the Data Page.

(14) **"Your ultralight"** means the **ultralight** shown in Item 4 of the Data Page. It must not be owned in whole or in part by anyone except **you**.

1.

PART I—YOUR ULTRALIGHT

COVERAGE A

BODILY INJURY AND PROPERTY DAMAGE LIABILITY FOR YOUR ULTRALIGHT

We will pay for **bodily injury** and **property damage** for which an **insured person** is legally liable. The **bodily injury** and **property damage** must be caused by an **accident**. Liability must arise from the ownership, maintenance or use of **your ultralight**. The **bodily injury** and **property damage** must not be expected or intended by an **insured person**.

ADDITIONAL PAYMENTS

When **bodily injury** and **property damage** are covered by this Part, **we** will also pay:

(1) Costs **we** incur settling a claim or defending a suit;

(2) Interest on that part of a judgment which does not exceed **our** Limit of Liability. Interest is paid from the date of judgment until **we** pay or offer to pay **our** part of the judgment;

(3) Reasonable costs an **insured person** incurs at **our** request to attend trials or hearings. **We** will not pay for loss of earnings;

(4) Costs an **insured person** incurs for first aid to others at the time of an **accident**.

We will settle or defend, whichever **we** feel proper, a claim or suit.

EXCLUSIONS APPLYING TO THIS COVERAGE

This Coverage does not apply to:

(1) **Bodily injury** or **property damage** liability an **insured person** assumes by contract or agreement, except an **airport contract**;

(2) **Bodily injury** or **property damage**:
   (a) when **your ultralight** is used for a **prohibited use**;
   (b) when **your ultralight** is used by a person not approved in Item 6 of the Data Page;
   (c) caused by noise generated by **your ultralight**;
   (d) which occurs outside the **policy territory**;

(3) **Bodily injury** to an employee of an **insured person** when workers' compensation is available or required.

LIMIT OF LIABILITY

The Limit of Liability shown in Item 5 of the Data Page for Coverage A is the most **we** will pay for all **bodily injury** and **property damage** combined in one **accident**.

The number of Data Pages, **insured persons, your ultralights**, claims or claimants does not increase this amount.

OTHER INSURANCE

When there is other liability insurance for **bodily injury** and **property damage** covered by this Part, **we** will pay **our** share. **Our** share will be the percentage that **our** Limit of Liability bears to the sum of all liability limits.

PART I—YOUR ULTRALIGHT

COVERAGE B

LOSS TO YOUR ULTRALIGHT

We will pay for **loss** to **your ultralight**. The **loss** must not be expected or intended by **you**.

ADDITIONAL PAYMENTS

When **loss** is covered by this Part, **we** will also pay:

(1) The cost of transporting **your ultralight** or its parts to the place of repair. After repair, **we** will pay the cost to return it to the place of **loss** or its home base, whichever is closer. Transporting will be by the least costly reasonable means;

(2) Reasonable costs incurred in providing protection for **your ultralight** after a **loss**.

EXCLUSIONS APPLYING TO THIS COVERAGE

This Coverage does not apply to **loss** to **your ultralight**:

(1) Caused by legal or illegal seizure or confiscation or during detention by any governmental body;

(2) When someone claiming a right of possession embezzles, converts or repossesses it;

(3) Due and confined to wear and tear, deterioration, or mechanical, structural, engine or electrical failure;

(4) When it is used for a **prohibited use**;

(5) When it is used by a person not approved in Item 6 of the Data Page;

(6) Which occurs outside the **policy territory**;

(7) Arising out of declared or undeclared war, civil war, riot or revolt.

LIMIT OF LIABILITY

Our Limit of Liability for **loss** is the least of:

(1) The actual cash value of **your ultralight**;

(2) The cost to repair or replace damaged parts with parts of like kind and quality; or

(3) The amount shown in Item 5 of the Data Page for Coverage B;

Less the applicable deductible shown in Item 5 of the Data Page for Coverage B.

NO BENEFIT TO OTHERS

This Coverage is for **your** benefit alone. It is not for anyone else.

CONDITIONS OF PAYMENT OF LOSS

We may pay for a **loss** in money. **We** may also repair or replace damaged parts. Before **we** pay for or replace missing property, **we** may return it to **you** with payment for physical damage. If **your ultralight** is stolen or disappears in flight and is not found, **we** will pay for the **loss** after 60 days.

When **we** pay for a **loss** the salvage will be **ours**. **You** must give **us** clear title to salvage when **we** pay for **loss**.

You or **we** may demand appraisal of the **loss**. Each will choose and pay a competent and disinterested appraiser. Each will share other appraisal costs equally. The appraisers will pick a third person to settle differences. An amount agreed to in writing by two of them will be the amount of **loss**.

LOSS PAYEE

Payment for **loss** will be made to **you** and the Lienholder shown in Item 2 of the Data Page.

OTHER INSURANCE

When there is other insurance for a **loss** covered by this Part, **we** will pay that part of the **loss** that **our** Limit of Liability bears to the total limits of all insurance.

PART II—NON-OWNED ULTRALIGHTS
COVERAGE C
BODILY INJURY AND PROPERTY DAMAGE LIABILITY FOR NON-OWNED ULTRALIGHTS

We will pay for **bodily injury** and **property damage** for which **you** are legally liable. The **bodily injury** and **property damage** must be caused by an **accident**. Liability must arise from **your** use of a **non-owned ultralight**. The **bodily injury** and **property damage** must not be expected or intended by **you**.

ADDITIONAL PAYMENTS

When **bodily injury** and **property damage** are covered by this Part, **we** will also pay:

(1) Costs **we** incur settling a claim or defending a suit;

(2) Interest on that part of a judgment which does not exceed **our** Limit of Liability. Interest is paid from the date of judgment until **we** pay or offer to pay **our** part of the judgment;

(3) **Your** reasonable costs when **we** ask **you** to attend trials or hearings. **We** will not pay for loss of earnings;

(4) Costs **you** incur for first aid to others at the time of an **accident**.

We will settle or defend, whichever **we** feel proper, a claim or suit.

EXCLUSIONS APPLYING TO THIS COVERAGE

This Coverage does not apply to:

(1) **Bodily injury** or **property damage** liability **you** assume by contract or agreement, except an **airport contract**;

(2) **Bodily injury** or **property damage**:

   (a) when **you** use a **non-owned ultralight** for a **prohibited use**;
   (b) caused by noise generated by a **non-owned ultralight**;
   (c) which occurs outside the **policy territory**;

(3) **Bodily injury** to **your** employee when workers' compensation is available or required;

(4) The legal responsibilities of the **non-owned ultralight** owner or the owner's agent or employee.

LIMIT OF LIABILITY

The Limit of Liability shown in Item 5 of the Data Page for Coverage C is the most **we** will pay for all **bodily injury** and **property damage** combined in one **accident**.

The number of Policyholders, Data Pages, claims or claimants does not increase this amount.

EXCESS INSURANCE

This insurance is excess insurance. If there is other insurance available to **you**, it shall apply first.

PART II—NON-OWNED ULTRALIGHTS
COVERAGE D
NON-OWNED ULTRALIGHT DAMAGE LIABILITY

We will pay for **non-owned ultralight damage** for which **you** are legally liable. The **non-owned ultralight damage** must be caused by an **accident**. Liability must arise from **your** use of a **non-owned ultralight**. The **non-owned ultralight damage** must not be expected or intended by **you**.

ADDITIONAL PAYMENTS

When **non-owned ultralight damage** is covered by this Part, **we** will also pay:

(1) Costs **we** incur settling a claim or defending a suit;

(2) Interest on that part of a judgment which does not exceed **our** Limit of Liability. Interest is paid from the date of judgment until **we** pay or offer to pay **our** part of the judgment;

(3) **Your** reasonable costs when **we** ask **you** to attend trials or hearings. **We** will not pay for loss of earnings.

We will settle or defend, whichever **we** feel proper, a claim or suit.

EXCLUSIONS APPLYING TO THIS COVERAGE

This Coverage does not apply to **non-owned ultralight damage**:

(1) Liability **you** assume by contract or agreement;

(2) Arising out of **your** use of a **non-owned ultralight** for a **prohibited use**;

(3) Which occurs outside the **policy territory**.

LIMIT OF LIABILITY

The Limit of Liability shown in Item 5 of the Data Page for Coverage D is the most **we** will pay for all **non-owned ultralight damage** in one **accident**.

The number of Policyholders, Data Pages, claims or claimants does not increase this amount.

EXCESS INSURANCE

This insurance is excess insurance. If there is other insurance available to **you**, it shall apply first.

GENERAL PROVISIONS

(1) POLICY CHANGE TO BE MADE BY US
No change may be made to this Policy except by Endorsement issued by **us**.

(2) SUIT AGAINST US
We may not be sued unless there has been compliance with all terms of this Policy. Under Coverages A, C and D, no one has a right to sue **us** until the duty of an **insured person** to pay is finally decided by a court. Bankruptcy or insolvency of an **insured person** or an **insured person's** estate does not relieve **us** of **our** obligations under this Policy.

(3) OUR RECOVERY RIGHTS
If **we** pay under this Policy, **we** have all rights of recovery of an **insured person**. That person must do all that is needed to help **us** exercise these rights. An **insured person** must do nothing to take away these rights.

(4) WHAT TO DO IN CASE OF AN ACCIDENT OR LOSS
An **insured person's** duties when an **accident** or **loss** occurs are shown in this Policy. An **insured person** must comply with them to the best of their ability.

(5) TRANSFER OF POLICY
Interest in this Policy may not be transferred without **our** written consent. If **you** die, the Policyholder will be:
(a) anyone who has custody of **your ultralight** until a legal agent is named; and
(b) **your** legal agent while carrying out his duties.

(6) NONRENEWAL
If **we** decide not to renew this Policy, **we** will mail **you** a notice of nonrenewal. This notice will be sent to the address shown in Item 1 of the Data Page. It will be sent at least 30 days before the Policy Period ends. Proof of mailing will be proof that **you** were notified.

If **we** offer to renew and **you** do not pay the renewal premium, **you** have declined **our** offer.

(7) CANCELLATION
To cancel this Policy, **you** must tell **us** in writing at what future date the cancellation should be.

We may cancel by mailing **you** a cancellation notice. This notice will be sent to the address shown in Item 1 of the Data Page. It will be sent at least 30 days before the cancellation date. Only 10 days notice will be given if **we** cancel for nonpayment of premium. Also, only 10 days notice will be given if the Policy has been in effect less than 60 days and is not a Renewal Policy. Proof of mailing will be proof that **you** were notified.

Upon cancellation, **you** may be entitled to a premium refund. **We** will send that refund to **you**. **Our** making a refund is not a condition of cancellation. If **you** cancel for any reason, the refund will be figured using the short-rate table shown. If **we** cancel because of **your** nonpayment of premium, **we** will use the same short-rate table.

If **we** cancel for a reason other than nonpayment of premium, the refund will be figured on a pro rata basis.

Our receipt and deposit of **your** premium payment after mailing a notice of cancellation will not reinstate the Policy. However, cancellation for nonpayment of premium will not be effective if the required payment is received before the cancellation date.

(8) POLICY CONFORMS TO YOUR STATE LAW
If terms of this Policy conflict with **your** state law, they are amended to conform to that law.

The President and Secretary of AVEMCO Insurance Company have signed this Policy and it is countersigned on the Data Page by an authorized representative.

John H. Ballard
John H. Ballard
Secretary

David E. Jensen
David E. Jensen
President

Short-Rate Cancellation Table		
Days Policy in Force	Per Cent of One Year Premium
1-146	50
147-149	51
150-153	52
154-156	53
157-160	54
161-164	55
165-167	56
168-171	57
172-175	58
176-178	59
179-182	60
183-187	61
188-191	62
192-196	63
197-200	64
201-205	65
206-209	66
210-214	67
215-218	68
219-223	69
224-228	70
229-232	71
233-237	72
238-241	73
242-246	74
247-250	75
251-255	76
256-260	77
261-264	78
265-269	79
270-273	80
274-278	81
279-282	82
283-287	83
288-291	84
292-296	85
297-301	86
302-305	87
306-310	88
311-314	89
315-319	90
320-323	91
324-328	92
329-332	93
333-337	94
338-342	95
343-346	96
347-351	97
352-355	98
356-360	99
361-365	100

WHAT TO DO IN CASE OF AN ACCIDENT OR LOSS

NOTIFY US PROMPTLY
The notice should give the time, place and circumstances. It should include names and addresses of witnesses and injured persons.

OTHER DUTIES
An **insured person** shall:
  • Cooperate with and assist **us** in matters concerning a claim or suit;
  • Promptly send **us** all legal papers received;
  • Authorize **us** to obtain medical and other records;
  • Provide proofs of loss **we** require;
  • Assume no obligation nor make any payment other than for first aid to others.
When **you** have Coverage for **loss** to **your ultralight**, **you** shall also:
  • Take reasonable steps after a **loss** to protect **your ultralight**;
  • Promptly report theft or vandalism to the police;
  • Allow **us** to inspect **your ultralight** before repair or disposal.

ASSOCIATED AVIATION UNDERWRITERS

AVIATION INSURANCE CONTRACT

Airport/Fixed Base Operator's Liability Policy   No. APL

(A Stock Insurance Company, Herein Called The Company)

In consideration of the payment of the premium, in reliance upon the statements in the declarations and subject to all of the terms of this policy, agrees with the **named insured** as follows:

DECLARATIONS

Item 1. NAMED INSURED...
....
Address...City...State.............................
The **Named Insured** is: individual ☐; partnership ☐; corporation ☐; joint venture ☐; other (specify) ....
....

Item 2. POLICY PERIOD: From...........................M,...to...
12:01 A.M., standard time at the address of the **Named Insured** as stated herein.
Audit Period: Annual, unless otherwise stated ....

Item 3. The insurance afforded is only with respect to such of the following Coverage Parts, as are indicated by specific premium charge or charges.

Coverage Parts	Advance Premiums
Comprehensive General Liability Insurance	$
Owners', Landlords' and Tenants' Liability Insurance	$
Contractual Liability Insurance	$
Completed Operations and Products Liability Insurance	$
Owners' and Contractors' Protective Liability Insurance	$
Premises Medical Payments Insurance	$
Personal Injury Liability Insurance	$
Hangar Keepers' Liability Insurance	$

Endorsements forming a part of this policy on its effective date:
....
....
....

Advance Premium Payable: Total Advance Premium $..
On effective date of policy $...............................; 1st Anniversary $........................; 2nd Anniversary $..................

The company has caused this policy to be executed by its President and Secretary or by its Managers at its principal United States Office but it shall not be valid unless approved by Associated Aviation Underwriters, countersigned by a duly authorized representative of the company and completed by the attachment hereto of (1) one or more Coverage Parts for which there is an advance premium indicated in this page, and (2) the Standard Provisions Part of the company's Airport/Fixed Base Operator's Liability Policy.

Countersigned...   APPROVED: ASSOCIATED AVIATION UNDERWRITERS
       Authorized Representative

By...   By...

Form No. APL-1

COMPREHENSIVE GENERAL LIABILITY INSURANCE — COVERAGE PART

I. COVERAGE A — BODILY INJURY LIABILITY
COVERAGE B — PROPERTY DAMAGE LIABILITY

The company will pay on behalf of the **insured** all sums which the **insured** shall become legally obligated to pay as damages because of

     A. **bodily injury** or

     B. **property damage**

to which this insurance applies, caused by an **occurrence,** and the company shall have the right and duty to defend any suit against the **insured** seeking damages on account of such **bodily injury** or **property damage,** even if any of the allegations of the suit are groundless, false or fraudulent, and may make such investigation and settlement of any claim or suit as it deems expedient, but the company shall not be obligated to pay any claim or judgment or to defend any suit after the applicable limit of the company's liability has been exhausted by payment of judgments or settlements.

Exclusions

This insurance does not apply:

(a) to liability assumed by the **insured** under any contract or agreement except an **incidental contract;** but this exclusion does not apply to a warranty of fitness or quality of the **named insured's products** or a warranty that work performed by or on behalf of the **named insured** will be done in a workmanlike manner;

(b) to **bodily injury** or **property damage** arising out of the ownership, maintenance, operation, use, loading or unloading of

  (1) any **automobile** or aircraft owned or operated by or rented or loaned to any **insured,** or

  (2) any other **automobile** or aircraft operated by any person in the course of his employment by any **insured;**

but this exclusion does not apply to the parking of an **automobile** on premises owned by, rented to or controlled by the **named insured** or the ways immediately adjoining, if such **automobile** is not owned by or rented or loaned to any **insured;**

(c) to **bodily injury** or **property damage** arising out of (1) the ownership, maintenance, operation, use, loading or unloading of any **mobile equipment** while being used in any prearranged or organized racing, speed or demolition contest or in any stunting activity or in practice or preparation for any such contest or activity or (2) the operation or use of any snowmobile or trailer designed for use therewith;

(d) to **bodily injury** or **property damage** arising out of and in the course of the transportation of **mobile equipment** by an **automobile** owned or operated by or rented or loaned to any **insured;**

(e) to **bodily injury** or **property damage** arising out of the ownership, maintenance, operation, use, loading or unloading of

  (1) any watercraft owned or operated by or rented or loaned to any **insured,** or

  (2) any other watercraft operated by any person in the course of his employment by any **insured;**

but this exclusion does not apply to watercraft while ashore on premises owned by, rented to or controlled by the **named insured;**

(f) to **bodily injury** or **property damage** arising out of the discharge, dispersal, release or escape of smoke, vapors, soot, fumes, acids, alkalis, toxic chemicals, liquids or gases, waste materials or other irritants, contaminants or pollutants into or upon land, the atmosphere or any water course or body of water; but this exclusion does not apply if such discharge, dispersal, release or escape is sudden and accidental;

(g) to **bodily injury** or **property damage** due to war, whether or not declared, civil war, insurrection, rebellion or revolution or to any act or condition incident to any of the foregoing, with respect to

  (1) liability assumed by the **insured** under an **incidental contract,** or

  (2) expenses for first aid under the Supplementary Payments provision;

(h) to **bodily injury** or **property damage** for which the **insured** or his indemnitee may be held liable

  (1) as a person or organization engaged in the business of manufacturing, distributing, selling or serving alcoholic beverages, or

  (2) if not so engaged, as an owner or lessor of premises used for such purposes,

  if such liability is imposed

  (i) by, or because of the violation of, any statute, ordinance or regulation pertaining to the sale, gift, distribution or use of any alcoholic beverage, or

  (ii) by reason of the selling, serving or giving of any alcoholic beverage to a minor or to a person under the influence of alcohol or which causes or contributes to the intoxication of any person;

but part (ii) of this exclusion does not apply with respect to liability of the **insured** or his indemnitee as an owner or lessor described in (2) above;

(i) to any obligation for which the **insured** or any carrier as his insurer may be held liable under any workmen's compensation, unemployment compensation or disability benefits law, or under any similar law;

(j) to **bodily injury** to any employee of the **insured** arising out of and in the course of his employment by the **insured** or to any obligation of the **insured** to indemnify another because of damages arising out of such injury; but this exclusion does not apply to liability assumed by the **insured** under an **incidental contract;**

(k) to **property damage** to

  (1) property owned or occupied by or rented to the **insured,**

  (2) property used by the **insured,** or

  (3) property in the care, custody or control of the **insured** or as to which the **insured** is for any purpose exercising physical control;

but parts (2) and (3) of this exclusion do not apply with respect to liability under a written sidetrack agreement and part (3) of this exclusion does not apply with respect to **property damage** (other than to **elevators**) arising out of the use of an **elevator** at premises owned by, rented to or controlled by the **named insured;**

(l) to **property damage** to premises alienated by the **named insured** arising out of such premises or any part thereof;

(m) to loss of use of tangible property which has not been physically injured or destroyed resulting from

  (1) a delay in or lack of performance by or on behalf of the **named insured** of any contract or agreement, or

  (2) the failure of the **named insured's products** or work performed by or on behalf of the **named insured** to meet the level of performance, quality, fitness or durability warranted or represented by the **named insured;**

but this exclusion does not apply to loss of use of other tangible property resulting from the sudden and accidental physical injury to or destruction of the **named insured's products** or work performed by or on behalf of the **named**

insured after such products or work have been put to use by any person or organization other than an **insured;**

(n) to **property damage** to the **named insured's products** arising out of such products or any part of such products;

(o) to **property damage** to work performed by or on behalf of the **named insured** arising out of the work or any portion thereof, or out of materials, parts or equipment furnished in connection therewith;

(p) to damages claimed for the withdrawal, inspection, repair, replacement, or loss of use of the **named insured's products** or work completed by or for the **named insured** or of any property of which such products or work form a part, if such products, work or property are withdrawn from the market or from use because of any known or suspected defect or deficiency therein;

(q) (1) to **bodily injury** or **property damage** arising out of

    (i) **aircraft noise,** or

    (ii) interference with the quiet enjoyment of property by overflight or other operation of aircraft in proximity thereto, or

  (2) to sums claimed or awarded as **damages** to the extent that such sums represent payment or compensation for the taking of or exercise of rights with respect to the property of others by overflight or other operation of aircraft in proximity thereto.

Each of the following is an **insured** under this insurance to the extent set forth below:

(a) if the **named insured** is designated in the declarations as an individual, the person so designated but only with respect to the conduct of a business of which he is the sole proprietor, and the spouse of the **named insured** with respect to the conduct of such a business;

(b) if the **named insured** is designated in the declarations as a partnership or joint venture, the partnership or joint venture so designated and any partner or member thereof but only with respect to his liability as such;

(c) if the **named insured** is designated in the declarations as other than an individual, partnership or joint venture, the organization so designated and any executive officer, director or stockholder thereof while acting within the scope of his duties as such;

(d) any person (other than an employee of the **named insured**) or organization while acting as real estate manager for the **named insured;** and

(e) with respect to the operation, for the purpose of locomotion upon a public highway, of **mobile** equipment registered under any motor vehicle registration law,

    (i) an employee of the **named insured** while operating any such equipment in the course of his employment, and

    (ii) any other person while operating with the permission of the **named insured** any such equipment registered in the name of the **named insured** and any person or organization legally responsible for such operation, but only if there is no other valid and collectible insurance available, either on a primary or excess basis, to such person or organization;

provided that no person or organization shall be an **insured** under this paragraph (e) with respect to:

(1) **bodily injury** to any fellow employee of such person injured in the course of his employment, or

(2) **property damage** to property owned by, rented to, in charge of or occupied by the **named insured** or the employer of any person described in subparagraph (ii).

This insurance does not apply to **bodily injury** or **property damage** arising out of the conduct of any partnership or joint venture of which the **insured** is a partner or member and which is not designated in this policy as a **named insured.**

Regardless of the number of (1) **insureds** under this policy, (2) persons or organizations who sustain **bodily injury** or **property damage,** or (3) claims made or suits brought on account of **bodily injury** or **property damage,** the company's liability is limited as follows:

Coverage A — The total liability of the company for all damages, including damages for care and loss of services, because of **bodily injury** sustained by one or more persons as the result of any one **occurrence** shall not exceed the limit of **bodily injury** liability stated in the schedule as applicable to **"each occurrence."**

Subject to the above provision respecting "each **occurrence**", the total liability of the company for all damages because of (1) all **bodily injury** included within **completed operations hazard** and (2) all **bodily injury** included within the **products hazard** shall not exceed the limit of **bodily injury** liability stated in the schedule as "aggregate".

Coverage B — The total liability of the company for all damages because of all **property damage** sustained by one or more persons or organizations as the result of any one **occurrence** shall not exceed the limit of **property damage** liability stated in the schedule as applicable to "each **occurrence**".

Subject to the above provision respecting "each **occurrence**", the total liability of the company for all damages because of all **property damage** to which this coverage applies and described in any of the numbered subparagraphs below shall not exceed the limit of **property damage** liability stated in the schedule as "aggregate";

(1) all **property damage** arising out of premises or operations rated on a remuneration basis or contractor's equipment rated on a receipts basis, including **property damage** for which liability is assumed under any **incidental contract** relating to such premises or operations, but excluding **property damage** included in subparagraph (2) below;

(2) all **property damage** arising out of and occurring in the course of operations performed for the **named insured** by independent contractors and general supervision thereof by the **named insured,** including any such **property damage** for which liability is assumed under any **incidental contract** relating to such operations, but this subparagraph (2) does not include **property damage** arising out of maintenance or repairs at premises owned by or rented to the **named insured** or structural alterations at such premises which do not involve changing the size of or moving buildings or other structures;

(3) all **property damage** included within the **products hazard** and all **property damage** included within the **completed operations hazard.**

Such aggregate limit shall apply separately to the **property damage** described in subparagraphs (1), (2) and (3) above, and under subparagraphs (1) and (2), separately with respect to each project away from premises owned by or rented to the **named insured.**

Coverages A and B — For the purpose of determining the limit of the company's liability, all **bodily injury** and **property damage** arising out of continuous or repeated exposure to substantially the same general conditions shall be considered as arising out of one **occurrence.**

This insurance applies only to **bodily injury** or **property damage** which occurs within the **policy territory.**

The insurance afforded is only with respect to such of the following coverages as are indicated by specific premium charge or charges. The limit of the company's liability against each such coverage shall be as stated herein, subject to all the terms of this policy having reference thereto.

COVERAGES AND LIMITS OF LIABILITY

Coverage A		Coverage B	
Bodily Injury Liability		Property Damage Liability	
each occurrence	aggregate	each occurrence	aggregate
$	$	$	$
Advance Premium $		Advance Premium $	
Total Advance Premium $			

GENERAL LIABILITY HAZARDS

Description of Hazards	Code No.	Premium Bases	Rates		Advance Premium	
			Bodily Injury Liability	Property Damage Liability	Bodily Injury Liability	Property Damage Liability
(a) Premises — Operations						
(b) Escalators		Number Insured	Per Landing			
(c) Independent Contractors		Cost	Per $100 of Cost			
(d) Completed Operations		Receipts	Per $1,000 of Receipts			
(e) Products		Sales	Per $1,000 of Sales			

GENERAL LIABILITY MINIMUM PREMIUMS

Bodily Injury Liability	Property Damage Liability	Bodily Injury Liability	Property Damage Liability	Bodily Injury Liability	Property Damage Liability
(a) $.	$	(c) $	$	(e) $	$
(b) $	$	(d) $	$		

Locations of all premises owned by, rented to or controlled by the **named insured**. (Enter "same" if same location as address shown in Item 1. of declarations.)
....

Interest of **named insured** in such premises. (Describe interest, such as "owner", "general lessee" or "tenant".)................................
....

Part occupied by **named insured**..
....

The foregoing discloses all hazards insured hereunder known to exist at the effective date of this policy, unless otherwise stated herein.

Policy Issued By...Policy No...

Named Insured...

This Coverage Part shall not be binding on the Company unless attached to the Declarations Page and Standard Provisions Part of the Company's Airport/Fixed Base Operator's Liability Policy.

When used as a premium basis:

1. **"admissions"** means the total number of persons, other than employees of the **named insured,** admitted to the event insured or to events conducted on the **premises** whether on paid admission tickets, complimentary tickets or passes;

2. **"cost"** means the total cost to the **named insured** with respect to operations performed for the **named insured** during the policy period by independent contractors of all work let or sub-let in connection with each specific project, including the cost of all labor, materials and equipment furnished, used or delivered for use in the execution of such work, whether furnished by the owner, contractor or subcontractor, including all fees, allowances, bonuses or commissions made, paid or due;

3. **"receipts"** means the gross amount of money charged by the **named insured** for such operations by the **named insured** or by others during the policy period as are rated on a receipts basis other than receipts from telecasting, broadcasting or motion pictures, and includes taxes, other than taxes which the **named insured** collects as a separate item and remits directly to a governmental division;

4. **"remuneration"** means the entire remuneration earned during the policy period by proprietors and by all employees of the **named insured,** other than chauffeurs (except operators of mobile equipment) and aircraft pilots and co-pilots, subject to any overtime earnings or limitation of remuneration rule applicable in accordance with the manuals in use by the company;

5. **"sales"** means the gross amount of money charged by the **named insured** or by others trading under his name for all goods and products sold or distributed during the policy period and charged during the policy period for installation, servicing or repair, and includes taxes, other than taxes which the **named insured** and such others collect as a separate item and remit directly to a governmental division.

OWNERS', LANDLORDS' AND TENANTS' LIABILITY INSURANCE
COVERAGE FOR DESIGNATED PREMISES AND RELATED OPERATIONS IN PROGRESS OTHER THAN STRUCTURAL ALTERATIONS, NEW CONSTRUCTION AND DEMOLITION

I. COVERAGE A — BODILY INJURY LIABILITY
COVERAGE B — PROPERTY DAMAGE LIABILITY

The company will pay on behalf of the **insured** all sums which the **insured** shall become legally obligated to pay as damages because of

A. **bodily injury** or

B. **property damage**

to which this insurance applies, caused by an **occurrence** and arising out of the ownership, maintenance or use of the **insured premises** and all operations necessary or incidental thereto, and the company shall have the right and duty to defend any suit against the **insured** seeking damages on account of such **bodily injury** or **property damage**, even if any of the allegations of the suit are groundless, false or fraudulent, and may make such investigation and settlement of any claim or suit as it deems expedient, but the company shall not be obligated to pay any claim or judgment or to defend any suit after the applicable limit of the company's liability has been exhausted by payment of judgments or settlements.

Exclusions

This insurance does not apply:

(a) to liability assumed by the **insured** under any contract or agreement except an **incidental contract**; but with respect to **bodily injury** or **property damage** occurring while work performed by the **named insured** is in progress, this exclusion does not apply to a warranty that such work will be done in a workmanlike manner;

(b) to **bodily injury** or **property damage** arising out of the ownership, maintenance, operation, use, loading or unloading of

(1) any **automobile** or aircraft owned or operated by or rented or loaned to any **insured**, or

(2) any other **automobile** or aircraft operated by any person in the course of his employment by any **insured**:

but this exclusion does not apply to the parking of an **automobile** on **insured premises**, if such **automobile** is not owned by or rented or loaned to any **insured**;

(c) to **bodily injury** or **property damage** arising out of (1) the ownership, maintenance, operation, use, loading or unloading of any **mobile equipment** while being used in any prearranged or organized racing, speed or demolition contest or in any stunting activity or in practice or preparation for any such contest or activity or (2) the operation or use of any snowmobile or trailer designed for use therewith;

(d) to **bodily injury** or **property damage** arising out of and in the course of the transportation of **mobile equipment** by an **automobile** owned or operated by or rented or loaned to any **insured**;

(e) to **bodily injury** or **property damage** arising out of the ownership, maintenance, operation, use, loading or unloading of

(1) any watercraft owned or operated by or rented or loaned to any **insured**, or

(2) any other watercraft operated by any person in the course of his employment by any **insured**:

but this exclusion does not apply to watercraft while ashore on the **insured premises**;

(f) to **bodily injury** or **property damage** arising out of the discharge, dispersal, release or escape of smoke, vapors, soot, fumes, acids, alkalis, toxic chemicals, liquids or gases, waste materials or other irritants, contaminants or pollutants into or upon land, the atmosphere or any water course or body of water; but this exclusion does not apply if such discharge, dispersal, release or escape is sudden and accidental;

(g) to **bodily injury** or **property damage** due to war, whether or not declared, civil war, insurrection, rebellion or revolution or to any act or condition incident to any of the foregoing, with respect to

(1) liability assumed by the **insured** under an **incidental contract**, or

(2) expenses for first aid under the Supplementary Payments provision;

(h) to **bodily injury** or **property damage** for which the **insured** or his indemnitee may be held liable

(1) as a person or organization engaged in the business of manufacturing, distributing, selling or serving alcoholic beverages, or

(2) if not so engaged, as an owner or lessor of premises used for such purposes, if such liability is imposed

(i) by, or because of the violation of, any statute, ordinance or regulation pertaining to the sale, gift, distribution or use of any alcoholic beverage, or

(ii) by reason of the selling, serving or giving of any alcoholic beverage to a minor or to a person under the influence of alcohol or which causes or contributes to the intoxication of any person;

but part (ii) of this exclusion does not apply with respect to liability of the **insured** or his indemnitee as an owner or lessor described in (2) above;

(i) to any obligation for which the **insured** or any carrier as his insurer may be held liable under any workmen's compensation, unemployment compensation or disability benefits law, or under any similar law;

(j) to **bodily injury** to any employee of the insured arising out of and in the course of his employment by the **insured** or to any obligation of the **insured** to indemnify another because of damages arising out of such injury; but this exclusion does not apply to liability assumed by the **insured** under an **incidental contract**;

(k) to **property damage** to

(1) property owned or occupied by or rented to the **insured**,

(2) property used by the **insured**, or

(3) property in the care, custody or control of the **insured** or as to which the **insured** is for any purpose exercising physical control;

but parts (2) and (3) of this exclusion do not apply with respect to liability under a written sidetrack agreement and part (3) of this exclusion does not apply with respect to **property damage** (other than to **elevators**) arising out of the use of an **elevator** at the **insured preimses**;

(l) to **property damage** to premises alienated by the **named insured** arising out of such premises or any part thereof;

(m) to loss of use of tangible property which has not been physically injured or destroyed resulting from

    (1) a delay in or lack of performance by or on behalf of the named insured of any contract or agreement, or

    (2) the failure of the named insured's products or work performed by or on behalf of the named insured to meet the level of performance, quality, fitness or durability warranted or represented by the named insured;

but this exclusion does not apply to loss of use of other tangible property resulting from the sudden and accidental physical injury to or destruction of the named insured's products or work performed by or on behalf of the named insured after such products or work have been put to use by any person or organization other than an insured;

(n) to property damage to the named insured's products arising out of such products or any part of such products;

(o) to property damage to work performed by or on behalf of the named insured arising out of the work or any portion thereof, or out of materials, parts or equipment furnished in connection therewith;

(p) to bodily injury or property damage included within the completed operations hazard or the products hazard;

(q) to bodily injury or property damage arising out of operations on or from premises (other than the insured premises) owned by, rented to or controlled by the named insured, or to liability assumed by the insured under any contract or agreement relating to such premises;

(r) to bodily injury or property damage arising out of structural alterations which involve changing the size of or moving buildings or other structures, new construction or demolition operations performed by or on behalf of the named insured;

(s) (1) to bodily injury or property damage arising out of

    (i) aircraft noise, or

    (ii) interference with the quiet enjoyment of property by overflight or other operation of aircraft in proximity thereto, or

    (2) to sums claimed or awarded as damages to the extent that such sums represent payment or compensation for the taking of or exercise of rights with respect to the property of others by overflight or other operation of aircraft in proximity thereto.

II. PERSONS INSURED

Each of the following is an insured under this insurance to the extent set forth below:

(a) if the named insured is designated in the declarations as an individual, the person so designated but only with respect to the conduct of a business of which he is the sole proprietor, and the spouse of the named insured with respect to the conduct of such a business;

(b) if the named insured is designated in the declarations as a partnership or joint venture, the partnership or joint venture so designated and any partner or member thereof but only with respect to his liability as such;

(c) if the named insured is designated in the declarations as other than an individual, partnership or joint venture, the organization so designated and any executive officer, director or stockholder thereof while acting within the scope of his duties as such;

(d) any person (other than an employee of the named insured) or organization while acting as real estate manager for the named insured; and

with respect to the operation, for the purpose of locomotion upon a public highway, of mobile equipment registered under any motor vehicle registration law,

    (i) an employee of the named insured while operating any such equipment in the course of his employment, and

    (ii) any other person while operating with the permission of the named insured any such equipment registered in the name of the named insured and any person or organization legally responsible for such operation, but only if there is no other valid and collectible insurance available, either on a primary or excess basis, to such person or organization;

provided that no person or organization shall be an insured under this paragraph (e) with respect to:

    (1) bodily injury to any fellow employee of such person injured in the course of his employment, or

    (2) property damage to property owned by, rented to, in charge of or occupied by the named insured or the employer of any person described in subparagraph (ii).

This insurance does not apply to bodily injury or property damage arising out of the conduct of any partnership or joint venture of which the insured is a partner or member and which is not designated in this policy as a named insured.

III. LIMITS OF LIABILITY

Regardless of the number of (1) insureds under this policy, (2) persons or organizations who sustain bodily injury or property damage, or (3) claims made or suits brought on account of bodily injury or property damage, the company's liability is limited as follows:

Coverage A — The total liability of the company for all damages, including damages for care and loss of services, because of bodily injury sustained by one or more persons as the result of any one occurrence shall not exceed the limit of bodily injury liability stated in the schedule as applicable to "each occurrence".

Coverage B — The total liability of the company for all damages because of all property damage sustained by one or more persons or organizations as the result of any one occurrence shall not exceed the limit of property damage liability stated in the schedule as applicable to "each occurrence".

Coverages A and B — For the purpose of determining the limit of the company's liability, all bodily injury and property damage arising out of continuous or repeated exposure to substantially the same general conditions shall be considered as arising out of one occurrence.

IV. ADDITIONAL DEFINITION

When used in reference to this insurance (including endorsements forming a part of the policy):

"insured premises" means (1) the premises designated in the declarations, (2) premises alienated by the named insured (other than premises constructed for sale by the named insured), if possession has been relinquished to others, and (3) premises as to which the named insured acquires ownership or control and reports his intention to insure such premises under this policy and no other within 30 days after such acquisition; and includes the ways immediately adjoining such premises on land.

V. POLICY TERRITORY

This insurance applies only to bodily injury or property damage which occurs within the policy territory.

SCHEDULE

The insurance afforded is only with respect to such of the following coverages as are indicated by specific premium charge or charges. The limit of the company's liability against each such coverage shall be stated herein, subject to all the terms of this policy having reference thereto.

Coverages	Limits of Liability	Premium
A. Bodily Injury Liability	$ each occurrence	$
B. Property Damage Liability	$ each occurrence	$
	Total Premium	$

GENERAL LIABILITY HAZARDS

Descriptions of Hazards	Code No	Premium Bases	Rates – Bodily Injury Liability	Rates – Property Damage Liability	Premium – Bodily Injury Liability	Premium – Property Damage Liability
(a) Premises — Operations (Designate **insured** premises by entering address. If address is same as Item 1 of declarations, enter "same".)						
(b) Escalators		Number Insured	Per Landing			

MINIMUM PREMIUMS

Bodily Injury Liability		Property Damage Liability	
(a) $	(b) $	(a) $	(b) $

Interest of **named insured** in **insured premises.** (Enter "owner", "general lessee" or "tenant")...

....

Part occupied by **named insured**...

....

Policy Issued By...Policy No...

Named Insured..

This Coverage Part shall not be binding on the Company unless attached to the Declarations Page and Standard Provisions Part of the Company's Airport/Fixed Base Operator's Liability Policy.

When used as a premium basis:

1. **"admissions"** means the total number of persons, other than employees of the **named insured,** admitted to the event insured or to events conducted on the **premises** whether on paid admission tickets, complimentary tickets or passes;

2. **"cost"** means the total cost to the **named insured** with respect to operations performed for the **named insured** during the policy period by independent contractors of all work let or sub-let in connection with each specific project, including the cost of all labor, materials and equipment furnished, used or delivered for use in the execution of such work, whether furnished by the owner, contractor or subcontractor, including all fees, allowances, bonuses or commissions made, paid or due;

3. **"receipts"** means the gross amount of money charged by the **named insured** for such operations by the **named insured** or by others during the policy period as are rated on a receipts basis other than receipts from telecasting, broadcasting or motion pictures, and includes taxes, other than taxes which the **named insured** collects as a separate item and remits directly to a governmental division;

4. **"remuneration"** means the entire remuneration earned during the policy period by proprietors and by all employees of the **named insured,** other than chauffeurs (except operators of mobile equipment) and aircraft pilots and co-pilots, subject to any overtime earnings or limitation of remuneration rule applicable in accordance with the manuals in use by the company;

5. **"sales"** means the gross amount of money charged by the **named insured** or by others trading under his name for all goods and products sold or distributed during the policy period and charged during the policy period for installation, servicing or repair, and includes taxes, other than taxes which the **named insured** and such others collect as a separate item and remit directly to a governmental division.

CONTRACTUAL LIABILITY INSURANCE — COVERAGE PART
(Designated Contracts Only)

I. COVERAGE Y — CONTRACTUAL BODILY INJURY LIABILITY

COVERAGE Z — CONTRACTUAL PROPERTY DAMAGE LIABILITY

The company will pay on behalf of the **insured** all sums which the **insured**, by reason of **contractual liability** assumed by him under a contract designated in the schedule for this insurance, shall become legally obligated to pay as damages because of

Y. bodily injury or

Z. property damage

to which this insurance applies, caused by an **occurrence**, and the company shall have the right and duty to defend any **suit** against the **insured** seeking damages on account of such **bodily injury** or **property damage**, even if any of the allegations of the **suit** are groundless, false or fraudulent, and may make such investigation and settlement of any claim or **suit** as it deems expedient, but the company shall not be obligated to pay any claim or judgment or to defend any **suit** after the applicable limit of the company's liability has been exhausted by payment of judgments or settlements.

Exclusions

This insurance does not apply:

(a) if the **insured** or his indemnitee is an architect, engineer or surveyor, to **bodily injury** or **property damage** arising out of the rendering of or the failure to render professional services by such **insured** or indemnitee, including

   (1) the preparation or approval of maps, plans, opinions, reports, surveys, designs or specifications and

   (2) supervisory, inspection or engineering services;

(b) to **bodily injury** or **property damage** due to war, whether or not declared, civil war, insurrection, rebellion or revolution or to any act or condition incident to any of the foregoing;

(c) to **bodily injury** or **property damage** for which the indemnitee may be held liable

   (1) as a person or organization engaged in the business of manufacturing, distributing, selling or serving alcoholic beverages, or

   (2) if not so engaged, as an owner or lessor of premises used for such purposes,

   if such liability is imposed

    (i) by, or because of the violation of, any statute, ordinance or regulation pertaining to the sale, gift, distribution or use of any alcoholic beverage or

    (ii) by reason of the selling, serving or giving of any alcoholic beverage to a minor or to a person under the influence of alcohol or which causes or contributes to the intoxication of any person;

   but part (ii) of this exclusion does not apply with respect to liability of the indemnitee as an owner or lessor described in (2) above;

(d) to any obligation for which the **insured** or any carrier as his insurer may be held liable under any workmen's compensation, unemployment compensation or disability benefits law, or under any similar law;

(e) to any obligation for which the **insured** may be held liable in an action on a contract by a third party beneficiary for **bodily injury** or **property damage** arising out of a project for a public authority; but this exclusion does not apply to an action by the public authority or any other person or organization engaged in the project;

(f) to **property damage** to

   (1) property owned or occupied by or rented to the **insured,**

   (2) property used by the **insured**, or

   (3) property in the care, custody or control of the **insured** or as to which the **insured** is for any purpose exercising physical control;

(g) to **property damage** to premises alienated by the **named insured** arising out of such premises or any part thereof;

(h) to loss of use of tangible property which has not been physically injured or destroyed resulting from

   (1) a delay in or lack of performance by or on behalf of the **named insured** of any contract or agreement, or

   (2) the failure of the **named insured's products** or work performed by or on behalf of the **named insured** to meet the level of performance, quality, fitness or durability warranted or represented by the **named insured;**

but this exclusion does not apply to loss of use of other tangible property resulting from the sudden and accidental physical injury to or destruction of the **named insured's products** or work performed by or on behalf of the **named insured** after such products or work have been put to use by any person or organization other than an **insured;**

(i) to **property damage** to the **named insured's products** arising out of such products or any part of such products;

(j) to **property damage** to work performed by or on behalf of the **named insured** arising out of the work or any portion thereof, or out of materials, parts or equipment furnished in connection therewith;

(k) to damages claimed for the withdrawal, inspection, repair, replacement, or loss of use of the **named insured's products** or work completed by or for the **named insured** or of any property of which such products or work form a part, if such products, work or property are withdrawn from the market or from use because of any known or suspected defect or deficiency therein;

(l) to **bodily injury** or **property damage** arising out of the ownership, maintenance, operation, use, loading or unloading of any **mobile equipment** while being used in any prearranged or organized racing, speed or demolition contest or in any stunting activity or in practice or preparation for any such contest or activity;

(m) to **bodily injury** or **property damage** arising out of the discharge, dispersal, release or escape of smoke, vapors, soot, fumes, acids, alkalis, toxic chemicals, liquids or gases, waste materials or other irritants, contaminants or pollutants into or upon land, the atmosphere or any water course or body of water; but this exclusion does not apply if such discharge, dispersal, release or escape is sudden and accidental;

(n) (1) to **bodily injury** or **property damage** arising out of

(i) **aircraft** noise, or

(ii) interference with the quiet enjoyment of property by overflight or other operation of aircraft in proximity thereto, or

(2) to sums claimed or awarded as **damages** to the extent that such sums represent payment or compensation for the taking of or exercise of rights with respect to the property of others by overflight or other operation of aircraft in proximity thereto.

II. PERSONS INSURED

Each of the following is an **insured** under this insurance to the extent set forth below:

(a) if the **named insured** is designated in the declarations as an individual, the person so designated and his spouse;

(b) if the **named insured** is designated in the declarations as a partnership or joint venture, the partnership or joint venture so designated and any partner or member thereof but only with respect to his liability as such;

(c) if the **named insured** is designated in the declarations as other than an individual, partnership or joint venture, the organization so designated and any executive officer, director or stockholder thereof while acting within the scope of his duties as such.

III. LIMITS OF LIABILITY

Regardless of the number of (1) **insureds** under this policy, (2) persons or organizations who sustain **bodily injury** or **property damage**, or (3) claims made or **suits** brought on account of **bodily injury** or **property damage**, the company's liability is limited as follows:

Coverage Y — The total liability of the company for all damages, including damages for care and loss of services, because of **bodily injury** sustained by one or more persons as a result of any one **occurrence** shall not exceed the limit of **bodily in-**jury liability stated in the schedule as applicable to "each **occurrence.**"

Coverage Z — The total liability of the company for all damages because of all **property damage** sustained by one or more persons or organizations as the result of any one **occurrence** shall not exceed the limit of **property damage** liability stated in the schedule as applicable to "each **occurrence.**"

Subject to the above provision respecting "each **occurrence**", the total liability of the company for all damages because of all **property damage** to which this coverage applies shall not exceed the limit of **property damage** liability stated in the schedule as "aggregate". Such aggregate limit of liability applies separately with respect to each project away from premises owned by or rented to the **named insured**.

Coverages Y and Z — For the purpose of determining the limit of the company's liability, all **bodily injury** and **property damage** arising out of continuous or repeated exposure to substantially the same general conditions shall be considered as arising out of one **occurrence**.

IV. ADDITIONAL DEFINITIONS

When used in reference to this insurance (including endorsements forming a part of the policy):

"contractual liability" means liability expressly assumed under a written contract or agreement; provided, however, that **contractual liability** shall not be construed as including liability under a warranty of the fitness or quality of the **named insured's products** or a warranty that work performed by or on behalf of the **named insured** will be done in a workmanlike manner;

"suit" includes an arbitration proceeding to which the **insured** is required to submit or to which the **insured** has submitted with the company's consent.

V. POLICY TERRITORY

This insurance applies only to **bodily injury** or **property damage** which occurs within the **policy territory**.

VI. ADDITIONAL CONDITION

Arbitration

The company shall be entitled to exercise all of the **insured's** rights in the choice of arbitrators and in the conduct of any arbitration proceeding.

SCHEDULE

The insurance afforded for **contractual liability** is only with respect to such of the following Coverages as are indicated by a specific premium charge applicable thereto. The limit of the company's liability against each such coverage shall be as stated herein, subject to all the terms of this policy having reference thereto.

Coverages	Limits of Liability		Advance Premium
Y. Contractual Bodily Injury Liability	$	each occurrence	$
Z. Contractual Property Damage Liability	$	each occurrence	$
	$	aggregate.	
	Total Advance Premium		$

Designation of Contracts	Code	Premium Bases	Rates		Advance Premium	
			Bodily Injury	Property Damage	Bodily Injury	Property Damage
			Total		$	$

Policy Issued By...Policy No...

Named Insured.. ....

This Coverage Part shall not be binding on the Company unless attached to the Declarations Page and Standard Provisions Part of the Company's Airport/Fixed Base Operator's Liability Policy.

When used as a premium basis:

1. **"admissions"** means the total number of persons, other than employees of the **named insured,** admitted to the event insured or to events conducted on the **premises** whether on paid admission tickets, complimentary tickets or passes;

2. **"cost"** means the total cost to the **named insured** with respect to operations performed for the **named insured** during the policy period by independent contractors of all work let or sub-let in connection with each specific project, including the cost of all labor, materials and equipment furnished, used or delivered for use in the execution of such work, whether furnished by the owner, contractor or subcontractor, including all fees, allowances, bonuses or commissions made, paid or due;

3. **"receipts"** means the gross amount of money charged by the **named insured** for such operations by the **named insured** or by others during the policy period as are rated on a receipts basis other than receipts from telecasting, broadcasting or motion pictures, and includes taxes, other than taxes which the **named insured** collects as a separate item and remits directly to a governmental division;

4. **"remuneration"** means the entire remuneration earned during the policy period by proprietors and by all employees of the **named insured,** other than chauffeurs (except operators of mobile equipment) and aircraft pilots and co-pilots, subject to any overtime earnings or limitation of remuneration rule applicable in accordance with the manuals in use by the company;

5. **"sales"** means the gross amount of money charged by the **named insured** or by others trading under his name for all goods and products sold or distributed during the policy period and charged during the policy period for installation, servicing or repair, and includes taxes, other than taxes which the **named insured** and such others collect as a separate item and remit directly to a governmental division.

COMPLETED OPERATIONS AND PRODUCTS LIABILITY INSURANCE

I. COVERAGE A – BODILY INJURY LIABILITY
COVERAGE B – PROPERTY DAMAGE LIABILITY

The company will pay on behalf of the **insured** all sums which the **insured** shall become legally obligated to pay as damages because of

A. bodily injury or

B. property damage

to which this insurance applies, caused by an **occurrence,** if the **bodily injury** or **property damage** is included within the **completed operations hazard** or the **products hazard,** and the company shall have the right and duty to defend any suit against the **insured** seeking damages on account of such **bodily injury** or **property damage,** even if any of the allegations of the suit are groundless, false or fraudulent, and may make such investigation and settlement of any claim or suit as it deems expedient, but the company shall not be obligated to pay any claim or judgment or to defend any suit after the applicable limit of the company's liability has been exhausted by payment of judgments or settlements.

Exclusions

This insurance does not apply:

(a) to liability assumed by the **insured** under any contract or agreement; but this exclusion does not apply to a warranty of fitness or quality of the **named insured's products** or a warranty that work performed by or on behalf of the **named insured** will be done in a workmanlike manner;

(b) to **bodily injury** or **property damage** for which the **insured** may be held liable;

    (1) as a person or organization engaged in the business of manufacturing, distributing, selling or serving alcoholic beverages, or

    (2) if not so engaged, as an owner or lesor of premises used for such purposes, if such liability is imposed

        (i) by, or because of the violation of, any statute, ordinance or regulation pertaining to the sale, gift, distribution or use of any alcoholic beverage, or

        (ii) by reason of the selling, serving or giving of any alcoholic beverage to a minor or to a person under the influence of alcohol or which causes or contributes to the intoxication of any person;

but part (ii) of this exclusion does not apply with respect to liability of the **insured** as an owner or lessor described in (2) above;

(c) to any obligation for which the **insured** or any carrier as his insurer may be held liable under any workmen's compensation, unemployment compensation or disability benefits law, or under any similar law;

(d) to **bodily injury** to any employee of the **insured** arising out of and in the course of his employment by the **insured** or to any obligation of the **insured** to indemnify another because of damages arising out of such injury;

(e) to loss of use of tangible property which has not been physically injured or destroyed resulting from;

    (1) a delay in or lack of performance by or on behalf of the **named insured** of any contract or agreement, or

    (2) the failure of the **named insured's products** or work performed by or on behalf of the **named insured** to meet the level of performance, quality, fitness or durability warranted or represented by the **named insured;**

but this exclusion does not apply to loss of use of other tangible property resulting from the sudden and accidental physical injury to or destruction of the **named insured's products** or work performed by or on behalf of the **named insured** after such products or work have been put to use by any person or organization other than an **insured;**

(f) to **property damage** to the **named insured's products** arising out of such products or any part of such products;

(g) to **property damage** to work performed by or on behalf of the **named insured** arising out of the work or any portion thereof, or out of materials, parts or equipment furnished in connection therewith;

(h) to damages claimed for the withdrawal, inspection, repair, replacement, or loss of use of the **named insured's products** or work completed by or for the **named insured** or of any property of which such products or work form a part, if such products, work or property are withdrawn from the market or from use because of any known or suspected defect or deficiency therein;

(i) to **bodily injury** or **property damage** arising out of the discharge, dispersal, release or escape of smoke, vapors, soot, fumes, acids, alkalis, toxic chemicals, liquids or gases, waste materials or other irritants, contaminants or pollutants into or upon land, the atmosphere or any water course or body of water; but this exclusion does not apply if such discharge, dispersal, release or escape is sudden and accidental;

(j) (1) to **bodily injury** or **property damage** arising out of

        (i) **aircraft noise,** or

        (ii) interference with the quiet enjoyment of property by overflight or other operation of aircraft in proximity thereto, or

    (2) to sums claimed or awarded as **damages** to the extent that such sums represent payment or compensation for the taking of or exercise of rights with respect to the property of others by overflight or other operation of aircraft in proximity thereto.

II. PERSONS INSURED

Each of the following is an **insured** under this insurance to the extent set forth below:

(a) if the **named insured** is designated in the declarations as an individual, the person so designated but only with respect to the conduct of a business of which he is the sole proprietor, and the spouse of the **named insured** with respect to the conduct of such a business;

(b) if the **named insured** is designated in the declaration as a partnership or joint venture, the partnership or joint venture so designated and any partner or member thereof but only with respect to his liability as such;

(c) if the **named insured** is designated in the declarations as other than an individual, partnership or joint venture, the organization so designated and any executive officer, director or stockholder thereof while acting within the scope of his duties as such;

(d) any person (other than an employee of the **named insured**) or organization while acting as real estate manager for the **named insured**.

This insurance does not apply to **bodily injury** or **property damage** arising out of the conduct of any partnership or joint venture of which the **insured** is a partner or member and which is not designated in this policy as a **named insured**.

III. LIMITS OF LIABILITY

Regardless of the number of (1) **insured** under this policy, (2) persons or organizations who sustain **bodily injury** or **property damage,** or (3) claims made or suits brought on account of **bodily injury** or **property damage,** the company's liability is limited as follows:

Coverage A — The total liability of the company for all damages, including damages for care and loss of services, because of **bodily injury** sustained by one or more persons as the result of any one **occurrence** shall not exceed the limit of **bodily injury** liability stated in the schedule as applicable to "each **occurrence**".

Subject to the above provision respecting "each **occurrence**", the total liability of the company for all damages because of all **bodily injury** to which this coverage applies shall not exceed the limit of **bodily injury** liability stated in the schedule as "aggregate."

Coverage B — The total liability of the company for all damages because of all **property damage** sustained by one or more persons or organizations as the result of any one **occurrence** shall not exceed the limit of **property damage** liability stated in the schedule as applicable to "each **occurrence**".

Subject to the above provision respecting "each **occurrence**", the total liability of the company for all damages because of all **property damage** to which this coverage applies shall not exceed the limit of **property damage** liability stated in the schedule as "aggregate".

Coverages A and B — For the purpose of determining the limit of the company's liability, all **bodily injury** and **property damage** arising out of continuous or repeated exposure to substantially the same general conditions shall be considered as arising out of one **occurrence.**

IV. POLICY TERRITORY

This insurance applies only to **bodily injury** or **property damage** which occurs within the **policy territory.**

SCHEDULE

The insurance afforded is only with respect to such of the following coverages as are indicated by specific premium charge or charges. The limit of the company's liability against each such coverage shall be as stated herein, subject to all the terms of this policy having reference thereto.

COVERAGES AND LIMITS OF LIABILITY

Coverage A Bodily Injury Liability		Coverage B Property Damage Liability	
each occurrence	aggregate	each occurrence	aggregate
$	$	$	$
Advance Premium $		Advance Premium $	
Total Advance Premium $			

GENERAL LIABILITY HAZARDS

Description of Hazards	Code No.	Premium Bases	Rates Bodily Injury Liability	Rates Property Damage Liability	Advance Premium Bodily Injury Liability	Advance Premium Property Damage Liability
Completed Operations		(a) Receipts	(a) Per $1,000 of Receipts			
Products		(b) Sales	(b) Per $1,000 of Sales			

Policy Issued By..Policy No..

Named Insured..

This Coverage Part shall not be binding on the Company unless attached to the Declarations Page and Standard Provisions Part of the Company's Airport/Fixed Base Operator's Liability Policy.

Form No. APS-4A Rev. 1-73   Page Three

When used as a premium basis:

1. **"admissions"** means the total number of persons, other than employees of the **named insured,** admitted to the event insured or to events conducted on the **premises** whether on paid admission tickets, complimentary tickets or passes;

2. **"cost"** means the total cost to the **named insured** with respect to operations performed for the **named insured** during the policy period by independent contractors of all work let or sub-let in connection with each specific project, including the cost of all labor, materials and equipment furnished, used or delivered for use in the execution of such work, wheth furnished by the owner, contractor or subcontractor, including all fees, allowances, bonuses or commissions made, paid or due;

3. **"receipts"** means the gross amount of money charged by the **named insured** for such operations by the **named insured** or by others during the policy period as are rated on a receipts basis other than receipts from telecasting, broadcasting or motion pictures, and includes taxes, other than taxes which the **named insured** collects as a separate item and remits directly to a governmental division;

4. **"remuneration"** means the entire remuneration earned during the policy period by proprietors and by all employees of the **named insured,** other than chauffeurs (except operators of mobile equipment) and aircraft pilots and co-pilots, subject to any overtime earnings or limitation of remuneration rule applicable in accordance with the manuals in use by the company;

5. **"sales"** means the gross amount of money charged by the **named insured** or by others trading under his name for all goods and products sold or distributed during the policy period and charged during the policy period for installation, servicing or repair, and includes taxes, other than taxes which the **named insured** and such others collect as a separate item and remit directly to a governmental division.

OWNERS' AND CONTRACTORS' PROTECTIVE LIABILITY INSURANCE – COVERAGE PART
COVERAGE FOR OPERATIONS OF DESIGNATED CONTRACTOR

I. COVERAGE A – BODILY INJURY LIABILITY
  COVERAGE B – PROPERTY DAMAGE LIABILITY

The company will pay on behalf of the **insured** all sums which the **insured** shall become legally obligated to pay as damages because of

A. **bodily injury** or

B. **property damage**

to which this policy applies, caused by an **occurrence** and arising out of (1) operations performed for the **named insured** by the contractor designated in the declarations at the location designated therein or (2) acts or omissions of the **named insured** in connection with his general supervision of such operations, and the company shall have the right and duty to defend any suit against the **insured** seeking damages on account of such **bodily injury** or **property damage,** even if any of the allegations of the suit are groundless, false or fraudulent, and may make such investigation and settlement of any claim or suit as it deems expedient, but the company shall not be obligated to pay any claim or judgment or to defend any suit after the applicable limit of the company's liability has been exhausted by payment of judgments or settlements.

Exclusions

This policy does not apply:

(a) to liability assumed by the **insured** under any contract or agreement except an **incidental contract;** but this exclusion does not apply to a warranty that **work** performed by the designated contractor will be done in a workmanlike manner;

(b) to **bodily injury** or **property damage** occurring after

  (1) all **work** on the project (other than service, maintenance or repairs) to be performed by or on behalf of the **named insured** at the site of the covered operations has been completed or

  (2) that portion of the designated contractor's **work** out of which the injury or damage arises has been put to its intended use by any person or organization other than another contractor or subcontractor engaged in performing operations for a principal as a part of the same project;

(c) to **bodily injury** or **property damage** arising out of any act or omission of the **named insured** or any of his employees, other than general supervision of **work** performed for the **named insured** by the designated contractor;

(d) to any obligation for which the **insured** or any carrier as his insurer may be held liable under any workmen's compensation, unemployment compensation or disability benefits law, or under any similar law;

(e) to **bodily injury** to any employee of the **insured** arising out of and in the course of his employment by the **insured** or to any obligation of the **insured** to indemnify another because of damages arising out of such injury; but this exclusion does not apply to liability assumed by the **insured** under an **incidental contract;**

(f) to **property damage** to

  (1) property owned or occupied by or rented to the **insured,**

  (2) property used by the **insured,**

  (3) property in the care, custody or control of the **insured** or as to which the **insured** is for any purpose exercising physical control, or

  (4) **work** performed for the **insured** by the designated contractor;

(g) to **bodily injury** or **property damage** due to war, whether or not declared, civil war, insurrection, rebellion or revolution or to any act or condition incident to any of the foregoing, with respect to (1) liability assumed by the **insured** under an **incidental contract,** or (2) expenses for first aid under the Supplementary Payments provision of the policy.

(h) to **bodily injury** or **property damage** arising out of (1) the ownership, maintenance, operation, use, loading or unloading of any **mobile equipment** while being used in any prearranged or organized racing, speed or demolition contest or in any stunting activity or in practice or preparation for any such contest or activity or (2) the operation or use of any snowmobile or trailer designed for use therewith;

(i) to **bodily injury** or **property damage** arising out of the discharge, dispersal, release or escape of smoke, vapors, soot, fumes, acids, alkalis, toxic chemicals, liquids or gases, waste materials or other irritants, contaminants or pollutants into or upon land, the atmosphere or any water course or body of water; but this exclusion does not apply if such discharge, dispersal, release or escape is sudden and accidental;

(j) to loss of use of tangible property which has not been physically injured or destroyed resulting from

  (1) a delay in or lack of performance by or on behalf of the **named insured** of any contract or agreement, or

  (2) the failure of the **named insured's products** or work performed by or on behalf of the **named insured** to meet the level of performance, quality, fitness or durability waranted or represented by the **named insured;**

but this exclusion does not apply to loss of use of other tangible property resulting from the sudden and accidental physical injury to or destruction of the **named insured's products** or work performed by or on behalf of the **named insured** after such products or work have been put to use by any person or organization other than an **insured;**

(k) (1) to **bodily injury** or **property damage** arising out of

    (i) **aircraft noise,** or

    (ii) interference with the quiet enjoyment of property by overflight or other operation of aircraft in proximity thereto, or

  (2) to sums claimed or awarded as **damages** to the extent that such sums represent payment or compensation for the taking of or exercise of rights with respect to the property of others by overflight or other operation of aircraft in proximity thereto.

II. PERSONS INSURED

Each of the following is an **insured** under this policy to the extent set forth below:

(a) if the **named insured** is designated in the declarations as an individual, the person so designated and his spouse;

(b) if the **named insured** is designated in the declarations as a partnership or joint venture, the partnership or joint venture so designated and any partner or member thereof but only with respect to his liability as such;

(c) if the **named insured** is designated in the declarations as other than an individual, partnership or joint venture, the organization so designated and any executive officer, director or stockholder thereof while acting within the scope of his duties as such; and

(d) any person (other than an employee of the **named insured**) or organization while acting as real estate manager for the **named insured.**

III. LIMITS OF LIABILITY

Regardless of the number of (1) **insureds** under this policy, (2) persons or organizations who sustain **bodily injury** or **property damage,** or (3) claims made or suits brought on account of **bodily injury** or **property damage,** the company's liability is limited as follows:

Coverage A — The total liability of the company for all damages, including damages for care and loss of services, because of **bodily injury** sustained by one or more persons as the result of any one **occurrence** shall not exceed the limit of **bodily injury** liability stated in the schedule as applicable to "each **occurrence".**

Coverage B — The total liability of the company for all damages because of all **property damage** sustained by one or more persons or organizations as the result of any one **occurrence** shall not exceed the limit of **property damage** liability stated in the declarations as applicable to "each **occurrence".**

Subject to the above provision respecting "each **occurrence",** the total liability of the company for all **damages** because of all **property damage** to which this coverage applies shall not exceed the limit of **property damage** liability stated in the schedule as "aggregate". If more than one project is designated in the schedule, such aggregate limit shall apply separately with respect to each project

Coverages A and B — For the purpose of determining the limit of the company's liability, all **bodily injury** and **property damage** arising out of continuous or repeated exposure to substantially the same general conditions shall be considered as arising out of one **occurrence.**

IV. ADDITIONAL DEFINITION

When used in reference to this insurance (including endorsements forming a part of the policy):

"work" includes materials, parts and equipment furnished in connection therewith.

SCHEDULE

The insurance afforded is only with respect to such of the following coverages as are indicated by specific premium charge or charges. The limit of the company's liability against each such coverage shall be as stated herein, subject to all the terms of this policy having reference thereto.

Coverages	Limits of Liability	Premium Bases	Rates	Advance Premium
A Bodily Injury Liability	$ each occurrence	Cost	$100 of Cost	$
B Property Damage Liability	$ each occurrence	Cost	$100 of Cost	
	$ aggregate			$
			Total Advance Premium	$

DECLARATION OF PROJECTS

Description of Projects	Code No.	Premium Bases	Rates		Advance Premium	
			Bodily Injury Liability	Property Damage Liability	Bodily Injury Liability	Property Damage Liability
☐ Special Provision Applicable						
☐ Special Provision Applicable						
☐ Special Provision Applicable						
☐ Special Provision Applicable						
☐ Special Provision Applicable						

PROJECT MINIMUM PREMIUMS

Bodily Injury Liability	Property Damage Liability	Bodily Injury Liability	Property Damage Liability	Bodily Injury Liability	Property Damage Liability
(1) $	$	(3) $	$	(5) $	$
(2) $	$	(4) $	$		

Designation of Contractor
Mailing Address
Location of Covered Operations

☐ Check here if the following provision is applicable:
The person or organization designated above as the Contractor has undertaken to pay the premium for this policy and shall be entitled to receive any return premiums and dividends, if any, which may become payable under the terms of this policy.

Policy Issued By..Policy No...

Named Insured...

This Coverage Part shall not be binding upon the company unless attached to Sections One and Two of the Company's Liability Insurance Policy.

When used as a premium basis:

1. **"admissions"** means the total number of persons, other than employees of the **named insured,** admitted to the event insured or to events conducted on the **premises** whether on paid admission tickets, complimentary tickets or passes;

2. **"cost"** means the total cost to the **named insured** with respect to operations performed for the **named insured** during the policy period by independent contractors of all work let or sub-let in connection with each specific project, including the cost of all labor, materials and equipment furnished, used or delivered for use in the execution of such work, whether furnished by the owner, contractor or subcontractor, including all fees, allowances, bonuses or commissions made, paid or due;

3. **"receipts"** means the gross amount of money charged by the **named insured** for such operations by the **named insured** or by others during the policy period as are rated on a receipts basis other than receipts from telecasting, broadcasting or motion pictures, and includes taxes, other than taxes which the **named insured** collects as a separate item and remits directly to a governmental division;

4. **"remuneration"** means the entire remuneration earned during the policy period by proprietors and by all employees of the **named insured,** other than chauffeurs (except operators of mobile equipment) and aircraft pilots and co-pilots, subject to any overtime earnings or limitation of remuneration rule applicable in accordance with the manuals in use by the company;

5. **"sales"** means the gross amount of money charged by the **named insured** or by others trading under his name for all goods and products sold or distributed during the policy period and charged during the policy period for installation, servicing or repair, and includes taxes, other than taxes which the **named insured** and such others collect as a separate item and remit directly to a governmental division.

PREMISES MEDICAL PAYMENTS INSURANCE

I. COVERAGE E — PREMISES MEDICAL PAYMENTS

The company will pay to or for each person who sustains **bodily injury** caused by accident all reasonable **medical expense** incurred within one year from the date of the accident on account of such **bodily injury**, provided such **bodily injury** arises out of (a) a condition in the **insured premises** or (b) operations with respect to which the **named insured** is afforded coverage for **bodily injury** liability under this policy.

Exclusions

This insurance does not apply:

(a) to **bodily injury**

    (1) arising out of the ownership, maintenance, operation, use, loading or unloading of

        (i) any **automobile** or aircraft owned or operated by or rented or loaned to any **insured**, or

        (ii) any other **automobile** or aircraft operated by any person in the course of his employment by any **insured**;

    but this exclusion does not apply to the parking of an **automobile** on the **insured premises**, if such **automobile** is not owned by or rented or loaned to any **insured**;

    (2) arising out of (i) the ownership, maintenance, operation, use, loading or unloading of any **mobile equipment** while being used in any prearranged or organized racing, speed or demolition contest or in any stunting activity or in practice or preparation for any such contest or activity or (ii) the operation or use of any snowmobile or trailer designed for use therewith;

    (3) arising out of the ownership, maintenance, operation, use, loading or unloading of

        (i) any watercraft owned or operated by or rented or loaned to any **insured**, or

        (ii) any other watercraft operated by any person in the course of his employment by any **insured**;

    but this exclusion does not apply to watercraft while ashore on the **insured premises**; or

    (4) arising out of and in the course of the transportation of **mobile equipment** by an **automobile** owned or operated by or rented or loaned to any **insured**;

(b) to **bodily injury**

    (1) included within the **completed operations hazard** or the **products hazard**;

    (2) arising out of operations performed for the **named insured** by independent contractors other than (i) maintenance and repair of the **insured premises** or (ii) structural alterations at such premises which do not involve changing the size of or moving buildings or other structures;

    (3) resulting from the selling, serving or giving of any alcoholic beverage (i) in violation of any statute, ordinance or regulation, (ii) to a minor, (iii) to a person under the influence of alcohol or (iv) which causes or contributes to the intoxication of any person, if the **named insured** is a person or organization engaged in the business of manufacturing, distributing, selling or serving alcoholic beverages or, if not so engaged, is an owner or lessor of premises used for such purposes but only part (i) of this exclusion (b) (3) applies when the **named insured** is such an owner or lessor;

    (4) due to war, whether or not declared, civil war, insurrection, rebellion or revolution, or to any act or condition incident to any of the foregoing;

(c) to **bodily injury**

    (1) to the **named insured**, any partner therein, any tenant or other person regularly residing on the **insured premises** or any employee of any of the foregoing if the **bodily injury** arises out of and in the course of his employment therewith;

    (2) to any other tenant if the **bodily injury** occurs on that part of the **insured premises** rented from the **named insured** or to any employee of such a tenant if the **bodily injury** occurs on the tenant's part of the **insured premises** and arises out of and in the course of his employment for the tenant;

    (3) to any person while engaged in maintenance and repair of the **insured premises** or alteration, demolition or new construction at such premises;

    (4) to any person if any benefits for such **bodily injury** are payable or required to be provided under any workmen's compensation, unemployment compensation or disability benefits law, or under any similar law;

    (5) to any person practicing, instructing or participating in any physical training, sport, athletic activity or contest unless a premium charge is entered for sport activities in the policy with respect to Premises Medical Payments Coverage;

(d) to any **medical expense** for services by the **named insured**, any employee thereof or any person or organization under contract to the **named insured** to provide such services;

(e) (1) to **bodily injury** arising out of

        (i) **aircraft noise**, or

        (ii) interference with the quiet enjoyment of property by overflight or other operation of aircraft in proximity thereto, or

    (2) to sums claimed or awarded as **damages** to the extent that such sums represent payment or compensation for the taking of or exercise of rights with respect to the property of others by overflight or other operation of aircraft in proximity thereto.

II. LIMITS OF LIABILITY

The limit of liability for Premises Medical Payments Coverage stated in the schedule as applicable to "each person" is the limit of the company's liability for all **medical expense** for **bodily injury** to any one person as the result of any one accident; but subject to the above provision respecting "each person", the total liability of the company under Premises Medical Payments Coverage for all **medical expense** for **bodily injury** to two or more persons as the result of any one accident shall not exceed the limit of liability stated in the schedule as applicable to "each accident".

When more than one medical payments coverage afforded by this policy applies to the loss, the company shall not be liable for more than the amount of the highest applicable limit of liability.

III. ADDITIONAL DEFINITIONS

When used in reference to this insurance (including endorsements forming a part of the policy):

"insured premises" means all premises owned by or rented to the **named insured** with respect to which the **named insured** is afforded coverage for **bodily injury** liability under this policy, and includes the ways immediately adjoining on land;

"medical expense" means expenses for necessary medical, surgical, x-ray and dental services, including prosthetic devices, and necessary ambulance, hospital, professional nursing and funeral services.

IV. POLICY PERIOD; TERRITORY

This insurance aplies only to accidents which occur during the policy period within the United States of America, its territories or possessions, or Canada.

V. ADDITIONAL CONDITION

Medical Reports; Proof and Payment of Claim

As soon as practicable the injured person or someone on his behalf shall give to the company written proof of claim, under oath if required, and shall, after each request from the company, execute authorization to enable the company to obtain medical reports and copies of records. The injured person shall submit to physical examination by physicians selected by the company when and as often as the company may reasonably require. The company may pay the injured person or any person or organization rendering the services and the payment shall reduce the amount payable hereunder for such injury. Payment hereunder shall not constitute an admission of liability of any person or, except hereunder, of the company.

SCHEDULE		
Coverage	Limits of Liability	Advance Premium
E — Premises Medical Payments	$ each person $ each accident	
(a) Premises and operations		$
(b) Escalators		$
(c) Sports activities		$
	Total	$

Policy Issued By .... Policy No. ....

Named Insured ....

This Coverage Part shall not be binding on the Company unless attached to the Declarations Page and Standard Provisions Part of the Company's Airport/Fixed Base Operator's Liability Policy.

When used as a premium basis:

1. **"admissions"** means the total number of persons, other than employees of the **named insured,** admitted to the event insured or to events conducted on the **premises** whether on paid admission tickets, complimentary tickets or passes;

2. **"cost"** means the total cost to the **named insured** with respect to operations performed for the **named insured** during the policy period by independent contractors of all work let or sub-let in connection with each specific project, including the cost of all labor, materials and equipment furnished, used or delivered for use in the execution of such work, whether furnished by the owner, contractor or subcontractor, including all fees, allowances, bonuses or commissions made, paid or due;

3. **"receipts"** means the gross amount of money charged by the **named insured** for such operations by the **named insured** or by others during the policy period as are rated on a receipts basis other than receipts from telecasting, broadcasting or motion pictures, and includes taxes, other than taxes which the **named insured** collects as a separate item and remits directly to a governmental division;

4. **"remuneration"** means the entire remuneration earned during the policy period by proprietors and by all employees of the **named insured,** other than chauffeurs (except operators of mobile equipment) and aircraft pilots and co-pilots, subject to any overtime earnings or limitation of remuneration rule applicable in accordance with the manuals in use by the company;

5. **"sales"** means the gross amount of money charged by the **named insured** or by others trading under his name for all goods and products sold or distributed during the policy period and charged during the policy period for installation, servicing or repair, and includes taxes, other than taxes which the **named insured** and such others collect as a separate item and remit directly to a governmental division.

PERSONAL INJURY LIABILITY INSURANCE

I. COVERAGE P – PERSONAL INJURY LIABILITY

The company will pay on behalf of the **insured** all sums which the **insured** shall become legally obligated to pay as **damages** because of injury (herein called "**personal injury**") sustained by any person or organization and arising out of one or more of the following offenses committed in the conduct of the **named insured's** business:

Group A – false arrest, detention or imprisonment, or malicious prosecution;

Group B – the publication or utterance of a libel or slander of other defamatory or disparaging material, or a publication or utterance in violation of an individual's right of privacy; except publications or utterances in the course of or related to advertising, broadcasting or telecasting activities conducted by or on behalf of the **named insured;**

Group C – wrongful entry or eviction, or other invasion of the right of private occupancy;

if such offense is committed during the policy period within the United States of America, its territories or possessions, or Canada, and the company shall have the right and duty to defend any suit against the **insured** seeking **damages** on account of such **personal injury** even if any of the allegations of the suit are groundless, false or fraudulent, and may make such investigation and settlement of any claim or suit as it deems expedient, but the company shall not be obligated to pay any claim or judgment or to defend any suit after the applicable limit of the company's liability has been exhausted by payment of judgments or settlements.

Exclusions

This insurance does not apply:

(a) to liability assumed by the **insured** under any contract or agreement;

(b) to **personal injury** arising out of the wilful violation of a penal statute or ordinance committed by or with the knowledge or consent of any **insured;**

(c) to **personal injury** sustained by any person as a result of an offense directly or indirectly related to the employment of such person by the **named insured;**

(d) to **personal injury** arising out of any publication or utterance described in Group B, if the first injurious publication or utterance of the same or similar material by or on behalf of the **named insured** was made prior to the effective date of this insurance;

(e) to **personal injury** arising out of a publication or utterance described in Group B concerning any organization or business enterprise, or its products or services, made by or at the direction of any **insured** with knowledge of the falsity thereof;

(f) (1) to **personal injury** arising out of

    (i) **aircraft noise,** or

    (ii) interference with the quiet enjoyment of property by overflight or other operation of aircraft in proximity thereto, or

    (2) to sums claimed or awarded as **damages** to the extent that such sums represent payment or compensation for the taking of or exercise of rights with respect to the property of others by overflight or other operation of aircraft in proximity thereto.

II. PERSONS INSURED

Each of the following is an **insured** under this insurance to the extent set forth below:

(a) if the **named insured** is designated in the declarations as an individual, the person so designated and his spouse;

(b) if the **named insured** is designated in the declarations as a partnership or joint venture, the partnership or joint venture so designated and any partner or member thereof but only with respect to his liability as such;

(c) if the **named insured** is designated in the declarations as other than an individual, partnership or joint venture, the organization so designated and any executive officer, director or stockholder thereof while acting within the scope of his duties as such.

This insurance does not apply to **personal injury** arising out of the conduct of any partnership or joint venture of which the **insured** is a partner or member and which is not designated in this policy as a **named insured.**

III. LIMITS OF LIABILITY INSUREDS PARTICIPATION

Regardless of the number of (1) **insureds** under this policy, (2) persons or organizations who sustain **personal injury,** or (3) claims made or suits brought on account of **personal injury,** the total limit of the company's liability under this coverage for all **damages** shall not exceed the limit of **personal injury** liability stated in the schedule as "aggregate".

If a participation percentage is stated in the schedule for the **insured,** the company shall not be liable for a greater proportion of any loss than the difference between such percentage and one hundred percent and the balance of the loss shall be borne by the **insured;** provided, the company may pay the **insured's** portion of a loss to effect settlement of the loss, and, upon notification of the action taken, the **named insured** shall promptly reimburse the company therefor.

IV. ADDITIONAL DEFINITION

When used in reference to this insurance:

"**damages**" means only those damages which are payable because of **personal injury** arising out of an offense to which this insurance applies.

SCHEDULE

Coverage	Limits of Liability
P. Personal Injury Liability The insurance afforded is only with respect to **personal injury** arising out of an offense included within such of the following groups of offenses as are indicated by specific premium charge or charges.	$ aggregate Insured's Participation..........%

Groups of Offenses	Advance Premium
A. False Arrest, Detention or Imprisonment, or Malicious Prosecution	$
B. Libel, Slander, Defamation or Violation of Right of Privacy	$
C. Wrongful Entry or Eviction or Other Invasion of Right of Private Occupancy	$

Minimum Premium $ Total Advance Premium	$

Policy Issued By...Policy No...

Named Insured...

This Coverage Part shall not be binding on the Company unless attached to the Declarations Page and Standard Provisions Part of the Company's Airport/Fixed Base Operator's Liability Policy.

When used as a premium basis:

1. **"admissions"** means the total number of persons, other than employees of the **named insured,** admitted to the event insured or to events conducted on the **premises** whether on paid admission tickets, complimentary tickets or passes;

2. **"cost"** means the total cost to the **named insured** with respect to operations performed for the **named insured** during the policy period by independent contractors of all work let or sub-let in connection with each specific project, including the cost of all labor, materials and equipment furnished, used or delivered for use in the execution of such work, whether furnished by the owner, contractor or subcontractor, including all fees, allowances, bonuses or commissions made, paid or due;

3. **"receipts"** means the gross amount of money charged by the **named insured** for such operations by the **named insured** or by others during the policy period as are rated on a receipts basis other than receipts from telecasting, broadcasting or motion pictures, and includes taxes, other than taxes which the **named insured** collects as a separate item and remits directly to a governmental division;

4. **"remuneration"** means the entire remuneration earned during the policy period by proprietors and by all employees of the **named insured,** other than chauffeurs (except operators of mobile equipment) and aircraft pilots and co-pilots, subject to any overtime earnings or limitation of remuneration rule applicable in accordance with the manuals in use by the company;

5. **"sales"** means the gross amount of money charged by the **named insured** or by others trading under his name for all goods and products sold or distributed during the policy period and charged during the policy period for installation, servicing or repair, and includes taxes, other than taxes which the **named insured** and such others collect as a separate item and remit directly to a governmental division.

HANGAR KEEPERS' LIABILITY INSURANCE – COVERAGE PART

I. COVERAGE K – HANGAR KEEPERS' LIABILITY

The company will pay on behalf of the **insured** all sums which the **insured** shall become legally obligated to pay as damages because of **loss** to an **aircraft** (provided, with respect to each **loss** each **aircraft,** there shall be deducted an amount equal to the applicable deductible amount stated in the schedule unless such **loss** results from Fire or Explosion or while the **aircraft** is dismantled and being transported) occurring while such **aircraft** is in the custody of the **insured** at the premises stated in the schedule for safekeeping, storage, service or repair, and the company shall have the right and duty to defend any suit against the **insured** seeking **damages** on account of such **loss,** even if any of the allegations of the suit are groundless, false or fraudulent, and may make such investigation and settlement of any claim or suit as it deems expedient, but the company shall not be obligated to pay any claim or judgment or to defend any suit after the applicable limit of the company's liability has been exhausted by payment of judgments or settlements.

The Supplementary Payments provisions of the policy are applicable to the insurance afforded for hangar keepers' liability, except the provisions with respect to the cost of bail bonds and expenses for first aid.

Exclusions

This insurance does not apply:

(a) to the liability of the **insured** under any agreement to be responsible for **loss;**

(b) to **loss** to robes, wearing apparel, personal effects or merchandise of any description, whether the aircraft in which they are contained is stolen or damaged or not;

(c) to an aircraft owned by or rented to

    (i) the **named insured** or a partner therein or a member thereof, or the spouse of any one of them, if a resident of the same household,

    (ii) an employee of the **named insured** or his spouse, if a resident of the same household, unless the aircraft is in the custody of the **named insured** under an agreement for which a specific pecuniary charge has been made;

(d) to **loss** by theft due to any fraudulent, dishonest or criminal act by the **named insured,** a partner therein, a member thereof or employee, trustee or authorized representative thereof, whether working or otherwise and whether acting alone or in collusion with others;

(e) to defective parts, accessories or materials furnished or to faulty work performed on an aircraft, out of which **loss** arises;

(f) to **loss** to an aircraft while **in flight;**

(g) to **loss** due to war, whether or not declared, civil war, insurrection, rebellion or revolution, or any act or condition incident to any of the foregoing;

(h) to **loss** due to radioactive contamination.

II. PERSONS INSURED

Each of the following is an **insured** under this insurance to the extent set forth below:

(a) the **named insured;**

(b) any employee, director or stockholder of the **named insured** while acting within the scope of his duties as such; and

(c) if the **named insured** is designated in the declarations as a partnership or joint venture, any partner or member thereof but only with respect to his liability as such.

III. LIMITS OF LIABILITY

Regardless of the number of (1) **insureds** under this policy, (2) persons or organizations who sustain **loss,** (3) claims made or suits brought on account of **loss,** or (4) aircraft to which this policy applies, the company's liability is limited as follows:

Coverage K – Subject to the applicability of any deductible, the limit of hangar keepers' liability stated in the schedule as applicable to "each aircraft" is the limit of the company's liability for all **damages** because of **loss** sustained by any one **aircraft;** but subject to the above provision respecting "each aircraft" the total liability of the company for all **damages** because of **loss** sustained by two or more **aircraft** at the same time or as a result of exposure to substantially the same general conditions shall not exceed the limit of hangar keepers' liability stated in the schedule as applicable to "each loss".

Repairs by the **named insured** shall be adjusted at actual cost to him of labor (at regular rates with no allowance for overtime or other premium payments unless authorized by the Company) and materials.

All of the terms of this policy apply irrespective of the application of any deductible amount and the company may pay any part or all of the deductible amount to effect settlement of any claim or suit and, upon notification of the action taken, the **insured** shall promptly reimburse the company for such part of the deductible amount as has been paid by the company.

IV. POLICY PERIODS; TERRITORY

This insurance applies only to **loss** which occurs during the policy period within the territory described in paragraph (1) or (2) of the definition of **policy territory.**

V. ADDITIONAL DEFINITIONS

When used in reference to this insurance (including endorsements forming a part of the policy):

"aircraft" means any aircraft including engines, propellers, operating and navigating instruments and radio equipment attached to or usually attached to or carried on the aircraft, including component parts detached and not replaced by other similar parts, and tools therein which are standard for the make and type of aircraft;

"in flight" means the time commencing with the actual take-off run of the aircraft and continuing thereafter until it has completed its landing run;

"loss" means direct and accidental loss of or damage to tangible property.

VI. ADDITIONAL CONDITION

Insured's Duties in the Event of Loss:

The insured's duties in event of **loss** shall be as provided in the condition with respect to an **occurrence,** claim or suit. In the event of theft or larceny, the **insured** shall also promptly notify the police.

SCHEDULE		
Coverage	Limits of Liability	Advance Premium
K. Hangar Keepers' Liability	$ Each Aircraft	
	$ Each Loss	$

HANGAR KEEPERS' HAZARDS

Description of Premises	Code No.	Premium Bases	Rates	Advance Premium

HANGAR KEEPERS' MINIMUM PREMIUMS

$

Policy No... of the...

Named Insured...

This Coverage Part shall not be binding on the Company unless attached to the Declarations Page and Standard Provisions Part of the Company's Airport/Fixed Base Operator's Liability Policy.

When used as a premium basis:

1. **"admissions"** means the total number of persons, other than employees of the **named insured,** admitted to the event insured or to events conducted on the **premises** whether on paid admission tickets, complimentary tickets or passes;

2. **"cost"** means the total cost to the **named insured** with respect to operations performed for the **named insured** during the policy period by independent contractors of all work let or sub-let in connection with each specific project, including the cost of all labor, materials and equipment furnished, used or delivered for use in the execution of such work, whether furnished by the owner, contractor or subcontractor, including all fees, allowances, bonuses or commissions made, paid or due;

3. **"receipts"** means the gross amount of money charged by the **named insured** for such operations by the **named insured** or by others during the policy period as are rated on a receipts basis other than receipts from telecasting, broadcasting or motion pictures, and includes taxes, other than taxes which the **named insured** collects as a separate item and remits directly to a governmental division;

4. **"remuneration"** means the entire remuneration earned during the policy period by proprietors and by all employees of the **named insured,** other than chauffeurs (except operators of mobile equipment) and aircraft pilots and co-pilots, subject to any overtime earnings or limitation of remuneration rule applicable in accordance with the manuals in use by the company;

5. **"sales"** means the gross amount of money charged by the **named insured** or by others trading under his name for all goods and products sold or distributed during the policy period and charged during the policy period for installation, servicing or repair, and includes taxes, other than taxes which the **named insured** and such others collect as a separate item and remit directly to a governmental division.

AAU **ASSOCIATED AVIATION UNDERWRITERS**

SPECIAL AIRPORT PROVISIONS

Applicable to Comprehensive General Liability Insurance and Owners', Landlords' and Tenants' Liability Insurance

With respect to the premises designated in the policy as an airport and all operations necessary or incidental thereto:

1. The "Persons Insured" provision is amended to include any airport manager of the **named insured** while acting within the scope of his duties as such.

2. Subdivision (3) of exclusion (k) relating to **property damage** to property in the control of the **insured** or **property damage** to property as to which the **insured** for any purpose is exercising physical control does not apply to **property damage** to aircraft when the insured's control is solely traffic control over the movement of such aircraft.

3. Exclusion (b) applies only to aircraft owned by or rented or loaned to the **insured** or **in flight** by or for the account of the **insured.**

4. The insurance does not apply:

   (a) (1) to the conduct of any contest or exhibition permitted, sponsored or participated in, by the insured, or

       (2) to the ownership, maintenance or use of

           (i) grandstands, bleachers or observation platforms other than observation decks or promenades which are part of permanent structures on the premises, or

           (ii) swimming pools, or

           (iii) lodging accommodations for the general public, or

           (iv) schools other than pilot training schools, or

       (3) with respect to restaurants operated by the **named insured** or by others trading under his name, to **bodily injury** or **property damage** arising out of

           (i) the **named insured's products,** or

           (ii) reliance upon a representation or warranty made with respect thereto

           if the **bodily injury** or **property damage** occurs after physical possession of such products has been relinquished to others,

       provided that any subdivision of this subparagraph (a) does not apply when specifically stated below or in the policy to be inapplicable.

   (b) to that portion of any loss arising out of the ownership, maintenance or use of aircraft or **automobiles** with respect to which the **insured** has other valid and collectible insurance, whether primary or excess.

5. The term **"in flight"** means the time commencing with the actual take-off run of the aircraft and continuing thereafter until it has completed its landing run.

STANDARD PROVISIONS PART — AIRPORT/FIXED BASE OPERATOR'S LIABILITY POLICY

SUPPLEMENTARY PAYMENTS

The company will pay, in addition to the applicable limit of liability:

(a) all expenses incurred by the company, all costs taxed against the **insured** in any suit defended by the company and all interest on the entire amount of any judgment therein which accrues after entry of the judgment and before the company has paid or tendered or deposited in court that part of the judgment which does not exceed the limit of the company's liability thereon;

(b) premiums on appeal bonds required in any such suit, premiums on bonds to release attachments in any such suit for an amount not in excess of the applicable limit of liability of this policy, and the cost of bail bonds required of the **insured** because of accident or traffic law violation arising out of the use of any vehicle to which this policy applies, not to exceed $250 per bail bond, but the company shall have no obligation to apply for or furnish any such bonds;

(c) expenses incurred by the **insured** for first aid to others at the time of an accident, for **bodily injury** to which this policy applies;

(d) reasonable expenses incurred by the **insured** at the company's request (in assisting the company in the investigation or defense of any claim or suit,) including actual loss of earnings not to exceed $25 per day.

DEFINITIONS

When used in this policy (including endorsements forming a part hereof):

"**aircraft noise**" means the noise of aircraft and the vibration associated therewith and also includes the phenomenon called sonic boom;

"**automobile**" means a land motor vehicle, trailer or semi-trailer designed for travel on public roads (including any machinery or apparatus attached thereto), but does not include **mobile equipment;**

"**bodily injury**" means bodily injury, sickness or disease sustained by any person which occurs during the policy period, including death at any time resulting therefrom;

"**completed operations hazard**" includes **bodily injury** and **property damage** arising out of operations or reliance upon a representation or warranty made at any time with respect thereto, but only if the **bodily injury** or **property damage** occurs after such operations have been completed or abandoned and occurs away from premises owned by or rented to the **named insured.** "Operations" include materials, parts or equipment furnished in connection therewith. Operations shall be deemed completed at the earliest of the following times:

(1) when all operations to be performed by or on behalf of the **named insured** under the contract have been completed,

(2) when all operations to be performed by or on behalf of the **named insured** at the site of the operations have been completed, or

(3) when the portion of the work out of which the injury or damage arises has been put to its intended use by any person or organization other than another contractor or subcontractor engaged in performing operations for a principal as a part of the same project.

DEFINITIONS (continued)

Operations which may require further service or maintenance work, or correction, repair or replacement because of any defect or deficiency, but which are otherwise complete, shall be deemed completed.

The **completed operations hazard** does not include **bodily injury** or **property damage** arising out of

(a) operations in connection with the transportation of property, unless the **bodily injury** or **property damage** arises out of a condition in or on a vehicle created by the loading or unloading thereof,

(b) the existence of tools, uninstalled equipment or abandoned or unused materials, or

(c) operations for which the classification stated in the policy or in the company's manual specifies "including completed operations";

"**elevator**" means any hoisting or lowering device to connect floors or landings, whether or not in service, and all appliances thereof including any car, platform, shaft, hoistway, stairway, runway, power equipment and machinery; but does not include an **automobile** servicing hoist, or a hoist without a platform outside a building if without mechanical power or if not attached to building walls, or a hod or material hoist used in alteration, construction or demolition operations, or an inclined conveyor used exclusively for carrying property or a dumbwaiter used exclusively for carrying property and having a compartment height not exceeding four feet;

"**incidental contract**" means any written (1) lease of premises, (2) easement agreement, except in connection with construction or demolition operations on or adjacent to a railroad, (3) undertaking to indemnify a municipality required by municipal ordinance, except in connection with work for the municipality, (4) sidetrack agreement, or (5) **elevator** maintenance agreement;

"**insured**" means any person or organization qualifying as an insured in the "Persons Insured" provision of the applicable insurance coverage. The insurance afforded applies separately to each **insured** against whom claim is made or suit is brought, except with respect to the limits of the company's liability;

"**mobile equipment**" means a land vehicle (including any machinery or apparatus attached thereto), whether or not self-propelled, (1) not subject to motor vehicle registration, or (2) maintained for use exclusively on premises owned by or rented to the **named insured,** including the ways immediately adjoining, or (3) designed for use principally off public roads, or (4) designed or maintained for the sole purpose of affording mobility to equipment of the following types forming an integral part of or permanently attached to such vehicle: power cranes, shovels, loaders, diggers and drills; concrete mixers (other than the mix-in-transit type); graders, scrapers, rollers and other road construction or repair equipment; air-compressors, pumps and generators, including spraying, welding and building cleaning equipment; and geophysical exploration and well servicing equipment;

"**named insured**" means the person or organization named in Item 1. of the declarations of this policy;

"**named insured's products**" means goods or products manufactured, sold, handled or distributed by the **named insured** or by others trading under his name, including any container thereof (other than a vehicle), but "**named insured's products**" shall not include a vending machine or any property other than such container, rented to or located for use of others but not sold;

"occurrence" means an accident, including continuous or repeated exposure to conditions, which results in **bodily injury** or **property damage** neither expected nor intended from the standpoint of the **insured;**

"policy territory" means:

(1) the United States of America, its territories or possessions, or Canada, or

(2) international waters or air space, provided the **bodily injury** or **property damage** does not occur in the course of travel or transportation to or from any other country, state or nation, or

(3) anywhere in the world with respect to damages because of **bodily injury** or **property damage** arising out of a product which was sold for use or consumption within the territory described in paragraph (1) above, provided the original suit for such damages is brought within such territory;

"products hazard" includes **bodily injury** and **property damage** arising out of the **named insured's products** or reliance upon a representation or warranty made at any time with respect thereto, but only if the **bodily injury** or **property damage** occurs away from premises owned by or rented to the **named insured** and after physical possession of such products has been relinquished to others;

"property damage" means (1) physical injury to or destruction of tangible property which occurs during the policy period, including the loss of use thereof at any time resulting therefrom, or (2) loss of use of tangible property which has not been physically injured or destroyed provided such loss of use is caused by an **occurrence** during the policy period;

CONDITIONS

1. Premium. All premiums for this policy shall be computed in accordance with the company's rules, rates, rating plans, premiums and minimum premiums applicable to the insurance afforded herein.

Premium designated in this policy as "advance premium" is a deposit premium only which shall be credited to the amount of the earned premium due at the end of the policy period. At the close of each period (or part thereof terminating with the end of the policy period) designated in the declarations as the audit period the earned premium shall be computed for such period and, upon notice thereof to the **named insured,** shall become due and payable. If the total earned premium for the policy period is less than the premium previously paid, the company shall return to the **named insured** the unearned portion paid by the **named insured.**

The **named insured** shall maintain records of such information as is necessary for premium computation, and shall send copies of such records to the company at the end of the policy period and at such times during the policy period as the company may direct.

2. Inspection and Audit. The company shall be permitted but not obligated to inspect the **named insured's** property and operations at any time. Neither the company's right to make inspections nor the making thereof nor any report thereon shall

constitue an undertaking, on behalf of or for the benefit of the **named insured** or others, to determine or warrant that such property or operations are safe or healthful, or are in compliance with any law, rule or regulation.

The company may examine and audit the **named insured's** books and records at any time during the policy period and extensions thereof and within three years after the final termination of this policy, as far as they relate to the subject matter of this insurance.

3. Financial Responsibility Laws. When this policy is certified as proof of financial responsibility for the future under the provisions of any motor vehicle financial responsibility law, such insurance as is afforded by this policy for **bodily injury** liability or for **property damage** liability shall comply with the provisions of such law to the extent of the coverage and limits of liability required by such law. The **insured** agrees to reimburse the company for any payment made by the company which it would not have been obligated to make under the terms of this policy except for the agreement contained in this paragraph.

4. Insured's Duties in the Event of Occurrence, Claim or Suit.

(a) In the event of an **occurrence,** written notice containing particulars sufficient to identify the **insured** and also reasonably obtainable information with respect to the time, place and circumstances thereof, and the names and addresses of the injured and of available witnesses, shall be given by or for the **insured** to the company or any of its authorized agents as soon as practicable.

(b) If claim is made or suit is brought against the **insured,** the **insured** shall immediately forward to the company every demand, notice, summons or other process received by him or his representative.

(c) The **insured** shall cooperate with the company and, upon the company's request, assist in making settlements, in the conduct of suits and in enforcing any right of contribution or indemnity against any person or organization who may be liable to the **insured** because of injury or damage with respect to which insurance is afforded under this policy; and the **insured** shall attend hearings and trials and assist in securing and giving evidence and obtaining the attendance of witnesses. The **insured** shall not, except at his own cost, voluntarily make any payment, assume any obligation or incur any expense other than for first aid to others at the time of accident.

5. Action Against Company. No action shall lie against the company, unless, as a condition precedent thereto, there shall have been full compliance with all of the terms of this policy, nor until the amount of the **insured's** obligation to pay shall have been finally determined either by judgment against the **insured** after actual trial or by written agreement of the **insured,** the claimant and the company.

Any person or organization or the legal representative thereof who has secured such judgment or written agreement shall thereafter be entitled to recover under this policy to the extent of the insurance afforded by this policy. No person or organization shall have any right under this policy to join the company as a party to any action against the **insured** to determine the **insured's liability,** nor shall the company be impleaded by the **insured** or his legal representative. Bankruptcy or insolvency of the **insured** or of the **insured's** estate shall not relieve the company of any of its obligations hereunder.

6. Other Insurance. The insurance afforded by this policy is primary insurance, except when stated to apply in excess of or contingent upon the absence of other insurance. When this insurance is primary and the **insured** has other insurance which is stated to be applicable to the loss on an excess or contingent basis, the amount of the company's liability under this policy shall not be reduced by the existence of such other insurance.

When both this insurance and other insurance apply to the loss on the same basis, whether primary, excess or contingent, the company shall not be liable under this policy for a greater proportion of the loss than that stated in the applicable contribution provision below:

(a) **Contribution by Equal Shares.** If all of such other valid and collectible insurance provides for contribution by equal shares, the company shall not be liable for a greater proportion of such loss than would be payable if each insurer contributes an equal share until the share of each insurer equals the lowest applicable limit of liability under any one policy or the full amount of the loss is paid, and with respect to any amount of loss not so paid the remaining insurers then continue to contribute equal shares of the remaining amount of the loss until each such insurer has paid its limit in full or the full amount of the loss is paid.

(b) **Contribution by Limits.** If any of such other insurance does not provide for contribution by equal shares, the company shall not be liable for a greater proportion of such loss than the applicable limit of liability under this policy for such loss bears to the total applicable limit of liability of all valid and collectible insurance against such loss.

7. Subrogation. In the event of any payment under this policy, the company shall be subrogated to all the **insured's** rights of recovery therefor against any person or organization and the **insured** shall execute and deliver instruments and papers and do whatever else is necessary to secure such rights. The **insured** shall do nothing after loss to prejudice such rights.

8. Changes. Notice to any agent or knowledge possessed by any agent or by any other person shall not effect a waiver or a change in any part of this policy or estop the company from asserting any right under the terms of this policy; nor shall the terms of this policy be waived or changed, except by endorsement issued to form a part of this policy, signed by a duly authorized representative of the company.

9. Assignment. Assignment of interest under this policy shall not bind the company until its consent is endorsed hereon; if, however, the **named insured** shall die, such insurance as is afforded by this policy shall apply (1) to the **named insured's** legal representative, as the **named insured,** but only while acting within the scope of his duties as such, and (2) with respect to the property of the **named insured,** to the person having proper temporary custody thereof, as **insured,** but only until the appointment and qualification of the legal representative.

10. Three Year Policy. If this policy is issued for a period of three years any limit of the company's liability stated in this policy as "aggregate" shall apply separately to each consecutive annual period thereof.

11. Cancellation. This policy may be cancelled by the **named insured** by surrender thereof to the company or any of its authorized agents or by mailing to the company written notice stating when thereafter the cancellation shall be effective. This policy may be cancelled by the company by mailing to the **named insured** at the address shown in this policy, written notice stating when not less than ten days thereafter such cancellation shall be effective. The mailing of notice as aforesaid shall be sufficient proof of notice. The time of surrender or the effective date and hour of cancellation stated in the notice shall become the end of the policy period. Delivery of such written notice either by the **named insured** or by the company shall be equivalent to mailing.

If the **named insured** cancels, earned premium shall be computed in accordance with the customary short rate table and procedure. If the company cancels, earned premium shall be computed pro rata. Premium adjustment may be made either at the time cancellation is effected or as soon as practicable after cancellation becomes effective, but payment or tender of unearned premium is not a condition of cancellation.

12. Declarations. By acceptance of this policy, the **named insured** agrees that the statements in the declarations are his agreements and representations, that this policy is issued in reliance upon the truth of such representations and that this policy embodies all agreements existing between himself and the company or any of its agents relating to this insurance.

NUCLEAR ENERGY LIABILITY EXCLUSION — (Broad Form)

I. Subject to the Provisions of paragraph III of this Endorsement, it is agreed that the policy and any endorsement used therewith, regardless of whether such endorsement makes the policy exclusions inapplicable does not apply:

A. Under any Liability Coverage, to **bodily injury** or **property damage**

(1) with respect to which an **insured** under the policy is also an **insured** under a nuclear energy liability policy issued by Nuclear Energy Liability Insurance Association, Mutual Atomic Energy Liability Underwriters or Nuclear Insurance Association of Canada, or would be an insured under any such policy but for its termination upon exhaustion of its limit of liability; or

(2) resulting from the hazardous properties of nuclear material and with respect to which (a) any person or organization is required to maintain financial protection pursuant to the Atomic Energy Act of 1954, or any law amendatory thereof, or (b) the **insured** is, or had this policy not been issued would be, entitled to indemnity from the United States of America, or any agency thereof, under any agreement entered into by the United States of America, or any agency thereof, with any person or organization.

B. Under any Medical Payments Coverage, or under any Supplementary Payments provision relating to first aid, to expenses incurred with respect to **bodily injury** resulting from the **hazardous properties** of **nuclear mate-**

rial and arising out of the operation of a **nuclear facility** by any person or organization.

C. Under any Liability Coverage, to **bodily injury** or **property damage** resulting from the **hazardous properties** of **nuclear material,** if

(1) the **nuclear material** (a) is at any **nuclear facility** owned by, or operated by or on behalf of, an **insured** or (b) has been discharged or dispersed therefrom;

(2) the **nuclear material** is contained in **spent fuel** or **waste** at any time possessed, handled, used, processed, stored, transported or disposed of by or on behalf of an **insured;** or

(3) the **bodily injury** or **property damage** arises out of the furnishing by an **insured** of services, materials, parts or equipment in connection with the planning, construction, maintenance, operation or use of any **nuclear facility,** but if such facility is located within the United States of America, its territories or possessions or Canada, this exclusion (3) applies only to **property damage** to such **nuclear facility** and any property thereat.

II. As used in this endorsement:

"hazardous properties" include radioactive, toxic or explosive properties;

"nuclear material" means **source material, special nuclear material** or **byproduct material;**

"source material", "special nuclear material", and **"byproduct material"** have the meanings given them in the Atomic Energy Act of 1954 or in any law amendatory thereof;

"spent fuel" means any fuel element or fuel component, solid or liquid, which has been used or exposed to radiation in a **nuclear reactor;**

"waste" means any waste material (1) containing **byproduct material** and (2) resulting from the operation by any person or organization of any **nuclear facility** included within the definition of **nuclear facility** under paragraph (a) or (b) thereof;

"nuclear facility" means

(a) any **nuclear reactor,**

(b) any equipment or device designed or used for (1) separating the isotopes of uranium or plutonium, (2) processing or utilizing **spent fuel,** or (3) handling, processing or packaging **waste.**

(c) any equipment or device used for the processing, fabricating or alloying of **special nuclear material** if at any time the total amount of such material in the custody of the **insured** at the premises where such equipment or device is located consists of or contains more than 25 grams of plutonium or uranium 233 or any combination thereof, or more than 250 grams of uranium 235,

(d) any structure, basin, excavation, premises or place prepared or used for the storage or disposal of **waste,**

and includes the site on which any of the foregoing is located, all operations conducted on such site and all premises used for such operations;

"nuclear reactor" means any apparatus designed or used to sustain nuclear fission in a self-supporting chain reaction or to contain a critical mass of fissionable materail;

"property damage" includes all forms of radioactive contamination of property.

III. The provisions of this endorsement do not apply to (a) family automobile, comprehensive personal and farmer's comprehensive personal insurance nor to (b) liability arising out of the ownership, maintenance or use of any automobile principally garaged or registered in the State of New York.

IN WITNESS WHEREOF, the company has caused this policy to be executed on the Declarations Page which is attached hereto and forms a part hereof.

AMENDMENT TO THE
COMPLETED OPERATIONS AND PRODUCTS LIABILITY INSURANCE — COVERAGE PART

It is agreed that:

(a) this insurance does not apply to **damages** because of **bodily injury** or **property damage** included within the **completed operations hazard** or included within the **products hazard** unless the operations or products are described in the schedule under hazards (d) or (e) — Completed Operations and Products.

(b) with respect to products, if any, described in the schedule under hazard (e) — Products as New Aircraft or Used Aircraft, the exclusion of "**property damage** to the **named insured's products** arising out of such products or any part of such products", shall not apply.

This endorsement is effective..

ALL OTHER TERMS AND CONDITIONS REMAIN UNCHANGED.

Attached to and made part of Policy No. .... of the ....

Issued to: ....

Countersigned ....
              Authorized Representative

By: ....

APPROVED: ASSOCIATED AVIATION UNDERWRITERS

By: ....

Endorsement No. ....

Form No. APL 8(1)A Rev. 1-73

SHORT RATE CANCELATION TABLES

Percent of one and three year premiums earned if policy is canceled during the first year.																	
Days Policy in Force	Policy Term One Year	Policy Term Three Years	Days Policy in Force	Policy Term One Year	Policy Term Three Years	Days Policy in Force	Policy Term One Year	Policy Term Three Years	Days Policy in Force	Policy Term One Year	Policy Term Three Years	Days Policy in Force	Policy Term One Year	Policy Term Three Years	Days Policy in Force	Policy Term One Year	Policy Term Three Years
1	5	2.	37-40	21	8.4	95-98	37	14.8	154-156	53	21.2	219-223	69	27.6	292-296	85	34.
2	6	2.4	41-43	22	8.8	99-102	38	15.2	157-160	54	21.6	224-228	70	28.	297-301	86	34.4
3-4	7	2.8	44-47	23	9.2	103-105	39	15.6	161-164	55	22.	229-232	71	28.4	302-305	87	34.8
5-6	8	3.2	48-51	24	9.6	106-109	40	16.	165-167	56	22.4	233-237	72	28.8	306-310	88	35.2
7-8	9	3.6	52-54	25	10.	110-113	41	16.4	168-171	57	22.8	238-241	73	29.2	311-314	89	35.6
9-10	10	4.	55-58	26	10.4	114-116	42	16.8	172-175	58	23.2	242-246	74	29.6	315-319	90	36.
11-12	11	4.4	59-62	27	10.8	117-120	43	17.2	176-178	59	23.6	247-250	75	30.	320-323	91	36.4
13-14	12	4.8	63-65	28	11.2	121-124	44	17.6	179-182	60	24.	251-255	76	30.4	324-328	92	36.8
15-16	13	5.2	66-69	29	11.6	125-127	45	18.	183-187	61	24.4	256-260	77	30.8	329-332	93	37.2
17-18	14	5.6	70-73	30	12.	128-131	46	18.4	188-191	62	24.8	261-264	78	31.2	333-337	94	37.6
19-20	15	6.	74-76	31	12.4	132-135	47	18.8	192-196	63	25.2	265-269	79	31.6	338-342	95	38.
21-22	16	6.4	77-80	32	12.8	136-138	48	19.2	197-200	64	25.6	270-273	80	32.	343-346	96	38.4
23-25	17	6.8	81-83	33	13.2	139-142	49	19.6	201-205	65	26.	274-278	81	32.4	347-351	97	38.8
26-29	18	7.2	84-87	34	13.6	143-146	50	20.	206-209	66	26.4	279-282	82	32.8	352-355	98	39.2
30-32	19	7.6	88-91	35	14.	147-149	51	20.4	210-214	67	26.8	283-287	83	33.2	356-360	99	39.6
33-36	20	8	92-94	36	14.4	150-153	52	20.8	215-218	68	27.2	288-291	84	33.6	361-365	100	40.

Percent of three year premium earned if a three year policy is canceled during the second or third year.											
Policy in Force One Year Plus Days	Percent Earned	Policy in Force One Year Plus Days	Percent Earned	Policy in Force One Year Plus Days	Percent Earned	Policy in Force Two Years Plus Days	Percent Earned	Policy in Force Two Years Plus Days	Percent Earned	Policy in Force Two Years Plus Days	Percent Earned
1-5	40.4	126-130	50.7	251-255	61.	1-5	70.4	126-130	80.7	251-255	91.
6-10	40.8	131-135	51.1	256-260	61.4	6-10	70.8	131-135	81.1	256-260	91.4
11-15	41.2	136-140	51.5	261-265	61.8	11-15	71.2	136-140	81.5	261-265	91.8
16-20	41.6	141-145	51.9	266-270	62.2	16-20	71.6	141-145	81.9	266-270	92.2
21-25	42.1	146-150	52.3	271-275	62.6	21-25	72.1	146-150	82.3	271-275	92.6
26-30	42.5	151-155	52.7	276-280	63.	26-30	72.5	151-155	82.7	276-280	93.
31-35	42.9	156-160	53.2	281-285	63.4	31-35	72.9	156-160	83.2	281-285	93.4
36-40	43.3	161-165	53.6	286-290	63.8	36-40	73.3	161-165	83.6	286-290	93.8
41-45	43.7	166-170	54.	291-295	64.2	41-45	73.7	166-170	84.	291-295	94.2
46-50	44.1	171-175	54.4	296-300	64.7	46-50	74.1	171-175	84.4	296-300	94.7
51-55	44.5	176-180	54.8	301-305	65.1	51-55	74.5	176-180	84.8	301-305	95.1
56-60	44.9	181-185	55.2	306-310	65.5	56-60	74.9	181-185	85.2	306-310	95.5
61-65	45.3	186-190	55.6	311-315	65.9	61-65	75.3	186-190	85.6	311-315	95.9
66-70	45.8	191-195	56.	316-320	66.3	66-70	75.8	191-195	86.	316-320	96.3
71-75	46.2	196-200	56.4	321-325	66.7	71-75	76.2	196-200	86.4	321-325	96.7
76-80	46.6	201-205	56.9	326-330	67.1	76-80	76.6	201-205	86.9	326-330	97.1
81-85	47.	206-210	57.3	331-335	67.5	81-85	77.	206-210	87.3	331-335	97.5
86-90	47.4	211-215	57.7	336-340	67.8	86-90	77.4	211-215	87.7	336-340	97.9
91-95	47.8	216-220	58.1	341-345	68.4	91-95	77.8	216-220	88.1	341-345	98.4
96-100	48.2	221-225	58.5	346-350	68.8	96-100	78.2	221-225	88.5	346-350	98.8
101-105	48.6	226-230	58.9	351-355	69.2	101-105	78.6	226-230	88.9	351-355	99.2
106-110	49.	231-235	59.3	356-360	69.6	106-110	79.	231-235	89.3	356-360	99.6
111-115	49.5	236-240	59.7	361-365	70.	111-115	79.5	236-240	89.7	361-365	100.
116-120	49.9	241-245	60.1			116-120	79.9	241-245	90.1		
121-125	50.3	246-250	60.6			121-125	80.3	246-250	90.5		

5

AAU-1 (10-82)

Appendix C

Endorsements

1. USAIG All-Clear Liability Coverage while Using Non-Owned Aircraft Endorsement

2. USAIG All-Clear Voluntary Settlement Endorsement

3. AAU Non-Owned Aircraft Endorsement

4. AAU Passenger Voluntary Settlement Endorsement

5. AAU Air Force Form 180 Endorsement

6. AAU Aircraft Engine and Auxiliary Power Unit Endorsement

7. AAU Additional Interest Endorsement

8. AVEMCO Breach of Warranty Endorsement

9. AVEMCO Commercial Purposes Endorsement

10. AVEMCO Commercial General Provisions Endorsement

11. AVEMCO Renter Pilot Extended Liability Coverage Endorsement

12. AVEMCO Commercial Use Pilot Endorsement

13. AVEMCO Seaplane—Amphibious Aircraft Endorsement

14. AVEMCO Component Parts Endorsement

15. AVEMCO Time Out of Force Endorsement

16. AVEMCO Additional Insured Endorsement

17. AVEMCO Hangared Aircraft Endorsement

18. AVEMCO Turbine Powered Aircraft Endorsement

19. AVEMCO Cancellation Change Endorsement—30 Days Notice

USAIG All-Clear
Liability Coverage While Using
Non-Owned Aircraft Endorsement

What this endorsement does. Your business needs may require you rent or borrow aircraft. For this reason, we've developed this endorsement to expand *Your Liability Coverage* to apply while you're using an aircraft you don't own.

Who's covered by this endorsement. The *Who's Covered* section appearing on Page 3 of your policy is changed to read:

   "*Who's covered*
   We'll cover the following organizations while they're using an aircraft which isn't owned in full or in part by them or registered in their name:

   _____

   _____

   We'll also cover employees and directors of the above organizations while they're using an aircraft in their professional capacity for your business. No person will be covered while using an aircraft they partly or wholly own or that is registered in their name or the name of any household member."

   Throughout this section, the words you and your, also include these other people and organizations.

   Each person or organization is covered separately. But we won't pay more for all injury and damage in any one occurrence than the Limit of Coverage shown on the *Coverage Summary Page.*

What aircraft are covered. We'll cover any aircraft you use in your business registered under a "Standard" Category Airworthiness Certificate issued by the Federal Aviation Administration, provided it isn't owned by or registered to any of the organizations stated in the *Who's Covered* section above.

This endorsement does not apply to aircraft covered in the *Your Coverage For Other Aircraft* section appearing on Page 5 of your policy. Nor, to aircraft covered elsewhere in your policy.

Aircraft Use. You agree not to charge anyone for using the aircraft covered under this endorsement. They can, however, reimburse you for operating expenses.

Pilots. The *Pilots* section of the *Coverage Summary Page* will not apply to this coverage.

Limits of your Coverage. You have those coverages under this endorsement for which a dollar amount is filled in. These coverages are the same as the coverages shown on your Coverage Summary Page.

Coverage	Limits of Coverage				
Combined Liability Coverage for bodily injury and property damage	$	Each Occurrence			
Combined Liability Coverage for bodily injury (except to passengers) and property damage	$	Each Occurrence			
Liability Coverage for bodily injury to anyone but passengers	$	Each Person	$		Each Occurrence
Liability Coverage for bodily injury to passengers only	$	Each Person	$		Each Occurrence
Liability Coverage for property damage	$	Each Occurrence			
Medical Coverage	$	Each Person			

See page 2 of this endorsement.

372-AC Rev 9/79

Claims we won't cover. Although this endorsement gives you broad liability coverage for your business use of aircraft you don't own, there are a few claims we won't cover:

We won't cover claims arising out of the use of any aircraft products you manufacture, sell, handle or distribute.

We won't cover damage to any property you own, rent, control or transport.

Reports. You agree to tell us whenever you use an aircraft you don't own for more than seven consecutive days. You will provide us with a detailed description of the aircraft and pay any additional premium.

If you have other insurance. This endorsement provides you with excess insurance. This means if you have other insurance covering a loss that's also covered by this endorsement, we'll pay claims only when all other valid and collectible insurance covering the loss has been exhausted. Of course, this restriction does not apply to any insurance you purchased in excess of this endorsement.

If any other insurance written through the Aviation Managers covers the loss, the Limit of Coverage under this policy will be reduced by the Limit of Coverage under the other insurance.

Additional Premium for this endorsement $

This endorsement does not change any of your coverage except as stated above. It is effective on the date and hour shown below, local Standard Time at the policyholder's address.

Policy issued to:

Endorsement No.	Policy No.	Date and hour endorsement takes effect

Approved: **United States Aviation Underwriters, Inc., Aviation Managers**

by _____

372-AC

USAIG All-Clear
Voluntary Settlement Endorsement

What this endorsement does. Your *Liability Coverage* section on Page 2 of your policy is expanded to include Voluntary Settlement Coverage. With this endorsement, we'll offer on your behalf and at the request of the policyholder, a sum to or for each passenger who receives certain injuries while riding in a covered aircraft with your permission. A passenger is anyone who enters the aircraft to ride in or operate it. It is a requirement of this offer that we receive a complete and final release of all liability for the injuries covered under your *Coverage for Bodily Injury to Passengers Only* or your *Combined Liability Coverage for Bodily Injury and Property Damage.*

What injuries are covered. Offers may be made to or for passengers who, immediately or within 90 days after an accident, die, suffer permanent loss of sight or have an entire hand or foot completely severed in an accident while riding in a covered aircraft with your permission.

What we won't cover. Although this endorsement provides extended coverage, there are a few things we will not cover:

We won't cover anyone acting as a crew member unless crew member is shown as "covered" in the Schedule shown on page 2 of this endorsement.

We won't cover a passenger in any aircraft not listed in the Schedule on Page 2 of this endorsement. But this coverage will apply to substitute aircraft and newly acquired aircraft as described in your *Coverage For Other Aircraft* on Page 5 of your policy.

We won't pay any settlement for loss which arises from declared or undeclared war, invasion, rebellion, or the seizure or detention of your aircraft by any government.

See page 2 of this endorsement.

Unlike *Your Liability Coverage*, the additional coverage under this endorsement applies to injuries covered by workers' compensation, unemployment compensation, disability benefit or similar law. But, the coverage under this endorsement may not be used to satisfy your or your insurance company's obligation under a workers' compensation, unemployment compensation, disability benefit or similar law.

Limits of Settlement. The *Limits of Settlement* shown below for "each person" is the most we'll pay to any one passenger. The *Limits of Settlement* for "each accident" is the most we'll pay for all passengers in any one accident.

If a passenger dies or loses both hands, both feet or both eyes, or a passenger loses one hand or foot *and* one eye, we'll offer up to the *Limits of Settlement* for "each person."

We'll pay up to one-half of the *Limits of Settlement* for "each person" if a passenger loses either one hand, foot or eye.

These *Limits of Settlement* are part of the *Limits of Your Coverage* shown on your Coverage Summary Page for *Bodily Injury to Passengers Only* or *Combined Coverage for Bodily Injury and Property Damage*, and are not in addition to those limits.

Covered Aircraft—Limits of Settlement Schedule

Make and Model	FAA Identification	Limits of Settlement		
		Crew	Each Person □Covered □Not Covered	Each Accident
		S		S
		S		S
		S		S
		S		S
		S		S

If the person to whom we offer a settlement does not accept the offer within 90 days of the time we make it, or brings a suit against you for the injuries which are the subject of the offer, we'll no longer be required to pay any settlement under this endorsement.

Additional Premium for this Endorsement $

This endorsement does not change any of your coverage except as stated above. It is effective on the date and hour shown below, local Standard Time at the policyholder's address.

Policy issued to:

Endorsement No.	Policy No.	Date and hour endorsement takes effect

Approved: **United States Aviation Underwriters, Inc., Aviation Managers**

by

LIABILITY
NON-OWNED AIRCRAFT ENDORSEMENT

In consideration of an additional premium of $ .... it is agreed that such insurance as is provided by Coverages A, B, C, D and E shall apply to the use of *non-owned aircraft* by or on behalf of the **Named Insured,** subject to the following provisions which are applicable only to the coverage afforded by this endorsement and which shall be in addition to all other applicable provisions not herein revised.

1. This insurance does not apply

    (a) while the *non-owned aircraft* is **in flight** unless the **pilot in command** holds a currently effective pilot's certificate issued by the **Federal Aviation Administration,** or

    (b) to **bodily injury** or **property damage** arising out of the *Named Insured's Products.*

2. *"Non-Owned Aircraft"* means any aircraft for which a "Standard" airworthiness certificate has been issued by the **Federal Aviation Administration** other than

    (a) aircraft described in Item 4 of the Declarations,

    (b) aircraft owned in whole or in part by or registered in the name of the **Named Insured,**

    (c) aircraft for which insurance is provided under Insuring Agreement V (Temporary Use of Substitute Aircraft), and

    (d) aircraft which are leased by the **Named insured** for a period in excess of thirty days unless such lease is reported to the company and an additional premium paid if required by the company.

3. *"Named Insured's Products"* means goods or products manufactured, sold, handled or distributed by the **Named Insured** or by others trading under his name.

4. The policy definition of *"Insured"* is revised to read as follows:
    The unqualified word *"Insured"* means (a) the **Named Insured** and (b) any director or executive officer of a **Named Insured** corporation or a partner of a **Named Insured** partnership while such person is acting in his capacity as such provided that no person shall be an *Insured* as respects any aircraft owned in whole or in part by, registered in the name of, or leased for a period in excess of thirty days by such person or any member of his household.

5. The policy provision with respect to Other Insurance is revised to read as follows:
    Except with respect to insurance specifically purchased by the **Named Insured** to apply in excess of this insurance, the insurance provided by this endorsement shall be excess insurance over any other valid and collectible insurance available to the *Insured,* either as an insured under a policy applicable to the *non-owned aircraft* or otherwise and, if such other insurance shall have been written through Associated Aviation Underwriters as primary insurance then the total limit of the Company's liability under all such policies shall not exceed the greater or greatest limit of liability applicable under any one such policy.

ALL OTHER TERMS AND CONDITIONS REMAIN UNCHANGED.

This endorsement is effective ....

Attached to and made part of Policy No. ....of the ....

Issued to: ....

APPROVED: ASSOCIATED AVIATION UNDERWRITERS

by..

Endorsement No. ....

Form 3 GW-(10/77)

LIABILITY

PASSENGER VOLUNTARY SETTLEMENT ENDORSEMENT

1. In consideration of the payment of the premium for Passenger Bodily Injury Liability Coverage, it is agreed that the following coverage is added to Insuring Agreement I:

   Coverage J — Passenger Voluntary Settlement

   (Crew ☐ included ☐ excluded)

   Irrespective of legal liability, to offer to pay on behalf of the **Insured** at the request of the **Named Insured,** benefits as set forth below, to or for the benefit of each **passenger** (excluding any *crew* member unless coverage for *crew* members is indicated above) who sustains **bodily injury** caused by an accident arising out of the ownership, maintenance or use of the *aircraft.*

2. Schedule of Benefits (applicable only when "X" is indicated in the appropriate box).

   If such **bodily injury,** directly and independently of all other causes shall result:

   ☐ (a) within one year of the accident, in (i) the death of the **passenger,** or (ii) the *loss* of any two *members,* then the Company shall offer to pay the sum requested by the **Named Insured** but not exceeding the *settlement limit;* or (iii) the *loss* of any one *member,* then the Company shall offer to pay the sum requested by the **Named Insured** but not exceeding one half of the *settlement limit;*

   ☐ (b) in the injured **passenger** becoming *permanently totally disabled,* the Company shall offer to pay the sum requested by the **Named Insured** but not exceeding the *settlement limit;*

   ☐ (c) in the injured **passenger** becoming *totally disabled,* the Company shall, within thirty days of payment, reimburse the **Named Insured** for payments made to the injured **passenger** for loss of earnings as a result of such disability, but not exceeding (i) eighty percent of the average weekly wage of the injured **passenger** based upon the twelve months period immediately preceding the date of accident, or (ii) one half of one percent of the *settlement limit* or (iii) $250 per week, whichever is the least, for the period of such continuous *total disability* up to a maximum of fifty-two consecutive weeks.

   The amount otherwise due and payable under any one of the foregoing benefits shall be reduced by the amount of any payments previously made under coverage J to or for the same **passenger** as a result of any one accident.

3. Definitions Applicable Only to Coverage J

   "Aircraft" means only the aircraft described in paragraph 4 of this endorsement and any aircraft for which insurance is provided under Insuring Agreements V or VII.

   "Member" means a hand, foot or eye.

   "Loss" means, with respect to a hand or foot, severance at or above the wrist or ankle; with respect to an eye, the entire and irrecoverable loss of sight.

   "Crew" means any person such as the **pilot in command,** co-pilot, flight engineer or flight attendant who is on board the *aircraft* for the purpose of assisting in the operation of the *aircraft.*

   "Totally Disabled" means the complete inability to perform each and every duty pertaining to one's occupation.

   "Permanently Totally Disabled" means the inability of the injured **passenger** after twelve months of being continuously *totally disabled,* to perform each and every duty pertaining to any occupation or employment for wage or profit for the rest of his life.

   "Settlement limit" means the amount set forth in paragraph 4 as the settlement limit for each **passenger.**

4.

DESCRIPTION OF AIRCRAFT		SETTLEMENT LIMITS		
Year, Make and Model	FAA Identification Number	Each Passenger		Each Accident
		Each Crew Member	Each Non-Crew Member	

The settlement limits for any *aircraft* insured under Insuring Agreements V or VII shall be the same as the highest limits set forth above for any one *aircraft.*

Form 2 GW (7/81)

APPROVED: ASSOCIATED AVIATION UNDERWRITERS

By: ....

5. Additional Exclusion applicable to Coverage J

Coverage J does not apply to **bodily injury** resulting directly or indirectly from war, invasion, civil war, revolution, rebellion, insurrection or warlike operations, whether there be a declaration of war or not.

6. Limits of the Company's Liability — Coverages B or D as applicable

The settlement limits set forth in paragraph 4 of this endorsement are included in and are a part of the limits of liability specified for Coverage B or D and are not in addition thereto. The Company's limit of liability, if any, as set forth in Coverage B for "each person" shall be reduced by the amount of any payment made under Coverage J to or for "each **passenger**" and the Company's limit of liability as set forth in Coverage B or D for "each **occurrence**" shall be reduced by the amount of payments made under Coverage J to or for all **passengers** as the result of "each accident".

7. Limits of the Company's Liability — Coverage J

The total amount which the Company shall offer to pay as respects any one injured **passenger** shall not exceed the amount set forth in paragraph 4 as the settlement limit applicable to "each **passenger**". The total amount which the Company shall offer to pay as respects two or more injured **passengers** in any one accident shall not exceed the amount set forth in paragraph 4 as the settlement limit applicable to "each accident". Payment of any amount to or for any injured **passenger** under the provisions of Coverage B or D shall operate to terminate the Company's obligations under Coverage J with respect to such **passenger.**

8. Additional Conditions applicable to Coverage J

(a) Liability Release Required

Except with respect to Weekly Indemnity Benefits which may be afforded by Coverage J, no payment shall be made until the injured **passenger** and all persons claiming by, through or under said **passenger** shall have executed, in a form acceptable to the Company, a full and final release of all claims for damages for which insurance is provided under Coverage B or D.

(b) Refusal to Accept Offer

If the injured **passenger** and all persons having a claim by, through or under such **passenger** refuse to accept the sum offered, or fail to execute the required release within 90 days of the date of the offer, or if claim is made or if suit is brought against an **Insured** for such **bodily injury,** then this endorsement shall become null and void as respects such **passenger** and the provisions of Coverage B or D shall apply as if this endorsement were not attached to the policy.

(c) Other Insurance

If any other Passenger Voluntary Settlement insurance (or Guest Voluntary Settlement insurance) which is available to or for the benefit of the injured **passenger** shall have been written through Associated Aviation Underwriters, the settlement limits specified in paragraph 4 shall be reduced by the amount of such other insurance.

(d) Physical Examinations and Reports

The injured **passenger,** or someone on his behalf, shall at the request of the Company furnish reasonably obtainable information pertaining to the injuries and execute authorization to enable the Company to obtain medical reports and copies of records. The injured **passenger** shall submit to physical examination by physicians selected by the Company when and as often as the Company may reasonably require.

(e) No admission

Any offer, payment or acceptance of benefits under Coverage J shall not constitute an admission of liability or any other type of admission whatsoever on the part of the Company or of the **Insured.**

(f) Employees of Named Insured

Benefits under Coverage J for any employee of the **Named Insured** shall be paid irrespective of whether such employee may be entitled to compensation or other benefits under Workmen's Compensation law.

9. Policy Provisions

All policy provisions applicable to Coverages B and D shall apply to Coverage J except the Limit of the Company's Liability section and Exclusion (c).

ALL OTHER TERMS AND CONDITIONS REMAIN UNCHANGED.

Attached to and made part of Policy No. ....This endorsement is effective ....

Issued to: ....Endorsement No. ....

LIABILITY — PHYSICAL DAMAGE
AIR FORCE FORM 180 ENDORSEMENT

It is agreed that:

1. The following coverage is added to Part I of this policy:

"Coverage J — Contractual Liability — to pay on behalf of the Insured all sums which the Named Insured by such indemnity provisions as are quoted below from a certain contract, hereinafter referred to, shall become legally obligated to pay as indemnification to the United States Air Force, but only to the extent that indemnification is against loss from (a) the liability assumed by the Named Insured with respect to personnel, equipment, or installations, of or under the control of the United States or (b) the liability imposed upon the United States by law, for damages, including damages for care and loss of services: because of bodily injury, sickness, disease or mental anguish including death at any time resulting therefrom, sustained by any person or because of injury to or destruction of property including loss of use thereof provided the said injury, sickness, disease, mental anguish or destruction is caused by an occurrence and arises out of the ownership, maintenance, or use of the aircraft."

2. The Company's limits of liability under Coverage J set forth in Paragraph 1 hereof are included in and are a part of the limits of liability expressed in Item 3 of the Declarations of this policy and in no event shall the provisions of this endorsement be construed in any way to increase the company's total limits of liability expressed in the said Item 3.

3. Waiver by the Insured of its rights of recovery against the United States of America under the provision quoted below from an agreement between the Insured and the United States Air Force for the use of Air Force Aviation facilities shall not prejudice the insurance afforded under Part III of this policy.

4. The following is a transcript of the provisions of the agreement referred to in Paragraphs 1 and 3 of this endorsement, such provisions being a part of the agreement between the Named Insured and the United States Air Force granting the use of Air Force Aviation facilities to the Named Insured:

"1. The User releases forever the United States, its agencies, and United States personnel, from every liability arising out of the use of any Air Force installation, supplies, or services, by the User. The User will defend, pay, or settle every claim or suit against the United States, its agencies, and United States personnel, by agents or employees of the User or persons claiming through them, or by third parties, and will hold the United States, its agencies, and United States personnel, harmless against every such claim or suit, including attorney fees, costs and expenses, arising out of the use of any Air Force installation, supplies, or services, by the User. EXCEPTION: Death, injury, loss or damage to persons or property resulting solely from the willful misconduct of United States personnel; and, in addition, if the use of the Air Force installation, supplies, or services, is in connection with the performance of an existing contract between the United States and the User, death, injury, loss or damage to persons or property resulting solely from the negligence of United States personnel.

2. The User will pay or settle every claim for death or injury to United States personnel, or for loss or damage to property of or under the control of the United States, arising out of the use of any Air Force installation, supplies, or services, by the User, unless the death, injury, loss or damage results solely from the negligence or willful misconduct of United States personnel.

3. For the purposes of this agreement, the term "United States personnel" shall include:

   a. Military and civilian personnel of the United States acting within the scope of their employment, and

   b. Heirs, successors, executors, administrators, and assigns of such personnel.

4. The User will comply with all pertinent parts of Air Force Regulation 55-20, which is hereby incorporated into this agreement."

5. This endorsement shall apply only with respect to loss or damage arising directly out of the use of the Air Force Aviation facilities described in the agreement referred to in Paragraph 4 of this endorsement and occurring during the period of the said agreement that falls within the effective date of this endorsement and the expiration date of this policy.

3 CHL-A

6. In the event the company, at its option, shall, subsequent to the issuance of a Certificate of Insurance with reference to Air Force Form 180, to the United States Air Force

    (a) reduce the limits of liability of this policy to less than the limits of liability referred to in the said Certificate; or,

    (b) restrict the territorial limits of this policy to less than those referred to in the said Certificate; or,

    (c) cancel the waiver of subrogation referred to in the said Certificate; or,

    (d) cancel this policy,

the Company agrees to notify HQ USAF (PRPO), Washington, D.C. 20330, when not less than 30 days thereafter such change or cancellation shall be effective. In the event the Named Insured requests such change or cancellation, the Company agrees to give such notification as soon as possible after the Named Insured requests such change.

This endorsement is effective ....

All other terms and conditions remain unchanged.

Attached to and forming part of Policy No. .... of the ....

Issued to ....

Countersigned ....   APPROVED: ASSOCIATED AVIATION UNDERWRITERS
                        Authorized Representative

By: ....   By: ....

3 CHL-A   Page 2   Endorsement No. ....

PHYSICAL DAMAGE

AIRCRAFT ENGINE AND AUXILIARY POWER UNIT ENDORSEMENT

In consideration of the premium for which this policy is written it is agreed that with respect to damage to aircraft engines and auxilliary power units insured under this policy

1. foreign object damage (damage caused by object(s) not a part of the engine or its accessories) whether resulting from ingestion or otherwise, shall be considered to be "wear and tear" unless such damage is the result of a single incident which is of sufficient severity to require immediate repairs in compliance with the requirements of the engine manufacturer;

2. damage caused by heat which results from the operation, attempted operation or shutdown of the engine shall be considered to be "wear and tear";

3. damage which is not "wear and tear" shall be subject to the same deductible if any, as is applicable to "in motion" damage;

4. damage caused by the breakdown, failure or malfunction of any engine component, accessory or part shall be considered to be "mechanical breakdown" of the entire engine.

ALL OTHER TERMS AND CONDITIONS REMAIN UNCHANGED.

This endorsement is effective ....

Attached to and made part of Policy No. .... of the ....

Issued to: ....

APPROVED: ASSOCIATED AVIATION UNDERWRITERS

By: ....

Endorsement No. ....

12GW

AA! ASSOCIATED AVIATION UNDERWRITERS

PHYSICAL DAMAGE

(COVERAGE F)

ADDITIONAL INTEREST ENDORSEMENT

In consideration of an additional premium of $_____, it is agreed that with respect to Coverage F of this policy:

1. _____of_____
_____ (hereinafter called the Lienholder) has (have) a financial interest in the **aircraft** described below under a mortgage, lease or other agreement, in the amount of $_____
_____ as of the effective date of this endorsement.

2. This insurance, as to the interest of said Lienholder(s) shall not be invalidated by any act or neglect of the *Named Insured* nor by any change in the title or ownership of the **aircraft;** provided, however, that conversion, embezzlement or secretion of the **aircraft** by the *Named Insured* is not covered hereunder.

3. In case the *Named Insured* shall neglect to pay any premium due under this policy, the Lienholder(s) shall, on demand, pay the same.

4. The Lienholder(s) shall notify the Company of any change of ownership or increase of hazard which shall come to the knowledge of said Lienholder(s) and, unless permitted by the policy, it shall be noted thereon and the Lienholder(s) shall, on demand pay the premium for such increased hazard for the term of the use thereof; otherwise the policy shall be null and void.

5. If the *Named Insured* fails to render proof of loss within the time specified in the policy, the Lienholder(s) shall do so within 60 days thereafter. The Lienholder(s) shall comply with and be subject to all applicable policy Conditions.

6. Whenever the Company shall become obligated to pay the Lienholder(s) any sum for loss or damage under Coverage F and shall claim that, as to the *Named Insured*, no liability existed therefor, the loss shall be adjusted with and payable solely to said Lienholder(s) in an amount not to exceed the lesser of the following:

    (a) the net amount owing to the Lienholder(s) by the *Named Insured* under such mortgage, lease or other agreement, as of the date of the loss or damage if any balance remains after the Lienholder has used all reasonable means to collect the amount due from the *Named Insured*, less (i) installments more than 30 days overdue, (ii) penalties, and (iii) unearned charges,

    or

    (b) the Insured Value of the **aircraft** less any applicable deductible.

7. In the event of a loss payment under the provisions of Paragraph 6 of this endorsement, the Company shall, to the extent of such payment, be thereupon legally subrogated to all the rights of the Lienholder(s) under all securities held as collateral to the debt, or may at its option, pay to the Lienholder(s) the whole principal due or to grow due on the mortgage, lease or other agreement with interest, and shall thereupon receive a full assignment and transfer of the mortgage, lease or other agreement and of all related securities; but no subrogation shall impair the right of the Lienholder(s) to recover the full amount due to said Lienholder(s).

8. The *Named Insured* agrees upon demand of the Company to reimburse the Company for the full amount of any payment made under the provisions of Paragraph 6 of this endorsement.

9. Any loss payable under Coverage F, other than loss payable under the provisions of Paragraph 6 of this endorsement, shall be adjusted with the *Named Insured* and payable to the *Named Insured* and the Lienholder(s) jointly, for the account of all interests.

10. The Company reserves the right to cancel this policy at any time as provided by its terms, but in such case the Company shall notify the Lienholder(s) at the address(es) shown above, when, not less than 30 days thereafter, such cancelation shall be effective as to the interest of the Lienholder(s). The Company shall have the right, on like notice, to cancel this endorsement.

11. As used in this endorsement "Named Insured" means only _____

ALL OTHER TERMS AND CONDITIONS
REMAIN UNCHANGED.

APPROVED:
ASSOCIATED AVIATION UNDERWRITERS

This endorsement is effective _____   By _____

Attached to and made part of Policy No. _____   Endorsement No. _____

Form 5 GW (5/83)

BREACH OF WARRANTY ENDORSEMENT

In consideration of the premium charged it is agreed that:

Loss, if any, under Coverage C of this policy shall be payable as interest may appear to the lienholder named in Item 8 of the declarations and this insurance as to the interest of the bailment lessor, conditional vendor or mortgagee or assignee of bailment lessor, conditional vendor or mortgagee (herein called the lienholder) shall not be invalidated by any act or neglect of the lessee, mortgagor or owner of the within described aircraft nor by any change in the title or ownership of the property; provided, however, that the conversion, embezzlement or secretion by the lessee, mortgagor or purchaser in possession of the property insured under a bailment lease, conditional sale, mortgage or other encumbrance is not covered under such policy, unless specifically insured against and premium paid therefor; and provided, also, that in case the lessee, mortgagor or owner shall neglect to pay any premium due under this policy the lienholder shall, on demand, pay the same.

Provided also, that the lienholder shall notify the company of any change of ownership or increase of hazard which shall come to the knowledge of said lienholder and, unless permitted by this policy, it shall be noted thereon and the lienholder shall, on demand, pay the premium for this increased hazard for the term of the use thereof; otherwise this policy shall be null and void.

The company reserves the right to cancel this policy at any time as provided by its terms, but in such case the company shall notify the lienholder when not less than 30 days thereafter such cancellation shall be effective as to the interest of said lienholder therein and the company shall have the right, on like notice, to cancel this agreement.

If the insured fails to render proof of loss within the time granted in the policy conditions, such lienholder shall do so within 60 days thereafter, in the form and manner as provided by this policy, and, further shall be subject to the provisions of this policy relating to appraisal and time of payment and of bringing suit.

Whenever the company shall pay the lienholder any sum for loss under this policy and shall claim that, as to the lessee, mortgagor or owner, no liability therefor existed, the company shall, to the extent of such payment, be thereupon legally subrogated to all the rights of the party to whom such payment shall be made, under all securities held as collateral to the debt, or may at its option, pay to the lienholder the whole principal due or to grow due on the mortgage with interest, and shall thereupon receive a full assignment and transfer of the mortgage and of all such other securities; but no subrogation shall impair the right of the lienholder to recover the full amount of its claim.

Nothing herein shall be held to vary, waive, alter or extend of any of the terms, conditions, agreements, or warranties of the below mentioned policy, other than as above stated.

(The information below is required only when this endorsement is issued subsequent to preparation of the policy.)

This endorsement shall take effect (mo./day/yr.)   at   standard time at the named insured's address as stated in the declarations.

Endorsement Number   attached to and forming part of Policy Number AV   issued by AVEMCO Insurance Company

to:

David E. Jensen PRESIDENT

Thomas H. Chere SECRETARY

Countersigned _____ , 19___

By:_____
Authorized Representative

AEE-11A (7/71) S

COMMERCIAL PURPOSES ENDORSEMENT

It is agreed that Item 6 "PURPOSES" of the Declarations is amended to read:

Item 6. Purpose for which the aircraft is to be used as defined herein is:

(a) "Pleasure and Business"—personal, pleasure, family and use in direct connection with the insured's business, but excluding (a) instruction of any person not specified by name in Item 7 or (b) any operation for which a charge is made;

(b) "Industrial Aid"—"Pleasure and Business" uses and including transportation of executives, employees, guest or customers but excluding (a) instruction of any person not specified by name in Item 7 or (b) any operation for which a charge is made;

(c) "Limited Commercial"—"Pleasure and Business", "Industrial Aid" uses and including instruction and rental to others, but excluding passenger carrying for hire or reward;

(d) "Commercial Ex Instruction or Rental"—including all of the uses under (a) and (b) above and use of the aircraft for the transportation of passengers and or freight for hire but excluding any use of the aircraft for instruction of or rental to others;

(e) "Commercial"—including all the uses permitted under (c) and (d) above;

(f) "Special Uses" is defined as:

Nothing herein contained shall be held to vary, waive, alter or extend any of the terms, conditions, agreements, or warranties of the below mentioned policy. other than as above stated.

(The information below is required only when this endorsement is issued subsequent to preparation of the policy.)

This endorsement shall take effect (mo./day/yr.)   at   standard time at the named insured's address as stated in the declarations.

Endorsement Number   attached to and forming part of policy Number AV   issued by AVEMCO Insurance Company

to:

                    PRESIDENT

                    SECRETARY

Countersigned _____ , 19 ___

By: _____

               Authorized Representative

AEE-51 (1-75) S

COMMERCIAL GENERAL PROVISIONS ENDORSEMENT

It is agreed that:

1. INSURING AGREEMENT III is amended to include:

   (e) while the aircraft is subject to any rental or lease.

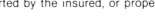

2. INSURING AGREEMENTS IV and VI are deleted in their entirety.

3. INSURING AGREEMENT VIII is amended to read:

   VIII—Policy Period, Territory, Purpose of Use. This policy applies only to occurrences, accidents and losses which happen during the policy period while the aircraft is within the United States of America, its territories or possessions and Canada, or while dismantled and is being transported between ports thereof, and is owned, maintained and used for the purposes stated as applicable thereto in the Declarations.

4. EXCLUSIONS (a), (b), (f) and (g) are amended to read:

   (a) Under Coverage A, to liability assumed by the insured under any contract or agreement;

   (b) Under Coverage A, to injury to or destruction of property owned or transported by the insured, or property rented to or in charge of the insured;

   (f) (4) with respect to starting of the insured aircraft engine(s), to any occurrence or to any loss or damage caused by or resulting from such aircraft moving under its own power or momentum generated there-from unless the aircraft is occupied by a person at the controls who is a properly certificated pilot or mechanic.

   (g) Under Coverages A and C, to any aircraft while in flight;

       (1) not bearing a valid and currently effective "Standard" Airworthiness Category Certificate issued by the Federal Aviation Administration, or

       (2) operated by a Student Pilot (i) carrying passenger(s) or (ii) without the direct supervision of and written approval of a Certified Flight Instructor;

       (3) if used for aerial spraying, seeding, dusting or fertilizing, banner or glider towing, powerline or pipeline patrol, fish spotting, hunting, herding or geological exploration or survey, unless such use is specifically declared and described in this policy;

       (4) involving intentional use, except emergency, of any location other than a designated airport;

       (5) while operated by a pilot renting or leasing the aircraft for any purpose other than as defined under "Pleasure and Business" in Item 6 of the Declarations.

5. DEFINITIONS—Is amended to include the following:
   7. Designated airport—The term "designated airport" means any area designed, generally maintained and customarily used for take-off and landing of aircraft of the same class and type as the insured aircraft, provided such area is approved or so designated by any township, city, county, state or federal authority.

Nothing herein contained shall be held to vary, waive, alter or extend any of the terms, conditions, agreements, or warranties of the below mentioned policy, other than as above stated

(The information below is required only when this endorsement is issued subsequent to preparation of the policy.)

This endorsement shall take effect (mo./day/yr.) _____ at _____ standard time at the named insured's address as stated in the declarations.

Endorsement Number _____ attached to and forming part of policy Number AV _____ issued by AVEMCO Insurance Company

to: _____

_____ PRESIDENT

_____ SECRETARY

Countersigned _____ 19 _____

By: _____

AEE-52 (9-77)   Authorized Representative

RENTER PILOT EXTENDED LIABILITY COVERAGE ENDORSEMENT

In consideration of the premium charged, it is agreed that:

1. Item (d) of INSURING AGREEMENT III—Definition of Insured is deleted in its entirety.

2. INSURING AGREEMENTS IV and VI are deleted in their entirety.

3. INSURING AGREEMENT VIII is amended to read:

   VIII—Policy Period, Territory, Purpose of Use. This policy applies only to occurrences, accidents and losses which happen during the policy period while the aircraft is within the United States of America, its territories or possessions and Canada, or while dismantled and is being transported between ports thereof, and is owned, maintained and used for the purposes stated as applicable thereto in the Declarations.

4. EXCLUSIONS (a), (b), (f) and (g) are amended to read:

   (a) Under Coverage A, to liability assumed by the insured under any contract or agreement;

   (b) Under Coverage A, to injury to or destruction of property owned or transported by the insured, or property rented to or in charge of the insured;

   (f) (4) with respect to starting of the insured aircraft engine(s), to any occurrence or to any loss or damage caused by or resulting from such aircraft moving under its own power or momentum generated therefrom unless the aircraft is occupied by a person at the controls who is a properly certificated pilot or mechanic.

   (g) Under Coverages A and C, to any aircraft while in flight;

       (1) not bearing a valid and currently effective "Standard" Airworthiness Category Certificate issued by the Federal Aviation Agency, or

       (2) operated by a Student Pilot (i) carrying passenger(s) or (ii) without the direct supervision of and written approval of a Certified Flight Instructor;

       (3) if used for aerial spraying, seeding, dusting or fertilizing, banner or glider towing, powerline or pipeline patrol, fish spotting, hunting, herding or geological exploration or survey, unless such use is specifically declared and described in this policy;

       (4) involving intentional use, except emergency, of any location other than a designated airport;

       (5) while operated by a pilot renting or leasing the aircraft for any purpose other than as defined under "Pleasure and Business" in Item 6 of the Declarations.

5. DEFINITIONS—Is amended to include the following:

       (7) Designated airport — The term "designated airport" means any area designed, generally maintained and customarily used for take-off and landing of aircraft of the same class and type as the insured aircraft, provided such area is approved or so designated by any township, city, county, state or federal authority.

Nothing herein contained shall be held to vary, waive, alter or extend any of the terms, conditions, agreements, or warranties of the below mentioned policy, other than as above stated.

(The information below is required only when this endorsement is issued subsequent to preparation of the policy.)

This endorsement shall take effect (mo./day/yr.) _____ at _____ standard time at the named insured's address as stated in the declarations.

Endorsement Number   attached to and forming part of policy Number AV   issued by AVEMCO Insurance Company

SPECIMEN

to:

_____ PRESIDENT

_____ SECRETARY

Countersigned _____ 19 _____

By: _____

Authorized Representative

AEE-59 (3-81)

COMMERCIAL USE PILOT ENDORSEMENT

It is agreed that Item 7 of the Declarations is amended to read:

Item 7. PILOTS: This policy applies when the aircraft is in flight, only while being operated by one of the following pilots who, (1) holds a valid and effective Pilot and Medical Certificate, (2) has a current and recorded Biennial Flight Review, (3) if carrying passengers, has completed at least three take-offs and landings within the preceding 90 days in an aircraft of the same make and model as the insured aircraft and (4) is operating the aircraft for the "Purposes" the aircraft is insured for as defined by this policy:

A. Pleasure and Business, Industrial Aid Use: (Owners and Pilots specified other than Renter Pilots or Commercial Use Pilots)
   (1) _____
   (2) _____ who shall hold a _____ Pilot Certificate and receive _____ hours dual flight instruction and approval of a Certificated Flight Instructor prior to solo of the insured aircraft.
   (3) _____
   _____
   _____
   _____

B. Limited Commercial Use: (Renter Pilots)
   (1) _____
   (2) Any pilot holding a _____ Pilot Certificate with _____ rating and who has not less than _____ Pilot hours, of which at least _____ hours were in _____ _____ type aircraft and _____ hours were in the same model as the insured aircraft.
   (3) Pilot renting insured aircraft shall complete a Check-Ride and receive written approval from a Certificated Flight Instructor prior to solo flight of the insured aircraft.

C. Commercial Use: (Passengers, Cargo or Special Uses Excluding Renter Pilots)
   (1) _____
   (2) Any pilot holding a _____ Pilot Certificate with _____ rating and who has not less than _____ Pilot hours, of which at least _____ hours were in _____ _____ type aircraft and _____ hours were in the same model as the insured aircraft.
   (3) _____
   _____
   _____

D. Any Commercial Pilot employed by an F.A.A. approved Aircraft Repair Station in connection with inspections or repairs to be or that have been performed on the insured aircraft, or by any F.A.A. Inspector, or by any Certificated Flight Instructor for the purpose of instructing anyone specified by this endorsement provided said Flight Instructor is current and qualified to give dual flight instruction in the insured aircraft.

SPECIMEN

This endorsement shall take effect (mo./day/yr.) _____ at _____ standard time at the named insured's address as stated in the declarations.

Nothing herein contained shall be held to vary, waive, alter or extend any of the terms, conditions, agreements, or warranties of the below mentioned policy, other than as above stated.

Endorsement Number _____ attached to and forming part of policy Number AV _____ issued by AVEMCO Insurance Company to:

PRESIDENT

SECRETARY

Countersigned _____ 19 _____

By: _____
Authorized Representative

AEE-53 (8-78) S

SEAPLANE—AMPHIBIOUS AIRCRAFT ENDORSEMENT

We agree with **you** that the following is substituted for Exclusion (1) (f) of **your** Policy:

This Policy does not cover:

(1) **Bodily injury, property damage,** or **aircraft damage** when the **non-owned aircraft** is:

    (f) operated into, on or from a landing area that is not designed, maintained and used as an airport. This exclusion shall not apply:

        (i) to a forced landing due to emergency flight conditions;

        (ii) to a float equipped or amphibious **non-owned aircraft** being operated into, on or from a body of water.

SPECIMEN

The charge for the Endorsement is $ _____.

The information below is required only when this Endorsement is issued after preparation of **your** Policy.

This Endorsement is effective Mo./Day/Yr. _____ at _____ Local Time at **your** address shown in Item 1 of the Data Page.

The Endorsement Number_____is a part of Policy Number _____ issued by AVEMCO INSURANCE COMPANY.

David E. Jensen PRESIDENT

John H. Ballard SECRETARY

COUNTERSIGNED _____ 19___

By: _____
           Authorized Representative

ERNE L (10-82)-1

COMPONENT PARTS ENDORSEMENT

The following is substituted for LIMIT OF LIABILITY in PART II — INSURANCE FOR DAMAGE TO OWNED AIRCRAFT on page 2 of **your** Policy:

LIMIT OF LIABILITY

Our Limit of Liability for **loss:**

(1) To any of the components of **your insured aircraft** shall not exceed the amounts determined by applying the percentage shown in the applicable table below, to the "insured value".

Components	A Fixed Gear Aircraft not equipped with flaps	B Fixed Gear Aircraft equipped with flaps	C Aircraft equipped with rectractable gear	D Biplane	E Multi Engine Aircraft	F Elective Option (Applicable only if percentages are filled in)
Fuselage	20%	20%	20%	15%	20%	
Engine	20	20	20	30	30	
Propeller	5	5	5	4	5	
Left Wing	15	15	15	20	15	
Right Wing	15	15	15	20	15	
Aileron	5	5	5	4	5	
Landing Gear	10	10	10	10	10	
Vertical Stabilizer	5	5	5	4	5	
Rudder	5	5	5	4	5	
Horizontal Stabilizer	5	5	5	4	5	
Elevator	5	5	5	5	2.5	
Flaps	—	5	5	—	2.5	
Instruments, Radios and All Else	15	10	10	5	5	
	125%	125%	125%	125%	125%	125%

The amount determined for each component part includes labor, transportation and other charges necessary to the repair or replacement of the part. If **your insured aircraft** has more than one of each of the components listed, the percentage shown for that component will be pro rated for each. The percentage for Instruments, Radios and All Else will not be pro rated. **Our** liability for **loss** shall not exceed the "insured value" however;

(2) To a replacement or additional aircraft is the highest "insured value" for any **insured aircraft**. But **our** liability is not more than the cost to **you** of the aircraft. In either case, the highest "deductible" applies;

(3) Is reduced by the amount of prior damage to **your insured aircraft**. It increases by the value of finished repairs until the "insured value" is reached.

The applicable "deductible" will apply to all **losses** except **loss** caused by a collision of **your insured aircraft** with another of **our** Policyholder's aircraft.

The information below is required only when this Endorsement is issued after preparation of your Policy.

This Endorsement is effective Mo./Day/Yr. _____ at _____ Local time at **your** address shown in Item 1 of the Data Page.

The Endorsement Number_____is a part of Policy Number NC _____ issued by AVEMCO INSURANCE COMPANY.

David E. Jensen PRESIDENT

John H. Ballard SECRETARY

COUNTERSIGNED _____ 19____

By: _____
Authorized Representative

ERPE 4 (9-81)-2

TIME OUT OF FORCE ENDORSEMENT

The Policy Period shown in Item 3 of the Data Page does not include the period:

Mo.	Day	Year		Mo.	Day	Year
			to			

_____   _____

(12:01 A.M. Local Time at **your** address)

Premium Refund: none.

EXPLANATION

Your Policy was cancelled for nonpayment of premium. This cancellation is subject to a short-rate premium penalty. The Policy was reinstated however, due to **our** receipt of **your** late payment. There is no premium refund or credit given for the time the Policy was out of force. This is because the premium **we** are keeping for the time out of force is less than the short-rate penalty **we** could have charged **you**.

Our use of this Endorsement allows **us** to restart **your** coverage. It avoids the extra expense to **you** of the short-rate cancellation penalty and inconvenience of making a new application for insurance.

The Endorsement Number_____is a part of Policy Number NC _____ issued by AVEMCO INSURANCE COMPANY.

David E. Jensen   PRESIDENT

John H. Ballard   SECRETARY

COUNTERSIGNED _____ 19____

By: _____
              Authorized Representative

ERPE 25 (9-81)-2

ADDITIONAL INSURED ENDORSEMENT

We agree with **you** that the following person or organization is insured under this Policy:

SPECIMEN

They are insured only while **you** are using a **non-owned aircraft** according to the Policy's terms. The addition of this person or organization as an insured does not increase the Limits of Liability shown in Item 3 of the Data Page.

The cost for this Endorsement is $_____.

The information below is required only when this Endorsement is issued after preparation of your Policy.

This Endorsement is effective Mo./Day/Yr. _____ at _____ Local time at **your** address shown in Item 1 of the Data Page.

The Endorsement Number_____is a part of Policy Number NC _____ issued by AVEMCO INSURANCE COMPANY.

PRESIDENT

SECRETARY

COUNTERSIGNED _____ 19____

By: _____
_____Authorized Representative

ERNE-G (7-82)-1

HANGARED AIRCRAFT ENDORSEMENT

You agree that **your insured aircraft** will be regularly hangared while at its home base, in a completely enclosed hangar which is normally either locked or guarded. **We** agree, because of this, to charge **you** the reduced premium for Coverage B — Aircraft Damage as shown on the Data Page.

If **you** have not honored this hangaring agreement, **your** deductible under Coverage B for any not **in motion loss** occuring at **your** home base will be 10% of the **loss**. In no event shall the deductible be less than that shown in Item 5 of the Data Page.

SPECIMEN

The information below is required only when this Endorsement is issued after preparation of your Policy.

This Endorsement is effective Mo./Day/Yr. _____ at _____ Local time at **your** address shown in Item 1 of the Data Page.

The Endorsement Number_____is a part of Policy Number NC _____ issued by AVEMCO INSURANCE COMPANY.

PRESIDENT

SECRETARY

COUNTERSIGNED _____ 19____

By: _____
Authorized Representative

ERPE 19 (9-81)-2S

TURBINE POWERED AIRCRAFT ENDORSEMENT

I. The following is added to the ADDITIONAL EXCLUSIONS in PART II — INSURANCE FOR DAMAGE TO OWNED AIRCRAFT on page 2 of **your** Policy:

This Coverage does not apply to **loss** to an engine of **your insured aircraft** which is:

1. caused by an object that is a part of an engine or its accessories;
2. caused by heat resulting from the starting, operation or shutdown of an engine;
3. caused by a breakdown, failure or malfunction of an engine component, accessory or part;
4. caused by an object not a part of the engine, or its accessories, unless the **loss** was sudden, and caused by a single recorded event that requires immediate repair to meet the requirements of the engine manufacturer.

II. The **in motion** "deductible" shown in Item 5 of the Data Page will apply to any **loss** to an engine of **your insured aircraft.**

III. The following is substituted for ADDITIONAL EXCLUSIONS applying to PART IV — INSURANCE FOR USE OF NON-OWNED AIRCRAFT on page 3 of **your** Policy:

ADDITIONAL EXCLUSIONS APPLYING TO THIS PART

This insurance does not apply to:

1. The operation of an aircraft furnished or leased to **you** for more than 30 days;
2. The legal responsibilities of the aircraft owner, or the owner's agent or employee;
3. The use of any aircraft which:
    (a) is owned by **you** in full or in part;
    (b) is flown without the owner's consent;
    (c) does not have a "Standard" Category Airworthiness Certificate;
    (d) has more seats than **your insured aircraft;**
    (e) is not a fixed wing aircraft.

IV. For the purpose of this Endorsement the term "engine" includes auxiliary power units.

The information below is required only when this Endorsement is issued after preparation of your Policy.

This Endorsement is effective Mo./Day/Yr. _____ at _____ Local time at **your** address shown in Item 1 of the Data Page.

The Endorsement Number_____is a part of Policy Number NC _____ issued by AVEMCO INSURANCE COMPANY.

PRESIDENT

SECRETARY

COUNTERSIGNED _____ 19____

By: _____
Authorized Representative

ERPE 35 (9-81)-2

CANCELLATION CHANGE ENDORSEMENT
30 Days Notice

The following is substituted for GENERAL PROVISION (7) CANCELLATION on page 4 of **your** Policy:

(7) CANCELLATION

To cancel this Policy, **you** must tell **us** in writing at what future date the cancellation should be.

We may cancel by mailing **you** a cancellation notice. This notice will be sent to the address shown in Item 1 of the Data Page. It will be sent at least 30 days before the cancellation date. Proof of mailing will be proof that **you** were notified.

Upon cancellation, **you** may be entitled to a premium refund. **We** will send that refund to **you**. **Our** making a refund is not a condition of cancellation. If **you** cancel for any reason, the refund will be figured using the short-rate table shown below. If **we** cancel because of **your** nonpayment of premium, **we** will use the same short-rate table.

If **we** cancel for a reason other than nonpayment of premium, the refund will be figured on a pro rata basis.

Our receipt and deposit of **your** premium payment after mailing a notice of cancellation will not reinstate the Policy. However, cancellation for nonpayment of premium will not be effective if the required payment is received before the cancellation date.

SPECIMEN

The information below is required only when this Endorsement is issued after preparation of your Policy.

This Endorsement is effective Mo./Day/Yr. _____ at _____ Local Time at **your** address shown in Item 1 of the Data Page.

The Endorsement Number_____ is a part of Policy Number NC _____ issued by AVEMCO INSURANCE COMPANY.

PRESIDENT

SECRETARY

COUNTERSIGNED _____ 19___

By: _____
Authorized Representative

Appendix D

Self-Tests

CHAPTER 1   SELF-TEST

MULTIPLE CHOICE: Circle the letter that corresponds to the best answer.

1. The first aviation insurance policy was written by:
   a. Associated Aviation Underwriters.   c. Lloyd's of London.
   b. Insurance Company of North America.   d. Aviation Office of America.

2. The Travelers Insurance Company eventually became a member of the following aviation insurance group:
   a. Aero Insurance Underwriters.
   b. Royal-Globe Insurance Companies.
   c. Aero Associates.
   d. United States Aircraft Insurance Group.

3. One of the earliest aviation insurance agencies was:
   a. Caroon and Black.   c. Johnson and Higgins.
   b. Barber and Baldwin.   d. Marsh and McLennan.

4. The Air Commerce Act of 1926:
   a. required minimum limits of liability for the air carriers.
   b. established the first airway rules and regulations.
   c. created the Federal Aviation Agency.
   d. provided subsidies for several of the early aviation insurers.

5. The first aviation insurance pool in the United States was:
   a. AAU.   c. ABC Plan.
   b. AVEMCO.   d. USAIG.

6. The individual who originated the idea of group aviation underwriting was:
   a. David C. Beebe.   c. Eddie Rickenbacker.
   b. Horatio Barber.   d. Owen C. Torrey.

7. The group approach to underwriting aviation risks was initially proposed for all of the following reasons, *except:*
   a. it appealed to American patriotism.
   b. it would create a monopoly.
   c. it was the most economical way to write aviation insurance.
   d. it would be staffed by specialists in aviation.

8. This company entered the aviation insurance market in 1949 as a direct writer and solicited business primarily from members of AOPA:
   a. Aviation Insurance Managers.   c. Aviation Office of America.
   b. American Mercury Insurance Company.   d. AVEMCO.

9. The investigation of the aviation industry by the Senate Subcommittee on Antitrust and Monopoly in 1960 resulted in:
   a. the breakup of USAIG.
   b. a number of penalties being imposed on the three leading markets.
   c. indictments of key officers of the two major pools.
   d. none of the above.

10. This company has become a leading source in assembling insurers of space policies:
    a. American Aviation Underwriters.
    b. International Technology Underwriters.
    c. Southern Marine and Aviation Underwriters.
    d. Aviation Office of America.

TRUE/FALSE: Circle *T* if the statement is true, *F* if it is false.

T   F   1. The Travelers Insurance Company was the first aviation insurer in the United States.

T   F   2. Most of the early aviation insurance policies did not include hull coverage.

T   F   3. J. Brooks B. Parker assisted in placing insurance for Pan American World Airways during that airline's formative years.

T   F   4. The Air Mail Act of 1925 required the first licensing of aircraft and airmen.

T   F   5. The USAIG and AAU were formed immediately following World War I.

T   F   6. The two predominant aviation insurance markets up to the end of World War II were Aero Insurance Underwriters and USAIG.

T   F   7. Established in 1932, the Board of Aviation Underwriters ceased operations in 1965 during the extremely competitive period in aviation underwriting.

T   F   8. The Royal-Globe Insurance Companies entered the aviation field in 1948 following its withdrawal from Aero Insurance Underwriters.

T   F   9. The Aircraft Builders Counsel, Inc., (ABC) was formed in 1952 to provide aircraft liability coverage.

T   F   10. The growth in all segments of the aviation industry during the 1960s and 1970s resulted in the establishment of a number of aviation insurers.

CHAPTER 2   SELF-TEST

MULTIPLE CHOICE: Circle the letter that corresponds to the best answer.

1. Companies like McDonnell Douglas, Boeing, RCA, and Ratheon are members of:
   a. ATA.   c. NBAA.
   b. AIA.   d. GAMA.

2. Companies like Cessna, Beech, Piper, and Gulfstream American are members of:
   a. ADMA.   c. AIA.
   b. AOPA.   d. GAMA.

3. The principal aviation insurance coverage purchased by the aircraft and component parts manufacturers is:
   a. aircraft liability.   c. products liability.
   b. aircraft hull.   d. construction and alterations.

4. Certificated air carriers such as Frontier, Ozark, and Hawaiian are classified as:
   a. major air carriers.   c. large regionals.
   b. national air carriers.   d. medium regionals.

5. Corporate operated aircraft flown by professional pilots are referred to as which of the following classes of business?
   a. business and pleasure.   c. industrial aid.
   b. commercial.   d. special use.

6. The nation's approximately 3,500 fixed base operators operate about _____ aircraft for airtaxi, instructional, and rental purposes.
   a. 20,000.   c. 44,000.
   b. 32,000.   d. 56,000.

7. The purpose of aircraft for "special use" would include all of the following *except*:
   a. police traffic control.
   b. flying club.
   c. powerline patrol.
   d. mosquito control.

8. Which of the following coverages is unique to airport owners and operators?
   a. non-ownership liability.
   b. airport premises liability.
   c. medical payments.
   d. air meet liability.

9. Special aircraft hull and liability policies have been designed for owners and operators of this fast-growing segment of the aviation industry:
   a. helicopters.
   b. ultralights.
   c. seaplanes.
   d. amphibians.

10. The personal non-owned aircraft policy is primarily designed for:
    a. corporate pilots.
    b. student pilots.
    c. private pilots.
    d. ultralight pilots.

TRUE/FALSE: Circle *T* if the statement is true, *F* if it is false.

T F 1. Major corporations are planning for the eventual industrialization of outer space, which is expected to increase the demand for new aviation insurance coverages.

T F 2. Virtually all of the major aerospace manufacturers are members of the Aircraft Distributors and Manufacturers Association (ADMA).

T F 3. Grounding coverage is frequently purchased by the major air carriers.

T F 4. Most general liability policies exclude aviation liability, and consequently many subcontractors who manufacture aircraft parts and components purchase aircraft products liability.

T F 5. The small non-certificated regional air carriers are one of the fastest growing segments of the airline industry.

T F 6. The airlines, as a class of business, represent a tremendous premium volume for relatively few insurance markets.

T F 7. Guest voluntary settlement (admitted liability) coverage is generally limited to industrial aid risks.

T F 8. The majority of civil aircraft in the United States are used for commercial purposes.

T F 9. Fixed base operators, as a class of aviation insurance, are considered excellent by underwriters because FBO's are all subject to strict FAA regulations.

T F 10. There are over 16,000 airports in the United States.

CHAPTER 3   SELF-TEST

MULTIPLE CHOICE: Circle the letter that corresponds to the best answer.

1. Combined aircraft hull and liability policies first appeared during the:
   a. 1950s.
   b. 1960s.
   c. 1970s.
   d. 1980s.

2. AVEMCO is an example of a:
   a. directing-writing company.
   b. underwriting group.
   c. multiple-line company.
   d. company who sells its policies through agents and brokers.

3. Based in St. Louis, this aviation insurer specializes in underwriting FBO's as well as helicopter and agricultural operators.
   a. Crump Aviation Underwriters.
   b. Aviation Office of America.
   c. National Aviation Underwriters.
   d. Associated Aviation Underwriters.

4. One of the two largest aviation insurance pools, this underwriter owned by Chubb and Son and The Continental Company was formed in 1929:
   a. American Aviation Underwriters.
   b. Associated Aviation Underwriters.
   c. Pacific Aviation Managers.
   d. Aviation Office of America.

5. Approximately how many aviation insurance markets are there today?
   a. 6.
   b. 18.
   c. 24.
   d. 36.

6. Which of the following reasons caused the number of aviation insurance markets to decrease in the last several years compared to the number in the 1960s and 1970s?
   a. Many of the competing companies merged.
   b. Lower rates were offered by Lloyd's of London.
   c. The variety of aircraft being produced was too much to develop an adequate spread of risks.
   d. Competition increased and there was a leveling-off of the number of active general aviation aircraft.

7. Which of the following statements concerning a Lloyd's underwriting member is *not* correct?
   a. The individual must be recommended by other members.
   b. The individual must be British.
   c. The individual must transact business with unlimited personal liability.
   d. The individual must satisfy the Council of Lloyd's of his or her financial integrity.

8. Which of the following qualities must a good agent possess?
   a. knowledge of the insurance business.
   b. good contacts with the aviation insurance markets.
   c. an effective claim follow-up service.
   d. all of the above.

9. In choosing among insurers, the nature of their services should be considered. In doing so, which of the following factors is/are important: (1) fairness of an insurer's claim service; (2) speed of claim service; (3) provision of additional services, such as loss prevention and safety where needed; (4) unquestioned claim payments to the insured.
   a. (1) only.
   b. (1), (2) and (4).
   c. (1), (2) and (3).
   d. (1), (2), (3) and (4).

10. Companies such as Frank B. Hall, Marsh and McLennon, and Rollins Burdick Hunter are:
    a. Lloyd's brokers.
    b. small aviation insurers.
    c. large domestic brokers.
    d. large domestic agencies.

TRUE/FALSE: Circle *T* if the statement is true, *F* if it is false.

T F   1. There are approximately 300 insurance companies in the United States which write aviation coverages, and the majority are members of some pool or association.

T F   2. Aviation Office of America is one of the two major direct-writing aviation insurance companies.

T F   3. Associated Aviation Underwriters is the designated insurer of the Aircraft Owners and Pilots Association (AOPA).

T F   4. Formed in 1928, USAIG is the largest of the domestic aviation underwriters, representing over 70 of the world's major insurance companies.

T F   5. Underwriting members at Lloyd's of London are known as Names.

T F   6. All Lloyd's brokers are formed into syndicates.

T F   7. Each Lloyd's syndicate generally accepts less than 100 percent of a particular line of business.

T F   8. Direct-writing companies always offer lower rates than companies selling their insurance through independent agents and brokers.

T F   9. Companies that pass off all or virtually all of a risk through various reinsurance arrangements are called captive agents.

T F 10. A broker is generally looked upon as the agent of the insured and not of the insurer.

MATCHING: Match the descriptor on the right with the aviation insurance company on the left.

_____ 1. USAU.

_____ 2. NAU.

_____ 3. INA.

_____ 4. AVEMCO.

_____ 5. AOA.

a. This company is the leading independent aviation underwriter specializing in industrial aid and business and pleasure risks.

b. Based in Dallas, this relatively new company is a leading underwriter of commuter air carriers.

c. This company is a major aviation insurer of airline risks.

d. This carrier specializes in writing FBO's.

e. This company is a leading underwriter of ultralight aircraft.

LISTING: List five factors which an insured should consider in selecting an agent or broker to handle aviation insurance.

1. _____

2. _____

3. _____

4. _____

5. _____

CHAPTER 4

SELF-TEST

MULTIPLE CHOICE: Circle the letter that corresponds to the best answer.

1. Risk is best described as:
   a. uncertainty.
   b. loss itself.
   c. cause of loss.
   d. chance of loss.

2. Losses resulting from destruction of property may be of what type(s)? (1) Direct loss; (2) Loss of use; (3) Additional expense
   a. (1) only.
   b. (1) and (2) only.
   c. (1) and (3) only.
   d. (1), (2) and (3).

3. Hazards are usually classified into three categories. They are:
   a. perils, risks, and uncertainties.
   b. physical, mental, and moral.
   c. moral, morale, and physical.
   d. personal, property, and liability.

4. Adverse selection is a term used to describe:
   a. the choice of the wrong insurance contract to fit a specific need.
   b. an underwriting error on the part of an insurance company.
   c. the tendency of poor risks to seek insurance.
   d. a loss situation in which the chance of loss cannot be determined.

5. Installation of an automatic sprinkler system in a hangar is an example of:
   a. reducing the risk.
   b. reducing the loss.
   c. reducing the peril.
   d. reducing the chance of loss.

6. Loss prevention means:
   a. self-insurance.
   b. reducing the hazard.
   c. purchasing insurance.
   d. reducing the loss.

7. According to the law of large numbers, as the number of exposure units is increased:
   a. the chance of loss declines.
   b. the chance or probability of loss increases.
   c. the accuracy of predictions should be better.
   d. the accuracy of predictions should remain about the same.

8. The goal of risk management is to:
   a. minimize insurance expenditures.
   b. make certain that uninsured losses do not occur.
   c. minimize the adverse effects of losses and uncertainty connected with pure risks.
   d. eliminate financial loss.

9. The risks most suited to treatment by insurance are those in which there is:
   a. a high probability and a low severity.
   b. a low probability and a high severity.
   c. a low probability and a low severity.
   d. none of the above.

10. Risk retention means that risk has been:
   a. avoided or ignored.
   b. identified and measured and a decision made to pay any losses out of company resources.
   c. retained by an insurance company.
   d. all of the above.

TRUE/FALSE: Circle *T* if the statement is true, *F* if it is false.

T   F   1.   Chance of loss is really the same as degree of risk.

T   F   2.   Pure risk can produce loss or gain.

T   F   3.   Personal loss exposures can result in loss of income, assets, and mental or physical suffering.

T   F   4.   The peril is the actual chance of loss.

T   F   5.   A hazard is anything that is likely to cause a loss, such as a fire, a windstorm, or a crash.

T   F   6.   Self-insurance is the same as no insurance.

T   F   7.   Assumption of risk may be conscious or unconscious.

T   F   8.   From an accounting standpoint, insurance is a device in which a small certain loss is substituted for a large uncertain loss.

T   F   9.   A hold harmless agreement can shift a legal obligation.

T   F   10.   The first step in the risk management process is identification of the risks facing the organization.

LISTING:

1. List five methods of dealing with risks.

   a. _____

   b. _____

   c. _____

   d. _____

   e. _____

2. List five requirements for an insurable risk.

   a. _____

   b. _____

   c. _____

   d. _____

   e. _____

3. List five uses of insurance.

    a. _____

    b. _____

    c. _____

    d. _____

    e. _____

4. List the five steps in the risk management process.

    a. _____

    b. _____

    c. _____

    d. _____

    e. _____

CHAPTER 5   SELF-TEST

MULTIPLE CHOICE: Circle the letter that corresponds to the best answer.

1. The principle of indemnity provides that:
    a. the agent must be paid a fair commission for his work.
    b. aircraft insurance cannot be written for minor children.
    c. those responsible for injury to others must pay them indemnity.
    d. one cannot make a profit from his insurance policy.

2. Which of the following would *not* have an insurable interest in an aircraft:
    a. the owner.   c. the lessee.
    b. the airport operator.   d. the mortgagee.

3. Which of the following statements concerning subrogation is *not* correct?
    a. It only applies after the insured has been indemnified.
    b. It prevents the insured from collecting twice.
    c. It only applies to property insurance.
    d. It is of great importance in the case of hull insurance.

4. Punitive damanges: (1) do not apply in liability cases; (2) are in excess of compensation for injuries; (3) are made to punish the defendant; (4) are made to discourage others from wrong.
    a. (1) and (2) only.   c. (1), (2) and (3) only.
    b. (3) and (4) only.   d. (2), (3) and (4) only.

5. Claims arising from torts are based on:
    a. negligence.   c. absolute laibility.
    b. intentional interference.   d. all of the above.

6. Which of the following is *not* generally considered to be one of the essential requirements of a negligent act?
    a. existence of a legal duty to protect the injured party.
    b. existence of a liability contract on trespassers.
    c. failure to exercise requisite care.
    d. reasonably close causal relationship between the breach of duty toward the claimant and the claimant's injury.

7. In most jurisdictions, a property owner owes the highest degree of care to:
   a. a trespasser.
   b. a licensee.
   c. an invitee.
   d. the degree of care owed is the same to all.

8. Vicarious liability refers to:
   a. res ipsa loquitor.   c. guest laws.
   b. imputed negligence.   d. sovereign immunity.

9. Which of the following is *not* generally considered a defense against allegations of negligence?
   a. assumption of risk.   c. comparative negligence.
   b. last-clear-chance.   d. tort-feasor.

10. In a liability case, the job of the jury is to:
    a. settle disputes over questions of fact.
    b. settle disputes over the law.
    c. interpret contracts.
    d. do all of the above.

11. Examples of intentional interference are: (1) assault and battery; (2) libel and slander; (3) bailment and conversion; (4) trespass and false arrest.
    a. (1) only.   c. (1), (2) and (3) only.
    b. (1) and (4) only.   d. (1), (2) and (4) only.

12. The doctrine of contributory negligence:
    a. has been replaced in many jurisdictions by the doctrine of comparative negligence.
    b. is a defense that benefits the injured party.
    c. is currently applied only in the field of employer's liability.
    d. applies only in the case of aircraft accidents.

TRUE/FALSE: Circle *T* if the statement is true, *F* if it is false.

T   F   1.   Administrative law consists of the great body of past court decisions.

T   F   2.   Under Public Law 15, insurance has been held to be subject to regulation by the federal government.

T   F   3.   When there is no insurable interest in an insurance policy, it becomes a gambling contract.

T   F   4.   In the property or liability field, insurable interest is generally only required at the time of loss.

T   F   5.   Proximate cause is a legal term which refers to the many factors which contribute to injury or damage.

T   F   6.   Loss of consortium means pain and suffering following an injury.

T   F   7.   A guest is usually defined as one who has not paid for his transportation.

T   F   8.   "The thing speaks for itself" refers to the doctrine of res ipsa loquitor.

T   F   9.   A breach of contract arises when one party to a contract refuses to fulfill his part of the bargain.

T   F   10. When property is given over to the case of another party, a legal relation of implied warranty arises.

T   F   11. Comparative negligence, when claimed, is a defense used by the plaintiff.

T   F   12. Negligence may be defined as the failure of a person to exercise the proper degree of care required by the circumstances.

CHAPTER 6   SELF-TEST

MULTIPLE CHOICE: Circle the letter that corresponds to the best answer.

1. An aleatory contract:
   a. is a contract of unequal exchange of value.
   b. is drawn by one party.
   c. is the result of long negotiations.
   d. none of the above.

2. A contract of adhesion:
   a. is drawn by one party.
   b. gives the benefit of the ambiguity to the insured.
   c. both a and b.
   d. none of the above.

3. An insurance contract may be:
   a. unilateral.
   b. conditional.
   c. personal.
   d. all of the above.

4. Representations:
   a. are part of the application for insurance.
   b. are about the same as warranties.
   c. do not exist in airport insurance.
   d. usually are continuing in nature.

5. Warranties:
   a. have the effect, in general, of waivers.
   b. are collateral inducements to a contract being formed.
   c. are part of the contract.
   d. may be oral.

6. Remaining silent when there is a duty to speak is:
   a. a misrepresentation.
   b. concealment.
   c. the parol evidence rule.
   d. fraud.

7. Which of the following would permit the insurance company to void your aircraft hull and liability policy?
   a. concealing the fact that it took you 80 hours to receive your Private Pilot's license.
   b. misstating the place where you first learned to fly.
   c. failure to indicate that you are flying subject to a waiver from the FAA.
   d. Both a and c would be cause to void the contract.

8. Which of the following is *not* generally considered among the agent's authorities?
   a. contractual authority.
   b. implied authority.
   c. assumed authority.
   d. apparent authority.

9. Waiver:
   a. is the same thing as estoppel.
   b. involves the relinquishment of a known right.
   c. is an obsolete doctrine, seldom used in insurance today.
   d. is an exception to the principle of indemnity.

10. Which of the following is *not* generally considered to be one of the essential requirements of a legally binding contract?
   a. offer and acceptance.
   b. contract must be in writing.
   c. legal object and consideration.
   d. competent parties.

11. Insurance policies contain exclusions in order to:
   a. eliminate duplicate coverage in other policies.
   b. eliminate coverage not needed by the typical insured.
   c. eliminate specialized coverage that the insurer is not qualified to offer or that requires special underwriting and rating.
   d. all of the above.

12. Changes in the contract are accomplished by adding:
    a. insuring agreements.
    b. conditions.
    c. endorsements.
    d. definitions.

TRUE/FALSE: Circle *T* if the statement is true, *F* if it is false.

T   F   1.   An insurance policy is a legal contract.

T   F   2.   Ambiguities in the contract are interpreted favorably for the insured because the contract is one of entirety and is unilateral in nature.

T   F   3.   Because of the nature of aviation insurance, any misrepresentation by the insured, intentional or otherwise, will normally be sufficient to void the policy.

T   F   4.   The pilot warranty would be an example of a promissory warranty.

T   F   5.   The parol evidence rule generally prohibits the incorporation of any warranty into the policy by reference.

T   F   6.   Warranties must be strictly complied with, whereas only substantial truth is required in the case of representations.

T   F   7.   Fraud is defined as remaining silent when there is a duty to speak.

T   F   8.   The doctrine of utmost good faith is applied more rigidly in the field of aviation insurance than in other fields of insurance because of the catastrophe exposure.

T   F   9.   A broker is generally considered to be the agent of the insured.

T   F   10.   Estoppel is the prohibition against asserting a right because of inconsistent action or conduct.

T   F   11.   The parol evidence rule refers to the right of a prisoner to give his word not to escape.

T   F   12.   The declarations include all of the pertinent descriptive material relating to the risk, such as the person covered, policy coverage, and limits.

CHAPTER 7   SELF-TEST

MULTIPLE CHOICE: Circle the letter that corresponds to the best answer.

1. The two most common aircraft hull coverages purchased are:
   a. all risks—ground and flight and all risks—not in flight.
   b. all risks—ground and flight and all risks—not in motion.
   c. all risks—not in flight and all risks—not in motion.
   d. all risks—not in motion and specified perils.

2. The definition of aircraft includes all of the following *except:*
   a. navigating or radio equipment while temporarily removed.
   b. an engine removed for overhaul.
   c. a spare engine.
   d. tools and equipment normally carried aboard the aircraft.

3. Deductibles are used for all of the following reasons *except:*
   a. to keep the rates in line.
   b. to eliminate small claims.
   c. to decrease the physical hazard.
   d. to decrease the moral hazard.

4. Which of the following types of deductible only applies to losses up to a stated amount? Once that amount is exceeded, the entire loss is paid in full.
   a. straight.
   b. disappearing.
   c. aggregate.
   d. franchise.

5. Which of the following hull losses would be covered?
   a. blown tire as a result of a rough landing.
   b. cracked windshield caused by freezing.
   c. damaged landing gear as a result of a hijacking attempt.
   d. electrical breakdown as a result of deteriorating wires.

6. Which of the following costs would *not* be covered in the event of a partial loss in which repairs were made by an FBO?
   a. new parts.
   b. transportation costs.
   c. labor expenses, including overtime.
   d. labor expenses, excluding overtime.

7. Which of the following is *not* a duty of the insured in the event of loss?
   a. have the damage appraised within 30 days.
   b. protect the aircraft from further loss or damage.
   c. file a sworn proof of loss within 60 days.
   d. assist and cooperate with the company.

8. If the insured and the insurer fail to agree on the amount of loss:
   a. the company can deny coverage.
   b. the insured can bring the company to court.
   c. each shall select a disinterested appraiser.
   d. the company shall select a disinterested appraiser.

9. Which of the following endorsements is of particular interest to lien holders?
   a. loss of use.
   b. component parts schedule.
   c. subrogation clause.
   d. breach of warranty.

10. Loss of use coverage:
    a. is generally provided under the basic hull coverage.
    b. is a separate coverage primarily designed for business and pleasure risks.
    c. includes all expenses associated with renting or leasing a substitute aircraft.
    d. does not apply if the insured has available another aircraft of similar type without charge.

TRUE/FALSE: Circle *T* if the statement is true, *F* if it is false.

T F 1. An aircraft might be "in flight" according to the aircraft hull and liability policy even though it is, in fact, on the ground.

T F 2. All risks—ground and flight coverage also provides for disappearance of aircraft if unreported 60 days after takeoff.

T F 3. The most common type of deductible is the aggregate deductible.

T F 4. A deductible, if applicable, is always subtracted in case of a total loss.

T F 5. Fire, lightning, explosion, and theft losses are not subject to a deductible.

T F 6. The hull coverage excludes any loss or damage to the aircraft caused by war.

T F 7. Hull coverage would not apply to an engine destroyed by fire while it was removed from the aircraft for an overhaul.

T F 8. If a policy were written on a valued basis, the company would pay the actual cash value of the aircraft in the event of total loss.

T F 9. Some policies provide for a return of any unearned hull premium in the event of a partial loss.

T F 10. Component parts schedules are normally attached to policies covering older aircraft.

T F 11. The value of all salvage following the payment of a total loss shall inure to the benefit of the company.

T F 12. Coverage for newly acquired aircraft is normally provided under hull insurance.

SELF-TEST

MULTIPLE CHOICE: Circle the letter that corresponds to the best answer.

1. The bodily injury excluding passengers coverage would cover all except one of the following accidents. Which accident would *not* be covered?
   a. An aircraft crashes into a farmhouse causing injury to several members of the household.
   b. An aircraft, while taxiing, blows debris causing eye injuries to several persons standing in the vicinity of the runway.
   c. A guest is injured when he trips and falls from the boarding platform of the aircraft on static display in an air show.
   d. An occupant (other than the pilot) of the aircraft suffers multiple fractures of both legs when the aircraft crashes.

2. Which of the following statements concerning medical payments coverage is *not* correct?
   a. Funeral expenses are included.
   b. It only applies to passengers.
   c. Payment is made regardless of legal liability.
   d. It discourages liability suits.

3. Admitted liability:
   a. must be at the written request of the injured party.
   b. requires a full release for all bodily injury after the payment is made.
   c. does not apply to the crew members.
   d. is designed primarily for employees.

4. The "omnibus clause," under definition of insured, covers liability incurred by all of the following *except:*
   a. another pilot flying the aircraft with the named insured's permission.
   b. guest passengers.
   c. employees of the named insured for suits other than fellow employees.
   d. any FBO who flies the named insured's aircraft.

5. Which of the following situations would *not* be excluded under the Liability coverage?
   a. bodily injury to a fellow employee.
   b. defending suits even if the suits are groundless.
   c. liability assumed under an agreement with an FBO.
   d. personal property of the named insured.

6. Temporary use of substitute aircraft applies:
   a. only when the named insured's aircraft is withdrawn from normal use because of its breakdown, repair, servicing, loss, or destruction.
   b. to any aircraft for any reason as long as it is not used for a period exceeding seven days.
   c. to any non-owned aircraft which is used as a temporary substitute.
   d. none of these.

7. A fairly standard territorial limit under an aircraft hull and liability policy would include the United States and:
   a. Central America.   c. Canada and the Caribbean islands.
   b. Canada and Mexico.   d. Mexico and the Bahamas.

8. Which of the following is *not* a reason for a company to purchase aircraft non-ownership liability coverage?
   a. Employees may rent, charter, or borrow non-owned aircraft.
   b. Employees may fly their own aircraft on company business.
   c. Limits of liability under other contracts may not be adequate.
   d. The company may lease a non-owned aircraft on an annual basis.

9. The named insured is required to waive subrogation rights and assume all liability when using:
   a. major hub airports.
   b. military installations.
   c. seaplane bases.
   d. general aviation airports.

10. No changes to the policy are allowed without approval by the:
    a. agent or broker.
    b. insurance company.
    c. FAA.
    d. local airport authority.

TRUE/FALSE: Circle *T* if the statement is true, *F* if it is false.

T F 1. Aircraft liability arising out of the ownership, maintenance, or use of an aircraft is, in general, based on the law of negligence.

T F 2. The term "occurrence" is broader than the term "accident."

T F 3. A single-limit of liability can be written either excluding or including passengers.

T F 4. Only reasonable expenses incurred for hospital and surgical procedures are payable under the medical coverage.

T F 5. Non-ownership liability provides the owner of aircraft with protection should he rent or lease his aircraft.

T F 6. Weekly indemnity can be included as part of the medical payments coverage.

T F 7. If medical payments coverage is provided, it can be used to satisfy a workers' compensation claim in the event of injury to an employee.

T F 8. "Use of other aircraft" only applies to the named insured (if an individual) and his spouse with respect to the operation of any non-owned aircraft.

T F 9. When two or more aircraft are insured under a policy, the terms of the policy apply separately to each.

T F 10. Because the insurance policy is a personal contract, an insured may assign it to another party in the event the aircraft is sold.

T F 11. If the named insured cancels his policy, a short rate penalty applies.

T F 12. Guest voluntary settlement limits of liability are not in addition to the legal limits of liability.

COVERAGE: Answer the following questions on the basis of the named insured having an aircraft hull and liability policy in force providing coverage under all liability insuring agreements. Indicate whether or not the policy would respond for the person seeking coverage by circling the *yes* or *no* preceding the question. Each numbered question gives a situation which stands by itself.

yes no 1. X, the named insured, is sued by the widow of passenger Y, who was killed in a crash.

yes no 2. X, the named insured, lends his plane to friends Y and Z. After the crash Y sues Z, the pilot, for injuries that Y sustained.

(3-5). X, the named insured, lends his plane to Y with instructions to let no one else fly it. Y, nevertheless, lends it to Z without the knowledge or implied consent of X. Z crashes the aircraft into a house and:

yes no 3. the occupants sue X.

yes no 4. the occupants sue Y.

yes no 5. the occupants sue Z.

yes no 6. X, an aircraft dealer, has sold an aircraft to Y, the named insured. Several days later after servicing, X flew the aircraft toward Y's home field and crashed into Z's home. Will X be covered under Y's policy?

yes no 7. The named insured instructs employee A to use the aircraft for business purposes. In the course of such use, A injures another employee, B. B sues A.

(8-9). X, the named insured, signs an agreement with the local FBO assuming all liability for any losses arising out of the use of the FBO's tiedown area. A windstorm occurs and X's aircraft is blown into Y's aircraft. Y sues X for tying down his aircraft in an insecure manner and enjoins the FBO for having poorly secured tiedown stakes.

yes   no   8.   Is X covered?

yes   no   9.   Is the FBO covered?

yes   no   10.   X, the named insured, while taxiing his aircraft on the ramp area injures an airport employee who sues X?

CHAPTER 9   SELF-TEST

MULTIPLE CHOICE: Circle the letter that corresponds to the best answer.

1. The declarations page of the airport premises liability policy includes all of the following *except:*
   a. the policy period.
   b. coverages and limits of liability.
   c. insuring agreements.
   d. description of premises.

2. Which of the following situations would *not* be excluded under the airport premises liability policy?
   a. liability arising out of an air show sponsored by the insured, for which a charge is made
   b. liability assumed under an agreement with a fuel supplier
   c. liability arising out of the operation of vehicles operated on the airport property
   d. liability arising out of work performed by independent contractors

3. Medical payments coverage is *not* designed to cover:
   a. the insured's employees.
   b. independent contractors employed by the insured.
   c. airline employees.
   d. answers a and b are not covered.

4. "Completed operations" under products liability includes:
   a. the sale of new and used aircraft.
   b. aircraft repairs, servicing and installation of parts and accessories.
   c. fuel and oil sales.
   d. sale of aircraft parts and accessories.

5. The following coverage is basically a form of bailee insurance:
   a. Products liability.
   b. Air meet liability.
   c. Contractual liability.
   d. Hangarkeepers liability.

6. Hangarkeepers liability:
   a. excludes coverage for aircraft in the insured's care, custody, or control.
   b. provides coverage for aircraft rented or loaned to the insured while the aircraft is on the ground.
   c. is written with a limit per aircraft and a limit per occurrence.
   d. only covers the insured's liability for maintenance and repair work done on aircraft.

7. A renter pilot may purchase individual non-ownership liability coverage for all of the following reasons *except:*
   a. the basic bodily injury and property damage liability includes physical damage to the non-owned aircraft.
   b. the limits of liability under the owner's policy may be inadequate for the renter.
   c. he may be excluded under the owner's policy.
   d. answers a and c are exceptions.

8. Consequential loss can best be described as:
   a. indirect loss.
   b. chemical liability.
   c. a large direct loss.
   d. non-ownership loss.

9. Many suppliers of aircraft components purchase aircraft products liability coverage because:
   a. their loss experience is very poor.
   b. most other products liability insurance policies exclude all aviation exposures.
   c. they need grounding coverage which is provided under the basic policy.
   d. most aircraft accidents involve minor aircraft components.

10. The basic ultralight aircraft policy provides:
    a. physical damage coverage.
    b. premises liability coverage.
    c. medical payments coverage.
    d. admitted liability coverage.

TRUE/FALSE: Circle *T* if the statement is true, *F* if it is false.

T F 1. The two prerequisites for determining the dividing point between premises operations and products completed operations are: (1) possession must be relinquished and (2) the occurrence must take place off the premises.

T F 2. Airport premises liability coverage is primarily designed for airport owners, not tenants.

T F 3. Many exclusions are included in the airport premises liability policy because there are other policies designed to cover such risks.

T F 4. The inspection and audit clause gives the company the right to inspect the insured's premises and to audit his books.

T F 5. Most airport liability policies provide automatic coverage for new premises and operations for 30 days.

T F 6. Contractual liability is normally provided on a blanket basis because of the numerous contracts between airport operators and tenants.

T F 7. Liability arising out of the work performed by independent contractors is automatically covered under the airport premises liability contract.

T F 8. An aggregate limit only applies in the case of products liability.

T F 9. Air meet liability is normally designed to protect the sponsor and the participants in an air show.

T F 10. Non-owned aircraft physical damage coverage is basically subrogation coverage.

MATCHING: Match the coverage applicable to each of the following accidents. (indicate a, b, c, or d)

COVERAGE

a. Airport premises BI.
b. Airport premises PD.
c. Hangarkeepers flight or ground.
d. Products BI or PD.

_____ 1. X's aircraft was tied down by FBO's employee on FBO's tiedown area. X's aircraft was destroyed by a windstorm.

_____ 2. A gasoline truck, operated by fueling service company T located at the airport, damaged A's automobile in the airport parking lot.

_____ 3. D slipped on some oil spilled on the apron area, which R's mechanic failed to clean up after working on an aircraft.

_____ 4. R's line employee lit up a cigarette after fueling E's aircraft. A fire ensued, causing considerable damage to E's aircraft.

_____ 5. R's counter employee failed to inform an incoming pilot, via unicom, that the county maintenance crew was cutting the grass landing strip. F's aircraft was damaged when he tried to avoid hitting the mower.

_____ 6. R's line employee pumped contaminated gasoline into Z's aircraft causing him to crash after takeoff.

CHAPTER 10   SELF-TEST

MULTIPLE CHOICE: Circle the letter that corresponds to the best answer.

1. Which of the following perils is not covered under the standard fire policy?
   a. fire.   c. lightning.
   b. explosion.   d. removal.

2. The general property form (GPF) covers which of the following property lines?
   a. buildings.   c. personal property of others.
   b. personal property of the insured.   d. all of these.

3. Comprehensive coverage under the business automobile policy includes:
   a. collision with another object.
   b. bodily injury and property damage.
   c. all physical damage losses from any cause other than collision.
   d. uninsured motorist coverage.

4. Which of the following statements is *not* correct regarding workers' compensation insurance?
   a. Negligence is not a factor in determining liability.
   b. The amount of benefits vary from state to state.
   c. In some states employees can sue their employer in cases of gross negligence.
   d. The basic limit of liability for coverage B is $25,000.

5. Extra expense insurance covers:
   a. the loss of profits during a period of shutdown.
   b. those normal expenses that continue during a period of shutdown or interruption.
   c. salaries of key employees.
   d. unusual expenses required to continue operations following damage to owned property caused by an insured peril.

6. Under a surety bond, the third party to whom the bonding company is answerable for the acts of the person bonded is called the:
   a. principal.   c. obligee.
   b. surety.   d. obligor.

7. Crime policies for businesses:
   a. cover robbery only losses.
   b. exclude any loss unless records have been kept.
   c. exclude any loss of money and securities.
   d. cover burglary only losses.

8. The three functional types of life insurance policies are:
   a. term, endowment, and whole life.
   b. annuity, whole life, and term.
   c. endowment, whole life, and limited payment life.
   d. whole life, annuity, and limited payment life.

9. The endowment insurance policy: (1) provides protection for the whole life; (2) has lower premiums than does term life insurance; (3) provides for a death benefit within the policy term; (4) pays to the owner if the insured survives the policy term.
   a. 1 and 2 only.
   b. 3 and 4 only.
   c. 1, 2, and 3 only.
   d. 2, 3, and 4 only.

10. Life insurance which provides for payment only if the insured dies within a specific time period is:
    a. term insurance.
    b. ordinary life insurance.
    c. endowment insurance.
    d. whole life insurance.

11. The large-loss principle is substitution of:
    a. a small certain cost for a small uncertain one.
    b. a small certain cost for a large uncertain one.
    c. an indefinite cost for a small uncertain one.
    d. an indefinite cost for a certain one.

12. Two essential coverages for an FBO would be:
    a. in-flight hangarkeepers and products liability.
    b. loss of license and the theft of mechanics' tools.
    c. airport premises and hangarkeepers liability.
    d. business-interruption and non-ownership liability.

TRUE/FALSE: Circle *T* if the statement is true, *F* if it is false.

T   F   1. The extended coverage endorsement increases the number of perils covered.

T   F   2. Contingent business interruption insurance requires physical damage to the insured's premises.

T   F   3. Coverage under the business auto policy may be provided on any automobile, or on specifically scheduled autos only.

T   F   4. Workers' compensation laws generally exclude from coverage those injuries that result from the worker's own negligence.

T   F   5. The major difference between the system of employers' liability and workers' compensation is that the former bases payment on negligence while the latter does not.

T   F   6. Today, most workers' compensation laws permit the employer or the employees to elect not to be covered under the law.

T   F   7. Fidelity insurance is written to protect the employer from employee dishonesty.

T   F   8. Employers nearly always pick up a portion of the premium expense for group health insurance.

T   F   9. The dividing line between essential, desirable, and available coverages for insureds engaged in aviation is quite clearcut.

T   F   10. Insurance companies often offer premium reductions for loss prevention and safety activities by an insured.

CHAPTER 11   SELF-TEST

MULTIPLE CHOICE: Circle the letter that corresponds to the best answer.

1. The basic function of underwriting is to:
   a. avoid insuring people who are likely to have losses.
   b. make certain that only very good risks are insured.
   c. generate as high a premium volume as possible.
   d. avoid adverse selection.

2. The aircraft hull and liability application requires all of the following information *except:*
   a. insured value of aircraft.
   b. the purpose for which the aircraft will be used.
   c. name of the home airport.
   d. hangar or tiedown charge per month.

3. The minimum pilot requirements for a single-engine retractible gear aircraft would normally include:
   a. any student pilot or better.
   b. any private pilot or better.
   c. any private pilot with a minimum of 200 total logged hours.
   d. any private pilot with a minimum of 50 total logged hours in the model.

4. Corporate aircraft flown by professional pilots would be classified as:
   a. business and pleasure use.
   b. industrial aid use.
   c. airline use.
   d. special use.

5. Air aircraft used for rental and instruction would be classified as:
   a. special use.
   b. industrial aid use.
   c. full commercial use.
   d. limited commercial use.

6. Products liability premiums are based on:
   a. the number of products sold.
   b. the gross receipts.
   c. the type and size of the FBO.
   d. the use to which the products are put.

7. Rate making in aviation insurance:
   a. is usually done on a cooperative basis.
   b. must be accomplished through rating bureaus and cannot be done by individual companies because of the limited spread of risk.
   c. differs from price setting in other businesses since prices must be set before costs are known.
   d. none of these.

8. The base rate for hull insurance is expressed as a rate per:
   a. $100 of insured value.
   b. $1,000 of insured value.
   c. number of estimated hours flown.
   d. days at risk.

9. Guest voluntary settlement coverage is available for:
   a. business and pleasure risks.
   b. industrial aid risks.
   c. commercial risks.
   d. airline risks.

10. A system by which one insurance company negotiates the terms of reinsurance with another company is called:
    a. treaty reinsurance.
    b. facultative reinsurance.
    c. pro rata reinsurance.
    d. excess reinsurance.

TRUE/FALSE: Circle *T* if the statement is true, *F* if it is false.

T   F   1.   The underwriting process includes preselection and postselection of risks.

T   F   2.   Underwriting sources include applications, agent's comments, and inspection reports.

T   F   3.   An aircraft's susceptability to loss can be a function of any number of factors relative to its age, construction, and general configuration.

T   F   4.   Underwriters often impose pilot standards in the form of minimum hours beyond those required by federal regulations.

T   F   5.   An aircraft used exclusively for charter purposes would be classified as limited commercial.

T   F   6.   Liability premiums for commercial risks are generally much higher than business and pleasure risks.

T   F   7.   The one item of the declarations which has the most significance for aircraft liability coverage is the certificated passenger capacity.

T F 8. The airport liability policy provides automatic coverage for all hazards connected with the operation of an airport.

T F 9. A corporation with no known aircraft exposure other than their employees' use of commercial airlines would have no need for non-owned aircraft liability coverage.

T F 10. The pricing problem in insurance is simpler than that in most other businesses.

LISTING:

1. An underwriter is interested in four principal areas when insuring aircraft hull and liability risks. They are:

    a. _____

    b. _____

    c. _____

    d. _____

2. List the correct purpose of use next to the following descriptions:

    a. An FBO provides aircraft and pilot to fly
        several executives on a business trip.   _____

    b. A sales representative uses his own aircraft to cover his
        territory.   _____

    c. A utility company uses a Cessna 150 for powerline patrol. _____

    d. A corporation rents its aircraft to another company for
        business and pleasure usage.   _____

    e. A corporate-owned aircraft is flown by corporate-employed
        professional pilots on flights in which no charge is made. _____

    f. A commuter air carrier is flown on regularly scheduled
        service.   _____

ANSWERS TO
SELF-TESTS, CHAPTERS 1-11

CHAPTER 1

Multiple Choice		True/False	
1. c	6. a	1. T	6. F
2. d	7. b	2. T	7. F
3. b	8. b	3. T	8. T
4. b	9. d	4. F	9. F
5. d	10. b	5. F	10. T

CHAPTER 2

Multiple Choice		True/False	
1. b	6. b	1. T	6. T
2. d	7. b	2. F	7. T
3. c	8. d	3. F	8. F
4. b	9. b	4. T	9. F
5. c	10. c	5. T	10. T

CHAPTER 3

Multiple Choice		True/False		Matching
1. a	6. d	1. T	6. F	1. c
2. a	7. b	2. F	7. T	2. d
3. c	8. d	3. F	8. F	3. a
4. b	9. c	4. T	9. F	4. e
5. b	10. c	5. T	10. T	5. b

Listing
a. knowledge of the insurance business.
b. type of aviation insurance written.
c. number of insurers represented.
d. knowledge of the aviation industry.
e. experience in handling aviation claims
(Other answers might include: continuing education; and respect of clients, competitors, insurers, and claim adjusters.)

CHAPTER 4

Multiple Choice		True/False	
1. a	6. b	1. T	6. F
2. d	7. c	2. F	7. T
3. c	8. c	3. T	8. T
4. c	9. b	4. F	9. T
5. b	10. b	5. F	10. T

Listing
1. a. avoided or ignored.
   b. loss prevention.
   c. loss reduction.
   d. shifted to another party.
   e. self-insurance.
   (Another answer might be: purchase insurance.)

2. a. large number of homogeneous risks.
   b. losses must be predictable.
   c. object must be of sufficient value.
   d. loss must be accidental.
   e. unlikely to occur to all insured risks simultaneously.
   (Another answer might be: must be definite.)

3. a. introduces security into personal and business situations.
   b. serves as a basis of credit.
   c. provides a means of capitalizing earning power.
   d. aids in the development of the economy.
   e. performs a social function by analyzing risks and making protection available at a reasonable cost.
   (Other answers might include: distributes the cost of accidents among a large group of persons; loss prevention is encouraged; provides a professional service; and reduces cost.)

4. a. identifying risks.   d. selection of specific techniques.
   b. risk measurement.   e. periodic evaluation.
   c. risk handling techniques.

CHAPTER 5

Multiple Choice

1. d		7. c	
2. b		8. b	
3. c		9. d	
4. d		10. a	
5. d		11. d	
6. b		12. a	

True/False

1. F		7. T	
2. T		8. T	
3. T		9. T	
4. T		10. F	
5. F		11. T	
6. F		12. T	

CHAPTER 6

Multiple Choice

1. a		7. c	
2. c		8. c	
3. d		9. b	
4. a		10. b	
5. c		11. d	
6. b		12. c	

True/False

1. T		7. F	
2. F		8. F	
3. F		9. T	
4. F		10. T	
5. T		11. F	
6. T		12. T	

CHAPTER 7

Multiple Choice

1. b		6. c	
2. c		7. a	
3. c		8. c	
4. d		9. d	
5. c		10. d	

True/False

1. T		7. F	
2. T		8. F	
3. F		9. F	
4. F		10. T	
5. T		11. T	
6. T		12. T	

CHAPTER 8

Multiple Choice

1. d		6. a	
2. b		7. b	
3. b		8. d	
4. d		9. b	
5. b		10. b	

True/False

1. T		7. F	
2. T		8. T	
3. T		9. T	
4. F		10. F	
5. F		11. T	
6. F		12. T	

Coverage

1. yes		6. no	
2. yes		7. no	
3. yes		8. no	
4. yes		9. no	
5. no		10. yes	

CHAPTER 9

Multiple Choice

1. c		6. c	
2. c		7. a	
3. d		8. a	
4. b		9. b	
5. d		10. a	

True/False

1. T		6. F	
2. F		7. F	
3. T		8. T	
4. T		9. F	
5. T		10. T	

Matching

1. c		4. b	
2. b		5. b	
3. a		6. d	

CHAPTER 10

Multiple Choice

1. b		7. b	
2. d		8. a	
3. c		9. b	
4. d		10. a	
5. d		11. b	
6. c		12. c	

True/False

1. T		6. F	
2. F		7. T	
3. T		8. T	
4. F		9. F	
5. T		10. T	

CHAPTER 11

Multiple Choice		True/False	
1. d	6. b	1. T	6. T
2. d	7. c	2. T	7. T
3. c	8. a	3. T	8. F
4. b	9. b	4. T	9. F
5. d	10. b	5. F	10. F

Listing
1. a. the type of aircraft to be insured.
   b. the abilities of the pilot.
   c. geographical considerations.
   d. the purpose for which the aircraft is to be used.

2. a. full commercial.
   b. business and pleasure.
   c. special use.
   d. limited commercial.
   e. industrial aid.
   f. airline.

Index